To Colette Delaney

Hope this is interesting read.

Regards
Prashant

Achieving Excellence in Retail Banking

'It's a great honour to be mentioned in this book – but even more important is that it gives us a unique opportunity to benchmark ourselves against others who are even better than us.'

Alessandro Profumo, CEO, Unicredito Italiano and European Banker of 2002

'The issues addressed in this book are very much on the mind of top management. It is not just theoretic but very pragmatic and it provides a lot of benchmarking opportunities. The book is very well structured, which makes it easy to refer to individual chapters when necessary. It is fun reading.'

Abdulkareem Abu Al Nasr, Deputy General Manager and Head of Consumer Banking Sector, The National Commercial Bank

'I liked the book because it was very practical about the opportunities and challenges.'

Adrian Hill, Managing Director, HFC Bank and First Direct. Member of Group Executive of Household International

'It is so unusual to have a book on retail banking so thoroughly researched and well written that I thought it would be important for my executive team to have the chance to read it as I have ... I encouraged my people to read and understand best practices of other banks.'

Benny Higgins, CEO, Retail Banking, Royal Bank of Scotland

'To my knowledge *Achieving Excellence in Retail Banking* is currently the most systematic and detailed analysis of banks that have a proven superior performance. Yet this book does not end with an analysis of the status quo. It is precisely the profound understanding of the new and competitive dynamic of the banking sector that challenges the business models of even the most successful banks, today and in the future, which makes this book a must for anyone with interest in the banking industry.'

Christine Licci, Chair, Citibank Privatkunden Board

'This book gives a good picture of the critical levers that matter in retail banking. I particularly liked the grouping into the five categories in the Excellence framework. This work gives us the opportunity to much better understand why and how some banks achieve outstanding successes and to act accordingly.'

Des Crowley, CEO, Retail Financial Services, Bank of Ireland

'This book is unparalleled in addressing comprehensively all the challenges retail banks are facing. It is a unique publication which has valuable insights and directions for all our businesses.'

Donal Forde, Managing Director, Allied Irish Bank, RoI

'The first book that stresses the success factors in retail banking so well. Leadership and performance and sales culture are also the focus of our future efforts.'

Dr Herbert Walter, Chairman of Board of Directors, Dresdner Bank AG

'The most practical and realistic book I have read in my life.'

Jamal Bin Ghalaita, Head Corporate Center, Emirates Bank

'I found the findings, the case examples and specific benchmarks, very helpful in looking at how to improve the performance of my bank.'

Jung-Tae Kim, President and CEO Kookmin Bank

'This book contains an enormous richness of retail banking experience and wisdom.'

Peter Buschbeck, Member of the Board, Sales, Citibank Privatkunden

'What I especially like in this book are the insights on the importance of corporate leadership and performance culture for achieving excellence.'

Peter Woicke, Executive Vice President, International Finance Corporation

Achieving Excellence in Retail Banking

Edited by Dr Reinhold Leichtfuss

WILEY

Published in 2003 by John Wiley & Sons Ltd, The Atrium, Southern Gate, Chichester,
West Sussex PO19 8SQ, England

Telephone (+44) 1243 779777

Email (for orders and customer service enquiries): cs-books@wiley.co.uk
Visit our Home Page on www.wileyeurope.com or www.wiley.com

Reprinted June, July 2003 and July 2004

Other Wiley Editorial Offices

John Wiley & Sons Inc., 111 River Street, Hoboken, NJ 07030, USA

Jossey-Bass, 989 Market Street, San Francisco, CA 94103-1741, USA

Wiley-VCH Verlag GmbH, Boschstr. 12, D-69469 Weinheim, Germany

John Wiley & Sons Australia Ltd, 33 Park Road, Milton, Queensland 4064, Australia

John Wiley & Sons (Asia) Pte Ltd, 2 Clementi Loop #02-01, Jin Xing Distripark, Singapore 129809

John Wiley & Sons Canada Ltd, 22 Worcester Road, Etobicoke, Ontario, Canada M9W 1L1

Wiley also publishes its books in a variety of electronic formats. Some content that appears in print may not be available in electronic books.

Library of Congress Cataloging-in-Publication Data

Achieving excellence in retail banking / edited by Reinhold Leichtfuss.
p. cm
Includes bibliographical references and index
ISBN 0-470-85827-3 (cased : alk. paper)
1. Banks and banking. 2. Bank management. 3. Strategic planning. I. Leichtfuss, Reinhold.
HG1573.A24 2003
332.1′068—dc21 2003043068

British Library Cataloguing in Publication Data

A catalogue record for this book is available from the British Library

ISBN 0-470-85827-3

Project Management by Originator, Gt Yarmouth, Norfolk (typeset in 10/12pt Times)
Printed and bound in Great Britain by TJ International Ltd, Padstow, Cornwall, UK
This book is printed on acid-free paper responsibly manufactured from sustainable forestry in which at least two trees are planted for each one used for paper production.

Contents

Preface

At the end of the 20th century, retail banking was not one of the banking sector's star performers. Rather it stood in the shadow of investment banking, asset management and private banking; indeed some banks considered reducing or even selling off their retail banking operations. The outlook was gloomy, with the capital markets not predicting much long-term growth for the retail business. The problem was compounded by the fact that many banks around the world were struggling to improve their retail banking performance.

Today, with the former stars like investment banking shining less brightly, more and more banks are once again turning their attention to the retail business and therefore must overcome their problems. We have always been convinced that retail banking can be a profitable business, lying as it does as a foundation stone of many banks' strategies; and there are banks that—even in the difficult times—have proved that substantial profits can be made while providing excellent customer service.

However, there is no doubt that achieving excellence requires top-flight performance in several competence areas. We have set these competencies into the Excellence in Retail Banking framework in order to clarify the multitude of areas that need to be developed and provide a platform from which to make the best prioritization decisions.

Achieving Excellence in Retail Banking is the result of a major research effort undertaken by McKinsey's European Banking Practice during 2001 and 2002—building on extensive experience from a series of Excellence in Retail Banking workshops with leading banks in the late 1990s.

We analyzed almost 100 retail banks around the world and, from these, nine emerged as the strongest performers between 1998 and 2001. The lessons to be learned from these banks, as well as from some others in certain competency areas, are not restricted to their individual situations, rather we consider them to be ingredients of long-term success. We will elaborate in this book on the importance of each competency and how the best performing banks have used them to reach their elevated status.

The book does not attempt to cover every possible aspect of retail banking (after all, we want you to read it, not use it as a doorstop!). Rather we focus on those areas of the greatest importance. In Chapter 1 we lay out the framework, and in Chapters 2 and 3 we discuss how today's best performing banks have achieved their success and what challenges lie ahead both for them and for those preparing to ascend to the top. We then move on to discuss competencies and concepts that are either of supreme long-term importance—such as having a superior performance culture and a relentlessly sales-driven organization—or are of current relevance to retail banking leaders—such as improving the cost position or adjusting credit management policies in the light of new regulation.

Acknowledgments

This book is a team effort of McKinsey's Banking Practice encouraged by the positive client feedback after the *Meeting Capital Market Expectations through Excellence in Retail Banking* conference in June 2002. Over 60 authors developed their views on how to achieve top performance along the 32 competencies of the Excellence in Retail Banking framework. But the team effort goes beyond the 60 authors; many colleagues around the globe contributed to individual chapters either by providing research or by challenging our views.

A major strength of *Achieving Excellence in Retail Banking* is that we have been able to discuss our findings and ideas with the leaders of high-performing retail banks across the world, all of whom have helped us refine our thinking. In particular we would like to thank Alessandro Profumo and Luca Majocchi (UniCredito Italiano), Francisco de Lacerda (Banco Comercial Português), Benny Higgins (Royal Bank of Scotland), Christine Licci (Citibank PK), Lars Grönstedt (Svenska Handelsbanken), and Ugo Ruffolo (Banca Fideuram).

To proffer a perspective from outside the immediate team of authors, a group of McKinsey directors from across the firm acted as an advisory committee, and their feedback went a long way toward improving the book and ensuring that we were not limited by our own experiences. In this regard we would like to thank Dominic Barton, Dominic Casserley, Roger Kline, and A. C. Reuter-Domenech.

We would particularly like to thank our colleagues Pedro Rodeia and Justo Alcocer who invested considerable time in several chapters and helped push the overall effort further.

We also express our gratitude to Vittorio Terzi and Pat Butler who without hesitation set up the introductions to some of the leaders of high-performing banks.

All this would have amounted to little if we had not had the support of our core team. Valentin Mihov, Ylva Bengtsson, Bertrand Bailey, and Martha Whitmore all worked tirelessly with the authors to develop each and every chapter and to make sure that we were never short-changing the reader. My assistant, Anja Bornschein, worked with her usual good grace—no matter how much work landed on her desk. Luis Oro, Matthew Bedford, Alexander Prokot, Alex Michel, Michael Vogt, and Raphael Schmidt helped to manage the process and provided superb research and administrative support.

Jonathan Turton edited the book, receiving substantial support on many chapters from Jody Doran and Graeme Jon Pearson. All three constantly challenged our logic and our thinking and of course undertook the not insignificant task of making the book enjoyable and easier to read.

Compilation of the charts called upon the talents of many visual aid professionals at McKinsey.

Finally, of course, we would like to thank Samantha Whittaker at John Wiley & Sons. Besides providing valuable early feedback, she ensured that the whole publication process ran smoothly.

However, with all this help, none of these individuals is responsible for what follows. All their advice and help was excellent; all the flaws that may be contained are of the authors. Specifically, although McKinsey sponsored the research on which this book is based, opinions expressed are our own and do not necessarily reflect those of the firm as a whole, our colleagues, or our clients. The examples used in the text are either drawn from public information or, where based on our professional experience, have been disguised to protect client confidentiality.

Reinhold Leichtfuss
and the McKinsey & Company Retail Banking Practice
Frankfurt 2003

List of contributors

Nick Adamus is a principal based in the Zurich office who has also worked in the New York and San Francisco offices. He is a leading member of the European Corporate Finance & Strategy and Banking Practices. Besides select industrial engagements, he is predominantly serving European financial institutions on a wide array of topics in retail, private, and corporate banking. His recent engagements include corporate strategy, growth strategy, sales stimulation, mergers and acquisitions (M&A), capital markets diagnostic, corporate transformation, and strategic due diligence.

Justo Alcocer is a principal in the Madrid office and has also served clients in Portugal, Morocco, and Latin America. He is responsible for the Financial Institutions Group in Spain. Together with Reinhold Leichtfuss, he is a leader of the European Retail Banking Practice. During his time with the firm, he has mainly served financial services clients, in both banking and insurance. Justo has helped retail banks in all areas, and his activities focus on segment strategies (affluent, mass market), distribution network management, marketing and segmentation, new product development, and credit risk management.

Dominic Barton is a director who has worked in Seoul for the past five years and before that was based in Toronto. He is a member of the Financial Institutions Practice and has served numerous financial services and public sector clients in Canada, the US, and Asia, addressing their most pressing challenges. Dominic has covered many different topics, with a focus on strategy, organization, M&A, corporate restructuring, and bank system restructuring. He has given numerous speeches to financial forums and written articles in a wide range of magazines, journals and newspapers. Dominic is the coauthor of *Dangerous Markets: Managing in Financial Crises*, published in September 2002 by John Wiley & Sons.

Carlos Beldarrain, an associate principal in the Madrid office, has served clients in the retail banking, energy, and postal industries. Carlos's banking projects cover global distribution strategy, network optimization, process redesign, and affluent banking.

Roman Binder works in the Zurich office as an associate principal. He is a leadership group member of the European Corporate Finance & Strategy Practice. He has served financial institutions, chemicals, and pharmaceuticals industries in the area of corporate finance and strategy as well as working on transformation programs ranging from supply chain management to marketing and sales.

Felix Budelmann is an associate in the London office who has mainly worked with financial institutions since he joined the firm. His focus has been on retail banking issues and credit.

Pat Butler is a director in London, where he is currently the office manager of the Kensington office. He has led the firm's London Financial Institutions Practice and the European Retail Banking Practice for a few years. During Pat's years with the firm he has had a wide range of experience in the banking and insurance sectors, working with clients in the UK, Europe, South Africa, and the US. In addition to banking and insurance, Pat has carried out strategy, marketing, organization, and financial work in a range of other industries, including pharmaceuticals, fast moving consumer goods, leisure, and property development.

Dominic Casserley is a director based in London. He leads the European Banking and Securities Practice. He joined McKinsey in New York, became office manager in Hong Kong in 1994, and moved to London in 2000. His career has focused on helping financial institutions in these markets improve their performance and make strategic moves. Dominic is the author of the books *Banking in Asia: The End of Entitlement*, published in 1999 by John Wiley & Sons, and *Facing up to the Risks*, published in 1991 by John Wiley & Sons.

Daniele Chiarella is an engagement manager based in the Milan office who has also spent time in the London office. He has worked on projects in investment banking, retail banking, and asset management. His major areas of experience include sales stimulation, structured products, hedge funds, organization, and strategy.

David Chinn works as an engagement manager in the Business Technology Office in London. He has focused on clients in the financial services and software industries. David has a broad range of experience in information technology (IT), strategy, retail brokerage, personal financial services, and online banking. He took an extended sabbatical from McKinsey from 1999 to 2002, during which he helped Credit Suisse launch a pan-European Internet bank.

Luís Cunha is a principal in the Lisbon office. He is a member of the European Retail Banking Practice. Although his main focus has been on serving financial institutions, he has also worked with telecommunications, pulp and paper, and ports companies. In the financial services sector, he has worked on a broad range of topics including strategy, M&A, operations, and efficiency improvement, and in a variety of segments, namely private, small- and medium-sized enterprises (SMEs), affluent, and retail.

Mario Daberkow is Head of Operations at Deutsche Postbank. He was previously an associate principal in the Business Technology Office of McKinsey. Mario had a key role in the research undertaken for the processes and IT section. He has served a wide variety of European clients in all major areas of operations and IT.

Jacob Dahl, a principal who works in the Copenhagen office, has experience in both the Brussels and London offices. Jacob is a member of the European Retail Banking Leadership Group. He mainly serves clients in the retail banking and investment banking industry throughout Scandinavia. He is an expert in the areas of distribution setup, strategy, organization, and performance improvement programs.

Maurizio Donato is a principal in the Milan office and a member of the European Retail Banking Leadership Group. Since he joined the firm, he has primarily served financial institutions on a wide range of topics. Maurizio has gathered broad experience in both strategy and operations. His major areas of expertise include corporate and business unit strategy, reorganization, post-merger management, implementation of commercial projects, and risk management.

Matthias Effinger, an engagement manager based in the Munich office, has served a number of clients in the banking industry. Matthias has extensive experience in credit risk management.

Andreas Etter is an engagement manager in the Business Technology Office in Zurich. He has focused mainly on retail banking, wholesale banking, and insurance. Andreas has a broad range of experience in operational effectiveness, process optimization, and IT.

Marcos Fernandes is a principal in the São Paulo office. During his time with the firm, Marcos has mainly served financial institutions, with a clear focus on retail banks and credit card companies. He has helped them in numerous areas, especially risk management, customer relationship management (CRM), strategy, M&A, and pricing.

Iacopo De Francisco works in the Milan office as an associate principal. Since he joined the firm, he has mainly served financial institutions, with a focus on retail banks. Iacopo's main areas of experience cover distribution strategy, process redesign, and affluent banking strategy.

Pius Fritschi is a Zurich-based principal who has also worked in the Mexico City and Sydney offices. He is a leader of the European Life and Asset Gathering Practice, a co-leader of the Swiss Financial Institutions Group, and a member of the European Banking Leadership Group. He has helped numerous clients in the banking and insurance industry. Pius has particular experience in life insurance and asset gathering, personal finance, and bancassurance.

Martin van Gemmeren is a principal in the Cologne office. He is a member of the Risk Management Practice Leadership Group. During his time with the firm, Martin has served a number of financial institutions in retail and wholesale banking, and insurance. His major areas of interest include risk, credit, asset allocation, capital markets, and capital management.

Greg Gibb, a principal in the Taipei office, serves domestic and international financial institutions primarily in Greater China. He has worked extensively with leading family-owned, regional commercial, and global investment banks to design and execute strategies, alliances, and acquisitions tailored to Asia. He is one of the authors of *Banking in Asia: The End of Entitlement*, published in 1999 by John Wiley & Sons.

Edoardo Ginevra, an engagement manager in the Rome office, has focused his consultancy work on corporate banking and personal financial services. Edoardo has served clients mainly in the areas of credit process, derivative products, financial adviser networks, and retail mutual funds pricing.

Roberto Lancellotti is a principal who works in the Milan office. He is a co-leader of the IT & Operations working group of the European Banking Practice. Roberto's clients are in the banking and insurance industries, where he has advised retail banks, life, and property and casualty (P&C) insurance companies mainly on operational issues. His activities focus on IT, operations, and post-merger management.

Wilm Langenbach, an associate principal in the Munich office, has served both banks and insurance companies. He is an expert in bancassurance, with a special focus on the personal financial service products of life and asset management. Wilm has also worked within the areas of corporate finance and strategy.

Reinhold Leichtfuss is a director based in the Frankfurt office and leader of the firm's European Retail Banking Practice together with Justo Alcocer. He is the founder of the Excellence in Retail Banking Framework and, in the late 1990s, conducted a number of Excellence in Retail Banking workshops with leading retail banks around the world. Reinhold has worked on numerous studies for banking and insurance clients, covering basically all areas within banking. Reinhold's major focus areas have been strategy, corporate leadership, marketing and sales, distribution, organization, merger management, controlling, and risk management. He has published numerous articles on a wide range of banking topics.

Paul ter Linden is a principal in the Amsterdam office who has also spent time in the Montreal office. He is a member of the European Retail Banking Leadership Group. Paul has served clients on strategic issues in a number of industries, namely banking, insurance, transportation, and telecommunication. In the retail banking sector, his major areas of expertise are products and distribution approaches for small- and medium-sized businesses.

Luís Lopes, an associate principal based in the Lisbon office, has worked mainly for clients in the financial institution and industrial sectors. He has been actively involved in turnaround situations and in enhancing the performance of retail banking businesses through pricing, product enhancement, sales stimulation, and efficiency programs.

Jens Lottner is a principal in the Kuala Lumpur office, having spent most of his time at the firm in Germany. He has a strong focus on financial services and is a co-leader of both the Asian Risk Management Practice and the South-East Asian Financial Institutions Practice. Jens's focus has been on a wide variety of core strategic and operational retail banking issues, as well as on corporate finance-related topics such as risk management, capital market products, and shareholder value management.

Miguel Lucas is a principal in the Lisbon office and a member of the European Retail Banking Leadership Group. Miguel has served several financial institutions, in both retail and corporate banking, although most of his work has been carried out in retail banking, where he has conducted numerous projects for the small business, affluent, and mass-market segments. In mass market, he has covered profitability turnaround, distribution network, products and pricing, and sales force effectiveness.

Fedele Di Maggio is a principal based in the Budapest office who has also spent three years in the Rome and Johannesburg offices. He is the leader of the Financial Institutions Practice in Eastern Europe and a core member of the Emerging Markets Financial Institutions Practice. Fedele is also a member of the European Retail Banking Leadership Group. He has worked mainly with financial institutions, and his areas of experience include corporate strategy, performance management, turnaround programs, affluent business, and credit.

Luca Martini is a principal in the Verona office and member of the European Retail Banking Leadership Group. He is also an active member of the European Asset Management Practice. He joined the firm after several years of working for another strategy consultancy and has focused mainly on retail banking and asset management since then. Recent projects include corporate strategy, product strategy, redesign of branch network, affluent banking strategy, operations, sales stimulation, and M&A.

Renato Martini, an associate principal in the Rome office, has focused on clients in the banking, insurance, and telecommunications sectors. His areas of expertise include marketing, customer service, sales force management, operations, IT, organization, and P&C insurance.

Pedro Mateache is a director in the Madrid office. Pedro has focused on serving financial institutions, working with nearly 30 different institutions located mostly in Europe and Latin America, and helping them meet their challenges in most areas. His main professional interests revolve around major transformation, change management, and growth-oriented processes, but he has also covered corporate and business unit strategy, as well as the functional areas of sales management, distribution, risk management, operations, and technology.

Lodovico Mazzolin is an associate principal with the Business Technology Office in Milan. His clients are mainly in the retail banking, corporate banking, and insurance industry, and he has covered a wide array of areas including customer segment strategies, distribution, financial advisers, IT, operations, credit management, sales force management, claims management, and life insurance.

Thomas Merkle works in the Munich office as an associate principal. He is a member of the German Financial Institutions Leadership Group and the European Retail Banking Leadership Group. Thomas has focused on both retail and wholesale banking in the financial institutions sector. His major areas of experience are pricing, asset finance, and investment products.

Jean-Christophe Mieszala is a principal in the Paris office but also worked in the Washington DC office for several years. He is a member of the European Retail Banking Practice. During his time with the firm, Jean-Christophe has worked mainly for banking and insurance clients. His major areas of expertise include consumer credit, payments, wholesale banking strategy and organization, risk management, post-merger management, sales force organization and management, and contact centers.

Andrea Mignanelli is an engagement manager based in the Milan office. His clients are within the financial services industry, with a particular focus on banking. Andrea has a broad range of experience in credit, organization, and business-building.

Valentin Mihov is a practice expert in retail banking based in the Frankfurt office. He is a member of the European Retail Banking Leadership Group. He has served his retail banking clients in the areas of distribution, strategy, organization, pricing, cost reduction, and product strategy. Valentin led most of the research for this book.

Bruno Montalvo, a principal based in the Madrid office, is a member of the European Retail Banking Leadership Group. Bruno has developed his professional activities in the financial institutions and telecommunications sectors, serving a number of clients in Portugal, Spain, the US, and several Latin American countries. His consulting experience covers a wide range of topics in the areas of corporate and business unit strategy, M&A, post-merger management, risk management, business-building and market entry, organization, marketing, and distribution.

Axel Müller-Groeling is an associate principal based in the Hamburg office. He works primarily with retail banks and utilities. Axel is an expert in risk management and corporate steering, and recent projects include credit risk, market risk, commodity price risk, risk-adjusted pricing, organization, balanced scorecards, and value-based management.

Gene Pappas is a principal based in Paris. He is the co-head of the European Wholesale and Investment Banking Practice. His work has focused largely on serving financial institution clients. Gene has served a number of commercial and investment banks, developing strategies for their corporate banking, investment banking and corporate finance businesses. He has also worked with different banking clients within operational product areas such as cash management, global custody, retirement services, securities processing, and corporate trust.

Wolfram Peters, an engagement manager based in the Frankfurt office, has served clients in the financial institutions sector on a wide range of topics including credit risk management, portfolio models, pricing, workout, capital markets, and post-merger management.

Alejandro Picos Losada is a principal who leads the Business Technology Office for Latin America. Since joining the firm he has worked in the Miami, São Paulo, New York, Toronto, Buenos Aires, and Istanbul offices. He is a core member of both the North American and Emerging Markets Financial Institutions Practices and leads the global hi-tech program for consultants in the financial industry. His work has focused on design, construction, and launch of new ventures, targeting innovative marketing concepts through state-of-the-art operations and information technology in the financial, telecommunications, electronics, and e-commerce sectors.

Diego Polo-Friz is a principal in the Milan office and the leader of the Banking work group of the European Risk Management Practice. Diego has served financial institutions on a variety of strategic and operational issues including risk management, sales and marketing, IT effectiveness, business process redesign, organization, post-merger management, value based management, growth, and privatization.

Gabriela Pueyo is an associate who started out in the Mexico City office and after a stint in the Buenos Aires office moved to the Madrid office. She has worked for clients in the banking, new technologies, telecommunications, nonprofit, and public sector areas, primarily helping them with marketing and growth strategies.

A.C. Reuter-Domenech is a director in the São Paulo office who has also worked in the Mexico City, Caracas, New York, and Milan offices. He was office manager in Caracas and has opened a number of McKinsey locations in South America. Since he joined the firm, he has led client service teams in most Latin American countries as well as North America and Europe. Among other areas, he has served clients in M&A and strategic and economic evaluation. He is currently the leader of the Emerging Markets Financial Institutions Practice and responsible for launching and leading the Corporate Finance & Strategy Practice across the region, serving both local and international clients.

Philipp Rickenbacher, an engagement manager in the Zurich office, also has experience of the London office. He has worked for clients in banking and securities, pharmaceuticals, agribusiness, and health care. Within banking and securities, his projects include post-merger management, bancassurance, new business-building, and mortgage strategy.

Pedro Rodeia is a principal in the Lisbon office who has also worked in the Chicago and Amsterdam offices. He is a member of the European Retail Banking Leadership

Group. Pedro has worked on numerous studies for banking clients, with a focus on retail banking, covering a wide array of topics including performance leadership and incentives, portfolio strategy, private banking, affluent, small business and mass market strategies, branch sales stimulation, organization, management information systems (MIS)/incentive systems, and credit underwriting and recovery.

Florian Reich-Rohrwig, an engagement manager in the Vienna office, has worked with a broad spectrum of financial industry clients including wholesale, investment and retail banks, asset managers, and public finance institutions. His major areas of experience include business strategy, operational excellence, efficiency improvement, and affluent banking.

Heinrich-Stefan Rolvering is a principal in the Stuttgart office. He is a member of the European Retail Banking Leadership Group. During his time with the firm, he has worked in almost all areas of consulting in banks and asset management companies. His major areas of expertise include marketing and sales, including CRM, developing value propositions, pricing and sales stimulation, as well as distribution network design, multichannel management, and private banking.

Piotr Romanowski is an associate principal based in the Warsaw office and has also spent a year in the New Jersey office. He is a member of the European Retail Banking Leadership Group. Piotr has developed his professional activities in the banking, insurance, and pharmaceuticals industry. His major areas of expertise include affluent banking and sales.

Anupam Sahay is a principal in the Business Technology Office in London. He also has international experience from the Mumbai, Chicago, and Melbourne offices. Anupam leads the Operations work group in the European Banking and Securities Practice and is a member of the European Retail Banking Leadership Group. He has served clients in the banking, insurance, and software industries on numerous issues. His major areas of expertise include international strategy, new distribution, and cross-border operations.

Alex Satchell, an associate principal in the London office, has worked in the retail and corporate banking, credit card, and leasing sectors. His consulting experience covers the major areas of overall strategy and transformational change.

Andrea Scerch is an associate principal based in the Milan office. He is mainly serving clients in the retail banking industry. Andrea has focused his activities on strategic planning, turnaround, sales force stimulation, and business-building.

Oliver Schein works in the Business Technology Office in Frankfurt as an associate. Since he joined McKinsey, Oliver has focused mainly on the financial services industry, where he has a broad range of experience in IT management, architecture, and operations.

Christian Schramm is an engagement manager based in the Cologne office whose work has focused largely on serving financial institution clients. His projects include sales stimulation, consumer banking strategy, pricing, credit and real estate workout, organization, and marketing.

Marcus Sieberer is a principal in the Vienna office and co-leader of the newly established South-East Europe office in Zagreb. He is a member of the European Retail Banking Leadership Group and the European Organization Practice. Since joining the firm, Marcus has concentrated most of his work on financial institutions and the public sector. His projects include post-merger management, strategy, profit improvement, back-office optimization, MIS, organization, credit, and performance culture.

Ernst Sonderegger is managing director, head TOP Corporate Center at Credit Suisse Financial Services. Until January 2003 Ernst was a principal in the Business Technology Office (BTO) in Zurich having joined McKinsey from IBM. He was a core member of the Swiss IT Practice and a leader of the BTO, within which he led the European Retail Banking Sector. He has particular expertise in IT for financial institutions and has served his clients on a broad range of issues, including front-end system strategy, IT production, cost reduction, transaction-processing strategy, e-brokerage platform, IT rearchitecture, and post-merger IT integration.

Volker Stadler is an associate principal in the Business Technology Office in Zurich. Within the BTO, he is member of the European Retail Banking Leadership Group. Volker has a broad range of experience in IT and operations outsourcing, strategy development, and business-building, focusing mainly on the financial services industry.

Uwe Stegemann is a principal in Cologne and a member of the Global Risk Management Leadership Group. Uwe has broad experience in risk management and banking issues and has served both retail and wholesale banks as well as bank regulators/central banks. His main areas of interest are risk-return-oriented capital allocation, market risk and asset liability management, credit portfolio management, credit rating, and Basel II.

János Strohmayer now works as an engagement manager in the Athens office, although he spent his first years in the Budapest office. He has focused on the financial and consumer goods sectors and has gathered broad experience in many different areas including growth strategies, marketing, e-banking, and distribution.

Vittorio E. Terzi is a director in the Rome office, which he helped establish in 1988. Before that he worked in the Milan office. He is a member of the leadership group of the European Banking & Securities Practice and of the Global Corporate Finance and Strategy Practice. Vittorio has recently managed a wide range of studies in the banking, insurance, and financial industries with Italy's major public and private institutions. Within these industries, he has focused particularly on corporate finance and strategy, M&A, performance enhancement, organization, and channel management issues.

Rita D'Uva is an associate principal in the Milan office. Her clients are mainly in the banking industry, and she has worked in a range of areas including strategy, M&A, capital structure management, financial engineering, marketing and sales, organization, pricing, asset management, and investment banking.

Vittoria Varianini is a principal in the Milan office, having also worked for a year in the London office. She is a member of the European Retail Banking Leadership Group. Vittoria is also one of the leaders of the European Marketing Practice, and her professional activities have a clear focus on marketing and branding issues. She has worked for clients in many different industries, including retail banking, insurance, consumer goods, telecommunications, and services. Her recent projects include strategy, marketing capabilities, organization, market entry, and branding/marketing spend effectiveness.

Stefano Visalli is a principal in the Milan office and a member of the European Retail Banking Leadership Group. Although he has spent most of his time serving financial institutions with a focus on retail banking and asset management, he has also worked with media and entertainment clients. He has a wide range of experience in both strategic and operational issues. The focus of his projects span from strategy, M&A, business-building and alliances to distribution, organization, and credit risk management.

Ulrich Voss is a principal in the Frankfurt office who joined and spent his first years with the firm in the Boston office. He is a member of the European Retail Banking Leadership Group. Ulrich has worked mainly for clients in the banking and insurance sector, with a special focus on retail banking. Although having covered most of the banking areas, his main focus has been on branch operations redesign, post-merger management, organizational setup, M&A, and international expansion strategies.

Cornelius Walter, a principal in the Munich office, has also worked for two years in the Budapest office. He has served a number of financial institution clients in both continental and Eastern Europe. Cornelius's consulting work has covered most areas of banking, with a focus on corporate and business unit strategy, performance management, turnaround, and affluent banking.

Part 1
Excellence and High Performers

1
Excellence in Retail Banking

Reinhold Leichtfuss

Retail banks around the world are having difficulty achieving good results, often despite their best efforts. They are introducing new strategies and organizational concepts, they are trying to increase cross-selling, and they are launching new channels and products. But not all can be certain that they are giving the most important actions the highest priority; and not all are following through with uncompromising implementation.

As a way to help banks structure their thinking, we have devised the Excellence in Retail Banking framework that consists of 32 competencies grouped in five competence categories (Figure 1.1). Banks that are world class in the most relevant set of competencies for their particular strategy can excel in retail banking. They can become the star to which the category arrows point, no matter whether they operate in Europe, America, or Asia. The five categories are:

- *Performance-oriented corporate leadership.* Relentlessly driving performance and establishing a performance culture throughout a bank are ultimately the cause of the greatest difference between the leading banks and the average performers.
- *Sophisticated marketing and sales.* This requires an approach that fluently translates customer information into effective marketing and sales strategies and subsequent revenue growth.
- *Differentiated and efficient distribution.* Banks must make the most efficient use possible of the multitude of distribution channels available to them.
- *Cost-efficient processes and information technology.* Although most banks have advanced in back office centralization, other fundamental process improvements still lag behind, not least in information technology (IT), in terms of becoming as cost-efficient as possible.
- *Superior credit policy and skills.* Without having the right organization in place to deal with risk and having advanced underwriting and portfolio management capabilities, no bank can remain at the top.

All these capabilities are important, but each bank will have a different set of priorities and a different emphasis on the individual competencies within each category depending on its own particular starting point and strategic goals.

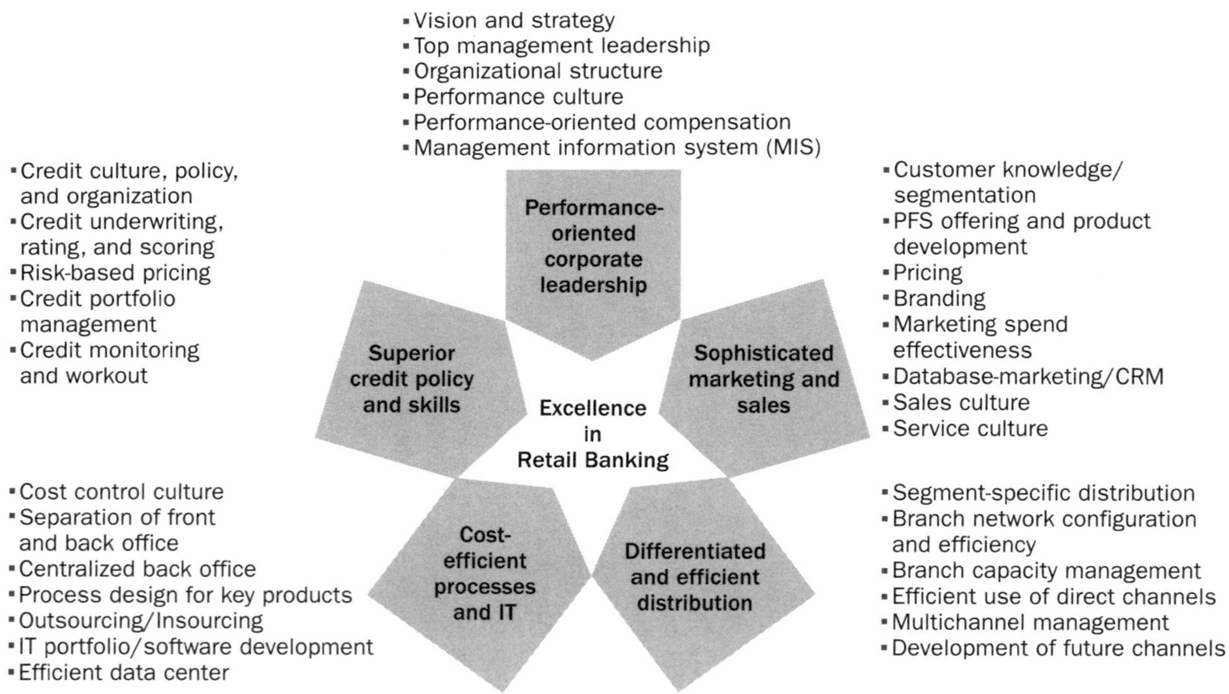

Figure 1.1 Excellence in Retail Banking Framework

Source: McKinsey

Most banks are naturally working to build these capabilities; many might argue they already have them. But our analyses show that in each category there is a substantial difference between world class and average. Leading banks tend to shine in all categories—not just corporate leadership and marketing and sales, but in distribution, operations, and credit as well. However, even these leading banks have scope for improvement and, of course, they are usually those that are least satisfied with their performance in weaker areas and that have the highest ambition to improve.

Performance-oriented corporate leadership

At the heart of strong corporate leadership sits a management team that is willing to initiate change, carry through implementation, and—when necessary—take tough decisions. It will be successful ultimately, however, only if a strong performance culture is embedded within the bank. By this we mean that the bank tolerates mediocrity neither in its aspirations and objectives nor in its everyday activities, but rather expects superior performance from everyone—from frontline salesperson to CEO—and rewards them accordingly. Merely improving is not enough for banks that have this sort of culture at their heart, they are constantly striving to be the best, not just better.

Leadership starts with setting the strategic direction. After all, there is little point in having high-performing units if they are pulling in different directions. A strategy should determine a specific superior market position and value proposition and, with that in place, it should be much easier to align everything else. The organizational structure of a bank then provides the frame within which responsibilities and accountabilities are made clear. Minimizing ambiguity here is important, otherwise performance targets can slip between the gaps and everyone passes the buck onto someone else. Too many banks do not demarcate units clearly enough, nor do they enforce adequate rules for cooperation.

Performance-oriented compensation systems are important in fostering a performance culture. Many leading retail banks pay their managers, and many less senior employees, a significant, variable, reward package that is linked to performance. In order to help managers achieve the highest performance possible, they must be equipped with a management information system (MIS) that shows them the key performance indicators—and they must also use it. Banks, however, should not be fooled into thinking that such a system can replace managerial action, it can help in reaching targets only if managers act decisively on the information it provides.

Part 2 (Chapters 4 to 9) deals with these topics in more detail.

Sophisticated marketing and sales

Marketing and sales competencies are the software that runs on top of the distribution system. Although such skills are not traditional hallmarks of banks, leading players are increasingly focusing on them. Having strong marketing and sales competencies plays an important role in developing the market position and delivering the value propositions that are set out in the strategy.

All the competencies within marketing and sales are highly interlinked, and indeed the connections spread out beyond this category into other areas of the framework

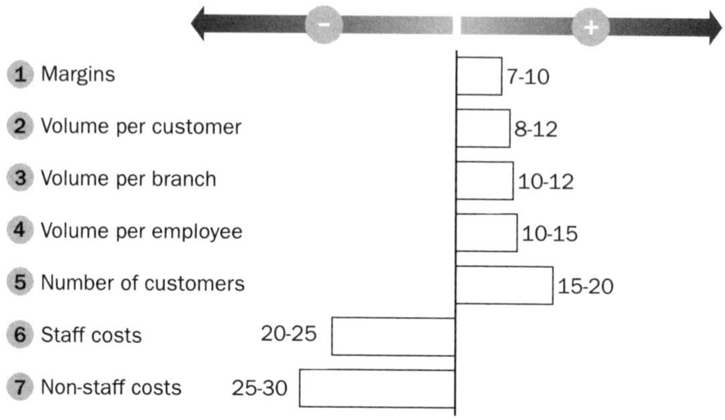

Figure 1.2 Hierarchy of factors to improve operating profitability by 25 percent (required percent of increase/decrease)

Source: McKinsey

such as performance culture, distribution, processes, and IT. They must all be directed effectively toward revenue growth.

The starting point for a more sophisticated marketing and sales operation is to specify the bank's overall value proposition for individual segments and target groups. This requires deep knowledge of the customer and state-of-the-art segmentation skills. Knowing the customer is a cornerstone of success in banking, just as it is in many consumer goods industries. Knowing the customers, their individual and life cycle needs, and their price sensitivities is also the basis for offering the most appropriate products and pricing.

Product development is still rarely seen as a core competency as replication is so easy in the financial services industry. However, some innovative providers have proved that it is possible to attract considerable numbers of customers with a new product, while those that see themselves only as followers miss out on potential revenue.

Working in tandem with having the right products is having the right pricing. Hardly any bank in the world today could claim to be excellent in pricing, yet given its impact on profits, the importance of improving pricing cannot be overemphasized. Financial services providers can take better advantage of price elasticities than they have in the past; best practice shows that in most markets, high profitability is connected to high pricing. Indeed, a *ceteris paribus* analysis based on a sample of typical retail banks shows that pricing has the greatest impact on profitability. A 25 percent increase in profits would take only a 7 to 10 percent increase in overall margins whereas the number of actual customers would have to increase by 15 to 20 percent to have the same effect (Figure 1.2).

Another strength of the consumer goods sector is branding, with some leading companies admired and envied for their brands. Banks have been slow to immerse themselves in this sort of intelligent branding, but the rewards can be substantial: the right brand can reduce the perceived risk for the customer, both attracting a greater share of wallet and more new customers. However, it is important to understand how budgets should be allocated in branding, as in other areas of marketing: some banks wonder whether they are throwing good money after bad, while others achieve the same impact at half the cost.

Banks can improve their product offering and their branding by making better use of the unique customer information they possess. Many are poor at exploiting such data, but effective database-marketing can create a powerful competitive advantage. It usually entails developing and refining systems, and cleaning and accumulating information over two to three years. No financial services provider is likely to excel in the future without this capability.

The difference between the most successful banks and the rest is the quality of the link between the marketing database and the frontline sales staff. Such an approach can support branch-based marketing in order to raise hit ratios and therefore reduce customer acquisition costs—especially important in the mass market where it can make the difference between profit and loss.

Of course, if all these marketing efforts are to succeed, then there must also be a superior sales culture in place. The most successful programs to develop this usually include a mixture of directives from above, staff empowerment, and specific on-the-job training. In those banks that have already gone through this stage, the sales culture has certainly improved, but nine out of ten of them still have plenty of room for further improvement in terms of both sales and profits. To ensure continuous improvement, the targeted monitoring and effective coaching of sales teams and individual salespeople is needed, as well as the database-marketing selling approaches mentioned above.

For a sales culture to flourish, it has to go hand in hand with a strong service culture, otherwise any increase in sales would be a short-lived event. The service challenge is particularly taxing because it requires the behavioral changes of thousands of people and a commitment to provide error-free service to customers. All service investments must naturally be cost-effective.

Part 3 (Chapters 10 to 14) discusses marketing, sales, and service skills in much more detail.

Differentiated and efficient distribution

The distribution channels are the hardware on which all marketing and sales efforts will build. Rising technological sophistication, the divergence of the needs of individual customer groups, and last but not least pure economics have made channel innovations and differentiated distribution crucial for many banks. Increasing differentiation does, however, mean rising complexity and cost, which in turn demands that the distribution channels are optimally set up and coordinated in order to achieve greater efficiency. One of the keys to differentiation is an intelligent active and passive segmentation (i.e., self-selection by customers) of both the existing and potential customer base. Indeed, service differentiation makes economic sense only if higher cost value delivery to some segments results in higher revenues.

Despite all their differentiation efforts, only a few banks in the world have successfully managed to develop distinctive separate business systems for different customer segments—offering standard services at low costs and low prices for the mass market and a value-oriented service for affluent customers.

Of all the multitude of options, branches have remained a bank's primary channel, and branch economics have improved lately as the branches themselves have become increasingly standardized. The death of the branch has certainly been a myth; the reality is that across Europe the number of branches fell by just 0.4 percent per year from 1993 to 2001, although the rate has been increasing, with a drop of 0.7 percent from 1998 to 2001.

The key to maximizing the effectiveness of a branch network is not just to shrink it but also to develop a differentiated network. This allows a bank to offer segment-specific benefits and be more cost-efficient by concentrating expertise rather than offering everything everywhere. A bank with a dense branch network can reduce costs by up to 10 percent by moving in such a direction. To cut costs further, leading banks have become far more flexible in their workforce utilization, drawing on a much larger share of part-time staff. This type of active capacity management can save 5 to 10 percent of staffing costs assuming that branch managers are able to match staffing levels to demand.

Retail banks are also taking a closer look at the potential benefits of embracing financial adviser networks. Banks that are seeking to expand their distribution capabilities and tap deeper into the profitable affluent segment can learn from the methods of these competitors, and some have even partnered with one or gone as far as acquiring a network.

Direct channels have gained enormous ground over the 1990s, and it is now well established that call centers can perform some tasks more efficiently than branches, but some banks have recently gone as far as moving entire customer segments to call centers. This not only saves the bank money but also allows them to offer customers a higher level of service at all times. However, it can also cause some customers to leave the bank.

The proliferation of new channels is causing headaches among bankers: online channels have brought efficiency gains but, in the short-term, overall costs have increased. Future channels such as interactive television, broadband, and mobile banking are yet to have a major economic impact. With this many channels at their disposal, banks now must consolidate them, acknowledging that their optimal setup will continuously evolve. There are tricky problems to be solved along the way, such as who owns the customer or whether all channels have equal rights to approach customers. Those banks that strike the right balance fastest and come up with intelligent solutions to these problems, will be able to capitalize on their 'hardware' efficiency.

Part 4 (Chapters 15 to 19) talks about what can be learned from distribution in the 1990s, before addressing the specific developments in branches, financial adviser networks, and direct channels and before finally offering an approach for successful multichannel management.

Cost-efficient processes and information technology

Cost-efficiency is clearly a major competitive strength, if not quite as significant as pricing and salesforce effectiveness given its size relative to revenues. On the other hand, process design and IT questions have gained more strategic relevance for banks because of increased outsourcing and insourcing opportunities and the capability of IT to build a competitive advantage through more efficient processes and innovative product offerings. Overall, the costs of an average retail bank—while varying from bank to bank and from country to country—are allocated as follows: 35 to 45 percent fall within the distribution network, 20 to 40 percent in operations, 10 to 20 percent on IT, approximately 10 percent on marketing, product development, and controlling and 10 to 20 percent on corporate overhead. In many banks it is immediately clear that the costs incurred by the corporate center and the nonsales- and distribution-oriented functions are too high. These functions are only indirectly productive and in many cases their costs should be reduced.

In order to keep costs down, a bank must have highly efficient and automated processes as well as a sound cost control culture. This means proactively controlling spending, rather than trying to cut back after the event. The capital markets also reward such a frugal culture, while tending not to appreciate stop–start cost-cutting measures. It may sound easy, but banks find themselves overrun by business pressures or technological developments.

A classic way to control costs is to centralize the back office and separate it from sales. Many banks did this during the 1990s, but not all completed the task. Some omitted important processes, others found that sales staff were creating new administrative activities, and still others floundered amid insufficient IT support.

The radical standardization and automation of processes will be a major challenge for many banks in the coming years, especially in the mass-market business. This will require a fundamental redesign of key processes. The overall goal should be to transform business systems, starting with simpler product design and including standardized sales approaches and a greater use of electronic transfers with the customer. Efficient back office processing is then essentially the result of improvements in earlier stages of the business system.

Many banks are increasingly considering outsourcing options more seriously, and several have already begun to outsource IT, securities-processing, payments, as well as loan-processing, both in mortgages and in consumer lending. However, progress tends to be slow. For the front-runners, the natural extension of outsourcing is to offshore processes and functions to lower cost locations such as India, where a skilled, but cheaper workforce is available. Some globally oriented banks are already taking substantial advantage of this.

Application development is essential for developing superior processes, but it can be an overwhelming challenge for many banks stuck with legacy systems. By contrast, efficient data centers are relatively easy to achieve, especially when compared with reaching true efficiency in software.

Part 5 (Chapters 20 to 23) expands at length on the cost issues that face retail banks.

Superior credit policy and skills

Credit, together with payments, has been the traditional core function of banks and therefore is a skill developed over hundreds of years. However, the credit business has undergone substantial regulatory changes over recent years. The new credit regulations have come sooner than expected and require the strict separation of credit sales and decision-making as well as separate workout units. These changes will have significant implications for banks' overall organization and processes. In addition, new legal arrangements require well-designed internal or external rating systems and more sophisticated portfolio management. The changes will certainly improve credit policies and offer chances for those banks that are prepared to tackle the challenge head on.

A well-defined credit policy and sound judgment are fundamental to retail banking success. It has long held true that the careful, conservative examination of credit risks lays a solid foundation for all credit management. Much of this comes from the unwritten expertise of bankers, and will always be important. However, superior credit capability will be determined in the future by the increasing use of systems for decision support, credit scoring, and credit rating. Systems capable of credit analysis not only increase the process efficiency but also improve decision quality, thereby reducing loan losses.

Credit underwriting is changing as rating and scoring become compulsory, forcing banks into adopting a much more systematic and transparent decision process. The radical standardization and automation of credit application processing is still a major challenge for European banks. Although consumer credit scoring systems do exist, the degree of success in implementation varies widely between best and average practice, and fully automated systems have yet to be developed properly in the area of small and medium commercial credits.

Robust rating and scoring systems can be a distinct competitive advantage for banks that have exposure to higher risk market segments. Despite existing for some time, scoring systems have been used rarely for differentiated risk-based loan-pricing, partly because their rigorous application and the statistical analysis were poor in many banks. Basel II will now enforce both the application of these instruments as well as their price relevance, as capital requirements will be based on credit risk classes.

In terms of credit portfolio management, banks have traditionally followed the 'buy and hold' strategy, with primarily US and UK institutions using securitization in the consumer credit and credit card business. Under Basel II, and with new technology available, portfolio management will start in credit origination and include more active controlling so that increasingly only target segments, risk classes, loan sizes, and maturities will be acquired and accepted.

Monitoring that builds on regular and more frequent rating updates as well as better data and analysis techniques will become standard, and workout units will be established as separate organizational units that try to manage the banks' collateral actively and more professionally. The most advanced banks in this area have even started to offer their services to competitors.

Part 6 (Chapters 24 to 28) offers much more detail on how to achieve excellence in this most fundamental area of banking given the new set of challenges.

The competencies elaborated upon in the framework are also followed very closely by the capital markets. Analysts and investors alike do not simply examine current financials, they also assess the underlying drivers of value creation (Box 1.1).

Raising the game to world-class levels

We have talked a lot about frameworks, processes, competencies, cultures, and only implicitly about people. But people are far from excluded from the Excellence

Box 1.1

Competencies: the capital markets' view

To identify what the capital markets monitor, we analyzed 50 broker reports and conducted a series of interviews with analysts in 2001 and 2002. Overwhelmingly, analysts pay the closest attention to corporate leadership, which together with a distinctive strategy was mentioned in no less than 86 percent of the cases (Figure 1.3). The second most common reference was to 'operating cost', understood as the ability to control costs and run efficient processes and IT systems. Credit skills were mentioned in 70 percent of the reports.

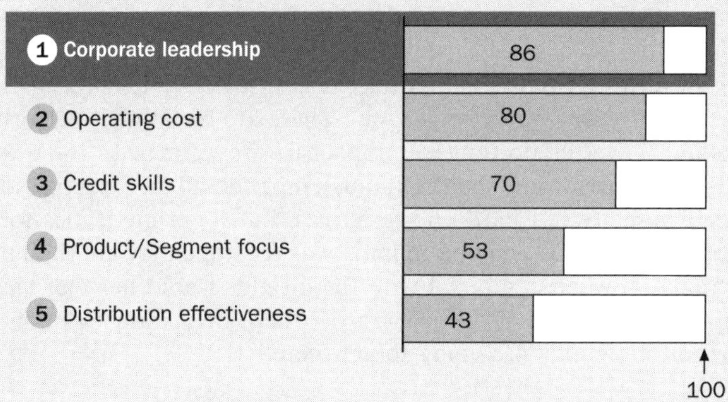

Figure 1.3 What analysts look for (percent of reports mentioning competence as important)

Source: analyst reports: McKinsey

The trustworthiness and credibility of the management team, distinctive strategies that can create sustainable competitive advantage, and the ability to deliver against expectations were all seen as essential components of corporate leadership. A shareholder value mindset is also highly regarded—and is reflected in the approach to management compensation and communication with analysts and investors—and a strong, independent board of directors seems to increase confidence in the top management. Performance-oriented corporate leadership not only enables current profitability, but seems to be the core driver of growth expectations.

The importance of this area is exemplified by the market impact of CEO changes, which when measured in terms of abnormal (10-day) returns has often been significant, though which way the share price moves will naturally depend on the market perception of the new and the old management.

Ongoing cost leadership was identified by 80 percent of the reports as an essential virtue, and it is clearly crucial in a mature industry such as retail banking. The key success factors in achieving cost leadership include ensuring that cost control is continuous, rather than a series of spectacular one-off measures. This is reflected in market reaction to announcements of cost reduction initiatives. Markets generally react favorably to such announcements, especially if the measures are taken in a consistent long-term context. Broker reports often refer to key process capabilities, IT-driven productivity gains, and IT efficiency are the major contributors to cost leadership.

As the economic environment deteriorates, both banks and analysts start to pay more vocal attention to risk management. And indeed in 2002, the difference between the best and the rest was crystal clear: top-quartile players by profitability had a ratio of nonperforming loans to loans outstanding that was three times lower than the ratio at bottom-quartile banks.

Marketing and sales as well as distribution competencies were mentioned less frequently, which is probably due to people's tendency to focus on whatever seems important at the moment. Nevertheless, about half the reports and all interviews mentioned that these skills are critical to revenue growth.

Although strong skills across these competency areas are fundamental to meeting market expectations, effective communication is just as indispensable. High-performing banks excel at delivering on promises—and managing expectations.

Nick Adamus, Roman Binder

in Retail Banking framework; they are included everywhere. Within every area, especially the critical ones such as corporate leadership, sales culture, and service culture, it remains the case that banking is about people and systems—and to be world class a bank needs world-class people.

But tackling all these topics would be a heavy burden to shoulder, even for top talent. Some might argue the task is too daunting, and that world-class performance in all these areas is not necessary. To an extent they are right. Best practice in every single element would be impossible to sustain. What does matter is how close a bank can get to top-flight performance in the most important competencies on which its strategy builds.

To give an idea of what is achievable, it is instructive to look at the best retail banks over recent years—the 'top league'. These are banks that perform strongly in most areas and have the bottom-line impact to show for it. In the next chapter we discuss these high-performing banks in much more detail and identify some formulae for success. These are not hard-and-fast rules, but more guidelines to what can be done by a bank that is determined to improve. We hope they are thought-provoking and inspiring and, when combined with the insights found in other chapters of this book, help banks to draw up the vision of where they want to be in three to five years' time and how they are going to get there.

2

High-performing Banks: Climbing to the Top

Reinhold Leichtfuss, Thomas Merkle, Valentin Mihov, Jacob Dahl[1]

Some banks excel in retail banking; they are at the top of their game. Others—the majority in fact—are still trying to work their way to the next level. In revealing what separates the high-performing banks from the rest, we can also help map the path to the summit. For banks still lingering at base camp, gazing up at those ascending above them, there will be satisfaction in knowing that there are ways to close the gap: but in banking as in mountaineering, climbing to the top takes an unbreakable will, the right skills, and enough stamina to complete the journey.

STAR-GAZING: IDENTIFYING THE BRIGHTEST

We analyzed almost 100 banks active in retail banking along a broad range of financial and organizational dimensions. The key financial performance indicators were cost–income ratio, return on equity (ROE), revenue growth, cost growth, and change in cost–income ratio. In parallel, to ensure a comprehensive understanding of what drives success, the banks were also mapped against the five categories of the Excellence in Retail Banking framework: corporate leadership, marketing and sales, distribution, processes and IT, and credit policy and skills.

Compared with traditional analyses of bank performance, our analysis is unique in two ways. This is the first time that reported retail segment financials have been analyzed for such a large number of banks in different countries.[2] We are aware of the significant effect that individual market characteristics have on cost–income ratios and, indeed, more broadly on performance. As many banks would agree,

[1] The authors would like to express their gratitude to Matthew Bedford, Rebecca Emerson, Alex Michel, Luis Oro, Alexander Prokot, Pedro Rodeia, Raphael Schmidt, Georg Schubiger, and Michael Vogt for their contributions to researching and shaping this chapter. We would also like to thank Michael Froehls from Citigroup for his valuable input.

[2] A total of 93 banks in 14 countries were analyzed. For 66 banks, retail segment reporting or retail banking subsidiaries were examined. For the remaining 27 without segment reporting (predominantly retail-focused banks) group financials were used.

such distortions render cross-border performance benchmarking quite ineffective. Therefore, the second unique element of this research was to estimate this effect and introduce country-specific adjustments to cost–income ratios.

Country-specific adjustments

Three factors in particular affect profitability in banking: price levels, the average gross unit labor costs in banking, and average customer volumes.

Price levels in banking are closely tied to competitive intensity, and thus banks cannot influence market prices in the short term, especially when industry concentration levels make collusion unlikely. In addition, the historical product mix and the general level of interest rates also affect revenue margins.

Gross labor costs are the single biggest driver of costs in banking, accounting for between 41 and 61 percent of total costs in the US and Spain, respectively. By examining unit labor costs, we can separate out the effect of specific labor market conditions from general productivity in banking.

Average customer volumes are calculated as total personal financial assets and liabilities held per capita. Higher volumes per customer help drive efficiency gains, although any improvement is mitigated somewhat by the need to match customers' growing sophistication with a higher spend on advisory services, and to pass some of these gains on to the customer in the form of lower margins. However, there remains a clear (although not particularly strong) negative relationship between average customer volumes and national cost–income ratios.

These three factors account for about 70 percent of the variance between the national cost–income ratios. Price levels account for 40 percentage points, labor costs account for 20 percentage points, and the remaining 10 are explained by differences in average customer volumes. Disregarding the effects of possible cross-correlation, the remaining 30 percent of the variance should be attributable to differences in productivity between countries, caused by the development level of the banking system, including specifics of the payment system, degree of consolidation, or density of the branch networks.[3] Furthermore, labor laws and the strength of trade unions (as well as cultural conventions) can cause a significant divergence in the conditions for developing a superior performance culture—for which adjustments are not possible. Although we recognize that differences between banks within the same country exist (e.g., based on product mix and labor costs), adjusting for this was not part of our remit.

The adjustments place banks from Benelux, Switzerland, and Germany, which suffer from low margins and relatively high labor costs, onto a level playing field with banks from the UK, Australia, and the US, where both revenue margins and customer volumes are high (Figure 2.1).

[3] The robustness of the analysis could be improved by explicitly incorporating country productivity in banking. However, comparable data across all countries is extremely hard to obtain, and we believe that the adjustments we have made would hold up directionally, even if their magnitudes were slightly reduced.

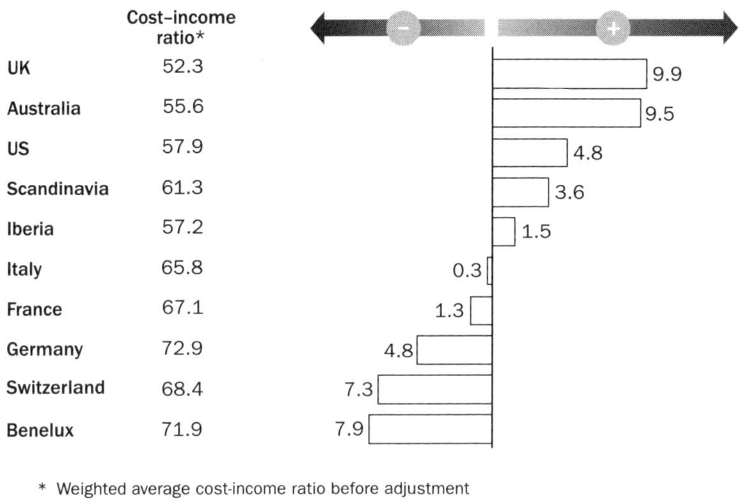

Figure 2.1 Adjustments to national cost–income ratios (percentage points)

Source: annual reports; central banks; OECD; McKinsey

Comparing the banks

A bank's market value is driven by both current profitability and expected revenue and profit growth. Together with cost–income performance, the ability to drive top-line growth over the long term is a key characteristic of successful banks. In Europe, where revenue pools in personal financial services grew by 4.5 percent between 1998 and 2001, the average revenue growth varies from country to country from 3 to 8 percent. However, the revenue growth disparities between banks *within* individual countries are much more significant: in all countries there are both banks that have grown by more than 10 percent on a merger-adjusted basis and those that have actually shrunk during the same period.

In our analysis we discovered that top performance on both country-adjusted cost–income and retail revenue growth goes hand in hand with excellent results on the other indicators that we have used. Combining these two major criteria then highlights those banks standing near the summit of excellence in retail banking. Nine banks enjoy both very attractive cost–income ratios and high revenue growth, adjusted for major mergers and acquisitions (M&A) activity: Citibank NA[4] in the US and Citibank PK in Germany (counted as two banks, given the extremely different environments each operates in), Banco Popular Español, UniCredito Italiano, Svenska Handelsbanken, Fifth Third, Banca Fideuram, Banco Comercial Português and Royal Bank of Scotland (Figure 2.2).

These banks have outstanding efficiency levels—achieving cost–income ratios below 50 percent in some cases—while still managing to grow by about 10 percent or more per year. This growth means that their cost–income ratios are improving

[4] Citibank NA is used here and throughout the book to refer to the banking/lending business of Citigroup's Consumer Group as defined in the Annual Report 2001 (Citibanking NA, Mortgage Banking, North America Cards, and CitiFinancial).

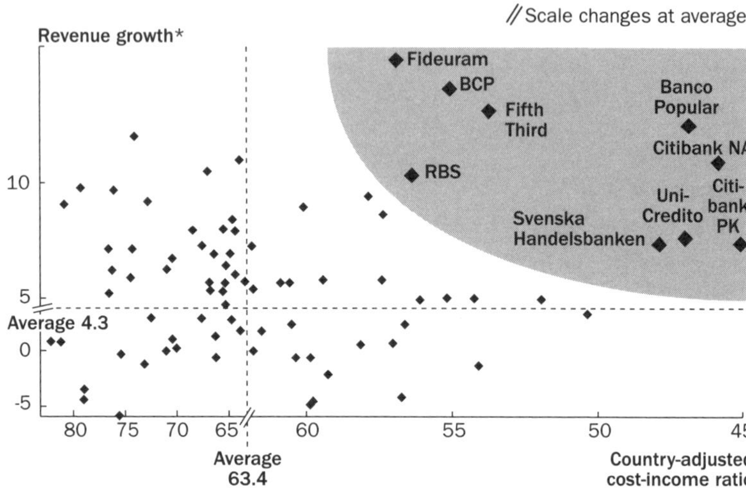

* Adjusted for major M&A activity

Figure 2.2 Revenue growth and country-adjusted cost–income ratios (percent, 1998–2001)

Source: annual reports; McKinsey

further and that at the same time they are earning higher-than-average returns on equity.

Alongside these financial criteria, we investigated the organizational capabilities of the banks along the Excellence in Retail Banking framework. The banks were assessed on all 32 competencies, on a scale from one (below-average performance, some serious weaknesses) to four (excellent, world-class skills) (Figure 2.3).

WHAT MAKES THE STARS SHINE

As mentioned in the previous chapter, exceptional corporate leadership is the strongest differentiator between the highest performing banks and the rest. The best banks have markedly higher scores for vision and strategy, which includes market-positioning and value proposition. All the top banks exhibit an outstanding drive for performance, striving relentlessly for bottom-line impact.

Nurturing the right attitude is also paramount in marketing and sales, where the presence of a strong sales culture marks out the winners.

The gaps to best practice in distribution are much smaller, with the notable exception of the effective use of direct channels. Interestingly, the top league banks actually score slightly below average in the development of future channels, suggesting that they tread cautiously when it comes to investing in new technologies.

High process and IT efficiency levels are already well established among the leading banks, which have separated sales from processing and centralized their back offices. Some of them also optimized their cost base through straight-through processing and the use of outsourcing where appropriate.

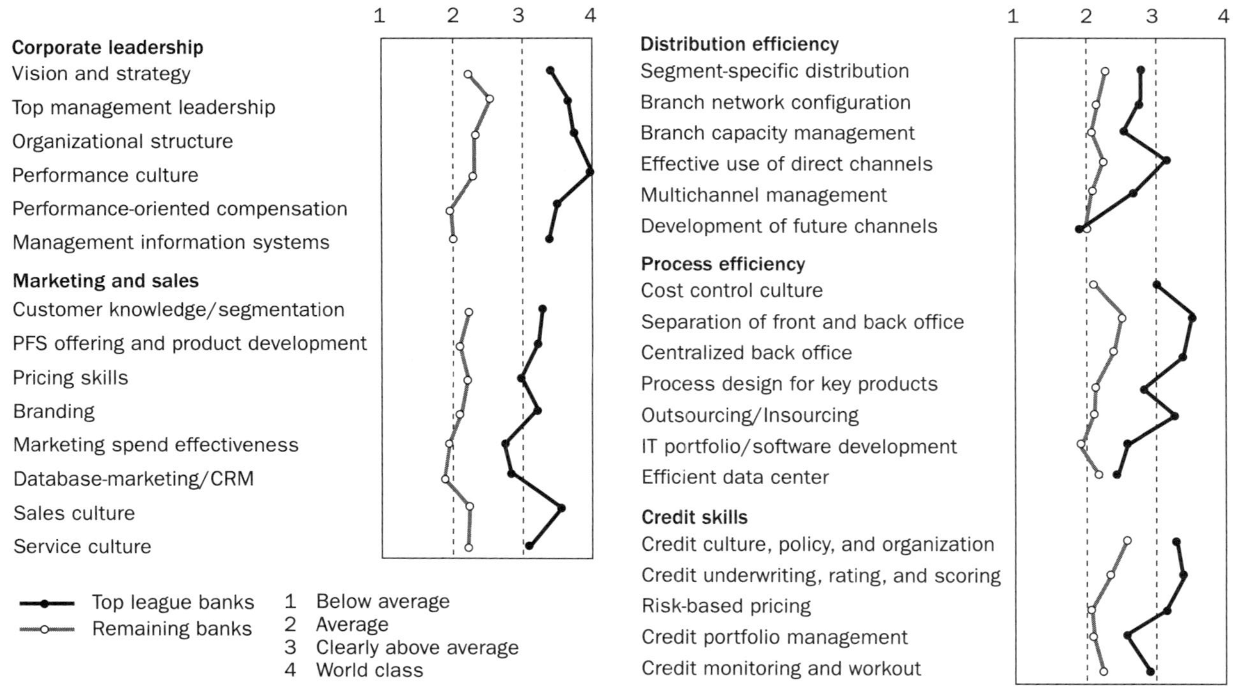

Figure 2.3 Assessment of banks' performance along Excellence in Retail Banking framework

Source: McKinsey

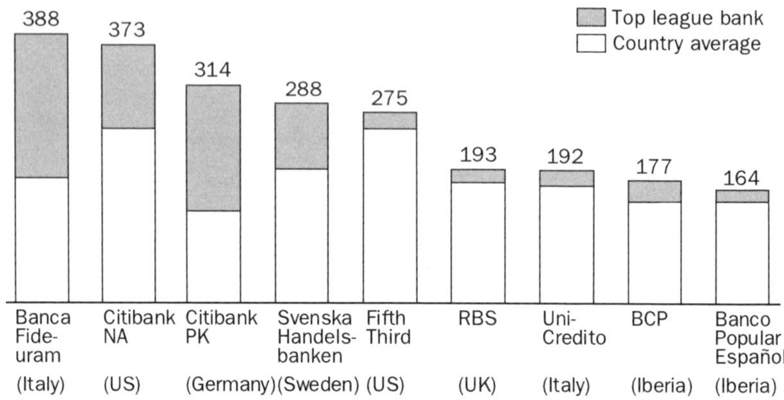

Figure 2.4 Income per full-time employee (€'000s 2001)

Source: annual reports; McKinsey

It will come as no surprise that the best banks manifest remarkable credit skills, scoring highly on their credit culture and policy as well as on their use of support models. They all have world-class skills in two to six areas of the framework and tend to outperform in several additional areas. Typically, they have very few weaknesses.

Together with these broad points, the best banks share other common ground. Most have evolved into outstanding performers over a period of more than 10 or 20 years. UniCredito is a more recent high-flyer—it only joined the elite in the late 1990s—demonstrating that those banks aspiring to excellence do not necessarily have to wait for ever to achieve it.

With a clear strategy in mind and a very strong sales culture, top banks usually outperform their national average in revenue per full-time employee (FTE) (Figure 2.4). The deep-seated sales culture also helps boost cross-selling ratios above those of their national peer group. For example, Citibank branches in the US that are piloting its new Citipro sales support tool, staff are selling an average of 6.7 products per household, compared with less than four products at non-Citipro Citibank branches and at other leading banks.[5]

Although we have seen that the top players control their costs well, this does not mean they are necessarily miserly. Rather, they are able to make better use of their fixed cost base and squeeze superior revenue growth out of it, thereby achieving a greater improvement in cost–income ratio (Figure 2.5).

Finally, the best banks' credit losses are generally lower than those of their peers, although they achieve this in different ways. Take Citibank: it is more risk-tolerant than many, but it also relies on very strong credit decision support systems and risk-based pricing. On the opposite side of the spectrum sits Svenska Handelsbanken, which has a lower appetite for risk and generally a more conservative credit culture. But, by combining this caution with better-than-average customer knowledge, it is able to outperform its national average (Figure 2.6).

[5] Citigroup, investor presentation, November 6, 2001.

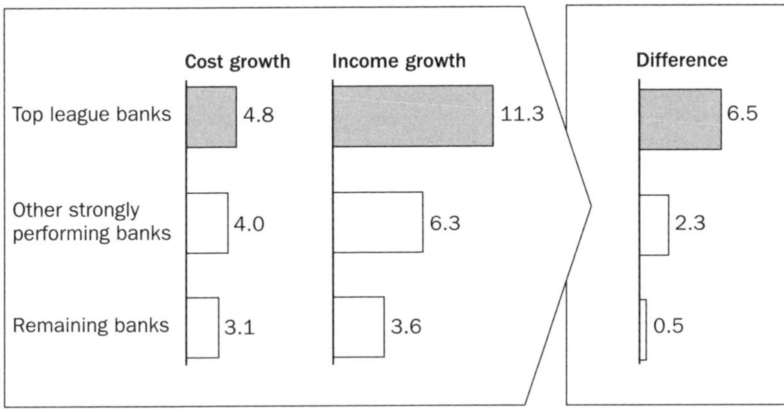

Figure 2.5 Merger-adjusted growth rates (percent, CAGR, 1998–2001)

Source: annual reports; McKinsey

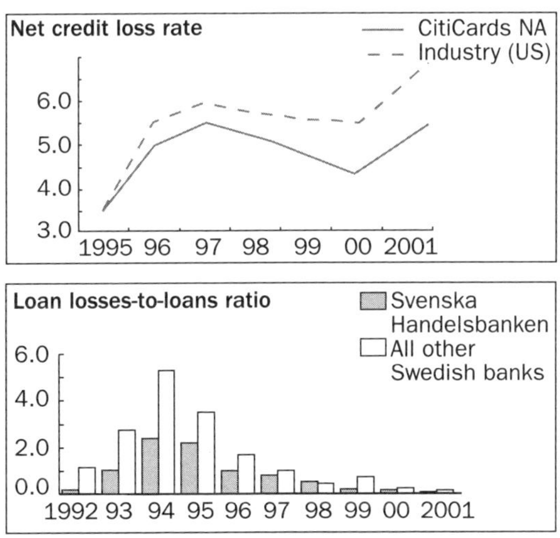

Figure 2.6 Comparison of net credit loss performance (percent)

Source: annual reports; analyst presentations; broker reports

SUCCESS FORMULAE IN RETAIL BANKING

Despite these commonalities, the precise bundle of strategy, skills, and focused efforts taken by the top banks varies. They use different combinations of organizational capabilities and concentrate on different core competencies, all aligned to their particular strategic orientation. All the leading banks are generally strong performers in most of the categories; the success formulae relate to their specific areas of

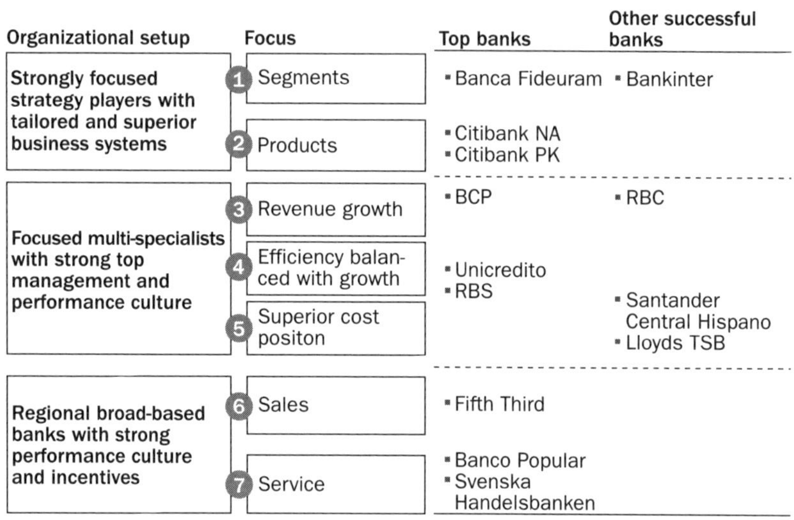

Figure 2.7 Success formulae in retail banking

Source: McKinsey

expertise—be it a powerful sales culture or an inspiring top management team. Of course, none of the banks started from the same base, the size of their operations differs, and corporate cultures vary. Indeed, there is no one 'correct' route to success, but rather a range of possibilities that might be appropriate for different banks at different times.

We can identify seven successful business models in three major groups (Figure 2.7). Not all are necessarily visible today, but their validity as successful strategies has been proven.

Strongly focused strategy players

These financial services providers succeed in building superior tailored business systems. Within this category are the *segment-focused specialists* (who may not necessarily be banks) and the *product-focused banks*.

Italy's Banca Fideuram (Box 2.1) is a segment-focused specialist. It homes in on the affluent and high-net-worth segment. It has almost 4000 entrepreneurial, sales-oriented independent financial advisors offering sophisticated and personalized advice to its customers. There is a strong performance culture driven primarily by high individual incentives that are combined with an extremely variable compensation package. The incentive system seeks to strike a delicate balance between new sales and customer retention and aligns advisor behavior with the articulated target of superior shareholder returns in both the short and long term. The business system is organized so that advisors are freed from lower value-added transactions and administration. Customers are encouraged to use online channels and call centers for simpler transactions, while the financial advisors use the direct connection to

Box 2.1

Banca Fideuram

- Founded in 1992 through the merger of Fideuram (an agent network) and Banca Manusardi.
- Leading asset manager in Italy among non-universal banks with market capitalization (end 2002) of €4.4bn; 610 000 retail customers in 2002.
- Mostly domestic business in Italy, private banking in Luxembourg and Switzerland; acquired Wargny in 2001 and Banca Sanpaolo Invest in 2002.
- Retail profits 2002: €201m; retail ROE: ~20.1%; retail C–I: 58.4%.
- Major achievements: fastest growing asset gatherer in Italy.

Box 2.2

Citibank Consumer Banking/Lending (North America)

- Formed in 1998 through the merger of Citicorp and Travelers Group.
- World's biggest bank with market capitalization (end 2002) of US$181bn (€203bn); retail assets: US$159bn (€178bn), 26 million retail customers.
- Present in over 100 countries.
- Retail profits 2002: US$9.8bn (€11.1bn); retail ROE: 63.5%; retail C–I: 35.9%.
- Universal bank, US personal financial services offered under several brands, focus on consumer finance through CitiCards and CitiFinancial.
- Major achievements: very high levels of automation and operational efficiency; outstanding ability to price and manage retail credit risks.

Box 2.3

Citibank PK

- German subsidiary of Citigroup, formed through acquisition of Kundenkreditbank in 1973.
- Retail assets: €10.2bn, 3 million retail customers.
- Retail profits 2001: €594m; retail ROE: ~77%; retail C–I: 49.7%.
- Retail subsidiary with strong focus on credit cards and consumer loans, although offers a broad product range.
- Major achievements: one of Europe's most profitable banks, despite difficult German market.

Fideuram's processing systems to feed the latest economic data into their financial planning tools and to send back sales and transactional information.

Other companies in this category are MLP in Germany and Bankinter in Spain.

Citibank (Box 2.2) belongs to the group of product-focused banks, both with its banking/lending retail divisions in the US and its German subsidiary, Citibank PK. Although Citibank offers a very broad range of products, the bank's revenues and profits demonstrate a strong focus: in 2001 almost 80 percent of its profits came from the consumer finance and credit card businesses (Figure 2.8). Citibank's focus is also reflected in its market shares, which are four to eight times higher in the high-margin credit card and consumer loan business than its overall market share in the US retail banking market. Citibank PK (Box 2.3) in Germany derives more than 60 percent of its revenues from consumer finance products and commands a market share of almost 9 percent in this business, compared with an overall German market share of 2 percent. Having such a strong focus on a small number of product groups has helped Citibank develop, implement, and fine-tune a tailored, exclusive business

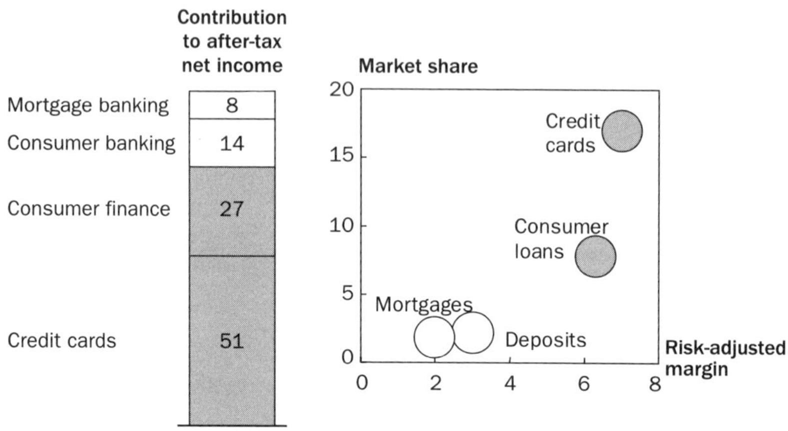

Figure 2.8 Product focus of Citibank NA (percent, 2001)

Source: annual report; analyst presentations; McKinsey

system built for efficient performance. The bank has optimized business processes, risk management, and pricing in consumer credit. Based on what is arguably the most extensive set of customer creditworthiness data and very high levels of automation in underwriting and processing, the bank has been earning higher margins on these products for years. It has been able to reduce risk costs, introduce exceptional speed and accuracy in credit decisions and efficiency in administration.

Standardized, well-designed processes at Citibank have laid the foundation for greater centralization, outsourcing, and offshoring of production, which in turn will pave the way for even more significant cost savings in the future. A global bank in this field can achieve higher cost savings than many of its competitors. CitiCards is present in more than 100 countries, but has only one center for global data entry in India, one global card manufacturing center (US), two transaction processing centers (US and Singapore), and three data network centers (US, UK, Singapore).

These business systems have been a major competitive advantage in the past and should continue to produce excellent results in the future. They can be leveraged to gain a broader customer penetration—a quest that Citibank is embarking on.

Focused multi-specialists

The top management teams at these banks have very compelling track records in instilling powerful performance cultures into their organizations and delivering excellent results year after year. All the top league multi-specialists have developed multiple value propositions and brands to match their target customer segments and have differentiated their distribution systems accordingly. There are three variations of this particular formula.

The first one is *revenue-focused* and targets specific value segments, implementing different strategies for each one. Banco Comercial Português (Box 2.4) is a leading exponent of this model.

Box 2.4

Banco Comercial Português

- Formed in 1985 by a group of Portuguese industrialists, BCP is Portugal's largest bank by market capitalization (end 2002) (€5bn).
- Retail assets: €70bn, 3.3 million retail customers, general market share of 27%.
- International operations in many countries, including significant retail exposure in Poland and Greece.
- Retail profits 2001: €814m; retail ROE: 26%; retail C–I: ~50%.
- Multi-specialist bank, leading Portuguese provider of mutual funds (market share 38%), credit cards, life insurance (33%), mortgages, current accounts, and deposits.
- Major achievements: building country's leading bank from scratch within 15 years; a successful track record of financial innovation starting with segment-specific distribution networks.

Box 2.5

UniCredito Italiano

- In 1995, Credito Italiano joined forces with Rolo Banca 1473 to form the Credito Italiano Group.
- One of Italy's largest banks with market capitalization (end 2002) of €23.8bn.
- Retail assets: €260bn, 6.5 million customers.
- Mainly operates in Italy, with operations in Poland, Croatia, Slovakia, Bulgaria, US, Germany, Czech Republic, and India.
- Retail profits 2001: €2.58bn; retail ROE: 34.3%; retail C–I: 46.5%.
- Multi-specialist with main focus on asset-gathering.
- Major achievements: transformation from a low-performer to one of the world's best performing banks within a period of just four to five years.

Box 2.6

Royal Bank of Scotland

- Founded by Royal Charter in Edinburgh in 1727.
- One of the UK's largest banks with market capitalization (end 2002) of £43.1bn (€69.5bn); retail assets: £82bn (€132bn), 12 million retail customers.
- Mainly operates in the UK, further presence in 10 European countries and in the US.
- Retail profits 2002: £2.9bn (€4.8bn); retail ROE (2001): ~78%, retail C–I: 40.6%.
- Multi-specialist with a leading UK position in private and offshore banking, retail banking, motor insurance, small- and medium-size enterprise (SME) business banking, and corporate banking.
- Major achievements: very rapid integration of NatWest—a bank twice its size—reducing combined cost–income ratio from 53.5% in 2000 to 45% in 2002. Innovations: Tesco, Direct Line insurance.

The second group seeks to *balance efficiency with growth*. Here we see banks such as UniCredito Italiano (Box 2.5) and Royal Bank of Scotland (RBS) (Box 2.6). Historically, RBS has prioritized growth, but has always been very cost-efficient. Recently it reduced costs at a tremendous pace by exploiting the synergies that arose following its merger with NatWest.

The third group focuses on *controlling costs*. Lloyds TSB was particularly good at this during the 1990s, and, more recently, Santander Central Hispano has managed impressive cost reductions without sacrificing revenues.

Most universal banks and multi-specialists, especially in Europe, can follow the routes of these banks to climb to the top.

All three top league banks with this multi-specialist approach have demonstrated their ability to fine-tune their value propositions to a range of different target segments. They have improved their market recognition with differentiated branding and aligned their cost-to-serve with segment profitability. Furthermore, this strategy gives them greater scope to explore new growth opportunities through alliances and the flexibility to reposition.

BCP—which excels in *strong revenue growth*—was the first bank in Europe to implement segment-specific delivery formats. From the outset, it has separated its branch networks into Banco Comercial Português, serving the high net-worth and small business segment, and NovaRede, which caters to the mass market. This segment-specific delivery system was a major factor in BCP's rapid rise from start-up to Portugal's most valuable corporation.

UniCredito Italiano seeks to *balance revenue growth with efficiency*. The Italian bank very recently moved from a federation of regional banks into a group of segment-focused banks that share a common umbrella brand, corporate center services, and infrastructure. Even before the separation of the retail, private and corporate banks, Unicredito had Xelion catering to the affluent segment through financial advisors and Clarima serving the mass market with a special emphasis on credit cards.

To capture the maximum benefit from its multi-specialist strategy, Unicredito has drawn on its world-class skills in leadership and performance culture. It is also innovative and successful in developing new products. To give one example, customers who own the 'Genius' product bundles have an estimated net present value (NPV) of the customer relationship that exceeds the NPV of an average customer by 60 percent.[6] Unicredito achieves impressive sales results building on the consistent and continuous monitoring of sales targets including customer relationship management-based (CRM) sales campaigns. Undoubtedly, the ambitious targets set by its top management also contribute to the bank's impressive performance.

Although Unicredito is still in the process of developing its business system and process efficiency to world-class levels, it managed to restrict cost growth in its Italian retail business to below 1 percent from 1998 to 2001. It did so by picking the low-hanging fruit first (e.g., decreasing tolerance for cost overruns) and capitalizing fully on the synergies from its Italian mergers (fully centralized back office, one IT system, etc.). In credit as well, Unicredito has preserved above-average asset quality and was the first major Italian bank to introduce a professional workout unit that also serves third-party lenders.

Not only are the achievements themselves impressive, the speed of transformation is even more astonishing. Most of the progress Unicredito made was accomplished over just four to five years.

Royal Bank of Scotland's management is also a critical part of the bank's emergence as a leading light. It delivers on its promises, and its promises of late have been to grow revenue, understanding that superior customer service and productive

[6] Unicredito, investor presentation, February 7, 2002. A Genius Extra bundle includes a current account with debit and credit cards, a securities account, an overdraft facility, a safe box, free online- and phone-banking, and discounts for a number of retail partners (restaurants, hotels, travel, newspapers, insurance policies, etc.).

employees are prerequisites for this. Management also sees a strong cost control environment as the basis for achieving high results. While prioritizing revenue growth, RBS has also achieved impressive cost savings (£1.3 billion in 2002—about 17 percent of the cost base) thanks to merger synergies.[7] RBS is, in fact, one of the very few banks that have managed to increase revenue by more than 10 percent while simultaneously reducing costs in retail banking.

RBS maintained the NatWest brand after the merger, knowing that customers do not like to lose touch with their brand too quickly. Its strong revenue growth is supported by innovations in distribution, such as joint ventures with Tesco and Virgin.[8] They appeal to new audiences that RBS would have found difficult to reach before, and have yielded revenue growth in excess of 40 percent per year.

In recent years, we have not been able to identify a multi-specialist bank that excels in *controlling costs*. Lloyds TSB was renowned for systematic and ruthless cost reduction during most of the 1990s and achieved impressive results in efficiency and profitability. However, the bank's significant increase in investments during 2000 and 2001—combined with stagnating revenues—lends credence to the hypothesis that it might have under-invested in building the service capabilities and functions required to compete successfully in a mature market.

Santander Central Hispano managed to reduce its costs in Spain by almost 3 percent per annum between 1998 and 2001. It did this through a massive branch network reconfiguration that shrunk branch numbers from more than 6440 in 1998 to 4700 in 2001. The 3.7 percent annual revenue growth that the bank enjoyed during this period is an indication of its ability to deliver value to the customers and manage customer migration effectively.

Regional broad-based bank

The third success formula has been less acknowledged historically; indeed, it has often been seen as the path to extinction. It is true that many of the regional banks operating today may disappear: they will fail and be rescued by a competitor, or merge to become marginally bigger. Nevertheless, there is a third way. They can define their own plan for success by cultivating an outstanding *performance and sales culture* that draws on their local knowledge and popularity, or by setting themselves up as a *customer service champion*. These business models must be supported by a deep-seated employee commitment to results.

Fifth Third (Box 2.7) and Svenska Handelsbanken (Box 2.8) are both good examples of this regional strategy, each focusing on a different element, while Banco Popular (Box 2.9) in Spain shares elements of both models. None of these banks focuses strongly on specific segments; their aim is rather to serve the customers in their community as best they can and at low cost.

The top regional broad-based banks consistently top the league tables on customer satisfaction, thanks to their proximity to customers and their ability to understand and consistently cater to their needs. Fifth Third's reputation for quality and consistency earned it the number one position among 40 banks in a financial services

[7] RBS, investor presentation, August 7, 2002.

[8] RBS now fully owns the joint venture with Tesco.

Box 2.7

Fifth Third

- Incorporated in 1975.
- Regional US bank with a market capitalization (end 2002) of US$34bn (€38bn); retail assets: US$25bn (€28bn), 4 million retail customers.
- Operates mainly in five US Midwest states.
- Retail profits 2001: US$806m (€903m); retail ROE: ~31%; retail C–I: ~51%.
- Universal bank, selling mostly traditional products such as checking/savings accounts, deposits, loans, mortgages, and credit cards.
- Major achievements: unparalleled earnings and dividend growth for 28 consecutive years at average annual rate of 16%.

Box 2.8

Svenska Handelsbanken

- Founded as Stockholm's Handelsbank in 1871.
- One of Scandinavia's largest banks with market capitalization (end 2002) of SEK82.6bn (€8.9bn).
- Retail assets (2001): SEK830bn (€89bn), 2.3 million retail customers.
- Mainly operates in Scandinavia and the UK; further limited presence in the rest of Europe, US, and Asia.
- Retail profits 2002: SEK9.4bn (€1bn); retail ROE: 23.9%; retail C–I: 44.7%.
- Universal bank with a focus on traditional banking, in particular lending. Primary target segments are upper mass market/affluent and small- and medium-sized companies.
- Major achievements: consistently excellent performer on most dimensions, especially in terms of profitability.

Box 2.9

Banco Popular

- Incorporated in 1926, Spain's third largest bank by market capitalization (end 2002) (€8.5bn); has 3.5 million retail customers and a general market share of 4.5%.
- Majority of revenues originated in Spain. International operations in France, Portugal, and Latin America.
- Retail profits in 2002: €1.01bn; retail pre-tax ROE: 39.1%; retail C–I: 42.3%.
- Universal bank, starting to focus more on private banking.
- Major achievement: highest ROE and lowest cost–income ratio in Spain over the last few years.

reputation survey in May 2001, commissioned by the *American Banker* magazine.[9] Banco Popular and Svenska Handelsbanken also regularly outperform their competitors in customer satisfaction.

Fifth Third's amazing profit growth of 16 percent per annum is a result of a focus on a *strong sales culture*, together with ambitious target-setting, transparency, and an inspirational management team that leads by example. The CEO follows the results of the numerous sales campaigns and plays a major role in generating a superior sales culture, which permeates all aspects of the workplace with even the screensaver

[9] The survey, conducted by Harris Interactive, Inc. and the Reputation Institute, ranked US financial institutions according to their reputation, name recognition, and customer service.

demanding of staff: 'What did you sell today?' Furthermore, individual and branch rankings are reviewed weekly and published company-wide, and the CEO sends out notes to local banks when targets are missed.

Svenska Handelsbanken does not focus on a centralized CRM system to drive sales campaigns. Instead, the bank aims at being a *customer service champion* by stressing local customer knowledge and proximity. Its unique corporate culture of empowerment goes as far as to allow branches to determine their marketing budgets, Internet appearance, and to retain responsibility for the biggest customers. Even if this introduces some inefficiency, the power of entrepreneurship is such that the bank consistently outperforms its Nordic peers.

A similar phenomenon also characterizes Fifth Third, which, after having acquired a number of smaller regional banks, gave them the operational freedom to shape their own approach and objectives within their natural local markets. Fifth Third's CEO George Schaefer considers that the bank operates as 16 affiliated banks instead of one, while Svenska Handelsbanken's top management speaks of 'a partnership type of culture'.

Banco Popular is well known in Spain for its consistent opposition to following the latest fads and investing in new technologies. Building on a culture of thriftiness, this bank—where even overhead projectors are considered unnecessarily lavish—has achieved cost–income ratios that are 10 to 20 percentage points lower than other Spanish banks. On the revenue side, the bank draws on its experience by building valuable partnerships with affinity groups, professional associations, and local businesses, while avoiding expensive mass marketing campaigns. By tailoring the product range to specific target groups, Banco Popular is able to sell up to seven products to some of those groups (compared with 2.7 on average) and achieve very high market shares, holding, for example, 45 percent of the mortgages of Spanish airline pilots.

Incentive structures are an important part of getting these models to work. In both Fifth Third and Svenska Handelsbanken, the employees own close to 10 percent of the bank. The underlying rationale is to align the interests of the employees with those of the shareholders, although the emphasis has its nuances. At Svenska Handelsbanken, explains CEO Lars Grönstedt, 'It is important that every employee receives an equal share in the Oktogonen Foundation.[10] This creates a partnership-like culture.'

Fifth Third also uses employee ownership to help it push for success. 'We want [our employees] to think they're owners first and employees second, so that the branch manager is acting like he actually owns the bank', explains George Schaefer, CEO[11]

Employee ownership and empowerment is a powerful motivational tool. It helps employees identify with and benefit from the success of the institution. Not

[10] The Oktogonen Foundation is an employee ownership vehicle that owns about 10 percent of the bank. Each employee receives an equal number of Handelsbanken shares every year, contingent on the bank's performance. These shares cannot be sold before employee retirement.

[11] Interview with *Money Magazine*, May 2002.

surprisingly, Fifth Third's Schaefer can claim: 'We measure and pay for performance. Some people play golf, some play tennis. Our people like to play banking.'[12]

PREPARING FOR THE ASCENT

All types of banks—be they monoliners or multi-specialists, regional banks or global powerhouses—have the opportunity to make it to the top. However, success depends on their ability to identify the most appropriate success formula and strategy and then equip themselves appropriately. The race for the summit positions in 2005 is open. Unicredito and Royal Bank of Scotland have both proven that it is possible to ascend to the peaks of performance within three to four years by exploiting merger synergies, as well as by unleashing organic improvement potential. But for banks like these, the top is no place to take a rest, as experience has shown.

Former leaders have been forced to descend from the summit for a variety of reasons. Some ran into difficulties following mergers that proved more challenging and more time-consuming than anticipated. Others found themselves unable to make the transition to a new industry paradigm. Some banks faltered when a new leadership introduced a strategy that was not aligned with the existing culture. Lastly, some banks simply could not maintain their pace, and slowing down means falling behind.

Challenges line the route

Banks that outperform today can expect to face significant challenges in the years to come. Some of the highly focused banks may already have exhausted their current route, and sustaining their present growth rates may not be possible. New competitive pressures may also arise in their specific area of focus, which could force them to enter segments and penetrate deeper into businesses in which they have yet to develop world-class expertise and which will divert top management attention away from the existing business.

The multi-specialists depend heavily on the management team that has guided them thus far. In order to stabilize, these banks will have to improve their business systems and process efficiency. They must also seek promising acquisition targets and integrate them smoothly. They can expect to be very busy in the next phase of their development. Some of today's internationally oriented multi-specialists may even decide to shrink and become regional players.

Today's regional players have to decide whether they want to remain in their region, which may have only limited growth opportunities in the long run, or whether they should expand into other markets. They should consider the limited transferability of corporate cultures across both geographies and organizations, which will certainly put obstacles in their path and could dilute top management's attention—and potentially any profits on new investments.

For those not yet in this elite group of high-performing banks, the task is to build their skills up to world-class levels.

[12] Interview with *Money Magazine*, May 2002.

As we move from segment-focused banks to regional broad-based banks, the importance of a strategic segment focus decreases. Although all banks pursue certain strategies, the focused banks have really taken strategic bets on their segments and products, forgoing the potential benefits of diversification but also saving on complexity and the costs of acquiring market share. Such a bet should not be placed lightly. If a bank is to focus, it must be sure that it knows what this means for all aspects of its business and that it has the right set of skills to succeed. For regional banks, for example, having the right 'can do' culture reverberating through the organization is the only way to stand out. Even the most ingenious and far-sighted strategies can be devastated by poor execution, and no bank can ever pay too much attention to it.

Consolidation is particularly important for the multi-specialists as mergers can improve cost–income ratios. Banks that have developed outstanding integration capabilities and mastered the skills-transfer process have a competitive advantage given the environment in Europe where banks are verging on merging. Top-notch post-merger management skills are vital for any bank with ambitions of excellence.

The approach is critical

The first step up the climb involves choosing the right route and thus committing to developing selected strategic capabilities that reflect the management's vision, market trends, and the bank's starting position. This decision will show the bank's willingness and ability to develop its competencies to a world-class level.

A corporate leadership team striving for success is always at the heart of any ambitious transformation program. Every competitor, irrespective of the success formula it follows, should take performance orientation by the top management and the generation of a world-class performance culture extremely seriously. They are indispensable for reaching the top.

Having an outstanding sales culture is vital in six of the seven success formulae; however, most banks are still a long way from installing such an environment. For the frontline to sell to its full potential, management must ensure that the drive for performance reaches right down through the organization and that it has an effective database-marketing system that continuously generates sales leads to achieve higher frontline productivity. This can be supported by a range of other marketing and IT tools.

Cost-efficiency is essential to the focused multi-specialist banks, for which cost control is a competitive advantage. In many banks, especially those with lower performance, cost control is seen as more of a tactical area to be tackled every few years with some short-term cost-cutting programs, but as we saw in the previous chapter the capital markets do not look on this favorably.

Taking the next step toward cost reduction will be harder for those banks that have already achieved good performance levels. These banks have to deal with topics ranging from end-to-end process optimization to developing superior transaction processing platforms. Some processes are outsourced—perhaps offshore where labor and infrastructure costs are lower. Such an undertaking is a serious challenge to all banks in view of the long-term time frame involved and the complexity. Any bank that rises to this challenge will gain a head start on the competition.

Banks driving performance through top-line growth—specifically, the segment-focused banks and the revenue growth-focused multi-specialists—should create benefits for the customers that outweigh the higher cost of servicing those customers. It is essential to build a value proposition that caters uniquely to the needs of their most valued (and valuable) customers, be it by providing extraordinary levels of service or by delivering the best financial advice.

Superior credit skills are essential for all approaches. At the most basic level this translates into a conservative credit policy coupled with an efficient credit process; there is still a lot of work that can be done in this area. More sophisticated banks, where consumer finance is at the core of banking profits, need state-of-the-art credit underwriting, decision support, and monitoring systems along with risk-adjusted pricing. Automated rating systems will play an increasingly important role as they incorporate robust quantitative analyses (providing real-time probabilities of default and loss-given-default distributions) directly linked into calculations of necessary economic capital and supporting risk-adjusted loan pricing.

The more relevant world-class capabilities a bank can develop, the greater the likelihood of success of a transformation program in terms of revenue growth, returns, and value creation. Banks should keep in mind that the current champions have already developed these and many other competencies to a level that exceeds the average across many developed countries. The contenders face a difficult journey, but it is well worth the effort and achievable for many.

The seven success formulae should not be considered a step-by-step ladder to the top; rather they are useful in structuring our thinking. They outline the specific combinations of strategy, organizational setup, and core capabilities that have been at the foundation of success for certain banks at certain points in time.

Any bank with high aspirations has to make its own choices—as a mountaineer has to choose the right team, time, and approach. The route, the skills needed, and the overall strategy are all critical. Moreover, once the first step is taken, the climb to the top must be decisive and relentless.

3

Winning in Emerging Markets: Taking Steps toward Stardom

Some of the high-performing banks in the developed markets are also active in emerging markets. This is especially true for UniCredito Italiano in Eastern Europe, Banco Santander in Latin America, and Citibank almost everywhere.

These emerging markets naturally have very different market conditions, and therefore we devote this chapter to banking in Eastern Europe, Asia, and Latin America.

In Eastern Europe, consolidation and specialization will certainly increase. From the perspective of a foreign strategic investor, the strongest East European banks will create significant value on the back of growth, scale, and filling gaps in the market. The revenue pool is small today, and an East European strategy will reward only those willing to commit long term to the region, to invest in restructuring and capabilities-building, and to dare to enter the less developed countries as they become ready for foreign investment.

Asian banks looking to capture the exciting growth opportunities in retail banking face a narrowing window of opportunity as competition intensifies. It is clear that many changes are needed at the frontline—especially in terms of developing 'soft' skills. Such a transformation will require a drive from the very top, for which Asian banks are often well suited given that many sprung from a family-owned background. These owners must however, shift their focus, investments, and excitement to the soft skills if they are to capture the growth that should be theirs.

On many dimensions Latin American financial institutions have moved toward global best practice, but there are still significant opportunities for them to push this further. The speed with which new management practices take hold may depend on whether existing structural conditions allow arbitrage opportunities—and hence relieve the pressure for change. We believe that a major shift is on the horizon at the top management level, as bank managers realize that closing today's gaps in operational excellence could give them a powerful and sustainable source of profits.

EASTERN EUROPE: LEARNING FAST FROM THE WEST

Fedele di Maggio, Piotr Romanowski, Cornelius Walter

East European banks' performance varies tremendously—in 2001, ROEs for large banks[1] ranged from –6 percent to more than 40 percent and cost–income ratios lay between 101 percent and 46 percent. However in Eastern Europe, traditional profitability metrics are sometimes not as reliable an indicator of truly excellent performance as they are in developed countries, as many banks lack a clear historical track record or sufficiently transparent reporting. Historical cost–income ratios, for instance, can be heavily influenced by mergers, state subsidies, the historical incumbent position, or the huge costs associated with developing a greenfield operation. On the revenue side, results might be artificially boosted by nonsustainable high deposit spreads and/or aging government bond investments (paying high fixed interest rates in markets where the cost of deposits is dropping fast).

What is clear though is that Eastern Europe is no easy ride for average performers from elsewhere looking to take advantage of the lower level of market sophistication and competitive intensity. First, several of the best performing East European banks are already owned by some of the top international banks, such as UniCredito Italiano and Citibank, as well as Erste, KBC, and HypoVereinsbank. These banks benefit from the direct transfer of knowledge from their foreign shareholders and can draw on their parent's scale in strategic areas such as IT, product development, purchasing, and asset management. Second, there are certain high-performing independent local players whose management has fully embraced international best practice and has a performance focus. These players—notably the Hungarian OTP—are often leading incumbents that began to modernize before their local peers and then successfully exploited their market position to outperform their competitors.

In this context, several differentiating features can be observed across the current best performers in the region along the five dimensions of the Excellence in Retail Banking framework.

Corporate leadership: grow and adapt

Two specific themes in corporate leadership are widespread in the region: rapid adaptability and a regional perspective.

Adaptability. East European banking sectors have undergone tremendous changes in terms of expanding product portfolios and service channels, often leapfrogging developments that took decades in the EU. Excellent banks have quickly launched retail brokerage operations, added mutual funds to their product-offering, and thus quickly gained market leadership in the new product categories. In addition, they lagged behind their Western peers only by a few years in introducing remote channels, such as call centers and Internet-banking. Rapid adoption of new services allows the best players to stay ahead of competition, which for local banks means

[1] In Bulgaria, Croatia, the Czech Republic, Hungary, Poland, and Slovakia. Analysis based on 2001 financial results of the largest banks in each country (>5 percent market share each).

Market Share: ○ <5% ◑ 5 - 10% ● >10%

	First wave EU applicants					Other countries		
	Czech Republic	Hungary	Poland	Slovakia	Slovenia	Bulgaria	Croatia	Romania
Citibank	○	○	◑	○	-	○	-	○
Erstebank	●	○	-	●	○	-	○	-
HypoVereinsbank/ Bank Austria	○*	◑	◑	○	○	○	○	○
Intesa BCI	○	◑	-	●	-	-	●	-
KBC	●	●	○	○	●	-	-	-
Raiffeisenbank	○	○	○	●	○	○	◑	○
Société Générale	●	-	○	○*	●	○	-	◑
UniCredito Italiano	○	-	●	○	-	●	●	○

* Through representation of a subsidiary bank in another CEE country

Figure 3.1 Regional players in Central and Eastern Europe (as of 2002)

Source: annual reports; McKinsey

quickly reaching a level playing field with foreign entrants, using their scale and experience in the home markets.

Regional players. Over recent years, several cross-regional banks have emerged, taking significant market positions across Eastern Europe (Figure 3.1). These banks pursue a variety of market entry strategies—from greenfield-focused such as Raiffeisenbank and Citibank, to pure acquisition-focused strategies such as Unicredito, Erste, or KBC. Not surprisingly, they often exploit their parent's skills in entering Eastern Europe. For example, Citibank draws on its leadership in credit cards, and Unicredito on excellence in improving both sales performance and operating cost-efficiency. Although the superiority of the regional approach remains to be proven, we think that at least some of these banks may turn into extremely exciting success stories given the following three conditions.

First, Eastern Europe needs to be sufficiently important within the parent bank's organization to ensure the strategic focus of senior management and the dedication of high-quality management talent.

Second, management skills and local experience need to be leveraged across several countries in the region—particularly by anticipating market developments in the less developed areas, building on first-hand experience from more advanced East European markets.

And, finally, there must be a relentless focus on capturing regional cost synergies wherever possible. Admittedly, achieving substantial benefits in this area is challenging given the difference in language and regulations. Nevertheless, several players are pursuing or contemplating measures such as group-wide procurement, card transaction-processing, product factories for more sophisticated products where individual markets lack sufficient scale (e.g., structured investment products, derivatives), or unification of IT platforms to limit maintenance and customization costs.

Marketing and sales: focus on affluent customers

The focus of sales efforts in retail banking in Eastern Europe is primarily aimed at capturing the emerging affluent opportunity due to the expected above-average growth of the affluent revenue pool. The top 10 percent of East European banking customers contribute about 40 percent of the retail banking profit pool, compared with 70 percent in Western Europe. With the increasing differentiation of wealth distribution, Eastern Europe is expected to gradually align with the West.

It must be noted that, as a direct consequence of the communist legacy, the majority of East European affluent customers tend to be high-earners, but not asset-rich. Hence, they require loans more than asset management. They are also younger, better educated, and often more entrepreneurial than their Western European peers. Those banks that have targeted this segment most successfully have recognized its peculiarity in the region and tailored their sales and service model accordingly.

Distribution: an abundance of formats

More advanced East European markets are characterized by the very rapid adoption of segment-specific offers and new distribution formats. Among Polish retail banks, the share of those offering dedicated service models and tailored product packages to affluent customers grew from 50 to 90 percent between 1998 and 2001, and in Hungary from 34 to 59 percent, respectively, over the same period. Adoption of novel distribution formats has been equally rapid, particularly in the Polish market. Mini-branch networks, first launched in 1998, now account for more than a tenth of all branches in the country.[2] Pure Internet banks, first launched in May 2001, commanded close to 300 000 customers by the end of 2001 and well above half a million, or 3 to 3.5 percent of the bankable population by September 2002.[3]

Processes and IT: unused potential

Average cost–income ratios for East European retail banks remained flat over the last four years (1998–2001). However, excellent players achieved a consistent improvement in their cost-efficiency. For example, Poland's Bank Pekao SA reduced its cost–income ratio by 18 percentage points between 1999 and 2001. In more advanced countries, such as Poland, costs came down mainly through headcount reduction and branch process redesign. In less developed markets, such as Bulgaria and Romania, efficiency improvement is primarily driven by rapid volume and revenue expansion with a roughly stable cost base. It should be stressed that a significant part of the operating efficiency improvement is not IT-related. Of course, the introduction of more efficient centralized IT solutions can bring additional efficiency gains, but their magnitude has to be weighed carefully against the largely fixed nature of IT investments and the relatively small scale of most East European banks compared with their EU counterparts.

[2] Excluding mini branches opened by universal banks as part of larger bank networks.

[3] Again, excluding universal banks' customers with online access to their accounts.

Credit: a long way to go

Credit skills are essential to capture the fast-growing retail credit business. So far, excellence has been achieved mainly by specialized nonbanking players, who have mastered the two key challenges in Eastern Europe: credit underwriting and credit workout.

In credit underwriting, Eastern Europe lacks credible historical credit information due to the absence of established central credit bureaus.[4] The challenge has been tackled most successfully by specialized point of sale credit companies (e.g., Lukas in Poland, Multiservis in the Czech Republic, and Budapest Áruhitel in Hungary[5]), that focused on building their own credit history databases for their customers through small-ticket lending and increasing ticket size following timely repayment.

In credit workout, a lax and often intransparent legal environment hinders the effective repossession of collateral. In addition, illiquid markets make it difficult to establish a realistic recovery price for many types of collateral. Best practice players tend to organize workout units as profit centers with clearly impact-oriented processes. Although specialized workout players have emerged, most successful workout operations tend to be internal given the high discounts/fees on external collection services.

We believe these specificities of 'Eastern European Excellence' are likely to hold true for the next five years. However, the names at the top of the performance list may change significantly. Looking forward, the one distinctive character of the East European banking environment that will likely redefine the performance map is the fluidity of its structure. Over the next five years, we expect to see a significant level of M&A activity. The emerging regional players will continue racing to expand their presence in all the more advanced countries and selectively in those that follow them. Several continental European players will be looking at the region with a renewed interest—either as the only realistic international growth option at their disposal or as a second home market justified by geographic proximity or by trade flows between their home market and the region. Others, that entered opportunistically over the past few years, may be reconsidering the strategic value of such moves and looking for ways to cash in their investment.

The large incumbents that still lack a strategic investor are slowly but surely being acquired. In addition, the wider consolidation of the European banking industry will also influence M&A activity in the region. Finally, greenfield banks will continue to emerge in both retail and corporate banking in the less developed countries and in specific products, such as mortgages and consumer-lending in the more advanced countries.

---

[4] Over the past two to three years, credit bureaus have been established, for instance, in Poland and the Czech Republic. However, they still lack full coverage of the banking system and do not include nonbanking lenders.

[5] Lukas is owned by Credit Agricole, Multiservis and Budapest Áruhitel by GE Capital; Cetelem is an important player in all three markets as well.

ASIA: SOFT SKILLS REQUIRED FOR LONG-TERM SUCCESS

Greg Gibb, Jens Lottner

Over the course of the last decade, retail banking throughout Asia has finally come into its own. Few banks, apart from some laggard state-owned institutions, continue to view retail banking merely as a way of accumulating deposits in order to support corporate lending. Indeed, today, some Asian countries have more branches and automatic teller machines (ATMs) per capita than the US and Europe.

However, in all this vigor, Asian banks are struggling to get a firm grasp on how to build sustainable profits. Most retail banks in the region have concentrated their growth and investment in the distribution 'hardware'; few have focused on developing the necessary skills or 'software' that drive business growth. As product margins compress with competition, the shortfalls within retail banking are becoming increasingly apparent.

Asian banks feeling the strain should not despair. Poor returns in retail banking do not have to be their destiny. In fact, the fundamentals are very attractive. High savings rates, exceeding 20 percent across the region, continue to build bank balances, and rising incomes in countries such as China and India will bring hundreds of millions of new households into the 'bankable' population. Asia's more developed economies such as Taiwan and Hong Kong are themselves still at the relatively early stages of a consumer finance boom and most households are less indebted than their Western counterparts. Even Japan's moribund economy holds promise of significant growth if its aging population wakes up to the fact that they can put their savings to better use. In 2002, only about US$400bn of Japan's US$12 trillion personal savings (i.e., about 3 percent) were held in mutual funds—a fraction of US and European levels.

So, the prospects look promising, but banks in Asia will take advantage only if they position themselves to generate sustainable profits. It is not too late for local Asian banks to strengthen their hand, but a new mindset will be required if some of them are to become truly high-performing banks. Developing new skills—either from scratch or in an alliance—lies at the heart of the challenge for Asian banks. The days of simply investing in hardware and building networks are over. For those that can master the challenge, there are few markets that can rival Asia for long-term growth opportunities.

Corporate leadership: the key to success

Many Asian banks have grown from small, entrepreneurial roots, and at many institutions ownerships are still very concentrated within a limited number of individuals, often serving on the board and actively involved in top management. Shareholder value orientation and performance mindset at the top—at least for Asia's private banks—is not an issue.

It is not that banks lack the desire to perform, they simply lack the culture and skills to achieve the sort of performance necessary, especially to translate aspirations at the top downward to every employee. Traditional management approaches based on senior managers' intimate knowledge of every single business are no longer feasible as banks consolidate and organizations become increasingly large and complex. The problem is that these banks do not have the proper processes to cope with large-scale operations. This is particularly the case when it comes to identifying true returns and evaluating the performance of business units down to the individual.

As a result, systematic performance management is not in place in most Asian banks. Incomplete internal and external information leads to vague target-setting at every level of the organization, which means consequence management can be neither justified nor enforced, thereby limiting profitable growth.

As a first step, some institutions have installed proper cost-of-funds and cost allocation systems in order to understand product and customer profitability and thus set more precise targets and monitor performance. However, it is perhaps only in Korea that true performance management has taken root, with Housing & Commercial Bank as the most outstanding example. In 1998, the bank publicly announced it was to focus on profit and shareholder value creation, and in the same year it introduced the country's first stock option-based compensation program. It also designed a state-of-the-art managerial accounting and costing system, and developed a system to measure and reward performance. By 2001, it was the biggest bank in Korea thanks to its merger with Kookmin Bank. As a testament to its performance aspirations, the share price rose by more than 40 percent annually from 1997 to 2001.

Marketing and sales: from volume to profits

During most of the 1990s, Asian banks' retail operations were little more than a net to capture deposits for corporate banking. The focus was therefore on generating customer volume, rather than customer quality and profit potential. As a result, many Asian banks today have extremely concentrated customer profitability. In the Western hemisphere, the rule of thumb is that a fifth of a bank's customers generate four-fifths of the profits. In Asia, many banks gain all their retail banking profits from less than 5 percent of the customer base. It is not surprising therefore that banks looking to improve earnings following the 1997 financial crisis have focused on cross-selling to retail customers.

In 2001, the Fubon Group—one of Taiwan's largest financial institutions—took advantage of a new financial holding company law to draw together its banking, insurance, securities, and asset management businesses. The Fubon Group plans to use its relationships with customers in all these businesses to build a financial supermarket that thrives on cross-selling. In communications to investors, Fubon noted that informal cross-selling before this new setup had already been yielding two to three products per customer. This places Fubon ahead of other financial institutions in Taiwan where the average number of products per customer is typically less than 1.5. Of course, there is ample room for the Fubon Group to extend its cross-selling to best practice levels of three to four products per customer.

For many banks, expanding the product range and generating higher profits per customer is proving to be a challenge. From the more developed markets such as

Taiwan to emerging markets such as Thailand, bank CEOs are beginning to ask why their investments in IT and CRM capabilities are not paying off.

There are three principal hurdles that Asian financial institutions need to overcome in moving to state-of-the-art marketing and sales practices.

At the top of the list is the lack of accurate customer information. In Taiwan and Hong Kong, for example, it is not unusual to find banks missing the correct phone numbers or addresses for up to 30 or 40 percent of their customers. In less developed markets like Thailand or Malaysia, this figure might even be 60 to 70 percent. In China, the problem is even more extreme: often the information exists, but in some cases it is tampered with in order to avoid tax liabilities or questions concerning the money's precise origin.

The second hurdle is finding the means to inject selling skills into the banks. The problem is particularly acute in countries such as China and India, where—in 2001—the largest players had 31 000 and 9000 branches, respectively. In smaller countries such as Malaysia, Taiwan, or Korea, the main problem is the high degree of branch autonomy. In many cases, branch managers resist central direction on how to sell to customers and ignore centrally prepared lists that might indicate the propensity of a customer to buy a certain product. However, as few banks have successfully centralized the leadership of the sales function, the head office is often at the mercy of the preferences of hundreds of independent branch managers, many of whom grew up in a corporate banking and not a retail banking world.

Faced with the difficulty of trying to convince branch managers to focus on certain customers or sell in a certain way, many Asian bank senior management teams retreat into isolation, choosing instead to design the perfect IT or CRM solution. Often, the plan is to devise the perfect customer segmentation approach in the hope that this will convince branch managers to change their ways. Unfortunately, after months of investment, the resulting segmentation often flops.

Herein lies the third hurdle Asian banks need to overcome in adopting marketing best practices. There is too often a strong focus on investing in new hardware, and not enough time spent on testing ideas and working out effective end-to-end processes. Banks must adopt a much more aggressive test-and-learn approach; although, if it is to be effective, internal divides between headquarters and branches will have to be dismantled so that people work together and really determine what will succeed.

The benefits of doing all this can be substantial. In 2002, one of the smaller Malaysian banks piloted a new approach to selling. The result: productivity per salesperson in the pilot branches jumped some 250 percent in less than six months. Asian banks that shift their focus away from acquiring sheer volume of customers and deposits to one that concentrates on customer penetration and profitability stand to reap substantial rewards.

Distribution: a hard look needed

Throw a brick out of a window in Taiwan and you are very likely to hit a banker on the head. So claimed a senior executive from a local bank in Taiwan, based on the fact that Taiwan, like many Asian countries, is over-banked and over-branched. In fact, in many Asian countries including Japan, South Korea, Taiwan, Hong Kong, and the Philippines, branches and ATMs per capita approach—and sometimes exceed—levels seen in the West. But with cost–income ratios in Asia often exceeding 80 to 90 percent within the mass retail businesses, most Asian banks could benefit from taking a long hard look at their distribution.

For much of the 1990s, aggressive branching in Asia was synonymous with growth. Asian banks set up in the 1980s and 1990s particularly found that branches were critical to obtaining balance sheet-funding. This model worked well as long as interest margins on deposits, mortgages, and corporate loans were substantially higher. Today, however, branch networks across Asia are looking rather expensive. The good news for many Asian banks is that they have the opportunity to optimize networks without immediately cutting the service reach that is important to many of their customers.

The first opportunity lies in reconfiguring branch locations. Asian cities have changed substantially over the last 20 years, while branch locations for any one bank have generally remained unchanged. And although some new branches in supermarkets, malls, etc. have been added to the network, old branches often remain due to regulatory pressure. The data are now available for banks to gain a more sophisticated understanding of where best to site their branches. Leading banks such as Standard Chartered in Hong Kong have already begun to reconfigure based on a better understanding of customer location and needs. They are, however, the exception rather than the rule.

Bank branches are often in expensive retail locations in Asian cities, and real estate costs alone are therefore very expensive. There are certainly opportunities to reduce branch sizes as well, especially as most banks have configured their branches to be autonomous in terms of transaction-processing. A branch at a typical government-owned bank in Taiwan often houses more than 50 employees, covering front and back office operations. Clearly, centralizing operations would help reduce branch size. Further cost savings can be achieved by employing part-time capacity in branches—at the moment, most branches are fully staffed despite the fact that customer volumes vary approximately 30 percent from month to month, and even more so through the course of any one day.

Ultimately, the size of many Asian banks' branch networks will have to shrink in order to generate attractive returns from the mass market. This will occur partly through consolidation, but, for the surviving banks, it will also be critical to increase customer usage of alternative channels to reduce reliance on branches. Consumers and branch managers alike must be educated and incentivized to favor phone-banking centers and ATMs over the more expensive branches. Asia's ubiquitous passbook savings accounts that result in people filing to branches for frequent updates, for example, will have to be phased out to change channel behavior.

Clearly, restructuring the distribution of Asian banks will not be an easy task. At the heart of the challenge lies the development of new skills and insights that will help banks locate branches and direct flows across channels more effectively. Fortunately, Asia's fast-growing urban populations are disproportionately young, outside of Japan, facilitating both change in behavior and the likely acceptance of new channels.

Processes and IT: a chance for leapfrogging

As a result of low labor costs, low customer sophistication, and limited competition from foreign financial services providers, Asian banks have to date made only limited investments in processing technology to achieve greater centralization and automation. As a result, productivity and consequently customer service significantly lag best practice.

Faced with a more demanding competitive environment, most have now realized that new technologies will ultimately change the traditional banking business models and have started to act. However, most attention is being directed at the customer interface, with offers such as PC-banking, mobile phone-banking, and call centers. Technological advances in the middle and back office are still dawdling, which might pose an even bigger competitive threat going forward.

Leading foreign banks such as Citibank, Standard Chartered, or HSBC have been using technology for some time to lower costs by centralizing and automating processes, allowing them to capture economies of scale and productivity gains. In the past, these banks consolidated processes primarily at the domestic level. In recent years there has been an increase in the offshoring of large-scale transaction processes to regional or in some cases even global hubs in low-cost countries such as India, China, Malaysia, or the Philippines.

Domestic Asian banks lack the scale to make significant investments in technology pay off, and the erosion of their traditional area of competitive advantage—low labor costs—means they are forced to define their own creative strategies for process-restructuring and use of IT. It is therefore possible that the large gap that exists today between them and best practice, as well as the offshoring wave in the US and Western Europe, will—at least in the medium to long run—be a blessing rather than a curse.

Their lack of scale is prompting even the largest Asian banks to look more favorably at outsourcing than most of their counterparts in more developed economies. IT-outsourcing is at the forefront, but more far-reaching business process-outsourcing models are also being both discussed and implemented. These can follow conventional structures, such as BCB in Malaysia which has set up a joint venture with EDS that sees EDS take over a significant part of BCB's back office operations and that intends to provide outsourcing services to other banks at a later stage. There are also more consortia-oriented models, where leading banks from different countries are exploring setting up joint pan-Asian transaction facilities to capture economies of scale. Ultimately, Asian banks could combine the best international systems from outsourcing with their lower labor costs to create some of the world's most cost-efficient banking platforms.

Credit: tremendous improvement potential

Most Asian banks have very weak credit skills: credit sales and approval are generally not strictly separated (with approval usually based exclusively on the credit officer's subjective judgment and not on statistically validated scoring models); rating models do not discriminate sufficiently; there is no connection between rating and pricing; and often there are no specialized collection and workout skills. To cover the risks that such weaknesses engender, collateralization is generally very high, which limits business opportunities especially in subprime and unsecured lending.

The main reason for this weak credit culture is the absence until very recently of competition from abroad. Local banks traditionally have had a huge advantage thanks to their well-established corporate banking networks, as well as their dense branch network. However, recently, foreign banks have strengthened their position in consumer finance and are expected to increase their position in commercial lending as well.

In most Asian markets, foreign banks dominate the credit card market, with a market share sometimes exceeding 40 percent, and they are expanding aggressively into other profitable areas such as mortgages. Along with their superior marketing and distribution skills, their success comes from their sophisticated scoring models, which make it easier to overcome problems of information reliability and screen risks more carefully.

With the imminent arrival of credit bureaus across Asia, the playing field is leveling making it easier for international players to fill up information gaps and bring their established credit underwriting skills and processes to bear.

Faced with increased competition, as well as emerging regulatory requirements following Basel II, some leading Asian banks have started to respond and strengthen their credit skills considerably. In fact, several leading banks in Korea are well on their way to installing state-of-the-art capabilities following the liberalization of consumer credit markets in the wake of the 1997 financial crisis. In Korea, banks that had no systems could leapfrog to the forefront unhampered by legacy systems. Across Asia, leading private banks are beginning to separate the marketing and credit functions, to invest in credit scoring systems, and are specializing their workout skills in separate workout units.

The practices of these leading private banks, however, are clearly the exception. Most Asian banks must now start—at least building the data-warehousing to store the required data history—to create a sustainable business in what will remain a volatile world.

LATIN AMERICA: READY FOR ACTION?

Marcos Fernandes, Alejandro Picos[6]

The diversity of Latin America's markets makes it hard to develop a single perspective on the region's retail banking industry. These markets are very disparate in size, level of economic stability, and degree of political maturity and, as a result, management practices and performance levels differ dramatically not just within the region, but within individual countries. Some are world class, others—where the market allows it—are suboptimal.

---

[5] The authors would like to thank, for their contributions, Alexandre Gouvea, Andrés Maldonado, Hugo Baquerizo, Tomas Elewaut, Guillermo Gómez, Justo Alcocer, and A.C. Reuter.

The best banks in the region have performance levels at least on a par with those of their high-performing US and European counterparts. They often embody best practices in a number of dimensions of excellence in retail banking. For the most part, these have been local banks. Banamex in Mexico (now acquired by Citibank), and Itaú in Brazil, for example, have, on average, outperformed other players in the region.

International banks started making bolder moves to enter the Latin American market at the end of the 1990s. Banks such as Santander Central Hispano, BBVA, and HSBC were initially rewarded in their home markets for their expansion, based on a series of successful local acquisitions; but efforts in strengthening performance and using their franchise to establish truly regional operations are still under way. Although they are busy turning around their local acquisitions, the transfer of skills and management practices takes time. However, where international players entered the market early and acquired top-perfoming local banks, they have been able to become market leaders and maintain that position.

Opportunities abound for Latin American institutions to develop excellence across all dimensions in retail banking. The industry is rapidly waking up to the need to step up performance, under the threat of intensified competition and the increasing presence of international capital.

Corporate leadership: laying the foundations

A focus on market performance has led excellent banks to deliver ROEs in the range of 25 to 30 percent compared with a level of 15 to 20 percent for second-tier performers. Top performers also trade at high market-to-book ratios of close to 2.

Local retail banks, however, still vary widely in how well they drive excellence in performance management. For the most part, they have yet to take bold steps toward developing appropriate performance measurements systems. Some do not have suitable transfer pricing mechanisms, which would allow them to measure profitability by product or segment type, and thus live with gaps in information that hinder decision-making. Furthermore, the lack of adequate performance metrics has inhibited the implementation of best practice incentive systems in many institutions, which reduces their ability to attract and develop the best managers.

Going forward, it will be even more important for banks to strengthen their performance culture. International and regional players alike should build on their efforts of turning around acquired banks to push for performance and for a merit-based approach to talent promotion. As competition intensifies and hopefully as regional economies stabilize, opportunities for improved performance will more likely be found in operational excellence.

Marketing and sales: customer segmentation on the horizon

Most Latin American banks have successfully implemented strong marketing programs focused on branding their value propositions. Brands in the region have become very valuable assets, and, in some countries, local brands command a higher premium than well-known international ones.

Banks are generally less skilled, however, when it comes to segmenting their customers and aligning their traditional banking operations with segment-specific offerings. Customer segmentation exists in very few banks, indeed many lack even reliable customer information. In some cases, banks have segmented their most valuable customers, but their understanding of customer behavior is insufficient to bridge the gap between theory and practice. A 'one size fits all' approach leaves upscale profitable segments relatively underserved when compared with mass market-banking offers. Efforts in these directions have started to emerge. For example, Banco de Crédito del Perú has created Banca Exclusiva, a dedicated brand for high-net-worth individuals that has a differentiated value proposition.

Even though many retail banks clearly understand the importance of customer penetration and retention, this lack of segmentation and customer knowledge has hindered the development of effective relationship management skills. However, as balances erode, attention is beginning to shift to CRM, and this whole area is rapidly becoming a core component of top management's agenda. In parallel, the greater penetration of lower income segments demands alternative, cheaper virtual relationship management models that move away from banks' traditional approach to account management.

The push to more sophisticated CRM models requires important changes in the way marketing functions. Banks must focus on building a customer information culture, where data availability and interpretation, and the modeling of customer behavior are ingrained in the marketing function.

Distribution: addressing complexity

Latin American banks have typically built dense distribution networks structured around a combination of physical and electronic channels. These networks have been effective in providing convenient banking for customers and have played an important role in fostering asset gathering and transaction capabilities. The attempts to offer segment-specific distribution formats have been timid at best, but they are now starting to be pursued with greater focus.

Banks have had little stimulus to tailor their service levels according to channel. They lack the knowledge of customer channel preferences, and high, stable margins do not provide an incentive to focus on cost-to-serve. Only a few leading banks have been able to turn high branch traffic into additional sales by turning branches into powerful sales offices. There are notable exceptions, where new brands were developed or acquired explicitly to target strategic segments. Fininvest in Brazil, for example, was acquired by Unibanco in order to focus on the low-income segment through a dedicated channel network.

Supermarket- or retail co-location-banking is still in its infancy, although increasingly popular as institutions begin to serve lower income customers and aim for higher efficiency levels. In Brazil, for example, bill payment, cash withdrawal, and other financial services are available in over 8000 lottery houses, a government business affiliated to Caixa Econômica, a state-owned bank. In Ecuador, Servipagos (owned by Produbanco) has reached higher efficiency levels by using dedicated business channels to streamline payments operations and reduce processing costs, serving retail customers through a proprietary branch network, telephone, and via the Internet.

Consumer finance at the POS is also increasingly penetrating retail outlets, broadening banks' loan reach. Elektra, the Mexican retailer that gradually evolved from a distributor of consumer finance loans to a personal financial services player including savings and money transfers, has recently taken the bold move of launching a fully fledged bank with brances in each of its almost 1000 stores. Variations of this model have been implemented successfully in other countries such as Brazil and Peru to reach low-income and credit-centric customers.

Latin American consumers have been quite receptive to new technologies. Many branches are highly automated with new ATM technologies enabling 24-hour banking, which customers have made clear they care about. Today, telephone- and Internet-banking are integral elements of the value propositions. The Internet in particular has quickly established itself as a legitimate banking channel; in Mexico and Brazil some institutions have over a fifth of their client base online, putting them near the top of the world league. Banco Mercantil in Venezuela is aiming to reach customers both in Latin America and the US through one single electronic regional platform—Todo1. As elsewhere, high Internet penetration has not lessened the reliance on branches—only a few institutions have been able to close branches or lower overall costs. As remote channels become ubiquitous, they will add further complexity to emerging segmentation strategies, and multichannel management skills will be crucial in order to ensure better customer service at lower cost.

Processes and IT: radical redesign still pending

Latin American financial institutions have been able to survive with below-par levels of operational efficiency: cost–income ratios are higher than in more developed economies, even for high-performing banks, despite significant labor cost advantages.

Paradoxically, the very factors that drove profitability in the past—historically high margins generated by basic transactional accounts and no-nonsense cheap labor manual processes—are possibly the reason that banks did not seek to upgrade their business delivery systems. Success was not associated with a push for sophisticated, risk-based products, nor with pursuing a segmented network approach to win market share; simply offering access to a basic product suite has been enough. Furthermore, in functional IT terms, the superb transactional capabilities created as a result of several inflationary crises have been enabled at the expense of levers associated with prospecting, sales, customer service, and retention.

In consolidating markets, the acquiring institutions have been able to justify their slow progress in cost reduction by rapidly building scale, thereby leaving plenty of room for substantial efficiency gains. However, with waning opportunities to boost revenues through acquisition and penetration at the current cost levels, banks are left with few alternatives other than to look at their own processes. They will have to address the need to enhance the functionality of their operations to address higher value-added commercial functions and dramatically improve the efficiency of their back office processes and IT delivery, in order to cap costs. They also need to squeeze the brakes on IT maintenance expenditure to align the levels with reality.

In the region's smaller economies, high-performing institutions started doing their homework sooner. Two of Chile's leading banks, Banco de Chile and Banco Santiago (owned by Banco Santander), centralized their back office operations and radically redesigned their processes, including the extensive use of process-outsourcing, as a way to build scale. These initiatives are starting to have impact on their efficiency indicators, which are approaching world class levels.

Some cost-efficient banks rely on standardized system solutions using IT platforms that are more efficient in terms of development, integration, and maintenance. Banco Santander has built a centralized software factory to serve its subsidiaries in Chile, searching for even bigger improvements in development and maintenance productivity and for the benefits of potential regional centralization of the activity. At the other end of the spectrum, some institutions in Brazil and Mexico have invested heavily in developing proprietary solutions. They have justified these investments based on the relatively low IT development labor costs, which in many cases have been lower than paying for a system license on an incremental basis.

Transformational operations strategies for proven and aspiring leaders in the region are twofold. On the functional side, the priority is to invest efficiently in information-processing tools that will enable key commercial performance levers—with CRM platforms and multichannel workflow tools at the core of the transformation. On the efficiency side, a radical effort is needed to optimize cost structures by reducing headcount and IT spend, which have shown steady progress, and embrace strategic transformational programs for an improvement of the cost base.

Credit: catching up with Basel

As credit markets continue to evolve and demand for consumer loans keeps growing, retail banks in Latin America are becoming aware of the importance of improving their credit risk management skills. Most banks have indeed implemented basic risk assessment tools in the form of credit scoring systems. The leaders in consumer finance have internalized and automated these capabilities and have integrated processes to approve credit rapidly at the frontline.

Far less attention has been paid to the monitoring and upgrading of these tools and policies, preventing institutions from validating and improving the models. Portfolio management tools, which are equally important and more sophisticated, are yet to be developed. Retail banks have limited knowledge of the probabilities of default for individual segments, and only a few of them have developed behavioral scoring models to monitor risk dynamically. Risk-based pricing skills are in their very early stages, leaving open many opportunities to enhance both volume and profitability. Developing a rigorous monitoring ('early warning') system, together with an effective workout organization and process, is important as the level of defaulted loans should increase as the credit market develops. Many Latin American institutions are seriously lagging behind their European and US counterparts in this respect: workout responsibility is often in the hands of salespeople; there is little systematic use of analytical tools to decide workout strategies; and institutions lack the data to assess expected recovery values.

Further hindering the development of strong credit skills is the lack of progress in establishing credit bureaus. Although negative credit information is being consolidated and structured for market use, the development of positive credit history is behind the curve. Some players, such as Serasa in Brazil, have made improvements in this area, and positive information is already available. However, local banks still seem to lack incentives to lead the process of sharing information as the overall benefits are perceived to be smaller than the competitive advantage their customer credit information represents. With decreasing M&A opportunities and increasing pressure for asset growth, the situation may revert, fostering the faster development of 'credit-positive' bureaus.

Some central banks (e.g., in Colombia, Mexico, and Brazil) have rapidly adopted the Basel II recommendations and are demanding a significant upgrading of institutions' internal risk assessment and management models, while creating separate legislation around provisioning and capital allocation. There is little doubt that banks will struggle with data availability and quality requirements, so, at this early stage, efforts should be put into building more robust data management platforms. Nonetheless, some top institutions see this as an opportunity to leapfrog to more advanced stages of credit risk management and are effectively reaching that level.

Part 2

Performance-oriented Corporate Leadership

4

Performance Culture: Realize the Hidden Value of Corporate Leadership

Reinhold Leichtfuss, Pedro Rodeia, Valentin Mihov[1]

A strong corporate leadership that strives for high performance is the most significant factor driving excellence in retail banking. Yet, despite many banks knowing this in theory, superior performance cultures in banking are mysteriously elusive.

There is no shortage of literature on organizational behavior and corporate leadership: the credo of some is to 'reach the hearts and minds of the people', while others favor the push approach of top management. The simple reality is that both are needed. Very few publications exist that explicitly address the task of building a performance culture in banking.

Here, we unravel the complexity of high-quality performance management in banking by offering an approach for enhancing performance culture throughout the bank. This approach is not just theoretical—it is based on and illustrated by observations at many retail banks around the world, whose leaders have discussed how they have achieved success in this field.

ILLUMINATING THE BUILDING BLOCKS

A performance culture is generally understood as one where there is a laser-like focus, inexorable energy, and the firm commitment of everyone in an organization

[1] The authors would like to express their gratitude to Lars Grönstedt (Svenska Handelsbanken), Benny Higgins (Royal Bank of Scotland), Francisco de Lacerda (Banco Comercial Português), Christine Licci (Citibank PK), Alessandro Profumo and Luca Majocchi (UniCredito Italiano), and Ugo Ruffolo (Banca Fideuram), for their time and insightful comments during our discussions on this topic. All quotations from them in this chapter come from conversations with us in 2002. We would also like to thank Michael Froehls (Citigroup), Matthias Beck, Maria João Carioca, and Vito Giudici for their contributions to our thinking.

to achieve extraordinary business results. Having a superior performance culture means consistently over-delivering and continuously raising the bar.

Fostering such a culture in any organization is a challenge, and for companies that traditionally have been less concerned with top performance, the task is even more daunting. Retail banks may well find themselves in this group, but should not be put off from attempting to achieve this goal. Without a performance culture that drives the bank, moving from average to world class will remain an insurmountable hurdle.

In the early 1990s, some banks believed that developing a management information system, monitoring target achievement, and introducing elements from performance-related incentive systems would be enough to do the trick. These can certainly help, but unless a bank takes a holistic approach to cultivating a performance culture, such attempts will inevitably be unsatisfactory. There are four categories of actions that can serve to turn unsatisfactory performance into world class. These building blocks are: clear direction-setting by top management, reinforcing the passion for achievement by managers throughout the organization (perhaps the most neglected of all areas), fine-tuning performance evaluation and incentive systems, and introducing performance-enhancing mechanisms that complement the first three cornerstones and that are focused on helping employees achieve superior results.

Broad category headings, of course, are of little value unless they are broken down. Here, we explain the precise actions needed in each category to achieve world-class levels rather than just average—there are 15 actions in total (Figure 4.1).

There are many useful combinations of individual actions within the four categories, giving banks some flexibility to adjust the change program to suit their specific situation and market conditions. However, to neglect one of these four categories, or to linger under the misapprehension that it is already in place and thus not strive aggressively enough to fulfill its requirements, will certainly bring about the downfall of the program.

On a scale from one to ten, the outperforming banks achieve performance levels of between eight to ten in 'top-management direction-setting' and score at least seven in the other categories. Comparing them with those players still striving for excellence reveals the extent of the difference: the average bank achieves scores between three and six. The difference is strongly reflected in the return on equity and the embedded future performance component of a bank's valuation.

Clear direction-setting by top management

If a performance culture within a bank is ever going to get a foothold, then senior managers must *demonstrate an indisputable will for superior performance*.

First comes a visionary CEO who is totally committed to performance. Such leaders need to strike a balance between subjecting the whole organization to a permanent state of tension and instilling a sense of fear in less performance-oriented managers, who are then likely to drift out of the core of the organization.

Once the manager is installed, the rest of the team has to be convinced of the merits of the approach and then share responsibility for overseeing its success. This can be a substantial hurdle, with aversion to change or lack of trust both potential problems. However, if a board decision is not universally upheld, and especially if

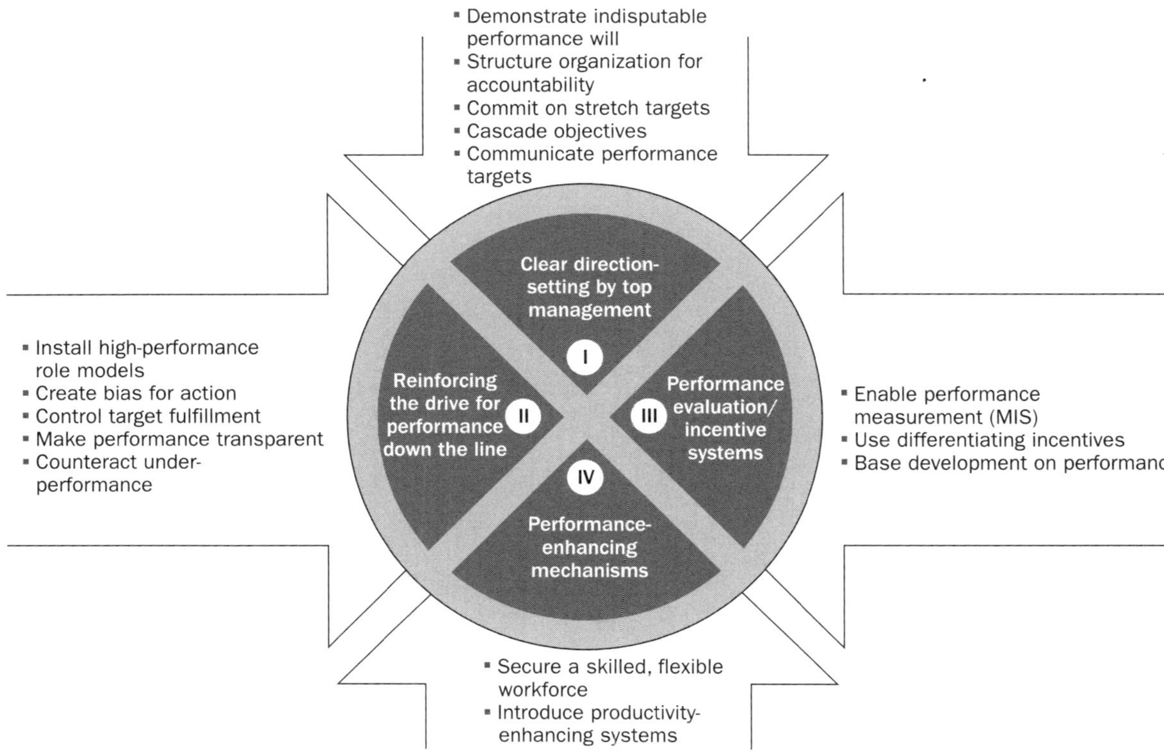

Figure 4.1 Performance culture framework

Source: McKinsey

employees receive mixed messages from board members, then any chances of operating as a homogeneous unit evaporate. This alignment is essential. If board members are seen to break ranks or are not fully in line with the key messages, there is a high risk of this discord filtering down through the organization breeding confusion and, consequently, no clear sense of direction is communicated.

Having a management team that has the strategy down on paper is one thing, but execution is another. Senior managers have to be able to walk the walk—not just talk the talk. They have to make it clear through their actions and their communications that performance goals are sacrosanct. To take one simple example, Banco Popular Español drives for cost containment and efficiency, and top managers live their own cost-conscious culture. Their spartan offices lack traditional corporate trappings: they do not buy expensive paintings, the furniture is upgraded only when absolutely necessary, and every executive makes an effort to fly economy class.

At another top-performing bank, Fifth Third, everyone, including the CEO and outside directors, has a target number of prospective customer calls to make per month and present the results to his peers and/or superiors.[2] Any contradictions between the impassioned speeches of senior managers and their subsequent behavior can rapidly become the topic of water cooler conversations and go on to spoil the entire process.

Walking the walk also means that every decision, be it a multimillion dollar corporate investment or just a simple transaction, is taken with performance at the forefront of the mind. Managers must not violate these standards themselves nor overrule an immediate subordinate who, for instance, refuses to sacrifice profitability for a prestigious customer or even a personal acquaintance of a manager.

Finally, success is even more difficult when it comes to tackling the politically sensitive issues that abound in every complex organization. Introducing a new regime into a bank means making tough decisions, and reorganization could well be imperative. Senior managers must have the courage of their convictions and solve these problems as swiftly as possible even when the decisions are painful. As Alessandro Profumo, CEO of UniCredito Italiano stresses, 'These are decisions that have to be taken, although it is tough from an emotional point of view, [but] we can deliver exceptional results only with exceptional people.'

When times are hard, it is the excellent banks that commit to making tough decisions and then carry them through—whether or not they are popular within the organization. The average banks meanwhile seek compromise in order to avoid creating dissatisfaction in the ranks. This is one of the factors that drive the big differences between the top league banks and other players when times get hard. As the stock market collapsed in 2000 through 2002, the high-performance banks were still able to grow their (merger-adjusted) revenues by an average of 8.9 percent while costs rose by just 2.2 percent. The rest had to put up with costs growing at almost the same rate as revenues: 3.7 and 4.5 percent, respectively.

Banking CEOs themselves stress repeatedly the importance of the role of top management teams. Alessandro Profumo claims that the most important factor

[2] First mentioned in Jeffrey Noe, 'Developing a sales culture.' *America's Community Banker*, August 1996, Vol. 5, Issue 8. This fact is emphasized in many interviews given by Fifth Third managers.

behind his bank's success has been the 'teams that we have been able to build and the fact that we have many different entrepreneurs who are able to work together.'

It is the CEO's role to bind these teams together and to ensure that the key initiatives remain at the center of management attention. 'The CEO must maintain the focus for the whole organization—day after day,' explains Ugo Ruffolo, CEO of Banca Fideuram. 'A CEO has to have the ability to simplify choices and implementation,' he adds.

Having a top team with an unquenchable thirst for superior performance is beneficial in any circumstance, but to reap the benefits at a bank-wide scale, the whole organization must be *structured for accountability and transparency*. In the words of Svenska Handelsbanken's CEO Lars Grönstedt, 'Organizational muddle is very expensive. If nobody is really responsible, there are a lot of things that will be done almost right, almost in time.'

Even though many banks today have established internal profit centers, the interfaces between units and the exact responsibilities of each unit are not always clear. Such a state usually arises from poor structuring or the inability to resolve political issues between units. In any restructuring, especially one that might not be welcomed universally, it must be made clear to every unit and organizational level that the purpose of the restructuring is the unambiguous allocation of responsibilities in order to reach specific targets. Once these areas of responsibility are clearly defined, their targets should be aligned with key corporate objectives.

A bank can check whether it is *setting the most ambitious targets possible* by answering the following questions:

- Do the targets focus on critical variables at the corporate level, linking them to value creation?
- Are they challenging enough to surprise the market?
- Are they accepted by the organization without endless discussions?

Royal Bank of Scotland (RBS) is an excellent example of a bank that set very ambitious targets and then exceeded them. Following its acquisition of NatWest, it set synergy targets that were in line with or exceeded international best practice. Many employees doubted whether this was achievable, but, inspired and motivated by their senior management, they still went about meeting and beating those figures. As a result, RBS exceeded its revenue synergy targets for 2001 by 75 percent and cost synergy targets by 33 percent. This in turn gave the organization the confidence to face ever more challenging targets as the bar was continually raised. The next logical step was to raise final synergy targets by 50 percent for revenues and 7.5 percent for costs from 2003.[3]

Fifth Third has a simple rule when it comes to instituting stretching income-growth and cost-reduction targets. George Schaefer, CEO, says, 'Our budget process consists of telling our managers "Get your revenues up 20 percent, keep your expenses single digit." You figure out how to do that.'[4]

---

[3] RBS, investor presentation, February 28, 2002.

[4] Robert A. Bennett, 'Happy warrior.' *U.S. Banker*, January 2002.

Overarching corporate objectives are not sufficient, however. They have to be broken down into specific individual targets, which in turn become a compelling story on how each employee can make a difference. *Cascading objectives down through the organization* is vital because a bank's vision can be seen through to fruition only with the support of its staff, and this means that each one of them should have their own personal mission. Naturally, these should align with the bank's grand plan, while allowing for a rewarding personal interpretation that helps the employee share ownership of strategic goals. Most of the excellent banks have deconstructed their corporate objectives into goals for individual teams and employees, implementing both implicit competition and explicit cooperation targets within and between units. These goals must reflect clearly the business and developmental responsibilities of individuals as well as their assumed ability to affect performance.

High levels of personal involvement throughout the entire bank are also supported by the *relentless communication of performance targets* and of the gaps to be closed. In most excellent banks, the objectives and their fulfillment are omnipresent—from the annual report to everyone's screensaver to canteen conversations. Moreover, if employees are constantly aware of what is happening, it is easier for them to understand what the bank's aspirations are and how it will achieve them.

Although many top managers may claim they are not doing so badly in direction-setting, clearly some banks are still struggling to reinforce the culture down the line—yet this is essential for success.

Reinforcing the drive for performance down the line

It starts with having *capable and highly committed role models* at all relevant leadership levels. If the people in pivotal jobs do not have the necessary capabilities and productivity rates to solve the upcoming problems, an institution will not become world class. Thus it is crucial for senior managers to maintain a clear understanding of the 50 to 200 pivotal jobs in their institution in both line and project management, as well as of the capabilities of the people doing these jobs and their potential successors. In the best organizations, the top managers have the specific responsibility to develop the next generation of leaders and are measured against their success.

Having the right people in place makes the next stage much easier. Role models can also make sure that there is *a clear bias toward action* rather than discussion. This requires a 'getting things done' mentality and fighting off the tendency to be overcautious, once so typical of bankers. All the top retail bank managers we interviewed were unanimous that execution—both doing the right things and doing things right—was very important. But, even more important was the ability to finalize decisions without procrastination and move to the implementation phase as quickly as possible. In the words of Benny Higgins, CEO of retail banking at RBS, 'We have to drive the change hands-on—not just talk about it.'

One way to speed up decision-making is to ensure that managers at all levels have the freedom to make decisions, such as how to strike the balance between working efficiently and ensuring high levels of customer satisfaction. If the decisions are not taken at the lowest possible level, a bank will find it extremely hard to be fast, responsive, and innovative. Thus, managers should receive the appropriate degree of entrepreneurial autonomy and relevant decision rights, together with the reassurance that there is tolerance for mistakes. Indeed, risk-taking should be encouraged, provided that it helps solve customers' problems—or the bank's—in a prompt, competent manner. Embedding such freedom in a personal mission that is aligned with the corporate objectives, and ensuring the right role models are in place, will be a tremendous driver of performance. Not doing so could be severely detrimental given the interdependence of all the areas within performance culture management.

Instilling such a culture also means introducing stringent rules of conduct, such as setting firm decision deadlines upfront or keeping meetings as small and short as possible. Some banks have even introduced a culture of stand-up meetings in order to push them along faster still.

Once goals are in place, it is important that banks *control target fulfillment closely*. This means monitoring performance daily, weekly, or monthly as appropriate—not just quarterly. If, for example, sales results are controlled only monthly with a time lag of three weeks, then the ability to respond to underperformance will be significantly inferior compared with that from shorter feedback cycles. To step outside banking for a moment, virtually all retailers, from the grocers round the corner to the biggest international chains, know exactly how much was sold the previous day, by outlet and often by product. This is part of their daily process for supply chain management but can also be used for performance management. By contrast, retail banks may be able to tell how many transactions were posted or what the balances are on the accounts, but they do not know exactly how many mortgages they sold in the previous week, or how many current accounts were opened, because their information systems focus on balances rather than sales. However, nothing proves the level of top management interest in frontline activities more than a Monday morning note from the CEO to the local market manager asking, 'Is this really the best we can do?'

One powerful way of ensuring that line managers are acutely conscious of the bank's vision is to *use rankings to make performance transparent*. Full transparency is not always easy to achieve, but a first step could be to introduce rankings for specific efforts such as sales campaigns. Rankings are much more useful if they are produced continuously for all business units and individuals along the relevant key performance indicators. Ideally, they would then be published openly within the organization in order to create internal competition. At Fifth Third, George Schaefer has his finger on the pulse, 'I keep score very well. I know the best and worst. We hold everyone accountable, every branch manager from the Sears Tower to Cleveland has stock options and bonuses tied to profit-and-loss performance. We rank them every week for loans, deposits, investments advisory sales, mortgage sales, credit card sales, annuity sales, and we hold them accountable. We follow the rankings very closely, looking to spot trends and identify laggards. They're measured on geographic areas as well as against each other.'[5]

[5] 'Wall Street's favorite banker.' *Money*, May 2002, Vol. 31, Issue 5.

Box 4.1

Hurdles to performance management

Strong corporate leadership commands a premium among analysts, but it is very difficult to build and sustain. European banks—and those operating in similar environments—face three main types of barriers:

1 They face *restrictive labor laws* that limit performance-oriented people management. In much of Europe, the fixed component of salaries cannot be reduced, making it harder to introduce performance-related pay; career progression is also often forced to take tenure, rather than performance, into account, and underperformance may not be a legally acceptable reason for dismissal.
2 The impact of this restrictive legal environment is compounded by *labor unions* that enforce compromises on staffing reductions, productivity requirements, work methods, or pay differentiation. In Germany, for example, where trade union representatives usually hold board positions, it is often difficult to measure, rank, and publish an individual's performance.
3 It can also be that a *bank's ownership structure* does not foster a focus on performance, as many are not publicly listed, but have shareholders who are not profit-oriented. This tends to reduce the pressure to maximize returns; the effect can be magnified by government influence, which tends to discourage unpopular measures such as layoffs, offshoring, or the bankruptcy of large corporations.

Although some senior bankers occasionally blame these barriers for the difficulties they have in creating a strong performance culture, the experience of excellent European banks demonstrates that many of these obstacles can be overcome or bypassed.

We would like to thank Gustav Adolf Schröder (SSK Köln) and Herbert Walter (Deutsche Bank) for their discussions and insights to overcoming such obstacles.

It is easier to implement completely transparent rankings in a North American bank, but some top-performing European banks have also found ways to exploit the power of rankings despite labor, legal, and cultural obstacles (Box 4.1).

Francisco de Lacerda, director at Banco Comercial Português, one of the excellent banks (and the sixth-ranked company in the 2002 Insead global report on competitive fitness[6]), underlines the importance of rankings, 'The high profile given to rankings worked extremely well,' he says. 'There was communication from the top, visits to the branch, and personal notes from the board to both the highest performers and to those falling behind. The results were put on the wall in every branch for every employee to see.'

Svenska Handelsbanken goes one step further by abandoning plans and budgets completely, and instead insisting that 'The responsible person must be able to compare his or her performance, not with something unreal like a plan or a budget, but with something tangible, such as the results achieved by people with similar responsibilities.'[7]

It is then the line manager's responsibility to *manage underperformers proactively*. Banks are in pretty bad shape if underperformance is not transparent, if it is disguised, or if managers turn a blind eye to it. Not that all forms of underperformance

[6] Larréché, Jean-Claude, *Measuring the Competitive Fitness of Global Firms 2002*. Pearson Education, 2002.
[7] Svenska Handelsbanken, *Annual Report*, 2001.

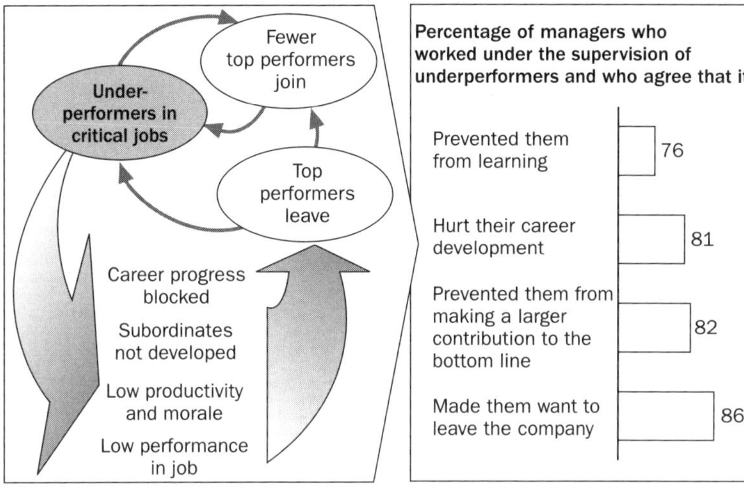

Figure 4.2 Damaging effects of underperformers

Source: McKinsey

management have the desired outcomes. For example, simply passing underperformers on to another department—especially with glowing references to encourage another manager to take them—merely shifts the problem; it does not solve it. Similarly, underperformers cannot be managed simply by eliminating pay rises and stalling on career progression. First, they should be trained and motivated by their immediate bosses in a practical, results-oriented way and improvement plans should be defined. But there must be clear penalties if disappointing performance continues, culminating in 'improve or leave' policies. In the end, only a limited number of periods of poor performance can be accepted, and, eventually, such people must be removed from management and leadership positions. Taking this step requires the clear, incontestable identification of those employees that are doing badly. If employees who consistently underperform—especially managers—are not removed from pivotal jobs, then the damage can be significant: apart from their own low performance, the mediocre manager dents the morale and decreases the productivity of his or her peers and subordinates (Figure 4.2).

The top banks have already made this leap. BCP's Francisco de Lacerda explains his bank's approach, 'We really should coach, train and work with people that are performing below average. But in the end, the organization must develop, and it can survive only if it rewards its shareholders properly. If we don't perform, then all of us will lose our jobs. Those who do not adapt after all the coaching and training will have to find other types of activity that they can fit into better.'

Counteracting underperformance also means that the insights gained through assessing and comparing performance must be transformed into actions. If specific customers, products, or units are unprofitable, then simply recognizing and monitoring them is not enough. We will elaborate further on the portfolio implications of underperforming units in Chapter 5 on corporate strategy, but the effect of weeding out such units on corporate results and on the organization's commitment to superior performance is enormous. As Luca Majocchi, CEO of Italian banking at UniCredito Italiano, states, 'If something is not working, then either you close it or you change it. You do not keep alive projects that are not working; they will take energy away from your organization.'

Fine-tune performance evaluation and incentive systems

We mentioned at the beginning that, during the 1990s, banks believed that announcing aggressive commercial objectives, installing an MIS to monitor target achievements, and developing an incentive system was all they needed to create a performance culture. However, this works only if the *MIS is linked explicitly to the value creation drivers*, if the links and interdependencies are transparent and if the managerial support structure is in place to react to the findings.

To be of any use, the MIS has to report promptly those performance indicators that are geared explicitly to value creation. In order to reach the highest levels of acceptance possible, the results must show a level of accuracy that is hard to challenge. It is unrealistic to expect that no one will ever complain about the results, but there should be reliable data behind the reports.

Once reliable performance data are available, achievements can be linked to incentives—both financial and non-financial. 'Top performers have to be rewarded and made to feel important,' says Benny Higgins from RBS. 'We have to celebrate success and we do celebrate success. I think we've got to look after people by the way we respond to them everyday, so it's not just once a year, it's not just in their pay packet, it's how we deal with them. Poor performers have to be coached, they have to be helped and if they remain poor performers they have to leave.'

Financial incentives have to be differentiated to be effective. If everyone gets the same, there is no true incentive. Instead, employees who have not reached their targets should receive no additional remuneration, whereas the overachievers should receive significant bonuses.

The excellent banks differentiate themselves from average banks by using variable compensation schemes that put a significant amount of an employee's pay at risk (Figure 4.3). In general, such schemes are well established, comprehensive, simple, stable, and include financial and other measures of performance. Bonus potential is known in advance, and the criteria for achieving it are clearly within the control of staff.

Francisco de Lacerda explains BCP's position, 'We set up targets, which we connected to incentives, and people began to talk in this type of language. Training and incentives are very clearly linked to performance, thus they really see the link between their performance and the money they will take home at the end of the month. People adapt their behavior believing that what is better for the bank is better for them, too.'

Another excellent approach is to encourage significant employee ownership. As Fifth Third's CEO George Schaefer points out, 'We pay good salaries and bonuses, but real wealth for our employees comes as a stockholder. We let them buy stock at a 10 percent discount to the share price. We want them to think they're owners first

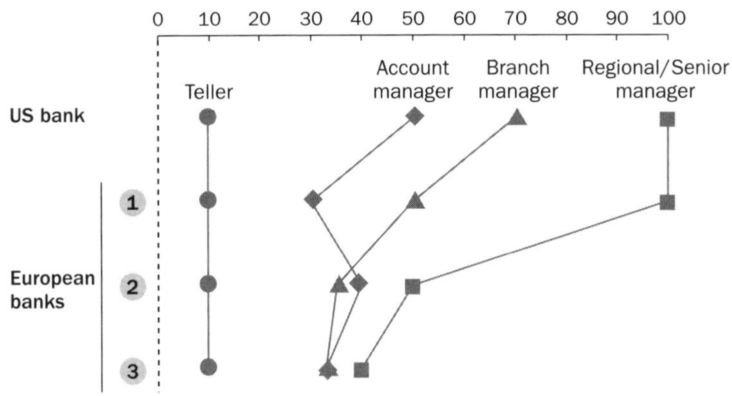

Figure 4.3 Maximum variable pay (percent of fixed salary)

Source: press clippings; McKinsey

and employees second, so that the branch manager is acting like he actually owns the bank.'[8] Under such circumstances, employees feel encouraged to go the extra mile and raise their performance targets themselves. Svenska Handelsbanken has a different, much more cooperative and egalitarian culture. Its employees receive, through a pension foundation, an equal annual share allocation based only on the bank's relative performance to its peer group. The employees have grown to be the biggest shareholder group within the bank, owning about 10 percent of the total capital.

Incentives often aim to foster the 'right' behavior, but they are not sufficient to elicit the full rewards of a superior performance culture. *Basing employee development on performance and potential* is essential if a bank is to make top performance its objective. But having a systematic approach to setting career paths is easier said than done. First, managers have to extract the different levels of performance, and, second, they have to avoid the pitfall of promoting based on power groups. Company politics must have limited influence, performance is all that matters, and this meritocracy has to operate at all levels of the organization.

Introduce performance-enhancing mechanisms

In environments with significant cultural or legal constraints, such as continental Europe or Asia, it is imperative to hire the right people in the first place and to provide them with the right productivity tools. If a bank cannot release underperformers, then it needs to be even more selective in recruiting so that it is able to cultivate *a skilled and flexible workforce*. Top managers and personnel departments have to work in a range of areas to achieve this.

First, they need to recruit genuine top performers for pivotal jobs, which means offering them an excellent package. Depending on the specific circumstances of both the bank and the recruits, its elements can range from a market-beating sign-on bonus to a rotational program that allows the employee to work in different loca-

[8] 'Wall Street's favorite banker.' *Money*, May 2002, Vol. 31, Issue 5.

tions. In all instances, however, it is the commitment of the bank to do what is best for the employee in return for his or her outstanding performance that characterizes the talent management of the successful banks.

Second, employers must train their staff to enable them to achieve a superior performance. Some financial institutions, such as MLP, take an average of 40 working days each year to upgrade employees' professional skills. Fifth Third invested in distance-learning systems in order to provide consistent and efficient new product and service training where and when it was needed. Its stated purpose was 'to continue to grow our business and retain our leadership in the industry.' To do this, the bank argued, 'We need ... technologies that increase employee productivity and performance. Highly skilled individuals will increase our revenues, make us faster, and ensure our success in the market.'[9] Unicredito stimulated employee computer literacy and self-teaching by giving every employee a high-performance desktop computer for home use.

Third, banks must create opportunities for the personal development of their brightest and best. Haphazard career progression will not deliver the full potential of these rising stars; rather, they need specific development programs and they should be monitored to ensure not just that performance levels persist but also that they are constantly stretched by ambitious targets. Certainly, the selection of personnel with very high potential should be based on clear, transparent evaluations, within a performance culture. Matching this talent to suitable opportunities is an art in itself that requires the personal involvement of the CEO, because the result should provide both a development challenge and have a substantive business impact.

The *introduction of productivity-enhancing processes and systems* that create productivity increases at the departmental or functional, rather than the individual level can be very powerful. These seek to replicate industrial-like production environments to improve performance: when an assembly line is introduced, the pace of work can be set for all employees alike. Banking is of course different to a manufacturer's shop-floor, but there are some mechanisms that can help boost performance.

A call center, for example, can be managed more effectively and supported more cost-efficiently than individual branches. In Germany, Citibank's call center has been scheduling the meetings for branch personnel for many years now, which has helped to boost productivity.

In the sales function, database-marketing information can be brought directly to frontline staff's screens offering sales reminders and leads. It also frees up time for sales preparation, sets a new pace for all salespeople, and ensures that customers are approached more often. The continuous search for productivity improvements must be made an explicit goal.

PAVE THE WAY TO SUCCESS

We have just gone through 4 categories and 15 dimensions, each with its own set of requirements. It may sound like too much effort, but if a bank wants to build a

[9] 'Fifth Third Bank's investment in Saba Learning supports rapid growth.' *PR Newswire*, September 9, 2002.

strong performance culture there is no other way. It is a long-term journey that will take at least three stages to complete: first, setting ambitions and prioritizing actions; second, defining a coherent set of targets in line with the ambition; and, third, implementing by overcoming obstacles while maintaining direction. Never forget that the goal should not be to improve a little along all 15 dimensions, but to achieve world-class levels in as many as possible.

Set the ambition and priorities

If you want to build a strong performance culture, you have to start with a vision, but, as Unicredito's Luca Majocchi explains, 'It is difficult to mobilize large organizations if you don't have a very strong sense of urgency.'

Although all top performers have very ambitious visions, not all can fulfill them within a reasonable time frame. Therefore, the first step should be to define a realistic position that can be achieved within two to five years. To know what is realistic requires benchmarking the bank against best practice in each dimension (Figure 4.4).

One thing needs to be made absolutely clear: identifying the real gaps for a given bank requires accurate, objective benchmarking. This is not easy. The exercise should be not only intellectual but also a practical group exercise, as not all top managers will share the same opinions and their assessments will vary across organizational levels and over time. The benchmarking needs to be driven by top management, but we have often found that internal assessments can be quite optimistic. Therefore, it can help to validate the internal view by introducing an external perspective, led, for example, by a non-executive board member. Once an objective assessment of the bank's relative position is complete, senior managers can set a realistic ambition and prioritize the overall improvement effort.

Many banks will find objective benchmarking on performance culture to be quite distressing, as the results can show them to be far from best practice in many dimensions. A CEO in this position should not panic; after all, even some of the top performers do not excel in all dimensions. But if a bank has large gaps in too many areas, then it needs to determine which ones are the most critical and should be fixed first. Although all 15 levels are very important and a score below average indicates significant handicaps in performance in general, prioritizing actions according to import and effort can help shave months off the journey.

According to the CEOs of the top-performing banks, it is the demonstration of indisputable will by the top management that is the number one priority and which, therefore, should be the starting point. Interestingly, making performance transparent is ranked second on the ladder of importance by top managers. Cascading operational stretch targets down the organization and creating a bias for action—which will place a bank close to the objective when others are still pondering how to start—as well as differentiated incentives also belong to the top five priorities. So, a bank that ranks low on these dimensions might do well to tackle them first. Banks that are unable to raise their game sufficiently in these five areas will not be able to reach the pinnacle of excellence, unless they can find some extremely successful substitutes.

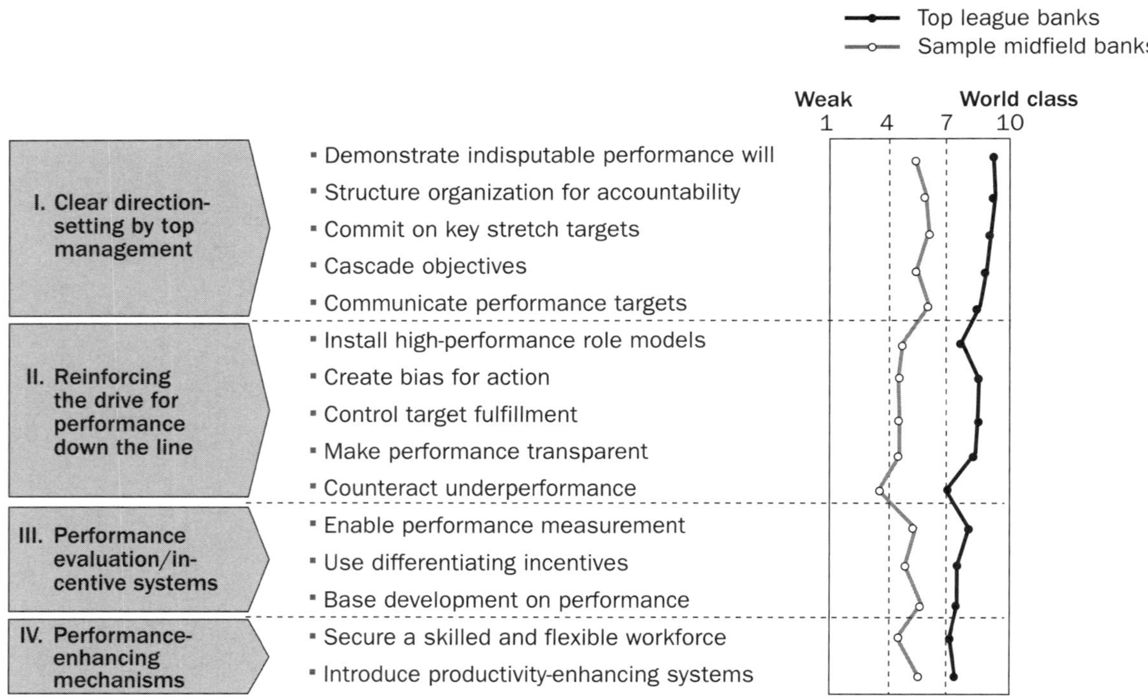

Figure 4.4 Benchmarking the performance culture

Source: McKinsey

Define the target system

With the priorities clear, it might seem quite straightforward to design a program that will fix these areas. Reality is, of course, more complicated. Many banks rank low in some dimensions precisely because they face significant barriers to implementation. Therefore, the next step is to identify and assess the critical barriers in the prioritized areas. For those that can be overcome, a credible plan can be designed to do just that. However, some banks will run up against structural or legal obstacles. For example, banks in Germany face contractual barriers in their collective agreements to making individual performance rankings available to the whole organization. In such cases, one option is to recognize that even if the ideal solution is not feasible, banks can achieve a similar effect with only a marginal reduction in impact. To continue the transparent rankings example, only some banks have gone all the way and made individual rankings transparent to all peers and superiors (Figure 4.5). Others have either created team-based rankings or made individual rankings known only to each individual and his or her superiors. One must be vigilant, however, and not dilute the impact too much. Rankings based solely at the branch level and made visible to only a few people may not be enough to create the necessary levels of internal competition.

Another option, particularly if slimmed-down versions of the ideal solution are not viable, is to look for substitutes. Take, for example, the management of underperformers in countries where it is illegal to dismiss employees for poor performance. One possible solution is to move underperformers out of critical functions without firing them and to be extraordinarily selective in recruiting. In addition, these banks should use productivity-enhancing mechanisms much more intensively. They have the benefit of improving performance, they signal to employees what is important, and, once in place, they become routine and do not need constant managing.

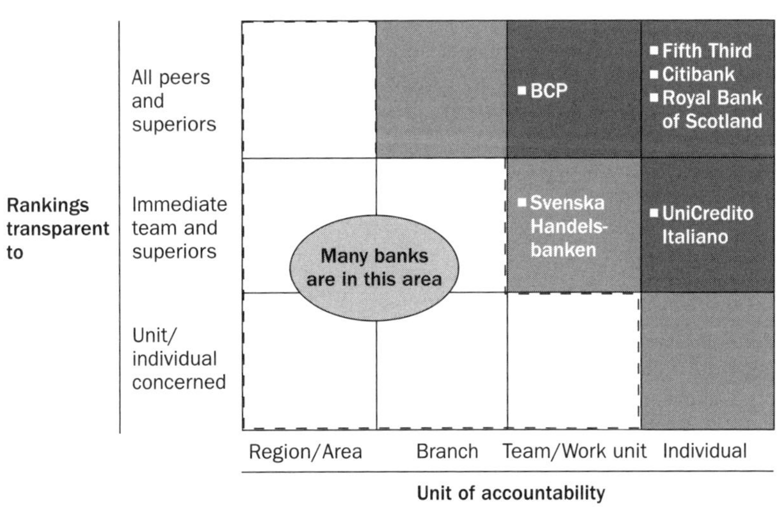

Figure 4.5 Transparency and reach of rankings

Source: McKinsey

Overall, each bank has to find its own profile (i.e., the right level for each of the 15 dimensions). Should a bank have only a basic MIS, then it should focus on managing only a very few, simple variables in order not to run into endless debates on the accuracy of reports.

Thankfully, there is not just one combination of levers that works. Rather, we have observed different performance culture profiles depending on the individual bank's traditions and strengths combined with market conditions. The following trade-offs and options may illustrate this point.

If a US-style 'hire and fire' policy is not feasible, then it is even more important to build a very strong performance ethic that includes not only hiring the very best people but also has an exceptional focus on the bottom-line impact of all measures. Establishing innovative ways of creating significant employee stockholdings in the bank can inspire people to work harder, as the example of Svenska Handelsbanken's Oktogonen Foundation shows. An inspiring vision and the ambition of beating the competition—be it on service, business systems, or products—can motivate employees enormously if executed well.

As Lars Grönstedt from Svenska Handelsbanken explains, 'It is inherent to the bank that it strives for the best customers and tries to improve the profitability of unprofitable customers rigorously. We have no problem reducing or abandoning service to constantly unprofitable customers. The branch responsible for the customer manages the whole process. There is absolutely no central edict that important or big customers must be serviced, if they are unprofitable. The branches are given absolute autonomy.'

At Citibank PK, the philosophy is focused on getting a fast return on investment. Christine Licci explains that 'payback periods of five or six years are not acceptable for us.'

The search for an overall system that overcomes the main gaps tends to be iterative, but it is important to remain alert to ensure that the system remains sufficiently aggressive. Getting the highest performance score possible means avoiding looking for substitutes just because the ideal course of action is too hard to implement. It also means ensuring that the target system is aligned with the desired profile and the intended vision. Many dimensions are interdependent (i.e., their impact is substantial only when they are applied in conjunction with each other). For example, cascading objectives down to the frontline may be effective only if they are then linked to visible rankings and differentiated incentives.

Execute the vision

With the target system clearly defined, the challenge is to kick-start the bank into action. This is often the most difficult part, as it requires mobilizing the whole organization and adjusting the path along the way without losing course.

Although choosing the right path depends on the exact situation, some general guidelines may be helpful. Five basic rules apply to the vast majority of situations.

1 *CEO involvement is critical.* It is absolutely crucial to allocate heavyweight management support to the effort, starting with the CEO. Unicredito's Luca Majocchi explains, 'As a CEO you can't delegate all the project management

down the organization; you still have to be the project manager of the most important areas. Try to act not only on the tactical improvements that can take three to five years, but focus also on the quick wins which can give a sense of mobilization and success in the organization. At the end of the day be very aggressive in defining your plans and looking at the results.'

2 *Carefully select and publicly support change champions.* Banks should also bear in mind the importance of other influential people within the organization. Consider, for example, the regional manager who has long been a 'father figure' for two-thirds of the bank's retail network, or the most successful sales agent for the past five years. These champions must be supported by the official celebration of success stories right from the beginning, generating a virtuous circle of change. This should then be reinforced with stories from managers who were not initially excited about the idea, but who then successfully turned around an underperforming team and are now willing to discuss with their peers how they did it. In one bank's change program, all branch managers met once a month to celebrate progress. In these meetings the best performers would sit at the CEO table and receive large green envelopes from the CEO to celebrate success. The worst performers meanwhile sat at the back and had to endure the gaze of their peers as they walked all the way to the front to receive a red envelope. All the meetings involved employees telling the group how they had improved. The stories with by far the greatest impact were from those who had received a red envelope in the previous meeting, but turned it into a green envelope in the next. It was then that the average employee started believing that he or she could do it as well.

3 *Reach all employees with a compelling story.* Often a clear vision and strategy does not materialize because it does not reach the frontline. Excellent banks translate it into a simple story that can be communicated persistently and understood by all employees and all other key stakeholders (customers, shareholders, unions). The head of retail banking at BCP, when facing a major challenge, often tells employees how similar situations were solved in the early days of the bank. This gives employees the confidence that problems can be overcome and gradually creates a culture of achievement.

4 *Expect and overcome resistance.* A strong performance culture is in place only when frontline employees change their everyday behavior. Such change often faces strong resistance, particularly during the initial stages. Entrenched middle managers may feel threatened, and underperforming employees could well oppose performance-based compensation and visible individual rankings. Often these sources of resistance lead to critical measures being diluted and compromise solutions being implemented. Excellent banks, however, manage to stay on course. Early on, they identify potential pockets of resistance and address their concerns and doubts proactively. Sometimes that is not enough and it becomes necessary to move aside persistent antagonists. Maintaining the will to go forward, not lose direction, and keep the focus on the things that matter most are all critical to success.

5 *Anticipate 'underwater obstacles'.* When developing a strong performance culture, one needs to realize that much of it happens below the waterline. Efforts fail when they focus only on what is really visible and tangible. For example, management may set ambitious performance targets, translate them into objectives for every

level right down to the frontline, and link them to powerful incentives; but for this to work several underwater obstacles need to be navigated around. First, when setting targets, one needs to fight those managers who try to beat the system by influencing targets so that they can be reached easily. If that fails, some managers may try to adjust how a given measure is calculated in order to make it fair—for them! If everything else fails, some may try to manipulate results. One of the excellent banks we interviewed created a ranking system visible to the whole network focused on sales and transaction migration to automated channels. Moving up the rankings became every employee's obsession on a daily basis. Some took it too far. After a couple of weeks ranking low on deposit migration, one branch suddenly achieved 100 percent migration. A visit to the branch revealed that the local manager had posted a notice saying, 'We accept no deposits. Try the ATM'. In another branch that jumped up the rankings, a survey to monitor customer satisfaction with the program showed that several customers, whose accounts showed automatic teller machine deposits, had never made them. Audits revealed that employees were making the deposits themselves after receiving the cash in person at the branch. Both offending branch managers were transferred to remote, much less important branches, sending the message to the whole organization that trying to beat the system was not the road to success.

Other guidelines apply only to specific situations. For example, in turnaround cases, the fundamental rule is to start by aggressively challenging the status quo, making inertia more painful than change. Frequently, in turnaround situations all focus is directed at quick wins, but although this generates positive momentum, it may also leave all the real breakthroughs buried for a long time. This raises questions over the true commitment to deep change and gives unwanted room to 'if we keep feeding them crumbs, they won't ask for the cake' attitudes. The challenge is to be bold and step into the arena to take on at least one of the organization's sacred cows.

However, when fine-tuning an organization that is already performing well, the key is to nurture smooth evolution, mitigating the disruption of aggressive change while introducing the elements that can take it a step further. At the end of the day, however, many of the basics don't change.

Finally, during implementation, it is crucial to monitor the results continually through a transformation program panel, recognizing that as much (if not more) happens beneath the surface as is really visible.

CORE SKILLS WILL REMAIN CRITICAL

Although many of the essential tasks for fostering a strong performance culture are relatively stable over time, it is likely that for more and more banks the international or interregional dimension will become increasingly important. This is likely to bring new challenges in terms of building a strong cross-border performance culture and sharing knowledge, as some of the top performers' leaders indicate when asked which capabilities a retail CEO will need in the future.

As the banking industry becomes more integrated—especially in Europe—bank leaders will need to refine their skills, explains BCP's de Lacerda, 'One very impor-

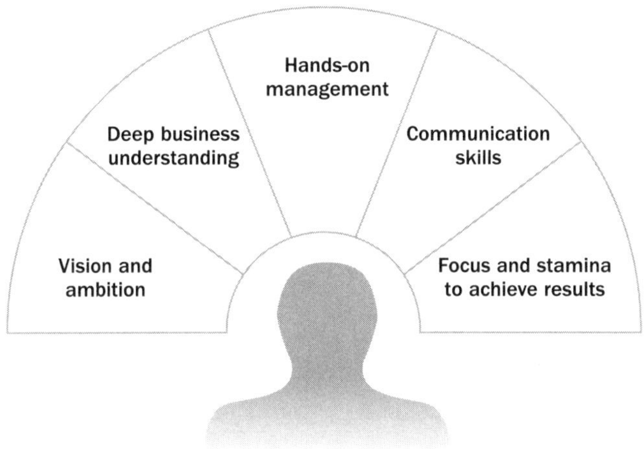

Figure 4.6 Key CEO skills

Source: McKinsey

tant skill will be to work effectively in multicultural environments and then to put people with different cultural backgrounds together and develop an organization that is based in more than one country. Transferring capacities and skills back and forth from one country to another will be a real challenge over time.'

In an era of intensive cross-border expansion, there is no doubt that the ability to adapt to changing environments will become increasingly important. However, retail bankers should not put the cart before the horse. The traditional competencies needed for driving performance: vision and ambition, a deep business understanding, hands-on management, communication skills, focus, and the stamina to get results will all be as important tomorrow as they are today (Figure 4.6).

5

Strategy Matters: Make the Whole Worth more than the Sum of Its Parts

Pedro Rodeia, Luís Cunha[1]

Historically, many banks have regarded themselves as one single business in which only execution mattered. Managers claimed that no segment, product category, or channel could be abandoned as all were linked. Furthermore, they have invested a significant portion of their capital in stakes in industrial companies, property and casualty insurance, or real estate—businesses with sometimes tenuous links to the core banking business.

Excellent banks recognize that their portfolios do indeed include a complex web of related, but distinct businesses that cut across multiple geographies, products (e.g., mortgages, consumer credit, asset management), segments (e.g., small business, affluent, mass market), and channels (e.g., branches, call centers, the Internet). They also understand that each of these businesses varies widely in its market attractiveness and competitive environment, both of which are often influenced by new, focused competitors such as credit card issuers, private banks, and online brokers.

These excellent banks stand apart from the rest by responding to these distinct conditions through 'de-averaging' their portfolio, aiming for above-average market share in those businesses that have the strongest value-creation potential, and below-average market share in all others. As a result, they allocate resources based on potential rather than on business unit demands.

This allows them to focus on the most profitable products, segments, or geographical markets, and helps them develop distinctive capabilities in these areas. There are at least three different formulae for achieving this goal. As outlined in Chapter 2, *strongly focused players* tailor their business system toward selected attractive segments or products; *focused multi-specialists* gradually steer their portfolios away from the average through their investment and capital allocation choices; and

[1] The authors express their gratitude to Ulrich Voss and Miklos Dietz for their contributions.

regional broad-based banks focus on limited geographical areas where they can exploit their superior customer knowledge and higher brand recognition.

This de-averaging, or unbalancing, has been a key factor behind the performance of many of the top league banks. Citibank NA is a particularly good example of how it works in practice. If, like most other banks, Citibank had an average market share in all its businesses then, naturally, its return on equity (ROE) would not differ significantly from the industry average. Instead, in 2001, the bank had a 16.5 percent market share in the very attractive credit card business, but only a 1.8 percent share of the less attractive mortgage business. This strategy is a strong contributor to Citibank's exceptional 30 percent plus ROE on its banking and lending operations.

De-averaging a portfolio is not just about numbers. Excellent banks shape their portfolios to create a vision that makes sense both internally (i.e., to employees) and externally (i.e., to customers and the capital markets). For Svenska Handelsbanken, their focus on proximity to customers, on being 'local', contributed to aligning the staff to providing excellent, personalized customer service. Focus also facilitates positioning a bank more clearly in the capital markets. For example, Fideuram's investment product focus helps it to be perceived as an 'asset gathering' specialist and to command multiples superior to those of universal banks.

Moreover, it is not enough to allocate only financial resources to the chosen few businesses. It is also necessary to allocate talent if these businesses are to achieve a strong competitive position. A prominent example has been BCP's aggressive, focused growth over its first 10 years. The bank followed a segmentation approach that established dedicated networks for each market segment, starting with the most attractive. 'BCP Particulares' for affluent, 'BCP Private Banking', 'BCP Corporate', 'BCP Empresas' for mid-market companies, 'BCP Comércios & Empresários' for small business and 'NovaRede' for the mass market. Each network had a dedicated top management team, separate accounts, a distinct brand, and pursued a clearly differentiated strategy. Top managers were rotated typically every two to four years across businesses and functions (on the basis of the fit of their skills with business requirements) to develop a rounded general management profile. Ten years after its launch, BCP had captured about 10 percent of the market in the most attractive segments and led the domestic consolidation process that resulted in its leading position in the Portuguese market.

When de-averaging, it is essential to avoid simply following the market, but rather to focus resources on those businesses that have the greatest value-creation potential and in which the bank can develop a truly distinctive competitive position. Although a corporate strategy will necessarily be specific to each institution, there are insights to be gained from looking at the best performing banks.

The first critical element is identifying which businesses could create the most value. Once they are identified, they need to be pursued aggressively to avoid being overrun by market trends that can draw all institutions toward the average. This exercise can be achieved in three straightforward steps. First, break up the bank to find where value can be created or destroyed; second, derive from that the priorities that each business unit must follow; and, third, ensure that the correct environment is in place so that everyone in the bank is pushing in the same direction.

BREAK UP THE BANK

In addition to measuring current profitability (essential for understanding the starting point), a bank needs to anticipate the relative value-creation potential of each business, its potential competitive position, and its potential contribution to other businesses in the portfolio. One relatively simple way of achieving this is to compare all units along two axes: intrinsic value-creation potential and the bank's ability to become the natural owner of the business (i.e., whether it is the best placed to extract the most value from it, given the potential competitive position and its execution capabilities).

Intrinsic value-creation potential. To rank business units by their value-creation potential, the first step is to define the baseline (i.e., the ability to generate returns over and above their cost of capital). This requires splitting the bank into economic units, as it is rare that all business units are separate companies. This is a shift from the traditional, aggregated method of measuring performance. The precise unit segregation will vary between banks, but, at the very minimum, it is necessary to understand product and segment profitability (some banks can break it down by channel as well). This often uncovers substantial cross-subsidies that undermine overall bank profitability.

However, banks have to go beyond current profitability if they want a more accurate, forward-looking perspective. One immediate refinement is to incorporate an estimation of growth and future profitability. These are very important factors since most institutions have portfolios that include a mix of growth and mature businesses, and the two need to be assessed differently. To avoid optimistic projections, any critical estimates should be translated into commercial objectives that are linked directly to the relevant managers' remuneration. Having a management information system structured around those businesses is vital here, as it allows a close monitoring of the degree to which those expectations are becoming a reality. Furthermore, it can provide a historical track record of each business leader's performance, which can help discourage excessive optimism and provides a basis for calibrating target-setting discussions.

A second and more difficult refinement is to incorporate the synergies that each business unit provides to the other parts of the bank. This is one of the most important differences between this approach and 'conglomerate' portfolio analyses. A European bank that followed this de-averaging approach realized that the value of its retail unit was 45 percent higher after taking into account the synergies it had with product and operation units. A stringent, quantitative approach can help avoid the pitfall of using synergies as an excuse for not taking decisive action when there are units that are clearly destroying value.

After these two refinements to the base profitability figures, a bank can make an integrated and comparable assessment of each business unit's contribution to value creation (see Box 5.1 for a European perspective on value creation).

Natural ownership. The second axis on which to base the portfolio relates to the opportunities and businesses that a bank is most suited to capture (i.e., in which it can achieve better returns or growth than its competitors). Specialization trends are increasingly forcing institutions to focus on areas in which they can claim natural ownership; otherwise, they will struggle to extend beyond the average. Banks

Box 5.1

Understanding market attractiveness: a European perspective

A prerequisite for assessing intrinsic value-creation potential is an understanding of market attractiveness at the geographic, segment, and product level. This is particularly relevant if a bank is considering entering a business for the first time.

Although retail banking accounts for almost 60 percent of operating profits[2] and 75 percent of value creation[3] (as a result of lower capital requirements than wholesale banking) of the Western European financial services industry, the degree of attractiveness varies widely across countries and between different products and segments.

In terms of national markets, it is not surprising that Europe's five largest economies account for almost 85 percent of financial services revenues. Overall, the UK and Italy are the most attractive European markets. The UK's market is highly efficient and draws on the strength of the capital markets, while Italy offers a combination of high growth, potential for increased penetration, operating efficiency opportunities and attractive margins. France, on the other hand, looks less attractive, with its biggest value creators, such as asset gathering, offering only slow growth. Spain can offer a combination of strong growth and high cash value created in certain segments, such as private banking and consumer finance. Germany has scale but, with its high levels of competition and its low margins and high costs, it has become a less attractive market.

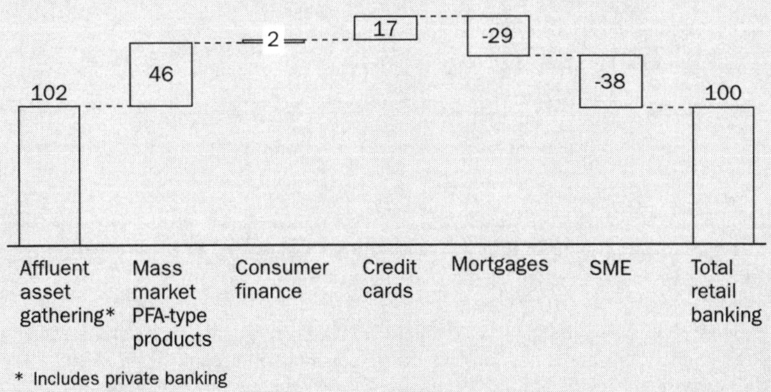

Figure 5.1 Cash value added by industry segment in Western Europe (percent, 2001)

Source: McKinsey

Value creation by segment and product group tends to vary over time and according to national markets; at times this variation is significant. For the big five European countries the variance can be quite high in any given year. For example, in 2001 with their economies on the brink of recession and in a relatively low interest-rate environment, their national banking system profits were dwindling (or at best stagnating). This was mirrored in the significant deficit of the aggregated small business banking

---

[2] After depreciation and loan loss provisions.

[3] Proxied by Cash value created = Operating cash flow (i.e., operating result adding back depreciation and provisions but subtracting normalized credit cash losses) − Cost of equity capital (i.e., cost of bank equity × capital required). In the case of a bank, this is a superior measure to economic value added since depreciation is often very dierent from reinvested capital, which is mainly a function of credit growth, and provisions often lag normalized cash credit losses.

profitability. However, the value destruction in this segment took place largely in Germany and to some extent in France. Mortgage banking did not perform well either, except in Italy, with German and UK mortgage banking the biggest contributors of red ink. Meanwhile, asset gathering continued to provide more than 30 percent of total retail revenues with roughly two-thirds coming from the affluent segment and the rest from high-net-worth customers (i.e., private banking). Asset gathering contributes 40 percent of total operating profits thanks to its structurally low cost–income ratio. Most importantly, because it is remarkably capital-light, it generates 102 percent of the total cash value created in retail banking (Figure 5.1).

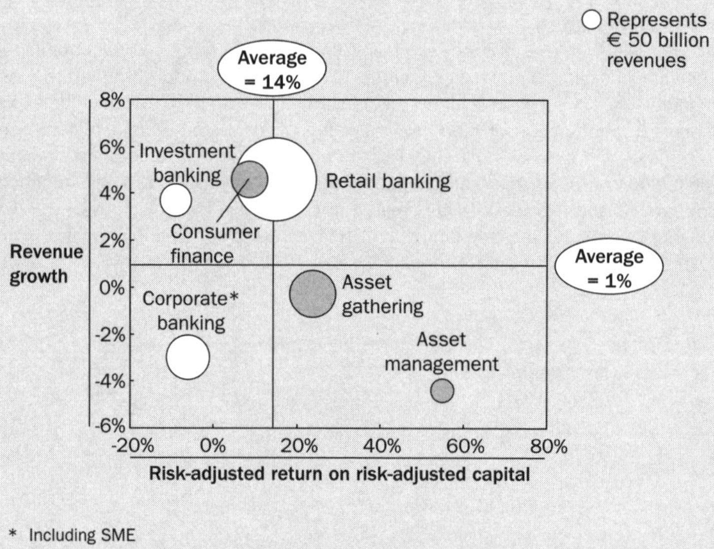

Figure 5.2 Business line attractiveness in Western Europe (percent)

Source: McKinsey

The importance of asset gathering will continue, as it is expected to drive revenue growth, together with retail lending. There are exceptions: in France, asset gathering and even private banking are predicted to grow more slowly, and the mortgage market could be flat or even contract.

The growth in asset gathering—especially in private banking—will be driven by strong growth in demand. It could accelerate even faster still if the European pension system is reformed, which would benefit the capital markets and thus help push asset gathering products, such as mutual funds and unit-linked life insurance. Even if the capital markets continue to perform poorly, it would be unlikely to slow volume growth in this segment, but could lead to a shift in asset mix toward bonds and fixed income—typically products with lower margins.

Revolving credit, especially in the form of credit cards, is expected to grow quickly, driven by strong demand, specialist leadership, and the high potential for penetration; but this is likely to be balanced by stagnation in the personal loan markets, which are generally mature and where high margins are under increasing pressure from nonbanking players entering specific product segments, such as car loans (Figure 5.2).

In the UK, there is about one card per person; in France, one for every two people; and in Europe as a whole, one card for every 10 people. Outstanding balances per card in Europe are around €340, compared with €1400 in the US, €980 in the UK and €720 in France. This shows that banks in most European countries have the opportunity to grow the market rather than simply battle for share. Just halving the gap to the UK would potentially yield profits for continental banks of €4bn. Indeed, credit card issuing earns a return on assets of 3 to 4 percent.

After the UK and France, Scandinavia has the most-developed card markets, but there is still room for growth here. In Germany, by contrast, credit cards are scarce even though consumer debt is high. Instead, consumers use substitutes such as cheap, easily available overdrafts for borrowing and electronic credit transfers (giros) for payments. On the other hand, credit cards could become the borrowing and payment vehicle of choice in southern and eastern Europe, as there are no entrenched substitutes.

There are market barriers hindering the development of credit cards, such as constraints on credit information and restrictions on marketing practices, but banks in markets like France have shown that they can be overcome and have reaped the rewards of a flexible product. Players in other markets have embarked in building the appropriate skills or partnering with credit specialists to mine this potentially rich vein.

Stefano Visalli, Jean-Christophe Mieszala

can determine the degree of natural ownership of their businesses along two indicators.

First, relative and absolute market shares are both reasonable proxies for a business's strength in its market. However, when calculating these, care has to be taken in defining each product's or segment's relevant market. This is especially true in Europe, where the euro has reshaped markets. Asset management is a good example: previously, each market had local leaders, but in the euro zone most of yesterday's leaders are now only marginal players.

Market share is important only if an institution is able to capture substantial economic benefit from it. Therefore, the second indicator that can help determine the degree of natural ownership is historical profitability. Natural owners tend to achieve superior returns while building or defending large relative market shares. But, as with value-creation potential, natural ownership is also dynamic—the bank has to understand whether natural ownership will be under threat in the near future given, for example, market deregulation, changing customer preferences, new competitors, etc.

After analyzing each business along these two axes, a bank can obtain a comprehensive view of its portfolio that allows for a richer understanding of where it should be investing its resources (Figure 5.3).

DEFINE STRATEGIC GUIDELINES FOR EACH BUSINESS

With Step 1 complete, the next step is to define the priorities of each business and select in which to allocate further capital and in which to decrease or even divest. This top–down approach differs significantly from most banks' typical planning process, which relies on a bottom–up approach. Usually, each business unit head presents a business plan and a budget to the CEO, and the planning department then compiles all these into a group business plan, subject to approval. If there is not enough money to go round, cuts are made across the board. We advocate that these decisions are made from an entirely different perspective: resources should be moved from businesses with low value-creation potential to those with high potential. This allows top management to allocate capital objectively.

Detailed business plans could then be made with an understanding of how much capital each business unit could expect to receive and what its priorities should be.

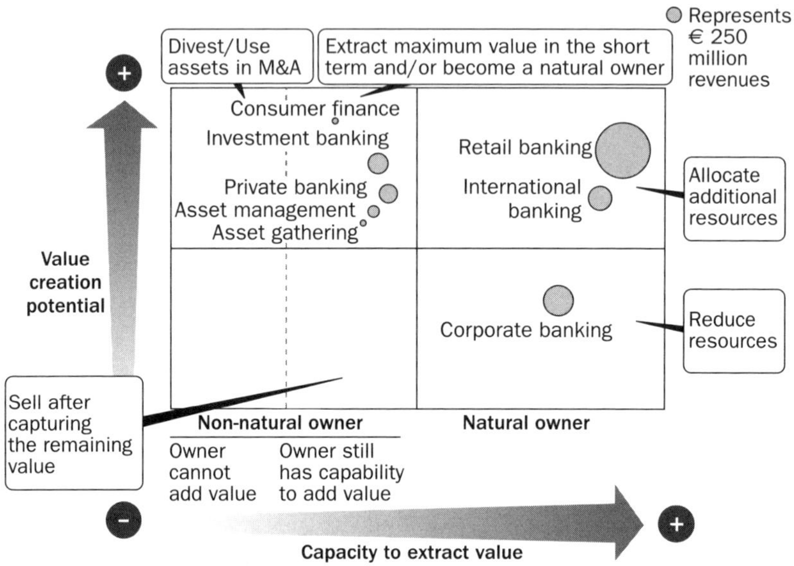

Figure 5.3 The business portfolio valuation matrix for a European bank

Source: McKinsey

Both capital and priorities will differ significantly according to the positioning that each business unit has in the bank's portfolio.

For businesses in the first quadrant (see Figure 5.3)—*high intrinsic profitability and weak competitive position*—the obvious priority would be to achieve natural ownership. This means identifying which capabilities the business unit lacks and are preventing it becoming a natural owner, such as a lack of scale, the wrong systems, inefficient commercial processes, etc. The business unit might then propose operational improvements, some M&A activity, the hiring of specific skills, or even creating a new group with the objective of developing and nurturing whatever is missing in-house. Solving this problem is the most important task in helping the business capture significant value. However, if the bank is convinced that it cannot bridge the gap, then it should consider cashing in through an alliance or a divestiture. Although it may seem counter-intuitive to divest a good business, the reality is that another institution may be able to extract more value and, hence, would be willing to pay a premium for the business. Again, asset management provides a good example. As previously mentioned, the introduction of the euro prompted several retail banks to think about their asset management operations. Some, aware that there are plenty of third-party offers and that asset management products can be white-labeled, decided to exit the business, usually selling their operations to larger institutions.

Royal Bank of Scotland (RBS), for instance, abandoned its asset management production. In its bid for NatWest, RBS recognized that it was not the best owner of NatWest's asset management business, and therefore sold it to Nationwide. Other banks have captured market share by trying to create a pan-European asset manager, as they realized they lacked the ability to build scale, which was needed to succeed in the new, enlarged asset management market. UniCredito followed a different approach—it relocated most of its European asset management operations from Italy to Ireland when it acquired Pioneer, an American asset management firm. So, solutions are out there. The important thing is that in all three situations, whether or not they have made the best long-term move, the banks have thought through whether to stay in the business in their quest to achieve natural ownership.

Banks must avoid the idea that businesses that are doing well should be left alone so that management attention can be diverted to turning around nonperforming operations. For these strong businesses in the second quadrant—*high intrinsic profitability and natural ownership*—the issue is how to invest in order to reinforce their market leadership. These businesses should be the bank's front-runners so the priority should be to develop their performance by providing additional capital (always taking into account the law of decreasing returns). Some institutions have found broader ways to reinforce leadership positions (e.g., by transferring knowledge to other geographical markets). Citibank built on the strength of its credit card operations in North America; first, to acquire and turn around other domestic operations and, second, to replicate that strategy in the rest of the world, either by pushing the credit card business of the retail banking operations it acquires (de-averaging its market share with a bias toward credit cards), or even by acquiring some credit card portfolios. Citibank's president, Robert Willumstad, has a clearly articulated vision: 'The biggest opportunity for us is taking what we do well here to other parts of the globe where margins are wider. Brokerage, consumer finance and credit cards—all of these businesses are so leverageable'.[4]

In the third quadrant—*low intrinsic profitability despite natural ownership*—the issue is how to shape industry economics while maximizing cash flow. If a bank is the natural owner of these businesses, then it is hard to believe that alternative owners could extract more value and would thus be willing to pay any premium on a possible acquisition. It is up to the bank itself therefore to promote initiatives to increase profitability. Some retail banks have found that their mass market retail operations fell into this category, and therefore to revamp profitability they developed initiatives aimed at reducing the capital invested in these operations. UBS's Private and Corporate Clients branch restructuring in Switzerland is an example. As stated in the company's 2002 third-quarter earnings presentation, its branch network was cut by a third and the headcount by 15 percent between 1999 and 2001. As a result, profitability has risen and the cost–income ratio over the same period has fallen from over 65 percent to around 60 percent.

Other banks have attempted to work on the income rather than the cost side, identifying additional opportunities to increase sales. Portugal's Banco Espirito Santo struck a partnership with Tranquilidade (a property and casualty insurance company) with the goal of selling retail banking products through the agent network. After three years, this was the bank's fastest growing channel and 10 percent of its mortgages were sold through this totally cost-variable channel. This

---

[4] John Birger with Nick Pachetti, 'What's ahead for Citigroup? Is a greater earnings multiple in Citi's future?' *Money Magazine*, May 30, 2002.

proves that the assurfinance model, although difficult to achieve, is possible. In Chapter 6, we shed some light on the complexities of bancassurance in Europe.

Finally, in the fourth quadrant—*low intrinsic profitability and weak competitive position*—the issue will usually be how to devise an exit strategy that maximizes the value from the business and frees up capital for other businesses. The first choice could be to pursue an outright sale to an institution that feels it could build natural ownership. For instance, Citigroup spun off Travelers P&C retaining a 9.9 percent holding and allowing Travelers to participate in any potential consolidation process. The transaction led to a market-adjusted increase in Citibank's value of almost 5 percent, which represents around half the value of the spun-off unit.

If divestiture is not an option, then a bank must reduce its exposure to that particular segment or product by using, for example, repricing and risk selection (thereby both reducing exposure and improving the economics of the remaining business). Barclays in Spain decided to move away from the traditional retail market as, according to its chairman Ernest Podesta, 'Our intention is to focus our activity towards traditional affluent clients. The bank will revisit its strategy regarding distribution channels, employee training, and product portfolio to offer a high-quality service.'[5] In fact, the bank reduced what already was a small branch network by Spanish standards by 26 percent (from 234 branches to 173 branches).

Even if a bank has assessed all its business units, has set the priorities, and allocated capital, success depends on having the right environment in place to support these decisions.

TRANSLATE PORTFOLIO PRIORITIES INTO ACTION

Banks now have to translate the boardroom discussions into action. There is a big gap between identifying the priorities and taking the right decisions, and the issue of how to establish an environment favorable to rapid and effective decision-making is very important. Such a conducive environment is built around four core tasks.

Install a disciplined process. Ensure that everyone involved, especially board members and other relevant managers, agree on the process and, more importantly, on the metrics to be used. Without this consensus there could be a tendency to revise the outcome once it is known by challenging the metrics, thus putting some of the conclusions at risk, especially the more radical ones. Then, link this corporate strategy process to the bank's budgeting and control procedures.

Align organization with business priorities. The closer the bank's organization follows a business unit logic, the more successful the implementation. The fact that there is someone, or a team of people, who can take on a specific segment or product as their challenge is a very important boost toward achieving an impact and promoting change. Banks that lack such a structure will find it difficult to maximize the impact from the corporate strategy process.

Manage talent proactively. As we said earlier, these decisions are about resource

---

[5] 'Barclays España entra en un período de ajuste y mayor especialización.' *Expansión*, December, 26, 1995.

allocation of all types, including staff. This is particularly important for businesses in the third and fourth quadrants, which will, by definition, struggle to attract top talent. The CEO has a role here in ensuring that managers assigned to define and implement exit strategies remain confident that the bank will find them other opportunities and that their work, if successful, will be duly recognized. Another aspect of talent management is recognizing that even in low-performing businesses, there will be people that the bank will want to retain in the case of a complete divestiture. Letting those people know that they are expected to remain will reduce the levels of anxiety that are natural in these situations.

Use smart pricing and aggressive cost-cutting as an alternative to divestiture. Sometimes divesting is not possible, either because no alternative owner can be found or because the entity is not separable from the bank (such as an internal department). However, one must be sure that an absence of potential buyers is not confused with a lack of willingness to proceed with the sale. If the business unit cannot be separated then an alternative is to reduce the capital allocated through the smart management of pricing and growth targets. Several banks have undertaken such initiatives, as the recent effort to reduce exposure to the corporate segment to concentrate on the retail segment proves. In the typical trade-off between growth and value, these initiatives clearly favor value, as the objective is actually to reduce exposure and hence foster profitability, even if at a smaller scale.

Banks that go through this three-step process will be positioned more firmly in the marketplace, as they will have a clear understanding of which parts of their business portfolio to over- or under-weight in terms of resource allocation. However, these exercises (ideally undertaken annually) need to be internally coherent and should not lead to a major change in direction every year. Each bank's strategy should become the articulated vision of the allocation decisions. As we explained at the beginning of this chapter, winning institutions have a stable formula over time, whether around a product (e.g., Citibank), a region (e.g., Svenska Handelsbanken), or in building a multi-specialist approach (e.g., UniCredito). Choosing and implementing the right formula for a given institution requires a lengthy commitment. One must not forget that running the exercise is good, taking the decisions—tough as they may be—is great, but excellence is achieved only when the required capabilities to turn opportunities into realizations are actually developed.

Most banks probably do not perform this kind of corporate strategy process. However, given the increased push for performance that the financial industry is expected to continue to face—with lower margins and lower growth—it should be clear that a corporate strategy that allows the CEO to optimize the value of the bank in an integrated way could be vital in raising the game to excellent levels.

6

Bancassurance: Chart a Path through the Fog

Pius Fritschi, Wilm Langenbach, Philipp Rickenbacher[1]

Bancassurance has played a major role in the development of today's European retail banking landscape, but the path forward seems shrouded in mist. Nevertheless, despite the prevailing uncertainties, there is a set of actions that will provide the cornerstones for the development of European bancassurance. These are based on an in-depth view of today's market, examining carefully what works and, just as importantly, what does not.

Over the past 15 years, bancassurance in its broadest sense has become a pervasive force in European retail banking. From the distribution of life insurance by retail banks to fully integrated bank/insurance companies, every European market today features one or more bancassurance player. Leading European players such as ING, Allianz, Fortis, or KBC have been able to draw a substantial share of profits from their combined banking and insurance businesses.

The greatest success story in European bancassurance comes from life insurance distribution. Here, retail banks have been very successful in capturing business across Europe, with market shares in 2000 ranging from over 70 percent in Spain and Portugal, through 40 to 60 percent in France, Benelux, and Italy, to rising, low, double-digit figures in most other European countries.

In property and casualty (P&C) insurance, by contrast, retail banks have not managed to achieve such a commanding position. Even in markets where retail banks have had most success in selling P&C, like France or Belgium, they have managed to gain only single-digit market shares.

Thus, despite its pervasive presence and a significant degree of success, the jury is still out on the future of bancassurance in Europe. Three major areas of uncertainty remain.

The first reflects the historical development of European bancassurance. Its success is based on individual stories, developed within national frameworks and driven by different rationales, ranging from favorable regulatory environments to

[1] The authors would like to express their gratitude for the contributions of Nils Beier, Oliver Bäte, Lieve Lowet, and Sopna Sury to this chapter.

defense against foreign takeovers. Convergence in both regulations and customer needs may ultimately weaken existing boundaries, but national frameworks will continue to determine the development of European bancassurance in the foreseeable future. The persistence of this fragmented market and the resulting constraints on cross-border developments are a serious source of uncertainty about the future.

Second, both between and even within individual markets, there is a wide range of bancassurance models. Players are using a variety of product ranges, distribution models, and ownership structures in their bancassurance businesses, and the resulting difficulties in identifying best practice are another major source of uncertainty for existing and potential bancassurers and investors alike.

Third, in the wake of the economic and capital markets turmoil since mid-2001, the question arises whether bancassurance is only a fair-weather strategic play. Bancassurers with ownership of insurance production have been hit particularly hard by the downturn: instead of combining the best of both worlds—delivering synergies and smoother earnings—bancassurance is seen today by many analysts as combining the worst of both worlds in terms of lending and asset management risks. The robustness of the bancassurance concept in terms of distribution (especially in life) is not in question, the advantages of ownership under adverse conditions remains to be proven.

In today's environment, it is essential for existing and potential bancassurers alike to grapple with these uncertainties and to chart a sustainable course through the fog and towards success. Such a route should be based on a full understanding of the European bancassurance landscape.

Analyzing a broad sample of European bancassurers, with a review of the internal and external conditions underlying each approach, reveals a pattern of what works today. This pattern can best be studied along three dimensions: product range, distribution model, and ownership structure.

PRODUCT RANGE: ACHIEVING A CLOSE FIT

The bancassurance product range is broad. It includes various types of life insurance and P&C insurance sold through banking channels, as well as—under the reverse term 'assurfinance'—any retail banking product that is sold through insurance channels. Although each of these three product families contains a vast array of single products, a pattern emerges at the product family level.

Cross-selling life insurance through the banking channel

The sale of life insurance by banks has been the strongest bancassurance success story so far, though continued success will not come automatically.

Life insurance has become an integral part of any financial planning offering, and especially of the retail banking product range. Not only does it meet clear customer needs—security, possible tax benefits, small recurring investments, and decent returns—but, perhaps most importantly, it has also enjoyed ease of distribution due to various bundling opportunities, its natural fit with the retail product range, and existing sales skills. In addition, from a bank's perspective, it has helped to make more use of fixed distribution capacity.

However, the profitability of traditional life insurance across Europe has come under substantial pressure in some countries since 2001 due to decreasing capital market performance leading to increasing capital needs. This has naturally had a serious effect on the many bancassurers who own life insurance production.

European bancassurers face three key challenges in life insurance; some successful institutions have already started to take action to overcome them.

First, many players find it hard to compare levels of value creation across life insurance, asset management, and banking products over the whole value chain. The result can often be a suboptimal product mix that takes no account of the producer or distributor perspective, or that adequately reflects customer preferences.

Second, few players have been able to adjust the product mix to reflect developments in product profitability. In practice, this means forgoing profitability by not sufficiently favoring traditional life insurance over bond funds in profitable life insurance markets, or incurring losses by not shifting quickly enough from traditional to unit-linked life or asset management products in less profitable markets.

Lastly, bancassurers who own life insurance production are confronted with the challenge of managing its profitability. The key here is improving asset management performance in terms of both skills and scale. Greater efficiency and more effective distribution geared toward profitable products may also help to compensate for any fall in profitability. Ultimately, in some markets, traditional life products and their guaranteed interest rate and bonus schemes may need to be revised on future contracts in accordance with the regulatory restriction.

Cross-selling P&C through the banking channel

Banks selling P&C insurance have not been as successful as they have in the life market, probably because of less favorable national market and competitive conditions and the greater difficulties involved in incorporating P&C into the retail banking business.

In general, P&C is a less natural fit with retail banking. As a risk product, it covers quite different customer needs compared with the asset gathering and lending business of retail banks and requires different sales approaches and capabilities. The key to success is a greater investment in intelligent product-bundling, sales capabilities, and customer perception, in order to use the existing natural touchpoints in retail banking for P&C distribution.

The example of Belgium illustrates the relative success of banks over traditional P&C distribution channels. Retail banks have managed to achieve visible market shares in all P&C product lines, ranging from 8 percent in health and accident to 17 percent in retail property in 1999. In addition, banks were able to gain 4 to 10 percent of market share per retail product line from 1994 to 1999, taking it away from the traditional broker channels. This relative success has been due mainly to external factors. The low service levels and excessive costs of incumbents have left substantial room for banks, as attackers, to excel with their lower costs and better service.

In most other European countries, however, such favorable external conditions have not existed. The low profitability of P&C, difficulties in switching providers, and a serious lack of both skill and will are often major barriers to P&C cross-selling. Perception issues, in claims management for instance, add to the negative picture.

One example of the impact of deteriorating P&C profitability is the Scandinavian market. By the end of the 1990s, banks had gained up to a fifth of the retail P&C market. Since then, however, major players have divested P&C production and partially also distribution. Sampo merged its P&C business with If, Danske Bank and Nordea sold their P&C subsidiaries, and SEB sold its P&C business to Codan. It may not be the last time that we see such moves in Europe. As Scandinavia is a very small and mature market, banks have been quicker than elsewhere in Europe to seek cross-border economies of scale. This is why they appear to be further advanced both in creating new business models and, in this case, in correcting them.

Making assurfinance work

The reverse approach—an insurance company offering retail banking products—is some time from really taking off in Europe. From an insurer's perspective, the market share of mutual funds through the agent channel has, until now, remained relatively low. After many years of developing mostly P&C-based agents into a P&C and life sales force, insurers have reached significant market shares in life. In asset management, however, there is still a long way to go with major players generally achieving well under a third of their life market share in asset management.

Although in some markets (such as Italy or to some extent Switzerland), regulations still complicate the sale of investment products through agent networks, it is the agents themselves—and their broad product range—that are the obstacle to success in both regulated and liberalized markets.

For even the most advanced insurers, bridging enormous skill and will gaps and managing the economics of a commissioned channel are all proving to be daunting tasks.

Other approaches to assurfinance, such as the greenfield creation of Banque AGF, face similar hurdles. In this particular case, starting from a loss-leading, single-product relationship it will take time and effort to broaden the product range, cross-sell (with credit, mutual funds, and life insurance) and develop the personal financial services (PFS) sales skills—although the first signs of success are visible.

Product range: future success factors

The first success factor undoubtedly lies in making the right choice of which products to sell. This is dependent not only on skills and customer needs but (in both life and P&C) also on local market conditions.

Given the choice of products, one of the most important success factors will be striking the right balance between the ease of selling and product complexity. Ease of selling usually increases the volume sold, while product complexity usually helps to tailor the product to customer needs and thus maintain profitability margins. But this is just the beginning of the product story. Product bundles with clear customer benefits (such as the combination of mortgages and home owner insurance) enable the best use of sales opportunities around life cycle events. A branding strategy that balances the same look and feel for bank, life, and P&C products with specific strengths and risks per product line (e.g., P&C claims) is essential. This could mean using the bank brand for life products and the insurance brand for P&C products. And, finally, embedding individual products in an optimized product mix (e.g., favoring life insurance over fixed-income mutual funds, where appropriate) maximizes the overall profitability of the bancassurance product range.

DISTRIBUTION: INTEGRATE OR SEPARATE

In bancassurance distribution, many successful retail banks have moved toward customer segment-specific channels, while refraining from integrating existing off-line distribution channels. Bancassurance distribution models can be classified along two dimensions: channel configuration (separate or integrated) and sales model (referrals or direct sales). Four distribution models result (Figure 6.1).

The *clear product focus* model uses separate channels to sell separate product ranges (e.g., bank branches sell asset-gathering products and agents sell P&C insurance). Bancassurance cross-sales occur through referrals only. This model is rarely observed in Europe and is best exemplified by Citigroup in the US.

Diagonally opposite is the *full integration* model, with direct sales of the entire bancassurance product range in one single channel. There is often one relationship manager who receives some assistance from specialists. MLP and SEB both use this approach.

In the mid-range, a *locally integrated* model (such as KBC's) aligns distribution channels through a single, local, sales manager and shared key performance indica-

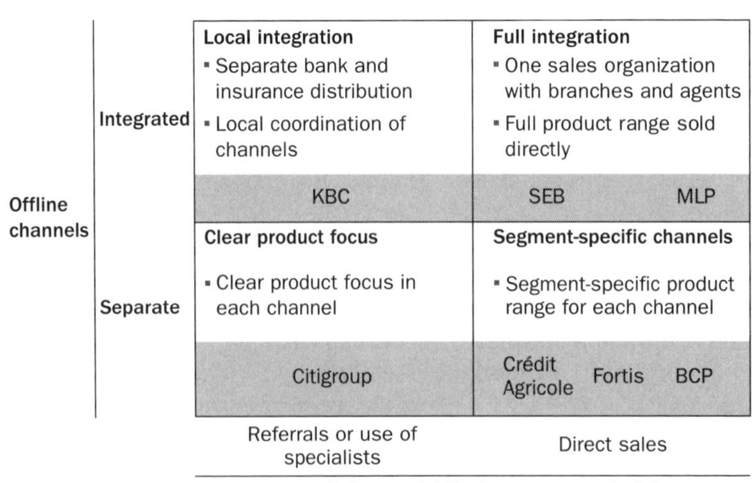

Figure 6.1 The bancassurance distribution matrix

Source: broker reports; annual reports; press clippings; interviews

tors. Although individual salespeople retain their channel and product identity, they work together at the point of sale and serve the customer jointly.

Lastly, in the *segment-specific channels* model (such as in Crédit Agricole, Fortis, or BCP), a complete, but segment-specific product range is sold directly by relationship managers, through separate channels, each focusing on one customer segment.

Of these four models, we believe that segment-specific channels are a natural starting point for bancassurance distribution involving more than one channel, for three reasons.

First, there is the positive impact on cross-selling. The concentration of each channel on one target market, combined with tailored products, creates a strong value proposition and simplifies sales. Customer handovers are also eliminated, reducing the risk of customer loss or dissatisfaction in the cross-selling process. Insurance products in the retail bank or banking products in the insurance channel thus become fully integrated in the normal selling process.

Second, such channels seem to be economically sound. Complexity costs are reduced through the channel's strict segment focus; and the direct sales model not only maximizes the relationship manager's expertise but also eliminates referrals to a more expensive agent channel.

Third—and often most important—implementing segment-specific channels reduces the integration risk related to merging separate off-line channels. Merging two different salesforce cultures, often with diverse incentive schemes and ways to operate, could easily result in a loss of the best, most performance-oriented sales representatives and consequently a loss in market share.

Having said this, there may still be good reasons for bancassurers to choose different distribution models. There may be a case for referral-based selling if products cannot be standardized or bundled, or if significant skill gaps reduce the ability to make direct sales. There may occasionally be a case for channel integration if a strong customer overlap would otherwise lead to significant conflicts and if two off-line channels have similar cultures or performance management systems.

Distribution: future success factors

Bridging the very large performance gap between the few top performers and the many low performers is the key to realizing the potential of a strong product offering. A combined set of measures needs to be implemented to achieve this objective.

At the individual level, the consistent and intensive development of sales skills, together with rigorous performance management are required, complemented by the use of sales-friendly screen displays for staff and easy-to-use forms for customers. Effective incentive systems can be geared toward channels and channel management, while making limited use of cash incentives for individuals to preserve profitability.

From a channel perspective, and in the medium term, the alignment of distribution with customer segments (and, possibly, the move toward segment-specific channels) will reduce complexity and increase focus. This also makes it easier to tailor the channel offering to customers' needs.

OWNERSHIP STRUCTURE: TO CONTROL OR NOT TO CONTROL

One important decision for retail banks has always been whether to focus solely on the distribution of bancassurance products or whether to pursue an integrated approach, owning production and distribution (especially in life insurance), and having clear control over the whole value chain. From the perspective of ownership and control, there has been a tendency toward integrated control models. This is mainly because control makes it easier to tailor the integration of bank and insurance businesses to their specific environment, and thus to maximize overall value creation and improve the chances of capturing a larger share of this value.

We quantitatively compared new life and P&C business per customer and per customer advisor across European players with different ownership structures. Ownership models that enable the bank to exert control over its bancassurance business—including both greenfield start-ups and acquisitions—seem to have outperformed arm's-length relationships such as distribution agreements by a factor of 2 to 3 in sales volume, depending on the precise product and metrics used.

We see five major advantages of the control model. First, the bank is free to tailor its bancassurance product offering and value proposition to the characteristics of its customer base, while prioritizing those products that generate the most value for the bank and the group overall. Second, the bank can tailor the degree of business integration (from product design through asset management to operations), thus maximizing efficiency and effectiveness. Third, it is easier to frame clear customer ownership rules. Fourth, it also generates a certain sense of urgency due to the major capital commitment, which is often not encountered in low-risk partnership settings. Lastly, the control model captures all the value creation, which is positive as long as both distribution and production actually do create value. From this point of view, it seems to have been worthwhile for bancassurers to own life insurance production.

The revenue split between distribution and production can serve as a first indicator of the value creation potential. Asset management, for example, is a distributor's market: distributors capture more than two-thirds of total fee income. In addition, most banks exert clear control over asset managers through ownership. The picture is very different in life and P&C insurance. The opaque nature of life products, together with their long-term perspective, seem to make it very hard for the customer (or distributor) to argue about or indeed understand the price of the products. In addition, a relatively high stickiness of P&C products and fragmented or even tied distribution have created barriers to market liquidity.

As a result, 50 to 65 percent of life and P&C product revenues stay with the producer. Depending on the efficiency of production—and the ability of a bank to attract and nurture the distinctive skills it requires—this revenue pool might be a significant source of value creation that could be captured through ownership. Up to now, the advantages of sales effectiveness, efficiency, and broader value capture of such models seem to have outweighed the higher demands of capital investment, management skills, and divestment of noncore businesses.

Many players have entered bancassurance directly through control models: through greenfield start-ups (e.g., Crédit Agricole with Prédica and Pacifica), outright acquisition (e.g., Svenska Handelsbanken), or a combination of the two (e.g., KBC). A second group of players, including Credit Suisse and Allianz, have moved from arm's-length relationships (joint ventures or stakeholdings) toward full ownership, in some cases through different, concurrent routes.

At the same time, there are moves in the opposite direction. Barclays, which entered life insurance through a greenfield subsidiary, today sources all new life products from a joint venture with Legal & General. Such a move exemplifies the notion of 'adequate' control, which can also be obtained with a well-structured joint venture.

Finally, looking forward, a whole set of new moves for existing and, especially, prospective bancassurers can be envisaged. Rising performance requirements for life insurers, combined with falling interaction costs and entry barriers, are creating pressure to disaggregate the life insurance value chain. Some sliver players, such as The Hartford in product-manufacturing and packaging, Schroders in asset management, or tecis and Banca Fideuram in distribution, have already emerged.

For existing bancassurers, this could mean applying the notion of adequate control to each sliver of their insurance value chain. And it may provide new opportunities for banks to enter bancassurance using a modular scheme that combines in-house control over critical value chain steps, such as product management, with strong partnerships for noncore capability operations.

Ownership: future success factors

It is critical for bancassurers to adopt an ownership structure that is tailored to their bancassurance strategy and core capabilities. The key to success is the consideration of all the relevant business objectives and parameters in the choice of the ownership structure, in addition to the bank's overall strategic aspirations and market conditions (Figure 6.2).

✓✓ Highly advantageous
✓ Positive

			Control	
Business parameters	**Cooperation**	**Joint venture**	**Greenfield**	**M&A**
Strategic objectives				
▪ Cross-selling revenues			✓✓	✓✓
▪ Capture of distribution and production margin			✓✓	✓✓
▪ Time to market	✓✓	✓		
Financial objectives				
▪ Capital efficiency (ROI)	✓✓	✓	✓	
▪ Synergy potential			✓✓	✓✓
▪ Risk diversification effects			✓	✓✓
Risk appetite				
▪ Capital requirements	✓✓	✓		
▪ Stability/Continuity			✓✓	✓✓
	Capital efficiency	Skill vs. control trade-off	Proven but limited	High risk, high reward

Figure 6.2 Imperatives for ownership structure

Source: McKinsey

There is no single, winning formula for doing this. Defining an ownership structure involves choosing the right trade-off between arm's-length models, with limited skill requirements, limited risk, and low capital investment, and stable control models, with higher skill and investment requirements, but also greater revenue and synergy potential and a larger share of the overall value created.

THE FUTURE FOR EUROPEAN BANCASSURANCE

European bancassurance today has many facets. But, despite its diversity, a surprisingly clear pattern of what works has emerged. Although it may be too early to derive a single success formula for European bancassurance, one common denominator has clearly crystallized: the need for action and the insight that success will not come automatically.

The bancassurance era of the recent past was characterized by growth, driven by M&A. The rationale for many entries into bancassurance, whether through joint ventures or greenfield start-ups, was to exploit the banking and insurance customer bases, and the quest for control through size gave rise to an unprecedented wave of bank/insurance deals in the mid- and late 1990s.

However, the environment in which bancassurers operate changed radically through 2001. The imperatives of operating in a downturn have returned with a vengeance. Operational excellence, a focus on the core business, and tangible bottom line impact are the essential ingredients in today's market, with its relentless focus on current earnings. These imperatives will determine the short-term future of both retail banking and bancassurance in Europe; and bancassurers need to take decisive actions in all three dimensions of the bancassurance business model and take them now.

One clear imperative for the future is 'Don't get stuck in the middle'. The performance gap between leaders and laggards among life insurers is already large, and it is likely to continue expanding. This leaves little room for maneuver for players who lack skill or scale to respond to the challenges of the competition and the demands of the capital markets.

There are two ways to achieve skill and scale in life insurance—the organic route and the partnership route. The organic route involves the aggressive acquisition of skill in the market, including product design, underwriting, processing, run-off management, and especially asset management. These skills can then be built up dramatically by moving to the next level of scale by acquiring underperforming players or portfolios. This is a hard route to navigate, requiring substantial commitment and management attention.

The partnership route allows bancassurers to exploit their competitive advantage and bargaining power over life insurers and to achieve skill and scale without building in-house capacity. The key to success lies in choosing the right partners and optimizing the collaboration model and ownership structure. The Barclays and Legal & General joint venture mentioned above is an example of this route.

On the P&C production side, it may be feasible for a profitable company in a profitable market to own P&C production. However, profitability is often low and management capacity scarce, and, if this is the case, bancassurers who now own P&C

production should seriously consider all the possible options, including spin-offs or sales. Here, the Scandinavian example might be followed in other European countries.

Overall, we see two basic strategic routes emerge. One sees retail banks positioning themselves as distributors, possibly even moving toward an open platform model. As such—especially if they focus on retail customers—they would need to capture a sufficient share of the customer wallet to maximize value creation from their predominantly fixed distribution capacity. Offering profitable life and P&C products to their customers would be crucial to their success, but they would not need to own life and P&C production as long as they were able to find a stable sourcing solution.

The other route sees retail banks positioning themselves as integrated financial services companies that own not only banking and asset management but also life production, and in some cases even P&C production. With sufficient skill and scale in distribution and production, these retail banks would differentiate themselves by means of a high-quality offering and greater sales effectiveness, deriving from the alignment of incentives between production and distribution.

Although the imperatives for bancassurers are very much focused on success in the next two to three years, it is important for European retail banks and bancassurers to start shaping their future role in the European market. Bancassurance could play an important role in many successful models in European retail banking in the future.

7

Mass Market: Mission Impossible

Miguel Lucas, Luís Lopes[1]

The mission, should you choose to accept it, is to transform up to half your customer base from being a drain on your resources to being a profitable segment. Sounds impossible? For the vast majority of retail banks across Europe, this is an all-too-real problem. Despite undertaking numerous improvement initiatives, the overall profitability of the mass market segment is still low or even negative.

The mass market comprises about two-thirds of the European population, who between them own roughly one-third of personal financial assets and almost two-thirds of personal financial liabilities.[2]

Yet, despite its immense size, the mass market segment is often loss-making. Such significant numbers of customers are unprofitable that typical cost–income ratios can reach 90 to over 100 percent. An examination of a number of banks from several European countries showed that anywhere from 45 to 70 percent of their mass market customers are not profitable and that profitability within the segment varies extensively (Figure 7.1).

This abysmal track record stems from the fact that most business models fail to address two core issues: first, the unprofitable product mix (a high penetration of unprofitable payment products compounded by low cross-selling levels for the most profitable products); and, second, expensive distribution (high-cost channels together with excessive transactional behavior).

Cross-selling rates for the mass market segment are roughly half those of other segments: the average number of products owned by each mass market customer is two to two-and-a-half, compared with the three to five achieved for the affluent segment.[3] Furthermore, branches still account for more than 70 percent of the total cost of serving these customers, often driven by inefficient branch networks with heavy transaction volumes.

[1] The authors would like to express their gratitude for the contributions of Jean-Christophe Mieszala, Heleen Wachters, Fedele di Maggio, and Nici Audhlam-Gardiner.

[2] Based on the typical segmentation criterion of less than €30 000 in deposits and investments.

[3] Client interviews; McKinsey European Mass Affluent Retail Banking research, 2001.

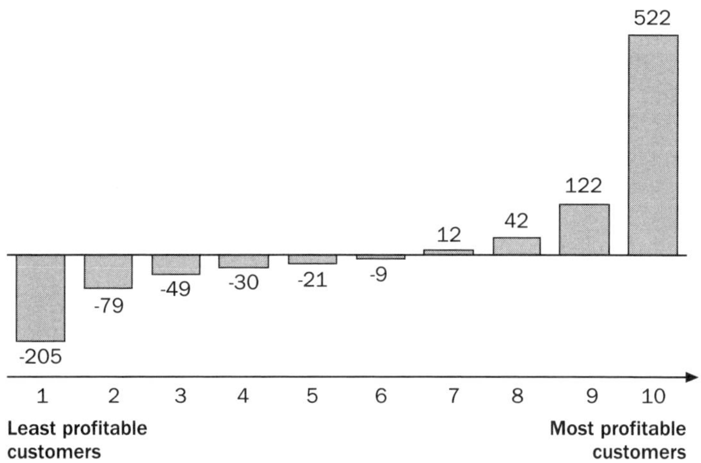

Figure 7.1 Typical profit structure of the mass market segment (average profit per customer by profitability deciles, €)

Source: McKinsey

Despite these problems, there are European banks that have found ways to serve the mass market profitably. Excellent practitioners have succeeded in achieving cost–income ratios of between 60 and 65 percent; some have managed to raise the average number of products per customer to three or four. This would suggest that the mission is not impossible for those able to find and follow the right route.

We interviewed more than two dozen industry insiders from all over Europe for examples of successful banks serving the mass market. This research brought to light two routes that can lead to substantially improved mass market profitability.

The first, which we have called the *traditional route*, consists of dramatically improving the traditional branch-based business model. This is the most common path taken by European banks, but has mixed results. We have analyzed in detail the most successful cases and integrated our findings into a series of must-dos. The second approach, called here the *alternative route*, makes use of innovative retail banking business models (in terms of product offering and/or distribution channel) to serve the mass market and covers everything from tellerless branches to product specialist models.

THE TRADITIONAL ROUTE: BUILD ON WHAT YOU HAVE

Enhancing the traditional branch-based business model remains a largely unexplored option for the average retail bank. Although many have sought to adapt and improve existing models, most have failed to tailor their model to the needs of the mass market. The most successful banks that have embarked down the traditional path have acted in four key areas: they have subsegmented the mass market, improved product design and pricing, dramatically increased distribution and operational efficiency, and created an aggressive sales culture. Banks often act on some of these levers with limited success, but acting on all of them simultaneously and implementing change to the full extent is what separates the mass market winners from the rest of the pack.

Empirical evidence shows that excellent retail banks that pursued the traditional route had a significant positive impact on cost, margin, and volume, resulting in major increases in the profitability of individual customers and of the mass market as a whole. In one extreme example, the share of profitable customers rose from 42 to 75 percent and the cost–income ratio dropped by 32 percentage points to 56 percent. In sum, banks executing the four must-do levers can make money in the mass market segment using a traditional branch-based business model.

Subsegment the mass market

By splitting up the mass market, banks can address the specific profitability issues affecting the segment. Given the wide range of needs and potential profitability levels of individual mass market customers, it would be naive to treat them as a single homogeneous collective. Simply ranking customers by profitability is not sufficient, however. Rather, segmentation must lead to an understanding of the root causes of profitability.

Best practice banks use this detailed subsegmentation to make decisions on channel strategy, product design, and pricing. One southern European bank uses transactional behavior and banking involvement (volume of deposits, funds, and loans per customer) to define customer segments (Figure 7.2). Armed with this knowledge, it has developed specific products for the highly unprofitable, transactional customer segment and actively migrated them to a new ATM-only account.

Often the criteria used in these customer segmentations can be even more sophisticated. Another bank uses not only transactional and banking involvement

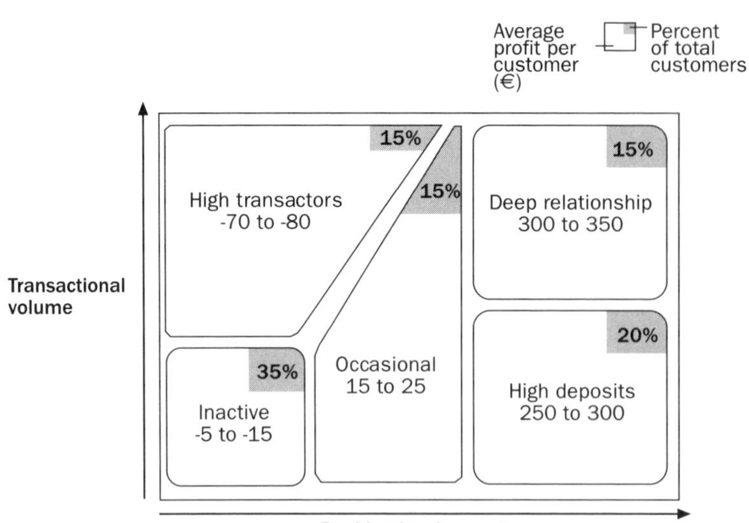

Figure 7.2 Mass market segments of a southern European bank

Source: McKinsey

criteria but also lifetime customer valuations. Its data showed that its mass market customers between the ages of 19 to 25 were loss-making for the bank, but had a positive net present value (NPV). This prompted the bank to develop products aimed at increasing loyalty while trimming transaction costs. One of these products—also an ATM-only account—offers reduced maintenance fees, as well as a free credit card for the first year and half the annual fee thereafter, but charges higher fees for each branch transaction.

Improve product design and pricing

Together, product design and pricing is a fundamental lever for improvement, but it has been a major stumbling block for many banks. The trick lies in finding a balance between addressing the specific needs and characteristics of each subsegment and avoiding over-complex product lines and pricing—a sure profit-killer in this segment. In general, banks have product portfolios that are too complex and too costly for the mass market and that fail to exploit the full potential of pricing.

The product portfolios of the most successful mass market banks offer a simple menu of easy-to-explain bundled products designed to meet the needs of the biggest segments of the population. They often heed the following six rules regarding product design: (1) differentiate the product across subsegments to avoid having an adverse effect on profitable customers and to meet customer needs; (2) simplify and streamline the number of products; (3) reduce development and handling costs; (4) increase cross-selling by using bundled products; (5) facilitate migration toward lower cost channels by bundling with a built-in transaction component; and (6) simplify communication with the aim of increasing product knowledge and the understanding of bank staff. One German savings bank that followed these rules managed to simplify its mass market product offer by eliminating more than 80 percent of its products, without suffering any loss of volume.

Innovative product bundles have been explored by a number of successful mass market banks. A southern European bank introduced a set of new products that bundle transactions, credit cards, and current account features, spurring on a 7 percentage point increase in customer satisfaction and boosting the average NPV per customer by 66 percent. Brazil's Banco Itaú is offering current accounts bundled with free credit lines and a transaction component that limits the bank's cost-to-serve. Transactions in some low-cost channels are free, and fees are increased for the more expensive channels (Figure 7.3). UniCredito has designed its Genius accounts (Light, Smart, Plus, and Extra), which bundle an increasing number of products into the basic current account, from debit cards to credit cards.

Finally, another southern European bank offers another example of an interesting bundled product for the mass market. It is a prepaid card concept designed to avoid costly branch transactions; for some subsegments (e.g., low-income and young people), this has become an attractive, economically viable solution. The card is sold with a corresponding current account. The card may be reloaded with funds only through an ATM or other automatic channel. There is no maintenance fee and a limited number of free transactions. One mass market subsegment suited to this product is low-income employees, who are generally low-revenue but high-transaction customers.

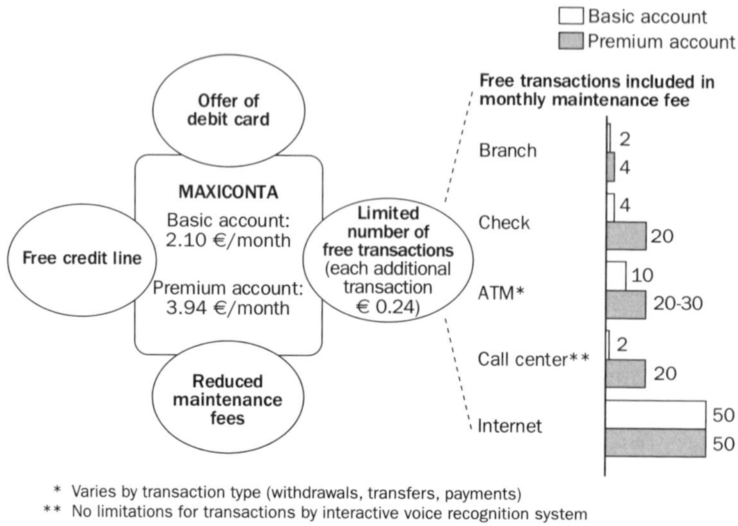

Figure 7.3 Maxiconta product bundle at Banco Itaú

Source: company website

Pricing—the other critical aspect of product design—can have the greatest impact on mass market profitability. Retail banks should strive to price products to reflect the real cost-to-serve and exploit consumer surplus by differentiating between different subsegments, as well as considering pricing on products that are less visible or less important to customers (Chapter 11 contains a more extensive description of pricing possibilities in retail banking). Such practices can lead to significant revenue increases with minimal volume losses. One southern European bank, for example, introduced a 150 percent increase in check fees after market research showed that people were not aware of the amount they were paying. There was no loss in business volumes and only minimal complaints from customers.

The particularities of each country and its competitive environment can play a major role in a bank's decision whether to raise pricing. An unfortunate pricing move can subject banks to the double peril of alienating customers and taking a beating in the press, as some banks have discovered. There are, however, measures to smooth the way. Successful examples show that one viable solution, even in difficult markets, has been to differentiate transaction costs by account type and bundle free transactions for different types of accounts.

Banks should avoid the pitfall of believing that pricing is the only solution or some sort of one-step remedy for low mass market profitability. The reality is that banks cannot successfully solve their mass market profitability problems through pricing alone. Nevertheless, a logical and well-implemented pricing program can give profitability a solid boost.

Dramatically increase distribution and operational efficiency

For mass market banks, distribution and operational efficiency is critical to improving profitability, since it reduces the cost of serving the transaction-heavy customers, while freeing up time for tellers to cross-sell.

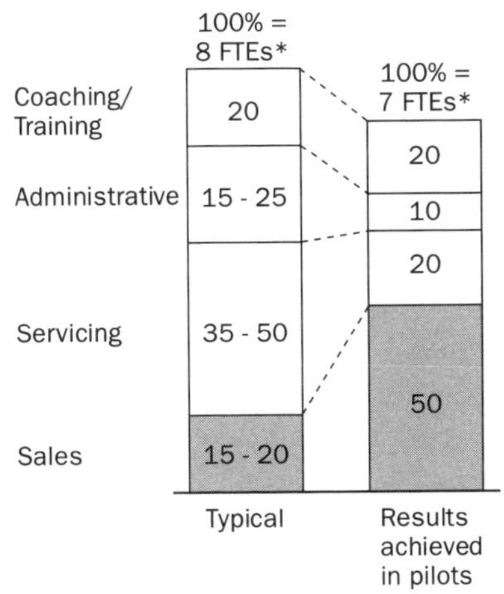

* Full-time employees

Figure 7.4 Typical split of activities for a mass market branch (percent of employee time in branch)

Source: McKinsey

Often branch capacity—an expensive asset—is wasted on low value-added activities. Our experience suggests that transactions remain by far the most important reason for branch visits, accounting for more than 85 percent of all visits. Banks frequently operate under the mistaken belief that migration to automatic channels is almost complete and that the remaining transactions in branches are conducted by unsophisticated customers who will never change their behavior. The reality is that the vast majority of banks still handle far too many transactions in branches, making branch and teller transactions a major source of costs. Typically, 40 to 50 percent of the transactions and 75 percent of the transaction costs of a bank originate in the branch. Many banks are struggling to achieve dramatic reductions in this nonvalue-added time spent by personnel in their branches. Time allocated to sales in the mass market is less than 20 percent in a typical European bank (Figure 7.4). In the new paradigm, tellers should become sellers, with the goal of increasing the percentage of their time dedicated to sales to over 50 percent. Hence, it is key to streamline branch capacity by reining in the number of branch transactions and by optimizing branch operations.

Best practice shows that a mid-term target of migrating 80 to 90 percent of all transactions to automatic channels is possible. Players that have achieved these migration levels have used a combination of tools. These have included the introduction of additional functionalities to ATMs and other channels, increasing the pricing of branch transactions, adding transactional components to products, internal incentive systems, branch staff training to explain the new functionalities to customers, and, in some situations, an important change in the branch layout. These tools must be used in combination in order to shift the existing branch usage rates (Figure 7.5). Successful mass market banks have migrated 60 to 70 percent of cash deposits and 90 to 95 percent of cash withdrawals and transfers to automatic channels. In one specific case, teller transactions fell by 30 percent within two years.

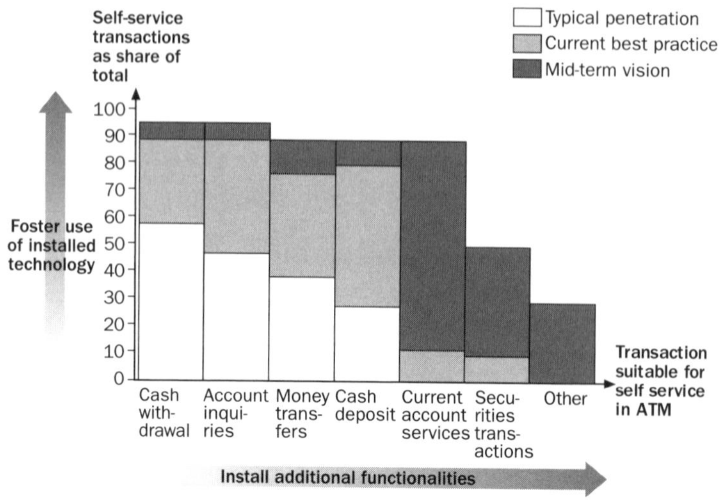

Figure 7.5 Remaining challenge to migrate transactions

Source: interviews; McKinsey

In addition to migrating transactions, mass market banks need to improve operational efficiency by customizing operations and addressing the peculiarities of the segment. This is especially true for operations that can directly influence the efficiency of the distribution channels and impact front office time spent on non-value-added activities. One European bank, for example, adopted image-processing technologies to process checks (redesigning the back office operations) and managed to more than halve the front office time spent per check deposit transaction and free up 12 percent of teller capacity on this transaction alone.

Another mass market bank transformed its operations in two ways. First, it migrated transactions to new ATMs that took deposits and sold new ATM-only current accounts, backed up by incentives for branch staff (paid holidays for the top-performing branches after a couple of months, reinforced by weekly rankings). Second, it undertook a significant process redesign in branches—eliminating most back office, paper-based transactions, removing any activity that could be centralized and automating branch credit-related processes. As a result, it increased sales time by almost a half for tellers and reduced branch personnel by a quarter.

In reducing the frontline to appropriate levels, some idle capacity might remain due to fluctuations in customer traffic throughout the day. Apart from using part-time tellers, this can also be used for sales activities. For example, some banks use the idle capacity at low-traffic hours to turn branches into decentralized outbound call centers to push sales.

Create an aggressive sales culture

Mass market customers tend to buy a small number of low-margin products, such as current accounts, so selling even a few high-margin products, such as credit cards or personal loans, can have a significant impact on overall profitability. Thus, creating a strong sales culture to drive cross-selling should be a priority for all mass market banks (Chapter 13 provides a more in-depth treatment on maximizing sales power).

A common assumption is that the mass market offers limited sales opportunities, and often sales campaigns address only one customer profile, completely overlooking much of the mass market. The best performing banks, however, know how to use aggressive sales organizations to capture more of this segment, while maintaining their service levels.

Building an aggressive sales-oriented culture can run the risk of scaring some customers away. But to paraphrase one bank executive, 'If some of our unprofitable customers are offended by our sales tactics, so be it.' The rewards should more than offset the risks. The process of building a strong sales culture also takes time and often entails making a few drastic decisions. Common features of mass market programs of this sort typically include measuring and publishing individual sales performance, awarding significant variable compensation, launching systematic sales campaigns based on low-cost customer relationship management (CRM) tools, using sales aid tools and implementing practical sales-training programs.

One northern European bank implemented such a program to improve mass market profitability. It set branch-level targets for sales growth and began announcing individual and branch performance figures. Both tellers and customer service representatives were given cash incentives for meeting sales growth goals. In addition, they used a simple CRM model to generate leads and sent direct mail to likely sales prospects. Lastly, the sales culture was fostered by training branch personnel in sales skills and product features and hiring new personnel experienced in sales. The number of branch-based weekly product sales jumped by 47 percent.

Another European bank changed the compensation system of its branch employees by including an individual performance component that could represent up to 100 percent of fixed compensation and a ranking system based on product sales (each product is worth a number of points proportional to the expected NPV). The result was a doubling in the value of products sold.

THE ALTERNATIVE ROUTE: INNOVATE TO WIN

The use of alternative business models in retail banking is nothing new. They have been widely used for at least the past decade. But the question of whether these business models are better than the traditional path for serving the mass market remains open. The most common alternative models are categorized along two axes: product- or segment-focused and channels (Figure 7.6). Both types are briefly described below.

Focused mass market models

Product-focused players. There are literally hundreds (if not thousands) of examples of banks in this category. Typically, they focus on product categories more relevant to the mass market segment, such as consumer credit or credit cards. Although Citibank PK is no longer a purely product-focused player, it illustrates how an initial product-focused strategy can succeed. The bank's strategy has expanded

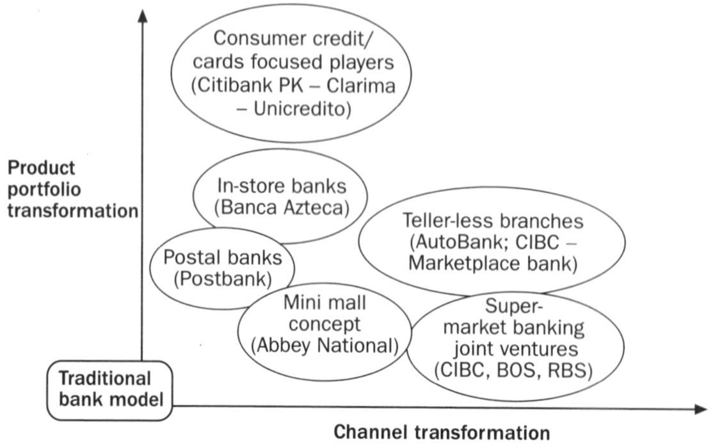

Figure 7.6 Alternative mass market business models

Source: press clippings; annual reports; broker reports; interviews

from an initial credit card and consumer credit focus to offering current accounts, insurance, and other financial products, although credit cards and consumer credit still account for a significant portion of its revenues. The level of process efficiency (achieved through its focus on a smaller number of products) can be seen in its cost base and service levels. Citibank PK is now one of the most profitable mass market players with 300 retail branches and a 2 percent share of the German market, boasting a cost–income ratio below 50 percent.

Segment-focused players. Of specific interest are the models that target the low-income segment of the mass market. These tend to be rare in western Europe (not surprising, given the average income in the region), but in countries where there is a large low-income population, they have become quite common. Peru's Mibanco is one such bank. It offers savings accounts as well as micro-credit loans and is in the process of expanding its ATM network as part of its policy to offer the latest technology to its low-income clients. The bank set up an agreement with Visa International in 2002 and expects to have more than 50,000 debit and credit cards in circulation by the end of 2003.[4]

Alternative distribution mass market models

Tellerless branches. This is a model whereby all transactions are handled by automatic channels. One example, AutoBank, serves the mass market in South Africa with efficient, very low-cost branches (typically 40 percent lower than a traditional branch). AutoBank branches have two or three sales assistants and serve between 8000 and 10 000 customers. All transactions are handled through ATMs, and sales

[4] *Business News Americas*, February 10, 2003.

assistants can only open accounts and sell products. In addition to the bank's own financial product offering, it sells third-party products (e.g., prepaid phone calls, micro-credits, funeral insurance). Efficiency is paramount, so processes are highly streamlined and product range relatively limited.

Supermarket banks. Numerous supermarket banks have been created in recent years, following what was arguably the first supermarket bank founded by Wells Fargo. A recent success story is the alliance between Royal Bank of Scotland and Tesco; launched in 1995, it has more than one million transaction account holders acquired at a tenth of the cost per customer of traditional branches.

In-store branches. This is similar to the supermarket bank concept. Banks like Banca Azteca (in Mexico) or Marks & Spencer Financial Services were built as extensions of retail businesses (in the case of Azteca, inside a consumer electronics and retail store group in Mexico). Banca Azteca is a highly profitable banking operation with a cost–income ratio of 33 percent. It has no branches (instead using the 950 Elektrim retailer outlets) and started by focusing on consumer credit, later expanding through partnerships into a fully-fledged banking offer.

Postal banks. Banks following this model have reduced their cost base by leveraging the existing post office infrastructure. The information on the success of these ventures is scarce and sometimes contradictory. The German Postbank claims to have achieved profitability in the mass market, whereas Banque La Poste (a joint venture between Fortis and the Belgian postal service) lost money because of high servicing costs and lower-than-expected revenues.

Mini-mall concept. Leasing branch space to third parties, though not feasible for all existing bank branches, can generate additional revenues and reduce the average cost of serving mass market customers. The recent venture between Abbey National and Costa Coffee in the UK is one example. The results for these types of concept remain to be seen.

For all seven models, the most successful players meet at least one—and often both—of the following criteria: highly cost-efficient distribution structures, often sharing a physical network; and a highly differentiated value proposition, typically offering a dramatic increase in convenience or innovation in a product category (e.g., credit cards to the mass market or in-store consumer loans).

In the medium term, there are other ways of serving the mass market, such as unbundling products from distribution (e.g., using third-party distributors or providing third-party products). Alternatively, transactional services could be completely automated by providing unmanned servicing in mass market branches, using technology such as voice recognition, advanced intelligence software, imaging, and others. Another model, already implemented in several cases, is to bundle nonbanking services and products into financial products (e.g., current accounts bundled with mobile phone services).

Alternative business models can be successful; however, an incumbent needs to consider carefully whether the cost of an alternative business model would be offset by the potential incremental revenue. In some cases, banks have launched new concepts and seen some customer migration, but they have not sufficiently moved away from their traditional branch-based model, resulting in higher total costs and little or no revenue growth. Alternative models may make sense for some players, but arguably are not the right answer for everyone.

Cracking this mission is undoubtedly challenging, but to reap riches from the traditionally fallow mass market segment requires decisive action based on a thorough analysis of the bank's current situation. Choosing and systematically following the right route—be it to enhance the traditional branch-based model or to adopt a bolder, more innovative model—are the key steps to achieving the impossible.

8

Affluent Banking: Roll out the Red Carpet

Marcus Sieberer, Florian Reich-Rohrwig, Pedro Rodeia[1]

Affluent banking has long been regarded as the goose that lays the golden egg for retail banking. The 15 percent of Europe's 263 million banking customers that qualify as affluent generate 44 percent of all personal financial assets (PFAs), 30 percent of total revenues, and 50 percent of the total PFA profits of Western European banks.[2] In the boom years from 1997 to 2000, the pool of affluent assets grew at 21.5 percent per year, significantly above the average banking business rate of 13 percent. However, the market correction has exposed the goose's sensitivity to unstable environments, interrupting this growth pattern, with total asset value stagnating or even declining in 2001 and 2002. As a result, several recent entrants are struggling to survive and established players face new challenges in reinforcing their position and restoring profitable growth.

But, looking further ahead, the long-term prospects for the affluent segment remain solid, rooted as they are in fundamentally favorable demographics, with an aging population pyramid in many European countries. This should result in the affluent customer base growing by 3 to 5 percent a year and the volume of affluent PFAs resuming growth rates of 6 to 8 percent a year until 2005 (assuming normal market returns). By then, it is expected that affluent customers will have increased their share of total PFAs to 50 percent and will be contributing about 60 percent of consumer banking profits (Figure 8.1).

OVERCROWDED COMPETITIVE LANDSCAPE

These fundamentally attractive prospects have driven new attackers to enter the business as well as encouraged traditional players to invest in order to retain and

[1] This contribution is based on our research conducted together with Cornelius Walter, Doran Schifter, João Mello Franco, and Jakob Haesler.

[2] The affluent segment is defined by either annual net income (the minimum in western Europe ranging from €22 000 to €36 000) or investable assets (the minimum ranging from €34 000 to €50 000 and the maximum—the cutoff point for moving into the high-net-worth segment—being €500 000).

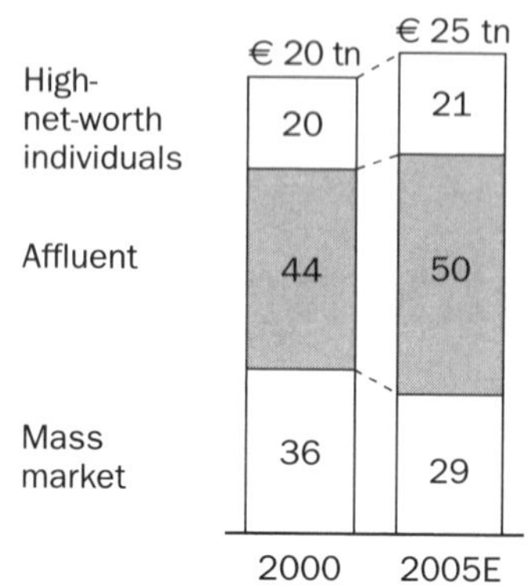

Figure 8.1 European PFAs split by segment (percent 2000–2005E)

Source: McKinsey

develop their affluent customer base. As a result, the market has become increasingly saturated with a proliferation of customer offerings that can be segmented along two critical dimensions: breadth of offering and access. This leads to five distinctive types of value propositions among established players and attackers (Figure 8.2).

Red carpet retail banks represent the account manager-based propositions of most of the leading established retail banks. They target customers (especially existing ones) who need comprehensive advice and who value a close banking relationship. This group includes most of the major European retail banks within their domestic markets.

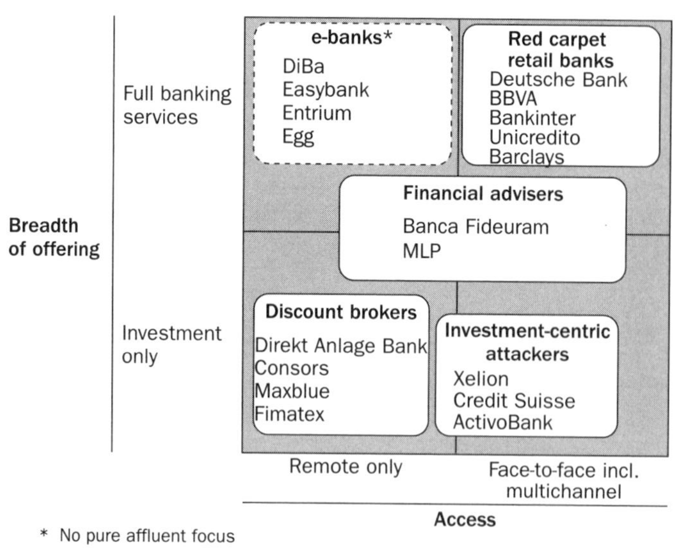

Figure 8.2 European affluent banking business models

Source: McKinsey

Financial advisers focus on customers who seek independent face-to-face investment advice. Their distribution relies heavily on a mobile sales force of well-trained and highly incentivized advisers. They offer above-average advisory quality based on broad approaches that are usually open to third-party products. They tend to be very selective in their offering, with a clear focus on highly profitable value-added products (e.g., investment and pension products).

Investment-centric attackers are often the international expansion vehicles of wholesale and private banks, dedicated to affluent customers (e.g., Credit Suisse in Germany). Their full-scale investment-centric offering is based on a distinct advisory proposition, building on the solid reputation of their parent institution. Distribution is centered on a limited number of flagship stores with well-trained personal advisers, who can offer regular advice sessions and financial checkups.

Discount brokers target self-directed investors and traders for their day-to-day transaction and investment needs. Although they offer a full range of discounted investment products as well as value-added research and limited advice, they are not exclusively dedicated to affluent customers and often lack transaction-banking products.

E-banks comprise the full-scale, discount-priced banking services of specialized remote-channel attackers. Although these models are targeted generally at self-directed customers and do not focus specifically on affluent customers, some have nevertheless been able to attract significant numbers of affluent customers through their aggressive pricing strategies, particularly on deposits.

Amid the recent market turmoil, it has been clear that, of these five distinctive value propositions, red carpet retail banks and financial advisers are the most resilient. Retail banks, in particular, have been able to build on their large existing customer base and still hold more than 90 percent of the primary bank deposits and more than 80 percent of the PFAs of all affluent European customers.

Financial advisers are retail banks' largest competitors in the affluent segment and it is the only example of an attacker model that has made serious inroads.[3] However, although financial advisers now hold a significant share in some markets—approximately 20 percent of all mutual funds in Italy and approximately 60 percent in the UK—overall, they still hold less than 10 percent of European affluent PFAs. In addition, wide differences exist between players following the same broad model. Some, such as MLP, have been able to increase their customer base significantly (MLP achieved growth rates of 19 percent per annum between 1998 and 2002), while others, such as Banca Fideuram, have recently seen a slight fall in customer numbers (although this is also a consequence of the company's move to attract more upscale customers).[4]

Most of the other attacker models have failed to capture significant market share, despite the fact that many offer comprehensive product and service packages at extremely aggressive prices. Investment-centric attackers have entered the market at a very difficult time, e-banks have so far accumulated considerably fewer affluent assets than planned, and online brokers are strongly dependent on developments in

[3] This is true despite the fact that their dramatic growth has recently slowed, due to the market downturn as well as internal problems (e.g., rumors surrounding MLP's accounting policies).

[4] MLP annual report 2001; Banca Fideuram investor presentation, July 2002.

capital markets. All of the players in these segments, therefore, have seen both their economics and their valuations dramatically deteriorate over the last two years.

WHAT AFFLUENT CUSTOMERS WANT

The first step to capturing a greater market share of this lucrative segment are understanding the specific needs of affluent customers and figuring out what business model is best suited to meeting them. McKinsey research reveals that affluent customer characteristics have been evolving toward a more demanding profile.[5] The survey revealed three elements that are particularly relevant for a successful affluent proposition: professional, trusted advice, personalized financial planning and integrated reporting, and top quality investment products and faultless banking services. Looking at how the specific model outlined above perform in these elements helps us understand more clearly why retail banks and financial adviser models have been the most successful models in the affluent segment. Although neither can completely fulfill each element, overall they appear to be more oriented toward their customer's fundamental needs than are their less successful competitors. This does not mean, however, that retail banks can rest on their laurels.

Professional, trusted advisers

Almost three-quarters of the affluent customers use some type of financial adviser, and almost 60 percent of those claiming to need financial advice would be willing to pay for it. Affluent customers place a high value on professional, personal advice through a relationship with an institution they trust. Indeed, failure to build trust among customers will undermine even the most brilliant value proposition. This is dramatically illustrated by the failure of many e-offerings that had little trust-building history. The stock market correction has driven customers to stick even more closely to trusted institutions. In 1999, 43 percent of affluent customers turned to trusted staff at financial institutions as a main source of advice; by 2002 that had risen to 56 percent, with the share of nonprofessional advisers dropping from 21 to only 8 percent during the same period (Figure 8.3). Most affluent customers prefer face-to-face advice, with 63 percent saying that they do not trust financial institutions that lack branches. This was one of the reasons behind Charles Schwab's heavy investments in building a branch network for customer acquisition.

Personalized financial planning and integrated reporting

Affluent customers increasingly demand access to financial planning across all of their assets and asset classes (eventually covering credit and protection needs as well), to ensure that their portfolio fully meets their specific needs. Financial planning is therefore ranked as the number one topic for customers and is also the area

[5] McKinsey Pan-European Affluent Investors Market Research 2002 (10 countries, 6000 interviews).

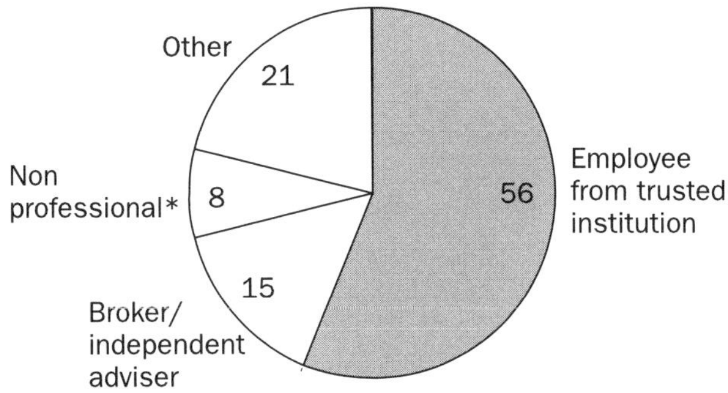

* E.g., lawyers, tax advisers, auditors

Figure 8.3 Sources of advice for affluent customers, 2002 (percent)

Source: McKinsey Pan-European Affluent Investor Market Research 2002

that banks touch on most often in their advice sessions (69 percent of all affluent customers receiving advice also receive financial planning). In addition, 60 percent of all affluent customers having a personal adviser want to set up a meeting at least once a quarter—with financial planning again one of the core topics. These financial planning models need to be updated over time to reflect changing risk preferences and to include an ever-widening range of asset classes and products.

Ideally, financial planning should be combined with integrated reporting on the overall portfolio status, as well as on the past and potential development of the customer's financial situation. Fully integrated tools can not only help support customer decisions but, more importantly, they can serve as a good excuse to set up regular meetings with the customer, as a better understanding of his or her overall financial situation (needs and total portfolio including assets held in other institutions) can help to push sales and to strengthen the bank–customer relationship.

Top-quality investment products and faultless banking services

On the product side, the key to reaching many affluent customers is to offer best-in-class investment products and error-free full banking services. As long as customers feel confident that they are being offered high-quality products at a fair price, it will be less important to them whether they are purely proprietary or also include third-party products.

The product portfolio must adapt to the changing needs of affluent customers. The downturn has not only made customers more risk-averse—approximately three-quarters now prefer safe, lower yield investments to higher risk alternatives, compared with just over half in 1999—but has also led them to consider new asset classes such as structured investment products with guaranteed capital.

HOW RETAIL BANKS CAN RAISE THEIR GAME

As mentioned above, the red carpet retail banking model has proved to be the most resilient in times of a market downturn; but there is still room for improvement. Retail banks' ability to defend current earnings is rooted primarily in their loyal customer base, their ability to draw on the power and trustworthiness of their brands, and their lower adviser cost per customer compared with financial advisers. This lower adviser cost—stemming from economies of scale and scope from existing retail operations—also ensures much higher and more stable income from previous sales. Although one could claim that this reflects only past performance, the model's resilience is confirmed when sales costs are compared with sales value. Our experience suggests that retail banks tend to maintain costs at about 40 to 50 percent of the sales value regardless of the economic cycle, whereas financial advisers' cost-to-sales fluctuate from a bull market (35 to 40 percent) to a bear market (50 to 70 percent). In bull markets, financial adviser models tend to sell more effectively, but best practice retail banks are better positioned to maintain sales volumes in bear markets by switching assets to deposits and capital preservation products.

In what follows, we describe the most important improvement measures a retail bank can make to its affluent business model in the areas of service and advice delivery, salesforce management, product offering, pricing, and branding. Some retail banks have already implemented many of the suggested measures and even achieved excellence in one dimension or another, but we have yet to find any bank that has reached excellence in all of them. The individual relevance of each of the measures may vary strongly by institution, so improvement programs need to be tailored to the starting point of each bank.

Improve service and advice delivery

Service and advice delivery is probably the most important area on which to work in improving the average retail bank's affluent proposition. The main challenge is to ensure a consistent advisory quality across a large institution by introducing a well-structured financial planning process. This process is often supported by affluent-specific tools that can be either information technology-based (IT) or mainly paper-based.

Most banks have realized the need for financial planning tools and processes, and, consequently, have developed them in-house. For example, a recent study revealed that 80 percent of all German banks have defined a structured advisory process.[6] However, only a few banks have managed to move successfully from development to implementation. We are not aware of any European bank that is state of the art in all aspects of financial planning, but our research shows that the leading players do share some commonalities.

First, to meet the more complex needs of the affluent segment effectively, successful financial planning approaches must be comprehensive enough to cover all major asset categories (including assets at other financial institutions as well as credit and

[6] *Exploration: Financial Planning*. Hochschule für Bankwirtschaft/HfB, Hamburg, February 2002.

protection needs), while remaining simple enough to be useful. Affluent customers do not expect comprehensive planning or a financial plan at each advisory session; usually discussions on specific products or needs are sufficient. Comprehensive financial planning is expected only once or twice a year or in times of market turmoil. Best practice tools can cope with these different requirements, usually by relying on a modular architecture that offers concrete product recommendations that can be seamlessly integrated with a full-scale solution. Banca Fideuram, for example, relies on an advanced tool by US asset management consultancy Frank Russell that can build a fully personalized financial plan based on customers' preferences with regard to the particular topics under discussion.

Second, to make best use of each advisory session, successful financial planning approaches actively try a step-by-step approach to boost the bank's share of each customer's wallet. Best practice examples, therefore, cover not only the current financial status of a customer but also include elements that simulate how the customer's needs might change over time. With every additional piece of information received from the customer in each advisory session, these tools provide additional cross-selling opportunities. One central European bank has developed a tool that reminds advisers during meetings to ask for further specific information on their customers that is missing from the database (e.g., expected date of birth of children, start of university education of children, etc.). This is also partly what lies behind MLP's concept of 'life cycle companionship', the (anticipated) lifelong personal relationship with advisers (in the same age group and with the same educational background) who understand the needs and backgrounds of their customers.

Third, best practice banks ensure that financial planning is used at all levels of the organization, not just as a tool but as a way to make the whole client interaction model more advisory-driven (as opposed to transaction-driven). The depth of the analysis, the functionalities and gimmicks of financial planning tools and processes, and the criteria for customers to qualify for access to advice sessions may vary among financial institutions; however, what does not change is that even the most sophisticated process will fail without the full commitment of management to implementing the new approach. Some large, well-respected banks have found this out the hard way. To reduce resistance within financial institutions, agreed processes must be mandatory for each individual advice session—and strictly enforced—but also easy to use (e.g., automated access to customer information and portfolios, minimal data input, etc.). Although heavy initial training requirements can create resistance to using any financial planning tool, without training, advisers will never become familiar with the instruments at their disposal. The trick is to make the tool an integral part of each training session from the outset. This way, advisers can become familiar with the way advisory work should be done quickly.

Finally, while offering best practice financial planning is one thing, getting customers to use it is more challenging still. The standard marketing vehicles such as TV or newspaper adverts have yielded conversion rates four to six times lower for financial planning offerings than for ordinary product sales. Successful players have understood that advice is a people business and have therefore relied heavily on both their existing customers (e.g., through customer referral schemes) and their advisers (e.g., through high incentives) to convince customers to use their premium affluent services. Banca Fideuram, for example, relies on a 100 percent variable compensation structure that is biased toward assets under management-related fees, rather than just pure sales commissions.[7] This guarantees staff remains keenly aware of asset gathering, the chances of which improve by offering best practice financial advice.

Aggressively manage the salesforce for sales and service

When it comes to sales, best-practice affluent banks have often been successful at drawing on their large retail branch networks, but they can still learn a lot from financial advisers with their highly incentivized and entrepreneurial salesforce. Financial advisers are able to reap significantly higher income from new sales per customer in healthy market environments, and their personnel costs structure is also more flexible in times of market downturn. This is mainly because financial advisers can rely on variable incentives and self-employed, entrepreneurial distribution partners with clear customer ownership.[8]

Bank employees serving affluent customers have to move from being pure product-sellers to being proactive, relationship-driven advisers who independently approach customers with targeted solutions and who maximize the time spent on value-adding customer services. Yet, turning account managers into financial advisers is not easy, therefore retail banks should not try simply to copy these models, as they are normally restricted by both a lack of suitable skills and by the boundaries of their compensation structure (with often more than 90 percent of compensation fixed, and only limited flexibility for changing compensation).

Nevertheless, there are important elements of the financial adviser model that could be adopted. First, the rigorous rationalization of branch processes would give affluent account managers more time to give advice. Some banks have seen net advisory time increase by 45 to 65 percent by off-loading administrative and servicing tasks and by streamlining processes. Second, banks can invest in building the relevant advisory skills of affluent account managers. Third, even within remuneration boundaries, there are often ways to incentivize affluent-customer account managers with a more flexible compensation structure and other nonfinancial rewards within existing agreements. This can often stimulate both their sales drive and overall results. Finally, a precise budgeting process with clear, mutually agreed individual targets and rigorous benchmarking of frontline peer groups can both motivate staff and help them learn from their best practice colleagues.

Implementing these changes will require a major commitment from top management and employees alike and will take a significant amount of time. However, the rewards can be substantial. Fending off the financial adviser threat by beating (or at least matching) them at their own game will help retail banks strengthen their position even further and keep them at the forefront of affluent banking.

Citibank is probably the best example of a bank that has succeeded in developing its salesforce in this direction. Its strong profitability and large share of the affluent

[7] Banca Fideuram analyst presentation, December 2000.

[8] The main challenge for financial advisers in times of a market downturn is to retain advisers when sales-based compensation is falling. This is especially true for top advisers who are not used to drastic cutbacks in their overall compensation.

segment in some countries (e.g., Turkey, Greece, and many countries in Asia via the Citibank Gold offering) stems, largely, from the strength of its salesforce. Citibank combines thorough salesforce training with a rigorously implemented financial planning tool (Citipro) that helps identify cross-selling opportunities as well as advanced database-marketing.[9]

Design an affluent-specific product offering

To create a more exclusive experience, retail banks have to offer affluent customers something beyond the regular retail product range. They can introduce (high-margin) products exclusively to affluent customers, either from within their own private or investment banking division or from third parties. Many of the most successful retail banks have opted for a combination of the two. Barclays in the UK, for example, offers proprietary 'Premier' products to its affluent customers, as well as full banking services combined with third-party funds. Deutsche Bank successfully introduced the Xavex hedge fund product line and targeted it primarily at the affluent segment. It is combined with a large range of third-party funds. Banca Fideuram is one of the few examples of a successful affluent player that relies solely on a small number of high-performing proprietary products in each product category. This does not mean that a bank should go down the third-party route without careful consideration, given the potential cannibalization effect on proprietary—and usually more profitable—products. The strength of this effect depends on the typical affluent customer's strategic asset allocation: the more conservative this is, the lower the average cannibalization rate, as third-party brands tend to be more appealing for higher risk products such as equities. On the other hand, offering third-party products should boost sales. Third-party products from well-known brands may also actually enhance the perception of performance and independence, which could attract new clients as well as decreasing churn rate and increasing share of wallet among existing customers. (See Box 8.1 on expanding the product offer with proprietary structured investment products.)

While banks contemplate this, many financial advisers have also started to broaden their product offering by adding selected high-margin banking products. This helps them stabilize their revenue streams, improve the revenues generated from each customer, and increase the comprehensiveness of their offering to affluent customers. This poses a substantial threat to retail banks in some of their most attractive product areas. MLP, for example, now offers credit cards as well as bank accounts and has become one of Germany's largest issuer of gold credit cards. However, where there is a threat there is often an opportunity. Financial advisers face the challenge of cost-efficient delivery when shifting to more transaction-oriented products, as they lack the synergies of scale and shared infrastructure of retail banks. Some retail banks might find that partnering with a financial adviser, offering existing economies of scale and transaction-oriented IT systems, might be an attractive option.

[9] Citigroup, investor presentation, November 6, 2001.

Box 8.1
Structured investment products: expanding the product-offering

Structured investment products are an important emerging revenue stream for European financial institutions that have access to both branch networks and capital markets and that possess a mix of skills in retail and wholesale banking. Although many have recognized these new opportunities, few have overcome the associated organizational hurdles to capture their full potential.

Structured investment products range in risk and complexity from hedge funds to private equity and from derivative-based products to covered warrants or reverse convertibles. Each has high-growth expectations (estimated to be between 20 and 60 percent over the next several years) compared with growth rates of traditional assets of between 5 and 10 percent.

These products are attractive first because they allow banks to increase their penetration of the customer base (they may help poach wallet share away from alternative financial services providers, such as equity brokers). They also complement banks' product ranges as the revenues from these products are often an addition, rather than an alternative, to those from mutual funds. Moreover, they can help build customer relationships by allowing distributors to establish a dialog with the customer throughout the economic cycle. Lastly, they also tend to be quite profitable. For example, many capital-guaranteed products can provide annualized pre-tax profits of around 120 basis points (of which 50 percent are for the distributors).

Customers like the products because they allow them to diversify risk, to protect the value of an equity portfolio, to go short (e.g., with covered warrants) or to cap the potential downside of their investments (e.g., with capital-guaranteed products), and they are relatively easy to understand.

To be able to sell these products successfully, it is important to segment investors in terms of their level of proactivity and risk appetite. Self-directed and support-seeker investors are proactive enough to be good targets for these products. Once customer segments have been targeted, marketing and sales should coordinate activities with the retail branch network.

Managing an attractive product portfolio across the economic cycle is crucial, so having a broad range of products will aid the dialog with a customer no matter what the market conditions. If a bank has interesting products in both bear and bull markets, the portfolio remains dynamic and the likelihood of meeting customers' risk/return preferences is higher.

The European retail capital markets business requires a unique combination of retail and wholesale banking skills. The retail side must offer strong branding and marketing, excellent customer interaction and product development, and a broad private distribution network. The wholesale business brings skills in product-structuring, trading and pricing, hedging and risk management, as well as IT and back office operations. Many European banks have these two sets of skills; the challenge is to blend the two sides together.

There are five key success factors in building a derivative-based business. First, install a full-time dedicated team with proven capabilities. Second, strong product-structuring and innovation are required. With a dynamic, state-of-the-art product, a bank needs to stay up to date with retail customers' needs, which demands a strong link to retail distribution channels. Third, the project requires motivated, entrepreneurial people supported by the marketing function of the retail business. Do not delegate sales and marketing responsibilities to other desks within the existing equity derivatives team. Fourth, create strong organizational interfaces—the business must be well represented within senior management. Finally, make sure that appropriate risk management systems are in place to avoid any undesired exposures.

Introducing derivatives-based products to retail clients is best undertaken in phases. In the first year, introduce a limited range of products (e.g., covered warrants and structured products) through the retail branch network, investing in increasing market awareness, and developing customer segmentation. In the second year, focus on expanding the product range, developing sales support tools, and refining the marketing strategy. Then, in the third year, complete the effort by enriching the product portfolio, drawing fully on third-party distribution capabilities, and developing all the necessary skills and abilities to understand clients' portfolio needs.

Unicredito took this approach and within three to four years it led the expansion of the covered warrants market in Italy and was at the leading edge of product innovation, pricing, marketing, and sales, and risk management for a variety of structured investment products. The bank built a distinctive product and service proposition by combining strong financial market skills with real retail market understanding. It hired a small, but highly motivated team with a strong entrepreneurial culture and created an autonomous business unit—Trading Lab—that had clear accountability and separate profit-and-loss statements. Its main strengths are product innovation, its state-of-the-art systems, a lean cost structure, an outstanding brand, and strong risk management tools. Although Unicredito started Trading Lab as recently as 1998, the division had reached revenues of €199m in 2001 according to its annual report.

Daniele Chiarella, Gene Pappas

Draw on the full range of pricing options

Pricing is often the single most powerful short-term lever for improving overall profitability. Getting pricing right can turn unprofitable customers into profitable ones by maximizing the overall amount charged for products and services. Successful and straightforward quick fixes in pricing include introducing minimum pricing to deter unprofitable customers and enforcing pricing discipline rigorously, with very limited leeway for discounts.

A typical pricing project in an (affluent) bank can result in overall revenue improvements of 10 to 20 percent within 12 months. Longer term pricing measures can have a substantial positive impact on profitability, but can be derived only from an in-depth analysis of all relevant aspects of pricing. This is discussed in much more detail in Chapter 11. There is little evidence that most financial institutions have used the full range of pricing options in their affluent business; by doing so, they could generate substantial value.

One European bank identified savings in excess of 0.5 percent on overall, new fund sales volumes just by limiting discretion on price discounts among its affluent advisers (e.g., defining and controlling different maximum discount levels per customer segment).

Another European bank improved profits by 15 percent within a year—and by 26 percent in the longer term—by increasing price levels in those products to which customers were less price-sensitive, by differentiating price levels between channels (e.g., raising prices for more expensive channels, while ostensibly paying customers to use cheaper ones) and by raising hidden fees rather than fees on products such as current accounts, which could cause customers to defect.

Retail banks should also monitor the pricing policies of financial advisers, so they can potentially react to short-term changes. So far, most financial advisers offer their services for free, so the introduction of advice-related fees, as seen at Merrill Lynch in the US, might be one way for them to increase overall profitability in Europe. If this starts to happen on a larger scale, it could pave the way for retail banks to start charging explicitly for advisory services in the affluent segment.[10]

Build a strong brand

Branding is essential in communicating the additional customer benefits of an affluent value proposition. Established retail banks have three main options for branding

[10] In Germany, for example, approximately 85 percent of banks say they charge customers extra for financial advice; however, this was mostly through implicit fees rather than commissions for financial planning.

their affluent business. First, they can use the power of a strong universal brand highlighting the attributes aimed at the affluent market segment (e.g., Deutsche Bank or Barclays). Second, they can establish a subbrand (e.g., BBVA Privanza or Santander Central Hispano's BSN BANIF). Third, they can launch an independent brand with a clear and distinct value proposition for the affluent segment. BCP has done this by using the BCP brand itself for affluent customers and the NovaRede brand for the mass market.

The decision as to which approach to choose should be based on a thorough assessment of the opportunities to increase margins, market power, and efficiency. In most circumstances, a strong, traditional universal brand is the most cost-efficient option. This is especially true in a market downturn, when trust is a prerequisite for attracting customers. The major downside of this approach for the affluent segment is the more limited chance to increase margins compared with mass market customers, particularly if the infrastructure is also shared and the offer is not clearly differentiated. In these circumstances, a subbrand can offer a way to combine trust and differentiation with sufficient degrees of freedom.

Red carpet retail banks have proved to be the most successful providers to the affluent segment even in a market downturn. Although their success is based on a distinctive affluent-specific value proposition, this model has also profited from some of the weaknesses of other value propositions (e.g., lack of trustworthiness, mediocre advice, no access to full banking services). In the light of renewed competition (especially from financial advisers), retail banks must constantly improve their affluent offerings to build on their excellent starting position. By implementing best practice measures, retail players can make the lucrative affluent market even more profitable.

9

Small-business Banking: Hunting down Elusive Profits

Paul ter Linden[1]

The small-business banking segment is rarely the focus of retail banks, stuck as it is between the consumer segment and mid-sized corporate clients. Yet it is still a constant source of headaches, sapping up a considerable amount of management attention, but failing to deliver healthy profits—or indeed, in some cases, any profits at all.

The US market demonstrates that small businesses can be served profitably and that they can become a source of profitable growth for banks. Success in small-business banking depends on the excellent execution of a few core processes. Very few banks rank as excellent in this segment in Europe, so there are interesting opportunities for determined players.

A DIVERSE SEGMENT SHARING COMMON NEEDS

The segment consists of all those smaller businesses that are served from the retail bank network because they are too small to justify the dedicated relationship-based sales approach and complex product offering of medium- and large-corporate banking. The exact parameters vary from country to country and bank to bank depending on, among other things, the maturity of the local economy and the profitability of the banking sector. This makes a pan-European analysis of this segment especially challenging.

Nevertheless, for the purposes of analyzing these customers as a whole we have established a practical working definition of the small-business segment that we believe applies to the majority of banks: business customers with up to about 50 employees and €10m in turnover, including enterprises such as farms, shops, hotels and restaurants, small service firms, and others.

In most European countries, the small-business customer segment as defined here represents roughly between 35 and 45 percent of the total pool of revenues from

[1] The author would like to express his gratitude for the contributions of Georg Schubiger, Gene Pappas, Nici Audhlam-Gardiner and David Hajman.

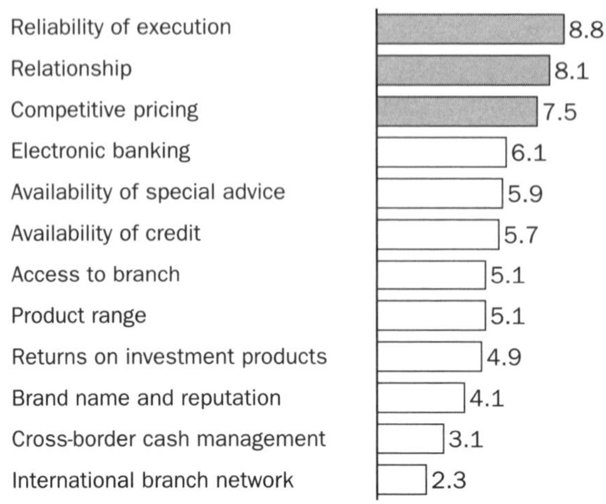

Figure 9.1 Key buying factors for small businesses (range from 1 [least] to 10 [most important)]

Source: McKinsey interviews

small-, medium-, and large-corporate banking customers. Perhaps surprisingly, in view of this important share of total banking business, little pan-European research documents the specific product and service needs of small-business customers. The majority of publicly available research has focused on the mid-sized corporate segment—one notch up from our focus here—largely because mass customer segments have traditionally appeared less attractive. To fill this gap, we conducted in-depth interviews with small businesses to assess their needs.

Despite the diversity within the segment, our research shows that small businesses share a number of common product and service needs. They all have a strong need for four clusters of products: transaction services (100 percent of all businesses surveyed), insurance (80 percent), commercial loans (70 percent), and asset finance (70 percent). Local market circumstances aside, no other product cluster than these four scores higher than 30 percent. As a result, in terms of profit potential, these customers rarely warrant a personal account manager spending substantial time on relationship-building.

Small-business customers also generally share a number of service preferences. Compared with their mid-sized corporate peers, they tend to be less financially experienced, typically lacking a dedicated (or even part-time) chief financial officer; so bank matters are often dealt with by the owner-manager. Banking products are seldom essential to small business processes, so banking services are mostly seen as unavoidable rather than exciting. Our research shows that the three strongest buying factors are the reliability of banking services, the quality of the banking relationship, and price (Figure 9.1). The importance of these factors shows that it is critical to develop an offer with consistent quality to a fair cost to satisfy small-business customers. Trailing surprisingly far behind are such elements as the availability of advice and the proximity of branches—service features that small-business bankers have traditionally seen as cornerstones of their service propositions and that, we would argue, often create an unsupportable cost base in many retail banks.

MEETING THE PROFIT CHALLENGES

As we set out to find examples of excellence in small-business banking, we were struck by how hard it was to find profitable players in Europe. Compared with average risk-adjusted returns on capital in consumer banking, which are around 20 percent, the small-business banking units we researched have an average performance of around 7 percent. Variance is much higher too, with some banks actually generating negative returns on capital. Of the few European banks that generate attractive returns on capital, most are active in markets with high price levels (such as the UK) or enjoy very focused, regional positions that give them an almost captive client base. Only a very small minority in Europe manages to outperform its peers through independent, focused efforts.

It would be wrong, not to say patronizing, to say that most banks have simply failed to give this segment enough management attention. In fact, most banks have made conscious efforts to boost profitability here. However, the fact that the small business segment is wedged uncomfortably between consumers and mid-sized corporates repeatedly raises the question of how the business model can be differentiated to avoid under-serving the segment within the retail bank and over-serving it within the corporate bank.

We have analyzed numerous small-business banking operations across Europe and North America to identify what constitutes excellence in small-business banking. Surprisingly, unlike consumer banking, where certain banks clearly outperform on many dimensions, there is no one European small-business bank that has found the answers to all challenges and that could serve as a role model for other banks. Nor is there a unique, new concept available that will turn around small-business banking.

The whole Excellence in Retail Banking framework certainly applies to the small-business segment, but our research suggests that the road to success in this segment mainly comes from excellence in the following two areas: *segmenting small-business customers* and the *passionate execution of operational levers.*

This is not a business that rewards effort only. Achievement is everything. This requires elevating the image of small-business banking from the activity of junior salespeople and trainees to the domain of dedicated professionals. The professionals in small-business banking simply need different skills from those in mid-corporate banking. They require state-of-the-art product development capabilities for simple, cheap, and value-adding bundling. Rather than relationship management skills, they need sophisticated marketing campaign management and remote channel sales capabilities. Unless these skills are supported by a dedicated organization that keeps track of targets and achievements and instills pride in what small-business banking managers do, profitability in small-business banking will remain elusive.

Banks that have managed to transform their small-business banking have harvested substantial profit improvements. One European bank increased it ROE by 15 percent by focusing on the aggressive repricing of products and services, improving distribution, and introducing new products. It also homed in on consistent sales efforts to exploit the full banking potential of both small businesses and their owners. Another European bank recently applied an integrated performance improvement program with an emphasis on better execution of existing policies. It improved operating profits by as much as 60 percent, which translated into absolute profit increases of over €60m. In both examples, the strongest improvements came from upgrading commercial practices: up to two-thirds from more streamlined, lower cost sales activities; one-third from product redefinition, bundling, and pricing; and a small remainder from distribution, processes, and operations.

SEGMENT SMALL-BUSINESS CUSTOMERS

Segmentation is critical in small-business banking because it lays the foundation for improving operations. It serves as a point of reference for determining the extent to which a bank can successfully implement products, distribution methods, sales approaches, and back office processes that strike the right balance between cost-to-serve, profit potential, and service needs for each of the subsegments.

Segmentation is actually a two-layer process. The first layer consists of defining which customers should be included in a small-business banking approach, and the second, subsegmentation, is an aid to determining the right service delivery approaches to be taken within small-business banking.

Define the small-business customer

The importance of correctly defining which customers to include in the small-business segment cannot be overemphasized. Banks that get it wrong can end up with too many small-business customers allocated to regional centers with a distribution approach tailored to mid-sized corporates. In many cases, this is due to an inaccurate perspective of customer profitability and potential, a misperception of required service levels and attention, or inappropriate expectations regarding the efficiency of the client service approach offered to mid-sized corporates. Furthermore, business customers who were once rightfully placed in the mid-sized corporate segment, but have lost profitability or potential, are rarely returned to the small-business segment. The fact is, however, a sizable number of clients that are only marginally profitable in the mid-sized corporate segment could be highly profitable in the small-business segment (assuming that a cheaper service approach is used there, as should be the case). Without these customers, the small-business banker (and the bank as a whole) misses out on an important profit opportunity.

At the other end of the spectrum, many of the smallest small businesses behave like retail consumers and keeping them in the small-business segment may force them to use products that are too expensive for the bank to produce, and they may receive levels of attention that they neither warrant nor need.

Subsegment based on product usage

Once this overall segmentation has been established, the resulting customers should be subsegmented. This should take into account typical bank profitability metrics regarding current and potential profits on products and services, as well as customer service needs and key buying factors. Most banks use industry sectors or customer size (e.g., client turnover, number of employees) to make crude segmentation cuts,

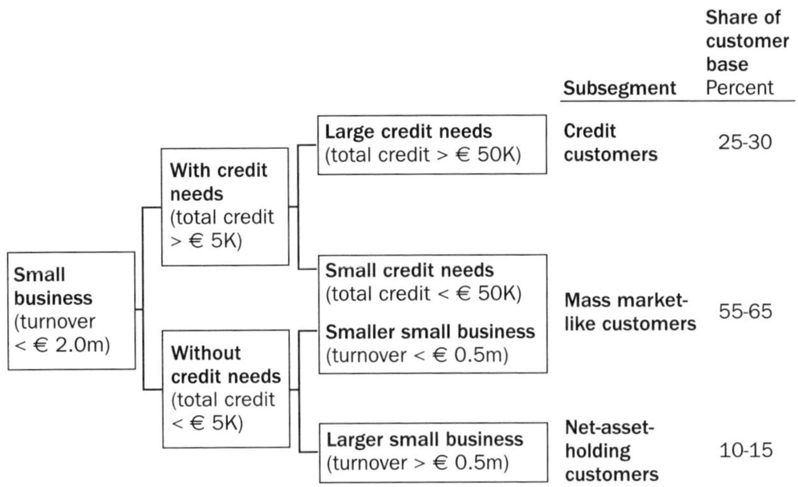

Figure 9.2 Subsegments of a leading small-business bank

Source: McKinsey

but the small-business subsegmentation with the highest impact we have seen is based on product usage and follows two fundamental rules.

First, keep the number of subsegments small, as the costs involved in over-differentiating customer service approaches rapidly outweigh the commercial benefits. A segmentation based on product usage should rarely result in more than four or five subsegments. Second, the segmentation method applied should facilitate proactive selling, rather than a relationship-based, demand-driven sales approach. A segmentation focused on specific product needs is well suited for this, as it groups together customers with similar requirements, making it easier to data-mine and develop targeted marketing and sales campaigns.

The subsegmentation then forms the basis for a highly differentiated client service setup. One successful European bank chose to discriminate between, among others, credit-focused, mass market-like, and net-asset-holding customers (Figure 9.2).

For the mass market-like customers, the bank has developed an integrated product package that allows only online transactions and strongly supports cross-selling of a product set consisting of basic financial services. Although it does provide for personal contact, customer group managers oversee up to 700 customers and most interactions take place by phone. Prices are set to stimulate cheap channel usage, limited transaction frequency, and additional product usage.

For credit-oriented customers, however, the bank designated specific branches as bases for small-business credit specialists with portfolios of up to 150 customers. In addition to corporate credit products, the salespeople are capable of selling PFS products aimed at owner-managers and employees. However, the key processes are aligned with the core credit product, with pricing focused on customer-specific risk, which is largely assessed using automated credit expert systems.

For its net-asset-holding customer subsegments, the bank has designated financial advisers who have a thorough understanding of cash management, savings, investments, and other related asset-side products, rather than a deep understanding of financing options. The impact of moving from a general small-business service model to this subsegment-specific approach has been huge. In fact, this is one of the few banks that we know of which is making healthy profits on mass market small businesses. The key has been the meticulous, aggressive development of multiple, differentiated service models that match the business needs and profit potential of specific subsegments.

EXECUTE WITH PASSION

Once the proper segmentation has been firmly established in the organization, the bank is in a position to consider the more operational elements of its offering. Whichever levers are chosen, they should be operated with a clear view as to how they will affect each of the defined subsegments. Above all, any measures undertaken should be executed with passion; otherwise, results will prove tough to come by.

Sales: no room for the half-hearted

Achieving excellence in the sales function can pave the way to substantial improvements in profitability. Many of the actions required to maximize sales power in small-business banking are no different from those applied in consumer banking (Chapter 13 talks about this in more detail). The two specific challenges that we see are: to exploit all contacts for additional sales, especially the owner-manager, and to drive all sales campaigns as aggressively as possible.

Fully exploit potential for cross-selling to owners. One of the hurdles banks face in the small-business segment is cross-selling to owners and employees. Common problems include customers being served out of different divisions, owners who are reluctant to use the same bank for personal and professional needs, or a lack of knowledge transfer between retail and corporate relationship managers. But experience has shown that these issues can be tackled successfully.

One European bank managed to cross-sell to its small-business customers and almost doubled the value of servicing them in the process. First, it identified the total cross-selling potential by scouring existing databases to match retail customers with small-business owners and to identify passive small businesses and individual customers with small-business potential. This gave the bank a clear picture of the overall cross-selling potential and a database of individual customers to target. In parallel, the bank aligned its value proposition with these specific subsegments, offering, for instance, integrated relationship management services for the small businesses and personal customers, as well as developing joint product bundles. In addition, it made its pricing more transparent (including discounts based on the strength of the relationship between the owner-manager and the bank) and developed new application forms with tick-off features to ensure that branch personnel target an owner's personal banking needs when a new customer is acquired. Finally, selected banking processes/systems were also tailored to the effort, specifically introducing a single customer view for performance management. As a result of these measures, the bank was able to grow the absolute profits from its small businesses and owner-manager customers by as much as 15 percent through more effective cross-selling and retention.

Aggressive selling. One important way of improving profitability is to deepen the relationship between the customer and the bank. The key to success here is to focus on a push-based sales approach.

In radical implementations, this could consist of centrally supported marketing and database-mining efforts that are followed up locally with outbound calling by small, integrated sales teams. The teams typically have two, dedicated, remote, small-business relationship managers and three to four product specialists for core products. The highly qualified remote relationship managers make outbound calls, respond to inbound calls, and attempt to close as many deals as possible. Specialist salespeople only follow qualified leads for more complex product sales opportunities that are generated by the relationship managers on the basis of the campaigns or customer inquiries.

To make this setup work, a segmentation based on product needs (as described above) is crucial. Moreover, any move to such a sales model must be all or nothing. Half-hearted implementation will leave the door open for salespeople to revert to traditional relationship-driven selling, which is both ineffective and too expensive in this segment.

Aggressive and creative marketing and sales campaigns can also help substantially in selectively acquiring new, attractive small-business customers and deepening the relationship with them.

Product design and pricing: find the right fit

Small businesses may be less sophisticated than mid-sized corporates, but they are still no-nonsense buyers with very specific needs. Hence, product design and pricing offer significant potential for profitability improvement. The four key areas that we have identified for achieving excellence in product design and pricing are to simplify and standardize products, offer targeted products and product bundles, outsource low-volume, specialty product offers, and aggressively pursue all pricing opportunities.

Simplify and standardize products. Key to keeping costs down in the small-business segment is to have a limited portfolio of standardized products that cover basic customer needs. Interestingly, although a significant benefit from portfolio rationalization is the reduction of product factory costs, the majority of the impact comes through simplification of the sales process. Complex products require consultative, specialist sales processes that are, in most product categories, uneconomical for small-business customers.

Create specific value propositions based on sector-specific needs. Many small business banks have developed an expertise in a particular industry sector. For example, those with a credit cooperative background have a strong franchise in the agriculture sector, while merchant banks typically have a strong customer base and brand image among professionals and trading firms. It could well pay off to create focused value propositions for only those sectors in which a bank has—or can quickly attain—critical mass. Such value propositions typically revolve around sector-specific products, but can and should be augmented by dedicated marketing efforts and possibly dedicated sales units. Unfortunately, most large banks tend to pursue the 'usual suspects', making it hard for all but the largest to really stand out from the crowd as the natural owner of any one sector. Yet there are interesting smaller sectors that can be attacked. Finland's OKO bank, for example, concentrates on the forestry sector. Moreover, some smaller banks have found it possible to defend an attractive and profitable niche position on the basis of targeted products, outstanding industry knowledge, and an almost captive clientele. The Apotheker- und Ärztebank in Germany, for example, caters to the needs of pharmacists and doctors; and the Antwerpse Diamantbank in Belgium caters to the needs of the local and international diamond industry.

Offer specific product bundles. Many small-business banks have been disappointed with the results of product-bundling and have consequently abandoned (at least partially) the idea. Excellent players, on the other hand, have been highly successful in this field, since they design products with a focus on making business life easy for small businesses and their owners. They also calculate the product economics rigorously and tailor product parameters to avoid cannibalizing net interest margins. They then push the sale of these bundles hard, largely eliminating the offer of single products, and communicate the benefits to their customers. Of these elements, a radical focus on consumer needs is usually the most critical. Small businesses do not generally have a dedicated corporate center, which makes them highly receptive to service offers that aim to make their lives simpler and enable them to focus on day-to-day business. This creates a huge opportunity for banks that can offer easy-to-use, internally reinforcing bundles of products.

A remarkable example of such a small-business-specific product bundle is Merrill Lynch's capital management account.[2] It bundles together an investment account, current account, and credit line, all with features designed specifically for small-business needs. The account automatically manages cash flows between the three account types, based on execution parameters defined by the customer. For instance, it includes an automatic sweep feature whereby balances exceeding a certain limit in the current account are transferred to the investment account on a predefined day of the week or month. The product offers various advantages for both small-business clients and for the bank. It lowers the bank's servicing costs for one thing, but, more importantly, it increases assets under management and can even be used to acquire additional customers. For its small-business customers, the product reduces the cost of financing, simplifies cash management, and maximizes the value of treasury surpluses. However, such products need to be introduced with care, since there is a potential cannibalization impact on netting revenues. This can be minimized with good product design (e.g., minimum tranches for netting and well-thought-through pricing of all elements of the product), as well as by targeting sales toward new customers or low-profitability customers.

A similar illustration of the strength of the bundling concept can be found in the employer–employee relationship. In addition to the hard-to-tackle area of employee benefits, employers face a huge administrative burden concerning their financial obligations to employees, typically working with salary administrators, pension providers, social security funds, absenteeism and disability insurers, workplace design specialists, absentee rehabilitation service providers, and more. In countries such as the Netherlands, legislation has shifted a lot of the burden of providing income to ill

[2] Company website; press clippings.

or otherwise disabled employees from the government onto corporations. Now, large financial institutions such as Rabobank, ING, and Achmea are starting to offer integrated product packages that provide a single transaction interface for all these services, connected to their own insurance and credit services, as well as to third-party service providers. Aimed at reducing the time owner-managers spend on noncore processes, these bundles are proving very successful.

Outsource production of low-volume specialty products. If it is economically justifiable for the bank to offer some specialty products, outsourcing can be an attractive option. Depending on the scale of the bank and the characteristics of its small-business customer franchise, this can apply to asset finance, small-business insurance coverage, group pension services, and others. At the moment, most European banks opt to produce almost all relevant products in-house, whereas in North America, the use of third-party product providers is much more widespread, and a number of North American blue-chip banks have outsourced product factory activities and sales support for small-ticket leasing to third parties. European product specialists (e.g., in leasing and invoice-discounting) are becoming more powerful and are gaining increasing access to small-business customers. This should lead many European banks to reconsider whether they can remain competitive in these areas.

Exploit the full potential of pricing. A broad set of pricing levers can be applied in small-business banking. In our experience, a moderately performing small-business bank that achieves excellence in pricing can enjoy an increase of up to 10 to 15 percent in total fees. Even though many of these levers are generally known, banks typically apply only a few of them rigorously, leaving much of the potential untapped. Many banks, for example, generate detailed studies of competitors' list prices and adjust their own prices to market levels. However, banks typically shy away from raising prices across the board for fear that increases on products that are often perceived as a public service, such as payments, will attract negative press coverage. Yet even without making visible list price increases, small-business products can still offer opportunities for creative pricing. Specifically, raising prices for nonshopped fees has huge potential. In addition, in the highly dispersed branch setup that forms the typical basis of small-business banking, enforcing adherence to pricing standards is often a simple, but very important profit improvement approach. (Chapter 11 talks about pricing in more detail.)

One continental European bank achieved a 40 percent increase in most fees by enforcing list prices more firmly (Figure 9.3). Before the project, decisions on waivers, discounts, and refunds were managed at a local level, often in branches with very limited checkups. As a result, the average price charged for account maintenance was 40 percent below the list price. The introduction of a rigorous process for centrally managing discounts, waivers, and refunds for small businesses increased profits. Nevertheless, without aggressive implementation (i.e., ensuring that no more discounts, waivers, and refunds are offered) and perseverance in execution (i.e., holding management fully accountable for implementation results), the impact would have been substantially lower.

Distribution: keep costs at bay

We have already touched upon aspects of distribution in various instances above, but there are three areas worth discussing in more detail: developing and offering

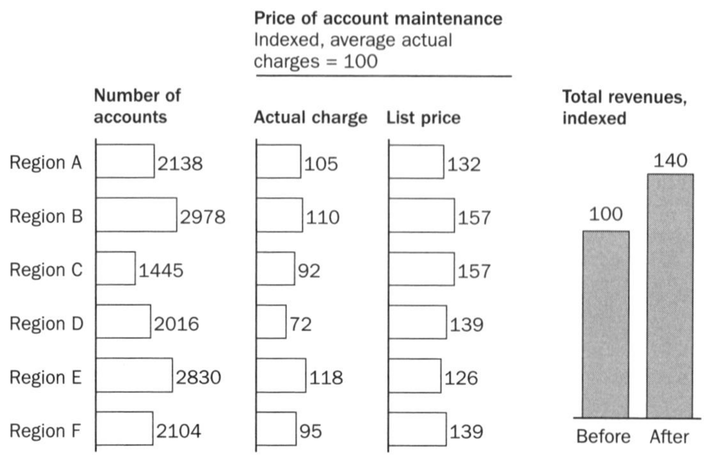

Figure 9.3 Impact of enforcing list prices at a European bank

Source: McKinsey

low-cost channels; active migration of customers to low-cost channels; and improving the capacity management of high-cost channels such as branches.

Develop and offer low-cost channels. Small businesses have traditionally been served out of retail branches, and the dominant interaction mode for most banks is still the face-to-face business service desk conversation. However, there are significant opportunities to deploy low-cost channels in small-business banking relationships. These not only include multi-functional ATMs but also remote telephone- or Internet-banking facilities.

The multi-purpose ATM pilots launched by many of the banks we reviewed have met with, at best, limited success and, at worst, failure. However, a few banks worked consistently at improving the introduction of these ATMs, exploiting new technological functionalities, such as improved deposit features, and forthcoming changes in European cash-handling regulations. They also supported a broader roll-out with a clear and overt migration program, including incentives for staff and customers, repricing, effective communication, and tailored network design (e.g., deposit ATMs at high-frequency cash branches combined with Internet-banking and the complete abolition of mainstream cash transactions at counters). With such aggressive, thorough implementation, some individual banks have been able to migrate up to 90 percent of small-business cash withdrawals and 75 percent of small-business cash deposits to direct channels.

Although European banks were relatively slow to pick up on the online banking opportunity in the small-business segment, most now have an Internet-banking facility that offers basic payment functionality. Some, such as Citibank and Barclays in the UK, Rabobank in the Netherlands, and OKO bank in Finland, have taken bigger strides to offer fully fledged online banking services to small businesses. In Citibank's case, these have been combined with selected nonbanking business services to increase the attractiveness of its overall service offer.[3]

[3] Review of websites of small-business banks.

Migrate customers to low-cost channels. It is one thing to offer low-cost channels, but quite another to get customers to use them—and, equally importantly, to stop them using expensive channels. Many banks shy away from pricing customers out of the branch, but they are often left paying for parallel channels, both of which remain underutilized.

Banks that get it right adopt creative, but aggressive approaches to migrating customers. Key elements in such approaches include: positioning remote channels as advantageous for the customer; pricing all channels to cost; repricing services that are not directly affected by the channel transition to give customers price breaks in areas of less relevance to the bank (e.g., account maintenance fees); designing transparent incentive structures for frontline personnel to shift customers to remote channels; and so on. As we have seen in practice at many banks throughout Europe, using such a suite of pricing concepts can hike Internet- and ATM-banking adoption rates significantly.

Improve capacity management in high-cost channels. With a needs-based segmentation in place, the logical next step is to review the geographical coverage approach. In undifferentiated client service approaches, where generalist small-business bankers cover all types of customers, banks are more or less tied to maintaining a full presence in all important branches because cash-intensive customers, such as local shops, demand a physical presence in most bank locations. These services can be provided by machines and relatively low-cost frontline staff, however, and do not necessitate the presence of skilled small-business advisers.

Therefore, one way to improve distribution costs for face-to-face interaction is to optimize the geographical coverage separately by subsegment. It is likely that financial advisers for net-asset-holding companies will find their customers in more varied locations than their colleagues who manage credit relationships—in fact, they may make more on-site visits to solicit business, whereas credit specialists are usually found in the branch. Excellent banks limit the number of customers who get real relationship management attention to about 25 percent of the total client base and limit the number of locations where relationship managers sit, basing their decisions on detailed financial and geographical data and regularly reviewing them.

Operations and credit: automate and streamline

There are four typical shortfalls relating to excellence in this field: limited credit process efficiency; insufficiently active credit risk management, including workout; cumbersome small-business-specific processes with difficult interfaces to the consumer bank; missed opportunities to streamline and share back office processes with retail.

In the small-business segment, with its thin margins, the challenge is to create an effective yet highly standardized credit process. We focus here on two examples of enhanced credit process efficiency. (For coverage of general approaches to credit challenges, see Part 6.)

Automating credit processes typically offers great improvement potential in terms of reducing both operating costs and credit defaults. However, banks often struggle to set up an effective and efficient process for small-business credits that strikes a balance between the more detailed, partly tailor-made credit processes for medium-sized corporates and the highly automated approaches prevalent in consumer lending.

One bank that has achieved a highly developed small-business credit process is Wells Fargo.[4] Competing against many small local banks that typically own the small-business credit relationship, it has developed a credit process that supports the targeting of small businesses, even in less intensively banked regions. Given the profitability potential and the physical remoteness of these customers, inquiry and application processes are based strictly on direct channels (i.e., Internet, phone, fax, and mail). This is facilitated by a highly standardized credit-offering that allows underwriting with limited client interaction and documentation processing. Underwriting and risk management are based on a clear understanding of RAROC loan models, including standard risk classes and credit-scoring models that allow risk-based pricing. As a consequence, front office staff have no discount possibilities, and total turnaround time (including making the funds available) is a matter of days, with instant feedback on the credit application, and slightly more time needed to complete the formalities. By applying this standardized, but highly sophisticated credit process, Wells Fargo has become number one in small-business lending in the US in terms of new loan volumes, with a very strong position in most states.[5]

Developing such an approach may not always be suitable, depending on the market conditions and the size of the bank. However, we have seen several smaller, more focused initiatives that can improve the overall credit process significantly. For instance, one European bank examined its disposition and reminder process for small businesses and found out that relationship managers were spending a significant amount of time every day (approximately 60 to 90 minutes) tracking overdrafts and issuing reminders. However, a large percentage of these reminders were unnecessary, given that they either fell within internal credit lines or were insignificant in size. By streamlining this process, significant relationship management time was released that could then be devoted to sales initiatives.

For most retail banks, being in small-business banking is not an option, but a given—albeit not one that most European banks are entirely happy with. Excellent small-business banks—of which there are but a few—distinguish themselves not through unique concepts, but through unique execution. Committed and aggressive executors who dedicate themselves to the segment can gain a competitive edge and build a banking business that may become an attractive platform for growth. Above all, they can help hunt down the profits that elude so many.

[4] Annual reports, company website, press clippings.

[5] Annual report, 2001.

Part 3

Sophisticated Marketing and Sales

10

Instilling Marketing Capabilities throughout the Bank

Vittoria Varianini, János Strohmayer[1]

Once, only consumer goods companies deemed it necessary to excel at marketing. Now, strong marketing capabilities are essential for company performance across a wide range of industries, including retail banking. Customers are changing and becoming ever-more demanding. They no longer expect purely functional benefits from their banks, they expect doing business to be easier and more convenient, and they expect their loyalty to be rewarded both financially and in levels of service.

At its core, marketing is about really understanding customer needs, translating this understanding into products and services that meet these needs, aligning the organization to deliver the promise to customers relentlessly, and effectively communicating the benefits of products and services to customers.

Indeed, building leading edge marketing capabilities is one of the few ways retail banks can grow and excel. Many, if not most, companies reach a point at which further growth is very tough to attain given the maturity of their markets. One of their few routes to competitive differentiation—and so to growth—is to look hard at their customers and to realign around their needs. In February 2001, Lloyds TSB's annual report stated that, 'Today, market segmentation has assumed even greater importance. We believe that over time competition on price alone is a losing strategy. The key to success is to find new, different and of course, better ways of serving each customer group. Ultimately, enhancing customer value for target customers is the primary means of delivering superior shareholder returns.'

Market leadership will depend increasingly on a bank's institutional capability to be customer-focused, which requires superior marketing capabilities and an organization that is aligned with customers. A laser-like focus on profitably delivering value to customers will allow players to outperform the market and outpace their competitors.

Those banks that have already succeeded have done so not because they made huge increases in their advertising budgets, but because they pinpointed the specific

[1] The authors would like to express their gratitude for the contributions of McKinsey's Marketing Practice, Péter Czágler, Marie Ford, and Grant Parkinson.

Figure 10.1 Key marketing capabilities in retail banking

Source: McKinsey

marketing skills that put them ahead of their competitors and then aligned their systems, organizational structures, and cultures to support their customer-focused marketing programs. These banks do not simply aim at having good marketing departments, but have instead developed a holistic approach that integrates all elements of the value chain: choose the value; deliver the value; and communicate the value. Banks face a particular challenge in doing this; after all, banking products are not neatly packed items on a supermarket shelf, they are actively delivered to the customer by often many hundreds of bank employees across dozens of different branches and in call centers. Establishing an integrated marketing model gives a company a solid platform for growth and usually unlocks significant revenue potential. In marketing, strategy and organization are inextricably linked and therefore the organization must possess an overall marketing mindset.

This breed of new marketers supports this holistic approach by going beyond a simple marketing department and looking instead at a range of underlying capabilities including customer knowledge/segmentation, branding, marketing spend effectiveness, personal financial services (PFS) offering and product development, pricing, database-marketing/customer relationship management (CRM), sales culture, and customer service (Figure 10.1). This chapter will cover the overall challenge to build marketing capabilities, whereas the rest of this section looks at pricing (Chapter 11), branding and the attendant marketing spend effectiveness (Chapter 12), sales culture (Chapter 13), and service culture (Chapter 14) as we believe these topics will be of the greatest relevance to banks over the next few years.

Sadly, there is no magic wand that can conjure up marketing capabilities. However, companies across a range of industries that are recognized as excellent marketers have found a way of institutionalizing marketing and subsequently bringing about success, based on the following six dimensions: (1) linking marketing goals to corporate objectives; (2) focusing on a few key capabilities; (3) developing an effective organizational structure; (4) attracting and developing marketing talent; (5) setting process rules in place; (6) designing self-funding programs.

Link marketing goals to corporate objectives

Setting marketing goals in line with overall corporate strategy allows banks to integrate specific marketing performance measures into the overall planning and performance management process. However, it is not enough simply to understand corporate objectives and try to move along the same lines. Marketing must link to the bank's operational plans by creating metrics that measure precisely what is happening all the way from the corporate level down to individuals at branch level. For retail banks, the major challenge is to create a series of metrics based on customers, not just products and channels. This could, for instance, create specific goals for branch staff, such as volume retention and customer satisfaction benchmarks for existing customers.

Driving marketing improvement efforts with concrete performance goals is important as it forces the entire organization to acknowledge the size of the marketing challenge, while giving clear benchmarks of success. Which benchmarks are used depends very much on which stage of the business they are in.

For a company growing its core business in an environment of competitive pressure, marketing should focus on developing, delivering, and communicating the distinctiveness of the value proposition. Customer acquisition and retention are crucial at this time, as are building and strengthening the brand. Once the business has reached a certain size and mass, it may be time to think about nascent, additional businesses. In this second phase, marketing can extend the brand into related markets and think about new products and services for new markets. Finally, when the business has matured, marketing can help to create viable options for the future. At this point, the marketing function needs to develop sufficient foresight into unmet customer needs in order to spot growth options for the business. It follows that marketing capability priorities should therefore be driven by corporate objectives.

In a number of retail banks, all individuals have their own performance plan that includes marketing goals and specific customer metrics. All benchmarks are tied closely to product-specific sales, reflecting the bank's stretching corporate objectives. These banks also make ambitious corporate objectives operational by having a central marketing unit that plans and develops segment-specific products to achieve the given targets. Indeed, planning is the major integrating process across functions, and it is crucial that marketing-specific objectives are integrated in the planning process. Marketing and financial planning must be developed jointly.

Focus on a few key capabilities

Once performance goals are set, the choice of which marketing capabilities to build in order to achieve them makes a big difference in how successful a bank will be. Simply aiming to become an 'excellent marketer' is far too broad; after all, as we saw in Figure 10.1, marketing involves a wide range of skills, and it is not feasible to be uniformly excellent at all of them. Although most companies can afford to excel in one or two, few can invest in building multiple skills. In fact, banks that try to build many capabilities will probably never lead in any. Strong marketing companies have typically developed two or three areas of expertise that, over time, have contributed to their reputation as leaders.

Outside financial services, Procter & Gamble is undoubtedly among the best companies in terms of continuous leading edge product development. This is mostly based on its outstanding ability to understand customer needs and install product improvement processes. For this model marketer, marketing comprises the entire value chain and, thus, includes product development.

Returning to the banking industry, Wells Fargo has managed—despite its size—to appeal to discrete customer segments and communities. Its success is built on the well-developed skill of driving research to gain deep insights into customer needs, as well as on its strength in identifying product needs leading to cross-selling or to the introduction of new services. Wells Fargo's stated strategy is to 'out-local the nationals and out-national the locals',[2] translated into offering better products and a broader product line than its local competitors, while staying close to its customers in each community, understanding their needs, and providing professional, personalized, timely service. One of Wells Fargo's declared objectives—as expressed in its vision statement—is to 'earn 100 percent of every creditworthy customer's business.'[3] The result is that today, this cross-selling (or needs-based selling) is much cheaper than attracting new customers, as insights from research generate better sales opportunities. Hence, a conscientious marketing effort results in better bottom line results from higher cross-sell ratios. Wells Fargo has a cross-sell ratio of 3.8 products per household compared with a North American industry average of 2.0.[4]

Develop an effective organizational structure

At the heart of meeting the overall marketing goal is the coordination and execution of a bank's promise to customers. It is no good having product development staff complaining how their great product is poorly sold in the branches, nor to have frontline staff claiming they are the only ones concerned with sales and could do better if they had better products. Such situations leave segment managers stuck in the middle. All this can generally be avoided through integration, reinforcing the culture that everyone in the bank is a marketer working toward the shared goal of delivering the product and service promises at the frontline.

Regardless of whether a bank has a matrix or divisional organizational model, there are a few basic principles that apply when developing world-class marketing capabilities. First, successful marketing companies decide which is the primary value-delivering dimension (e.g., segment, product, channel, or location) based on their strategy. They then place integrators in pivotal positions along the primary dimension to coordinate the delivery of products and services to customers. Finally, they support integrators with pools of world-class specialists skills in two or three core capabilities, such as market research, database-marketing, or pricing (Figure 10.2).

---

[2] 'The Vision and Values of Wells Fargo—How we intend to be one of America's great companies', by the Chairman, President, and CEO, Richard M. Kovacevich, April 2001.

[3] Ibid.

[4] Citigroup analyst presentation, November 6, 2001.

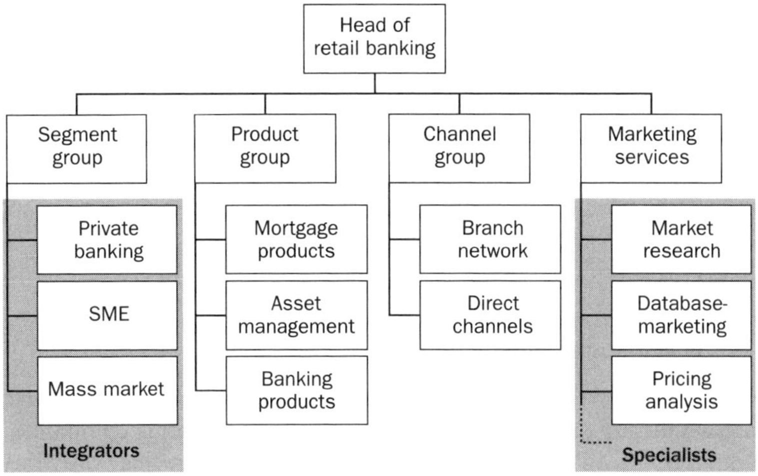

Figure 10.2 Integrators and specialists at bank with segments as primary dimension

Source: McKinsey

Integrators are marketing leaders with a broad generalist skill set, who are responsible for delivering the entire package to customers, even if they do not have line authority over people delivering all parts of the package. To date, few banks have effectively employed integrators consistently. Banks that do use them to enhance their institutional marketing capability also usually align their organizational structure and management processes to reinforce the integration.

A southern European bank, for example, chose segment-specific integration with different platforms for each level of the retail and corporate pyramid. Each platform has network managers and value proposition managers. The latter are segment integrators who ensure that each segment receives tailored products and services with adequate service levels through appropriate channels. They also make sure that the customer experience reflects the bank's overall aims, in conjunction with those of the particular platform.

Marketing specialists, on the other hand, are usually organized in functional rather than business units and provide integrators with focused marketing knowledge that enhances integration across channels, products, and segments. It is more efficient to pool specialists in order to create a critical mass, allowing them to be deployed as flexibly as possible and able to serve different segments or divisions. Skilled marketing employees, as with many creative industries, benefit tremendously from working together as they can nurture each other's ideas and help spark new innovations.

Financial institutions generally have at least some of the required specialists, and there are cases where they have contributed significantly to an organization's success. Two US financial services providers both hired specialists to achieve their marketing goals; both had the aim of using customer information more effectively, but they took different approaches to employing specialists.

The first grew revenues by developing successful cross-selling and consideration campaigns that employed modeling experts who extracted possible targets from in-house data and additional market research. Pooling CRM specialists together enabled the company to build economies of scale in customer-focused IT requirements.

The second institution uses two types of specialists: market researchers and service specialists. Their efforts in understanding and characterizing drivers of customer satisfaction are coordinated by integrators and ultimately passed on to frontline staff. Churn rates have fallen significantly thanks to the introduction of more effective ways to handle customer service issues. In both cases, these specialists are also pooled in order to build a critical mass and improve coordination.

Attract and develop marketing talent

A company can have a customer-focused mindset only if its management has it—and that means a majority of senior managers. In the best marketing companies, as many as three-quarters of all managers focus on the customer in their everyday job. To achieve such a shift, it is important to ensure that the best people are recruited, which means that the opportunities offered in banking must be at least as appealing as jobs in other industries. The choice to become a marketer in a bank should be comparable with that of joining a fast-moving consumer goods company where the long-term outlook would be that two-thirds of board members come from marketing. As long as marketing is considered a side road in financial institutions and not a path that can take its best people to the top, it will be challenging to recruit and retain talent.

If a retail bank is serious about building new marketing capabilities in a particular area, then typically over half the relevant hires should be made externally. However, this is not an easy task, and banks that have tried this road have often encountered two obstacles.

First, banks have found it hard to help outside marketing specialists fit into the banking corporate culture, where marketing is not generally perceived to be as critical as it is, for example, in packaged goods. The cultural fit will not come by itself, and whether the recruiting process is led by the marketing department or by HR, there should be screening for this as well as for specific marketing abilities. It is no less important that work is done to ensure that external hires are accepted by the existing organization. Second, banks have encountered difficulties in getting outside marketing specialists to understand fully and act decisively on the particular challenges faced by retail banks. It is a considerable leap from working in a consumer goods marketing environment with a long history and a well-oiled machinery to being part of a typical retail bank's marketing department, where processes are not as developed. In organizations that have successfully integrated these specialists, an emphasis has also been placed on talent management and development.

The southern European bank we mentioned earlier hired an entire group of marketing staff with nonbanking backgrounds and created a marketing unit in the broad sense that was supported by traditional bankers in product and service development. Its leader subsequently advanced to the bank's top echelons, while the department is now in the process of integrating employees who have been rotated into it, thus enlarging the skill base within the organization.

Another southern European bank places strong emphasis on continuous feedback and coaching, performing staff evaluations at least three times a year. The bank recruits many people with no previous banking experience and uses job rotations (across networks, as well as between frontline and central services) to strengthen the corporate culture as well as the individuals' identification with and understanding of their bank.

Set process rules

Beyond the world of banking, there are a number of examples of companies that have successfully created proprietary approaches to various aspects of marketing. Procter & Gamble—a company for which advertising is a critical task—has developed its own approach to briefing advertising agencies. This helps it work consistently and effectively across the world. There is nothing revolutionary about what it actually does, but the important point is that in all its locations, the company systematically applies a process that suits its particular business. Other companies do things such as implementing a standardized customer service experience or installing a clear, formalized product development process.

A large Spanish bank is a good example of an institution that worked on corporate marketing strategies and set up the infrastructure within which to achieve them. After rapid growth, the bank sought improved profitability through cross-selling. By no means a unique goal, but when looking at the bank's marketing organization, three things immediately stand out. First, customer service is deemed so important that two-thirds of staff are partially compensated according to customer satisfaction results. Second, the bank's marketing strategy involves an organization built around macro-customer segments, which is rare. Third, the bank did not have a large pool of existing bank staff and was therefore easily able to recruit the required skills, meanwhile creating its own culture. The results show the success: the cross-selling rate of 5.6 products per customer is one of the highest in Europe, while customer satisfaction is at 80 percent and brand awareness figures are among the highest in Spain.

Design self-funding programs to accelerate pace

Many attempts to build capabilities languish due to a lack of financing, enthusiasm, and support. Successful programs generate financially positive and morale-building quick wins, which also make programs self-funding. It is therefore important to decide in what order to tackle the various elements of a program.

As with many organizational change efforts, it typically takes two to three years to build a better marketing company. Therefore, long-term capability-building needs to be coupled with early wins. The best programs are designed around strategically significant projects (such as brand-building or new product development) with a view to setting up specific individual and institutional capabilities (such as pricing or salesforce stimulation) up front (Figure 10.3). The latter can generate revenue relatively easily, which can then fund subsequent phases of the program. Morale levels will also increase, leading to more widespread support of the program throughout the bank.

Pricing is a good example of a program that can be structured and implemented quite rapidly, typically having an impact within six months. Measures and programs

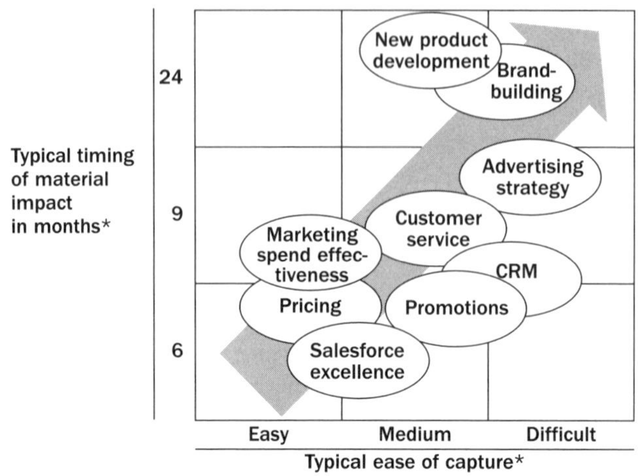

* Based on average observed across industries and geographies in over 500 engagements

Figure 10.3 Timing and ease of capture of marketing initiatives

Source: McKinsey

that affect the salesforce's performance or the effectiveness of promotions also bring quick results. Programs with longer lead times, such as new products or branding, can easily take up to two years before having an impact on the bottom line and are also harder to secure.

In addition, programs that are actively supported by the CEO have proven more successful for three reasons. First, the CEO's attention communicates a program's importance. Second, staff get the CEO's personal attention, which makes program participation a way to get increased visibility. Finally, individual accountability is increased as it is known that reports are made directly to the CEO.

Changing a company's culture is a long process, but it can be done. One financial services provider took more than 18 months to complete the transformation, but it moved from a position where it considered marketing superfluous to one where marketing was the driver of company performance. It also generated a 70 percent increase in the monthly customer acquisition rate and a 500 percent increase in new sales volumes.

Financial institutions have started to transform into customer-focused organizations. Marketing, however, has in many cases not yet been developed beyond a department. In order to become truly excellent, a more integrative approach and mindset are imperative. This is a mindset that links all processes to the main objective of being distinctive and relevant to customers whenever, wherever, and however they come into contact with the organization. We believe that the approach described allows an organization to tackle these challenges effectively.

11

Pricing: Capitalize on Opportunities

Justo Alcocer, Thomas Merkle, Gabriela Pueyo[1]

Setting the right price levels is a vital component of achieving revenue growth in retail banking. It can achieve a broad range of objectives, from long-term strategic changes such as altering a bank's overall positioning to short-term measures such as increasing current earnings. What is more, any changes in pricing have an immediate bottom line impact—especially when compared with measures such as cost reduction or sales stimulation programs. For a typical retail bank, a 1 percent increase in price levels can produce an increase of between 10 and 12 percent on the bottom line, while the impact of a similar cost reduction effort ranges from 3 to 8 percent. In fact, as shown in Chapter 2, differences in realized price levels are the single most important factor for explaining the variance in cost–income ratio performance across countries.

Despite its impact, banks often step carefully around pricing for fear of its effect on customer acquisition and attrition. However, market research carried out in Europe, Asia, and the US demonstrates that these fears are unjustified, as pricing often has relatively little bearing on customers' choice of a financial institution.[2] Indeed, customers often cannot recall the last pricing increase their bank introduced, and, of those who can, only a very small percentage shopped around for a different offer, with an even smaller percentage actually taking any action (Figure 11.1).

Given their reticence to use pricing to improve profitability, banks have fallen behind other industries, such as airlines or retail stores, in their pricing behavior. This is true in terms of both the tools and strategies used and the development of the organizational capabilities needed to implement them effectively. Thus, banks today must look outside their own industry for new pricing insights. Only a few leading banks have begun working on improving their pricing practices; for the vast majority, therefore, pricing presents a tremendous untapped opportunity.

[1] The authors would like to express their gratitude for the contributions of Bruce McEvoy and Ylva Bengtsson.

[2] McKinsey US Retail Bank Price Survey, 2001; McKinsey European Mass Affluent Retail Banking research, 2001; McKinsey PFS Survey Asia, 2001.

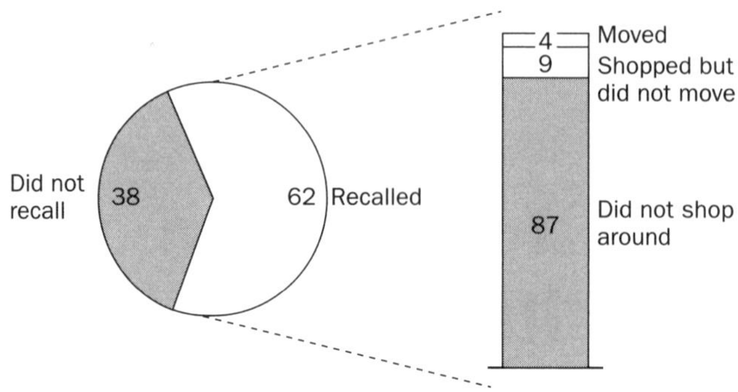

Figure 11.1 Recollection of last checking price change and action taken (percentage of respondents)

Source: McKinsey US Retail Bank Price Survey, 2001

FOUR LEVERS TO OPTIMIZE PRICING

Setting price levels means applying traditional research methods such as conjoint analysis and test markets as systematically as possible and giving pricing the right priority and focus. It is not rocket science; rather it entails institutionalizing pricing processes and skills. Although achieving pricing excellence can be broken down into many tasks, we believe that pricing excellence can be achieved by using the following four levers correctly (Figure 11.2).[3]

Pricing discipline is the simplest of the four to implement; it entails establishing clear rules and processes to ensure that value generated from a defined price structure is not then destroyed by frontline staff offering waivers and discounts. Banks can expect an impact on revenues of 1 to 4 percent by setting these processes firmly in place.

Optimizing the *price structure* across the product portfolio (between and within

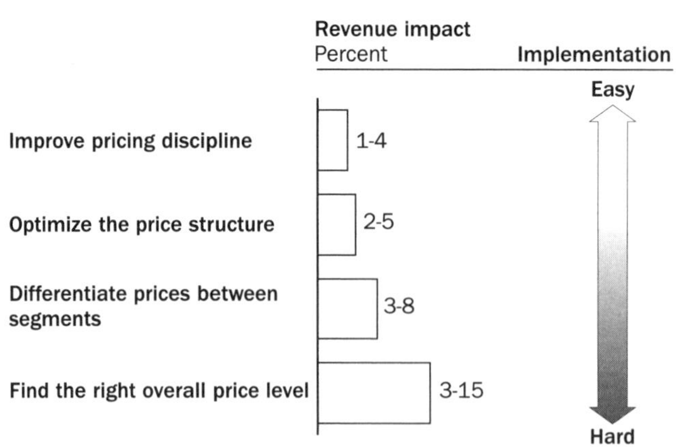

Figure 11.2 Key levers of pricing

Source: McKinsey

[3] Risk-adjusted pricing, a crucial skill for retail banks, is dealt with in Chapter 26.

products) entails understanding how customers shop (i.e., which prices they actually look at in making decisions to buy and which they do not). This can have an impact on revenues of between 2 and 5 percent.

Price differentiation involves tailoring the price structure for individual customer segments, based on their preferences and the alternatives available, in order to maximize the capture of consumer surplus. Price differentiation can have an impact equivalent to 3 to 8 percent of revenues.

Finally, defining the right *overall price level* is the most difficult lever to implement. It includes actions ranging from taking advantage of the price umbrellas offered by close competitors to identifying and occupying specific niches, to taking a price leadership role in the industry. This is closely linked with defining a bank's value proposition and its ability to make the most of its branding, and is therefore more difficult to implement. Although excellent banks can generally command significant price premiums, a typical bank's improvement potential based on the overall price level ranges, in our experience, from 3 to 15 percent, depending on its starting position.

As is apparent, these four are far from mutually exclusive; they can be used independently or in various combinations, depending on each individual bank's capabilities, opportunities, and objectives. All four depend on developing a deep understanding of customer price sensitivities. Furthermore, pricing excellence requires the institutionalization of processes, organization, and skills so that a sustainable competitive advantage can be built.

Improve pricing discipline

Although many banks believe they have established rules to prevent value being destroyed at the local level, analyses demonstrate that for many banks there are surprisingly wide variations in price discipline between branches (e.g., in the number of customers actually paying fees). In our experience, the lowest and highest discounts given by a branch or region of a retail bank can differ by more than a factor of 10. To counteract this, banks need to establish rules, processes, and incentive systems for granting waivers and discounts, as well as installing monitoring systems to ensure their implementation.

There is no set formula for designing discount rules, processes, and incentive systems: they will differ depending on a bank's segment focus, its price level strategy, and the degree of centralization of its market intelligence. For example, when focusing on the mass market segment, banks tend to have centralized market intelligence, which implies that prices are set centrally and the frontline should be given little leeway to grant waivers and fees. In the personal banking segment, on the other hand, banks may wish to provide individual customers with a more tailored solution and greater discretion should be granted to the frontline as they will have a clearer understanding of what an individual customer requires.

The first step any bank aspiring to pricing excellence should take is to understand its current situation, investigating what sort of discounts and waivers are granted, and under what circumstances. Armed with this information, banks can develop sets of rules for individual products and segments depending on their price elasticity. If a bank decides not to prohibit waivers and discounts completely, but to use them actively in its pricing policy in combination with high list prices, it is paramount to define a clear process of granting discounts at all levels of the organization: from the frontline staff, with limited authority to reduce prices, to senior management, who must approve any deep discounts. The incentive systems must be aligned accordingly, ideally discouraging discounting behavior no matter how small the discount might seem!

In the implementation phase, training the frontline is vitally important in order to dispel the belief that discounts are the most important means of capturing new business and retaining current customers. This can be overcome by demonstrating unequivocally that customers are willing to purchase products without these crutches (internal benchmarking, in particular, has proven extremely powerful here), as well as providing support tools to help frontline staff make the best discount decisions. Lastly, tools to track and monitor discounts need to be developed and sales force incentives tied to their use. This type of strategy can have a significant impact on revenues without appreciably increasing customer attrition.

Optimize the price structure across the product portfolio

Excellence in a bank's price structure involves finding a price configuration that strikes the best balance between customer perception and bank profitability. Price structure has two dimensions: first, the prices of different products within the overall offering and, second, the various price elements within an individual product. At the core of both must sit a thorough understanding of the price sensitivity for different products (Figure 11.3).

Banks can use their knowledge of customer price sensitivities to influence consumers' price perceptions. The sensitivity curve for shopped products (those about which customers care) is much steeper than for nonshopped products, leaving a substantially narrower zone of indifference for shopped products. Since shopped products and fees are price-sensitive, they should be priced according to the message they are supposed to communicate to the customers. These products help to establish the customers' perception of a bank's overall price level.

Nonshopped products and fees, however, to which customers are less price-

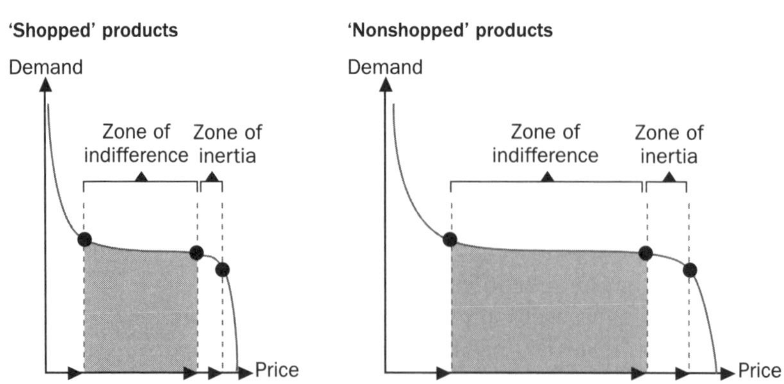

Figure 11.3 Price sensitivities of 'shopped' and 'nonshopped' products

Source: McKinsey

sensitive and which therefore have less influence on their perceptions, should be priced at least at the same level as competitors' prices and possibly higher. Banks rarely modify prices of nonshopped products, so competitors are unlikely to react to another bank's price changes on these products.

Ideally, to maximize profits for both shopped and nonshopped products, banks should strive to increase prices to the point that marks the end of customers' zones of indifference.

In addition, the communication of prices should depend on market transparency and competitive dynamics. In transparent markets, banks will want to signal their value proposition clearly through easy-to-understand pricing. In some instances, players can gain a competitive advantage by introducing a transparent pricing scheme into an otherwise opaque market. Generally, however, the most appropriate strategy is to use tactics such as hidden fees, where competitively shopped fees are extensively advertised and margins are made up through other, less visible fees.

Optimizing a price structure across products is common in other industries, yet it is not often used in banking. A best practice example comes from the world of retail: one leading US retailer carries out extensive market research and competitive benchmarking in order to set prices carefully relative to its main competitors and create the perception that its prices are lower. It sets prices based on an understanding of what product lines customers pay attention to (e.g., stationery and toiletries), which are then priced below their competitors, and what lines they do not (e.g., toys and sporting goods), which are priced at similar levels to competitors. This creates the perception that prices are significantly lower on a storewide basis when, in reality, overall profitability is increased because they are only lower along selected lines.

Banks can use similar strategies to differentiate their products and to optimize the pricing components of the various products. One central European bank is among the few that actively use this strategy. While its basic checking account is offered almost for free, all other components and products are priced at a clear premium. A US bank also demonstrates the impact of price-structure optimization: with a deep understanding of the price sensitivities of different elements of the checking accounts, it was able to generate a short-term impact of 15 percent on profits by simply switching from a high monthly fee to a low monthly fee plus a minimum balance requirement with a comparatively low interest rate.

Excellent banks understand in detail the factors that drive customer choice, which is especially important as price sensitivity differs by market (e.g., per-check charges are clearly more important in countries with high check usage). Some of the most important factors driving customer choice are product value, price transparency, frequency of purchase, and a product's public profile. Customers generally spend much more time shopping around and finding the best offer for high-value purchases, such as mortgages, than low-value purchases, such as foreign currency. Similarly, customers tend to focus their attention on purchases and pricing components that are transparent and frequent: account fees and per-check charges generally have more weight in a purchase decision than less transparent price components, such as interest rates and infrequent price components, such as foreign ATM fees (Figure 11.4).

Typically, consumers are significantly less price conscious regarding product extension decisions than they are for initial purchases. For example, while customers

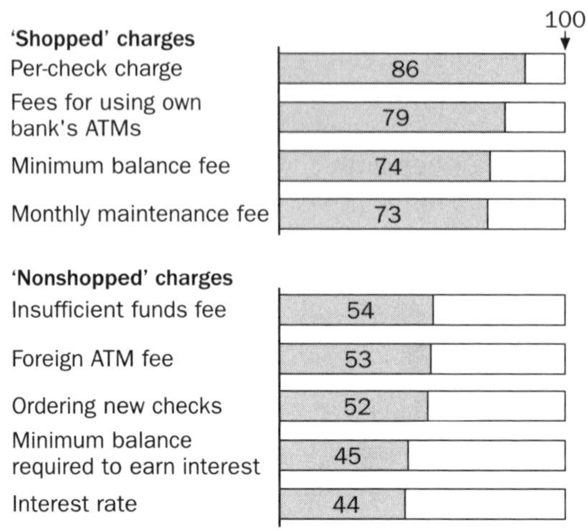

Figure 11.4 Decision criteria for checking-account purchase in the US (percentage of respondents)

Source: McKinsey US Retail Bank Price Survey, 2001

are extremely sensitive about their initial mortgage purchase price, mortgage extensions are among the least price-sensitive bank sales. Moreover, products or fees that are advertised heavily have staying power in consumers' minds—people recall transaction fees for brokerage accounts, for instance, but rarely recall the interest rate applied to funds in the account. Excellent banks reflect these different customer behaviors in their pricing system and update their understanding of customers' shopping behavior continuously through extensive market research.

The final point on price structure relates to cross-subsidization. Retail banking is very much about building a long-term relationship with a customer; however, successful banks, while recognizing a customer's lifetime value, should not use differences in price sensitivity to justify the cross-subsidization of unprofitable products. Given the typically low rates of cross-selling, cost coverage must obviously be considered the lower boundary in any sustainable pricing strategy.

Differentiate prices between segments to capture consumer surplus

Price differentiation involves maximizing the capture of consumer surplus by exploiting a given customer segment's willingness to pay, based on a thorough understanding of the alternatives these particular customers have available and the economic returns it provides to the bank. This implies differentiating the pricing of the overall offering by protecting the assets of price-sensitive, high-value customers and extracting higher margins from less sensitive, lower value customers (Figure 11.5). Although the concept is well known in principle, it is rarely used in a systematic, analytical way.

A systematic approach, used by sophisticated players in other industries, looks like this: the bank conducts thorough market research both to understand customers' willingness to pay for different products and to identify individual segments

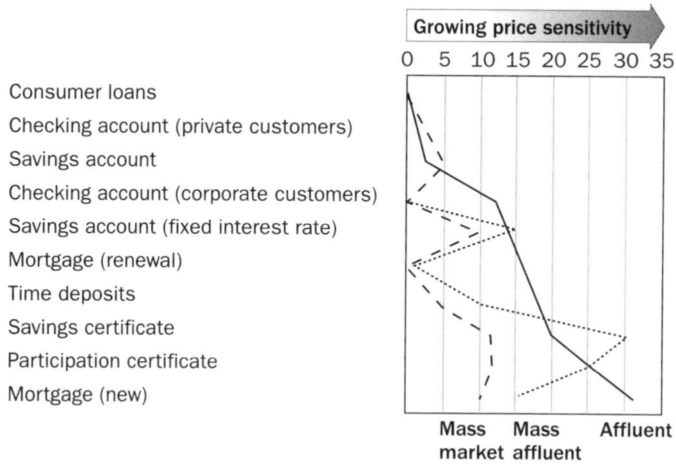

Figure 11.5 Price sensitivities for different customer segments in Germany (estimate of volume decrease [percent] if interest rate terms worsen for the customer by 50 basis points)

Source: McKinsey

based on grouping similar elasticities. Potential dimensions of segmentation could be demographics (e.g., age, income, or regional segmentation). At the same time, the institution performs an internal analysis of the profitability of these segments. Once the segments and their preferences are identified, the bank can modify the prices of existing products or, in market situations where adverse reactions can be expected, create new products to capture this increased potential willingness to pay. Before setting the price for these products, however, the information gathered needs to be cross-checked with the alternatives available to customers in their individual markets. A regional segmentation can be applied to small towns with only one bank, where prices can be set to capitalize on customers' willingness to pay. In more competitive settings, however, prices will probably be lower than the level of willingness to pay identified for a segment (e.g., in large cities with several competitors on every street corner). Although this is a simplified explanation, many banks still set price levels without taking into consideration either of these factors, which often translates into the loss of considerable potential value.

There are notable exceptions: one US retail bank has followed such a scheme successfully. First, it set national prices for each of its products according to the target segments' preferences and willingness to pay, as determined through market research. It then adjusted these national prices based on the competitive scenario of each branch. To implement price changes quickly, each branch submits an annual proposal to a central pricing committee as to the discount—or premium—it should have with respect to the national price, based on its local competitive conditions and the alternatives available to its customers. Thus, as soon as national prices are published, they are automatically adjusted for each branch.

UniCredito also uses exhaustive segmentation: it has repriced and repackaged all its standard products into segment-oriented bundles with various combinations of product features and components, such as checks, debit cards, number of transactions, overdraft facilities, and specific pricing, targeted to subsegments of its clientele.

All banks can use price differentiation tactics to improve profits, although they are particularly applicable to those with a diverse customer base who can then prevent niche players from cherry-picking particular segments. The success of such a scheme depends on a number of factors. First, segment definitions should be made specific and operational and the process as simple as possible so that it can be realistically implemented, since the key limiting factor for a price differentiation strategy is the sales capacity of bank employees. Banks should be aware that overly complex product portfolios can make it difficult for employees to sell the right product to the right customer. Also, a centralized aggregate view is crucial for a more objective analysis of relative differences between markets. Furthermore, banks should set top–down targets up front to serve as a check and ensure that they are meeting their objectives.

Find the right overall price level

Setting the overall price level entails establishing a bank's prices relative to individual competitors or the market as a whole in a manner that fulfills its value proposition and exploits its brand value, thus achieving the highest possible profitability. There are three ways a bank can do this, with increasing degrees of impact: incrementally increase pricing relative to competitors, occupy a new position in the market, or change the industry price structure.

First, opportunities for incremental price increases occur quite frequently—most obviously when the primary reference competitor's price level provides a price umbrella, allowing a lower priced player to raise prices while still remaining competitive. Thus, banks should have a clearly defined price position relative to their reference competitors and systematically scan competitor prices to identify price umbrellas. Although competitor price levels can serve as a proxy gauge for establishing a new price level, a detailed understanding of customers' zones of indifference between price levels allows a bank to set the price within a band delimited by the bank's and the competitor's price. These incremental adjustments demand a very dynamic approach, as the main cost factor (i.e., the market interest rate) changes daily. Consequently, setting price levels for banking products requires a price adjustment rule rather than a static pricing level definition. The execution of this pricing adjustment rule should be supplemented by close monitoring of market changes.

Second, incumbents trying to occupy new niches by adopting strategies such as second brands and new players seeking to capture customers by signaling a distinct value proposition may choose to increase or decrease prices relative to the market to target specific customers or occupy a new position in the market. A bank that targets niche markets through price increases needs to communicate its value proposition clearly and set up the organization and processes to allow it to deliver upon its promises. Banks that cut prices in order to enter market niches or capture clients or volume need to be aware that attacker strategies can be extremely hazardous, particularly for incumbents. Moreover, these banks must ensure that they capture enough business to offset the price cut—always taking into account possible competitor reactions. They also need to establish beforehand a clear strategy to cross-sell to new customers and retain them and what the timing will be of their eventual increase in prices back to sustainable levels.

Lastly, large players may identify an opportunity to change the industry's price structure by playing a price leadership role in a structurally unprofitable industry or—in some rare instances—by decreasing prices to take advantage of structural inefficiencies in the market or their lower cost structure. Becoming a price leader means having a clear understanding of competitors' cost structures and motives to ensure that they follow the lead and raise overall prices. Deutsche Bank, for example, changed its private banking pricing model from a transaction-based approach to a mainly asset-based model, thus aiming to offset the cost of offering its customers high-quality advice. Another example is the German mutual funds market, where almost all players reacted to decreasing profitability in 2001 by raising margins, initiated by one of the strong price leaders.

To implement a price decrease leadership strategy successfully, banks need to be aware of changing market dynamics and scan the horizon for opportunities, such as the deregulation of the industry or of a particular product. Price leadership strategies, whether moving prices up or down, are possible only rarely as they require a specific set of circumstances, and only large banks with enough clout to be able to shape the industry can carry them through. However, the benefits can be ample, so banks should remain vigilant for opportunities.

Whatever the situation, banks need to consider carefully not only their actual price level but also the perceived one. As mentioned, customers' perception of a bank's overall price level is based on the price of very few products and services—usually well advertised. An inadequate communication of prices, particularly when compared with competitors, may result in a completely wasted effort.

Although overall price adjustment is clearly the most difficult area to get right, it is also potentially the one with the greatest impact. It is clearly worth making a significant effort to get price-positioning right as the overall price level lays the foundation for the other pricing levers. Thus, once the overall price level is determined, all other pricing levers must be reconsidered to ensure they are in line.

INSTITUTIONALIZING PRICING EXCELLENCE

Pricing is not a question of intuition. It requires a rigorous approach and processes, even for issues that may seem relatively straightforward. Furthermore, it requires the right organizational structure and set of skills to support it. The markedly different organizational attention that pricing receives in other industries compared with retail banking is astonishing. In the retail goods sector, for example, one UK supermarket chain has institutionalized competitive monitoring and price adjustments as one of its regular key processes. Weekly competitor price checks are carried out on over 3000 lines, and the information acquired is condensed and promptly summarized for management. Decisions are then taken rapidly and price changes can be implemented nationwide within 24 hours.

The airline industry is also well known for its pricing capabilities, especially its price segmentation skills whereby customers can pay thousands of dollars or almost nothing for the same seat. These capabilities, which are crucial for airlines' success, do not come cheaply, however. One mid-sized European airline, for example, has its own pricing department of 250 full-time employees! The scope of pricing efforts at other airlines is similar.

As a further example, let us examine consumer goods producers—renowned for their outstanding market research capabilities. Procter & Gamble, for instance, carries out extensive national and local market research to understand the positioning of each brand in the market before negotiating price contracts with its retailers. Its continual commitment to improving pricing practices allows such companies to come closer to selling the right product to the right customer at the right price, anytime, anywhere.

For a retail bank, institutionalizing pricing excellence as defined by the four pricing levers has three aspects: an analytically sound approach; a clearly defined and continuous process rather than a one-time effort; and appropriate organizational capabilities.

Build a sound approach

First, the bank needs to understand customer price sensitivity; specifically customers' zones of indifference, zones of inertia, and the corresponding breakpoints. This may sound quite straightforward, but it is actually the most difficult single task in developing a pricing strategy. Only by using a broad range of analytic tools, such as statistical customer decision analysis, analysis of historical price change case studies, and extensive market research (particularly advanced forms of conjoint analysis and frontline expert interviews), can a bank attain a thorough understanding of price elasticity. Sensitivity also shifts dramatically with different market environments and when consumer expectations and requirements change. Perspectives on elasticity need to be reshaped whenever markets undergo major adjustments, such as the entry of a new player.

The most powerful way of understanding true price sensitivities is by institutionalizing price-testing processes. No other research method delivers such reliable information on consumer reactions, making limited-scope test-marketing the key to excellence in pricing. Direct Line in the UK, for example, uses price-testing continuously to test alternative prices against its current price so it can measure how different price levels affect the volume sold. This enables it to determine at what price level revenues are maximized (Figure 11.6).

Second, players must endeavor to understand the expected impact on both new business and the existing business portfolio, based on price sensitivity assessments. UK banks ran into severe trouble by neglecting this issue when they reduced new mortgage rates without considering the impact of this on their existing portfolio. In the end, banks were obliged by the courts to reduce rates for existing mortgages too, with a severe impact on their overall profitability. Additionally, the internal impact analysis considers the indirect impact of a pricing move on the bank's value proposition, as well as the option value of a strategic price move.

Third, competitive reactions to different price structures and levels should be simulated. Neglecting competitors' reactions is one of the most frequent causes of flawed pricing decisions: price cuts look much better on paper if similar moves from

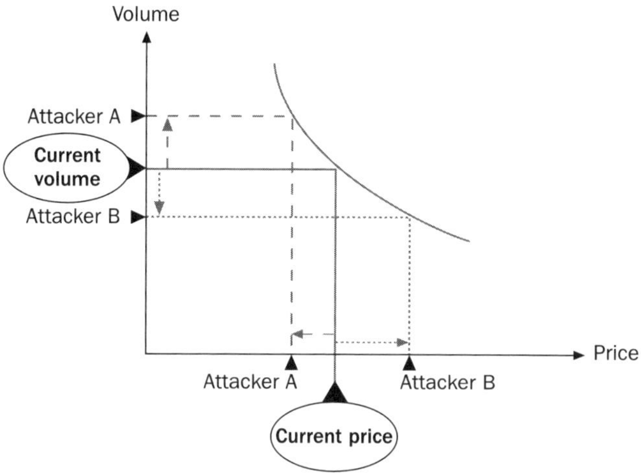

Figure 11.6 Price-testing process to measure price elasticity

Source: McKinsey

competitors are not factored in; price increases tend to look much worse, as competitors follow such moves upward more than is assumed. The assessment of competitive reaction is largely built on game theory, particularly in an oligopolistic industry setting that requires a solid understanding of competitors' cost positions and strategic plans. By simulating alternative moves, banks can assess best and worst case scenarios.

Introduce support processes

In addition to implementing this analytic toolbox, excellent retail banks have set up processes that ensure continuous and proactive pricing. To this end, banks need to search continuously for pricing improvement opportunities by monitoring, for example, product profitability, competitors' pricing behavior in relevant markets, internal discount behavior, and external changes/inconsistencies. Predefined triggers (e.g., a competitor launches a new product) then set off pricing reviews to ensure that pricing remains optimized at all times.

Furthermore, banks must perform regular, scheduled reviews of pricing assessments. The results of these need to be channeled into an efficient decision-making process. Therefore, banking organizations must assign clear responsibilities for decisions and put in place an efficient and effective implementation mechanism. This requires adequate system capabilities. Beyond that, good internal communication processes and internal processes in general are needed to ensure implementation discipline. Lastly, the bank must set up systematic impact-monitoring and codify the lessons learned.

Establish the right organizational structure and build pricing skills

Once the analytical approach and processes are defined, the bank must ensure that the necessary organizational capabilities are in place. Although each bank needs to define the optimal structure based on its individual needs and circumstances, pricing responsibilities must be clearly defined in any case. There are two basic organizational options: one is a centralized pricing department; the other consists of pricing specialists dispersed by product or by sales channel unit. Although there is no one-size-fits-all approach, our analysis of excellence in pricing suggests that in all excellent organizations there is at least a minimum degree of centralization. This is to enable some degree of coordination throughout channels and products (e.g., payment products and investment products), build economies of scale (e.g., market research), and monitor pricing discipline.

A further reason for centralizing pricing skills is the scarceness of pricing expertise, particularly in the banking industry. For most banks, it is neither apt nor feasible to build pricing departments, which would have to be of a size somewhere between those of airlines and retail chains. Banks must ensure that the limited number of pricing experts they employ have truly excellent pricing skills that are used efficiently. Banks need to combine in-house experience in the pricing of banking products with best practice pricing skills from other industries, and the existing pricing expertise must be advanced by access to the latest thinking on pricing. Lastly, the task must represent such a challenge for pricing management that talent retention does not become an issue. To this end, pricing managers must have decision-making clout together with appropriate compensation schemes and appealing career paths.

Improving pricing practices is not only a major challenge for retail banks today but can also be seen as a significant opportunity. Achieving pricing excellence must be approached methodically and thoroughly. Only the banks that manage to apply the four key levers correctly and that develop the necessary toolkit, processes, and skills to ensure sustainability will successfully rise to the pricing challenge and reap the rewards.

12

Marketing Spend Effectiveness: Getting the Best from Your Brand

Vittoria Varianini, Rita D'Uva[1]

Brands should be a company's most significant intangible asset: companies with strong brands consistently earn 2 to 5 percentage points more in total returns to shareholders than their industry counterparts.[2] Part of this higher return is due to better current performance; but much of it can be explained by the greater expectations of future performance as the brand is deployed into new channels, regions, customer segments and businesses, and its strength today naturally evolves into its strength tomorrow.

For too long, banks have managed with relatively weak brands, but the industry is changing, and to prosper in today's and tomorrow's challenging environment, retail banks must build stronger brands by dramatically improving the impact of their marketing spend.

UNDERSTANDING BRANDING

Brands are an important asset because they create value for the customer and, therefore, for the bank, both in terms of real economic returns today and by creating a platform for future opportunities in existing or new markets.

For the customer, brands play a key role in influencing purchase decisions in several ways. First, they simplify decision-making by enabling increasingly sophisticated, but busy consumers to sift through a proliferation of products, services, and information sources. A European survey of affluent customers revealed that 63 percent felt that the brand was more important than the product when it came to making their investment decisions.[3] Brands also help reduce risk, as they minimize

[1] The authors would like to express their gratitude for the contributions of McKinsey's Marketing Practice and of Reinhold Leichtfuss.

[2] David Court, Mark Leiter, and Mark Loch, Brand leverage. *McKinsey Quarterly*, No. 2, 1999.

[3] McKinsey European Affluent Survey, 1999.

uncertainty for customers who choose to rely on well-known and established product- or service-providers. Furthermore, brands can achieve commitment by creating community membership and empathy in consumers, often providing intangible benefits that strengthen the relationship with the product or service.

This value for the customers means that retail banks with stronger brands benefit from easier customer acquisition, superior customer loyalty, and better cross-selling ratios, as well as having the ability to charge a premium on their services. An example of the flow of capital into mutual funds shows this clearly: within US funds of the same type, with the same Morningstar rating and the same annualized returns for the last three years, those with strong brands had average net inflows of US$262m compared with net outflows of US$86m for those with weak brands.[4] It also means that retail banks with stronger brands are more successful in extending into new products, segments, channels, and geographies. When combined, all this translates into higher returns to shareholders.

However, despite the obvious benefits of having a strong brand, retail banks tend to have weaker brands than those in some other industries as a result of some unique brand-building challenges. A key characteristic of retail banking is that although its products and services are of high importance to customers, they tend to be of low interest and have a low emotional content, especially relative to other industries. This translates into high levels of inertia and procrastination, which is not the same thing as loyalty.

A study on brand health across a number of industries in the US aimed to understand the strengths and weaknesses of different brands in more detail.[5] Banks on average performed worse than other industries: when customers were asked to rate brands on various elements from 1 (worst) to 5 (best), bank brands scored between 2.5 and 3, whereas other consumer industries scored between 3 and 4. The banks in the survey performed badly in several areas based on service and experience (Figure 12.1). Very few bank brands had elements that served to differentiate them. Those differentiators that did exist were in areas concerning reliability.

Looking at the world's strongest brands irrespective of industry, it is rapidly apparent how few belong to financial institutions. Only Citibank and American Express appear, for example, in branding consultancy Interbrand's 2002 ranking of the top 100 global brands.[6] This is partly because banking is predominantly a domestic business, but the problems go much deeper than mere geography.

More than just a name

At its heart, a brand is not a name, but a relationship between customers and the products and services that a company provides. Building a winning brand is therefore fundamentally about building relationships that strengthen loyalty and create both a protected earnings stream and a perceived value for which customers are prepared to pay a premium, even for commodity products.

[4] Morningstar (a global investment research firm), McKinsey analysis.

[5] McKinsey US Brand Health, 2000.

[6] 'The 100 top brands.' *Business Week*, August 5, 2002.

Low → High

- Overall quality
- Flexible
- Reasonable fees and rates
- Will not let you down if there is a problem
- Strong relationship with customers
- Recommended by friends
- Caring; fun
- Premium priced
- Membership rewards program

- Good value
- Easy to do business with
- Good and consistent service
- Resolves problems
- Quality advice
- Delivers what it promises
- Good investment services
- Dominant brand
- Innovative
- Convenient hours
- Convenient branch locations
- Prestigious
- Classic

- Trustworthy
- Reliable
- Good phone-banking capabilities
- Up-to-date with trends
- Value-added/wide range of services
- Clear, accurate statements
- Serve customers in a timely manner
- Approachable
- Wide range of products/ offerings/content
- Global presence
- Convenient ATM locations
- Respected
- A leader

Figure 12.1 Average US bank-brand performance

Source: McKinsey US Brand Health Survey, 2000

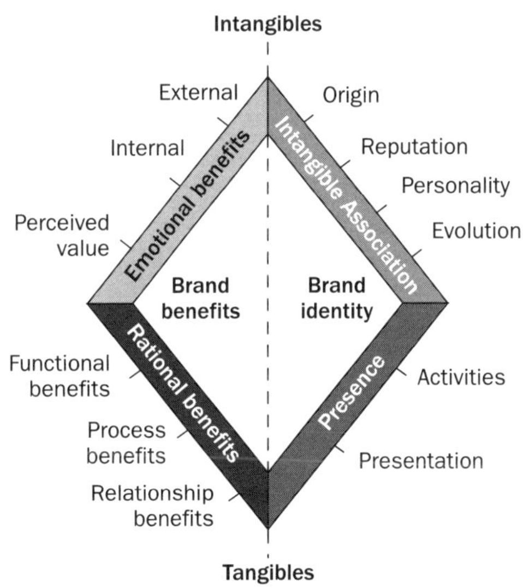

Figure 12.2 Brand equity elements

Source: McKinsey

A brand is characterized by its benefits and its identity. Both have tangible and intangible elements (Figure 12.2).

Brand benefits. Rational benefits are those that customers gain from the particular attributes of the product or service-offering. If a bank wants to understand how a brand works, it is not enough to list the attributes; it needs to uncover what the benefits behind them really are. There are functional benefits, which include the product range, performance, price level, and reliability; process benefits, which accrue from ease of access to product and services, transactional convenience and information delivery; and relationship benefits, which deepen customer commitment, such as getting better advice because the bank understands the customer or being rewarded for loyalty.

Emotional benefits revolve around how the brand makes the customer feel and are critical in driving loyalty and commitment. These emotional benefits are: external—what the brand communicates about the customer; internal—how the brand makes the customer feel; and the perceived value, which is the subjective interpretation of absolute and relative value between a brand's benefits and price. Abraham Maslow's classic concept of the 'hierarchy of needs' lays out a useful framework for this as it identifies different levels of emotional needs, from the need for security and safety (lower order) to self-esteem and self-actualization (higher order).[7]

Brand identity. This is the imagery and associations that are connected with the brand; in other words who and what the brand is. Intangible associations are driven by the brand's perceived or actual origin, the brand's perceived reputation, by the key personality and character traits associated with a brand, and by the evolution of the brand over time. Intangible associations can be created by past or present advertising, product endorsement, or by people associated with the brand, as well as by a host of other possible marketing activities.

Swiss private banks as a collective group provide an interesting example. They generally draw on their 'Swissness' with connotations of being reserved, private, and trustworthy, which are the key attributes their core clients expect and want. Many use classical iconography to reinforce their heritage and develop traits such as longevity and quality. But of course they also want to evolve, and therefore adapt their branding to new channels, such as the Internet. Only a few years ago, the online channel would have been perceived by many customers as not suitably secure, whereas now the same class of private bank customers expect online services as part of the bank's offering.

The presence of a brand's identity is formed by the company's actions (its communication and its activities, including promotions and alliances), as well as the presentation (the look, feel, tone, and iconography of the brand).

Habits of highly effective brands

Strong brands build emotional bonds with customers and tend to share a number of habits that help foster this bond.

First, they are able to distill their most salient attributes into a simple focused thought that clearly positions the brand to customers. Sportswear manufacturer Nike's 'Just do it' slogan is a good example. Second, they go to considerable lengths to ensure that the brand is relevant to the specific needs of clearly segmented target customers. Third, they synthesize the brand benefits and identity into a unique and compelling value proposition that distinguishes them clearly from their competitors. Fourth, they make sure they do what they say they will do—and crucially they do not make promises until they know they can deliver. Fifth, they deliver a

[7] Abraham Harold Maslow, Robert Frager, and James Fadiman, *Motivation and Personality*. Addison-Wesley, 3rd edn, 1987.

consistent customer experience across all channels and touchpoints. Sixth, they ensure that the benefits and communication are aligned with the brand's heritage. Finally, they ensure that the brand-positioning is sustainable and remains compelling over time.

A NEW APPROACH TO MARKETING SPEND EFFECTIVENESS

Boosting marketing spend effectiveness is critical in building stronger brands. It also has a positive effect on the bottom line, as it means the same impact can be achieved at a lower cost. Very few banks are actually able to demonstrate the impact of their marketing spend, yet there are companies that have made marketing effectiveness a source of competitive advantage while their peers have stalled amid clutter and rising costs.

In a period of earnings pressures, marketing dollars can be the first to be cut; but if this is done across the board then it could jeopardize the branding strategy and be disastrous for long-term growth. It is therefore vital to understand how to spend the right amount of money at the right touchpoints in the most effective and efficient manner.

The objective for any retail bank—regardless of the economic climate—is to improve its brand's performance along the consumer purchase cycle, or what we call the 'purchase funnel'. This moves from awareness to consideration to experience/selection to loyalty (Figure 12.3).

Typically, a bank will have a bottleneck at one or more of the funnel stages, as it struggles to move customers through to the next stage. It is at these bottlenecks that banks should focus both their spending and their messages; otherwise they risk wasting the marketing budget and diluting the impact of their brand. Naturally, different products or segments within a bank will have different bottlenecks. It is important to ensure that a value-based decision is made on where resources should best be allocated, which in turn needs an understanding of what creates the bottlenecks.

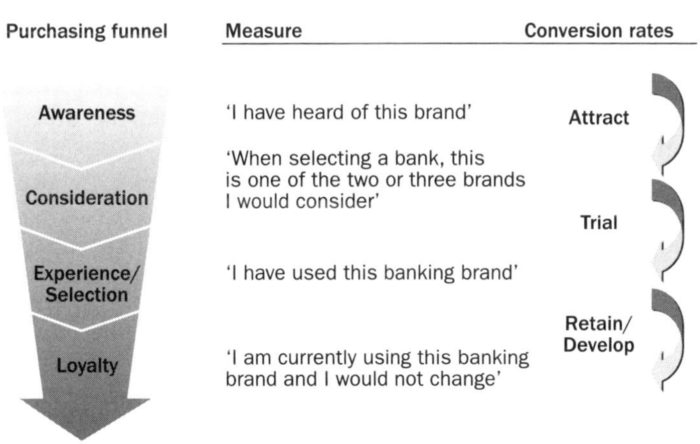

Figure 12.3 The customer purchasing funnel

Source: McKinsey

Successful marketers spend smarter and build stronger brands faster, cheaper, and more effectively than their rivals. The impact of the more effective and efficient management of marketing spend is very significant. First, it can reduce marketing costs (on average by 10 to 30 percent) without having a negative impact on revenues. Second, and most importantly, it can reallocate 30 to 50 percent of spend to activities that will have a greater impact. This, especially when combined with more effective messages, can lead to an 8 to 10 percent increase in revenues, coming from customer acquisition, increased loyalty, and greater profitability of existing customers.

Focus on the bottlenecks

Precise bottlenecks vary from situation to situation and depend on the target segment and life stage of the brand, but they can appear at any stage of the purchase funnel. In general, new brands will need to overcome barriers to awareness, while established brands may need to concentrate on encouraging experience/selection or building retention. Yet, if we look at how retail banks spend in practice we see that, on average, very significant investments are made to target awareness even though this is often not a priority (see Box 12.1).

Awareness. Media clutter is often a major bottleneck, particularly for new entrants. It is compounded by insufficient intensity or creative appeal in marketing communications. Breakthroughs can sometimes be achieved with sheer scale—simply outspend the competition. However, more cost-effective awareness can be achieved with creativity, such as innovative public relations and media events that deliver a high impact per marketing dollar spent.

Banks might argue that they already have high brand awareness levels, and it is true that major banks achieve levels above 90 percent. However, this may just be an awareness of the brand name rather than its distinctive proposition. Market research can usually determine this.

Consideration. When customers reach the consideration stage, they generally have two or three brands from which they select. To enter that small set of banks, the challenge is to make the brand relevant. McKinsey research shows that retail banks have significant opportunities to improve conversion rates from awareness to consideration, while some other financial service sectors are already more successful.[8] Conversion rates for retail banking brands range on average from 34 percent in the US to 39 percent in Germany. Credit card businesses, on the other hand, have conversion rates of 50 to 60 percent (Figure 12.4).

A brand may not be seen as relevant or distinct to the target segment because of real or perceived gaps in its emotional or rational benefits, or because of the brand's communication or delivery of these benefits. By gaining a full understanding of the target market, banks should be able to improve this.

Experience/Selection. Once the bank has been considered, it has to be distinctive enough to become the customer's choice. One way to clear the bottleneck from consideration to selection is to offer a substantial incentive. Retail banking has serious problems here as it suffers from a high level of customer inertia. E*Trade offered 25 free trades in an attempt to move customers from consideration to

[8] McKinsey US Brand Health Survey, 2000.

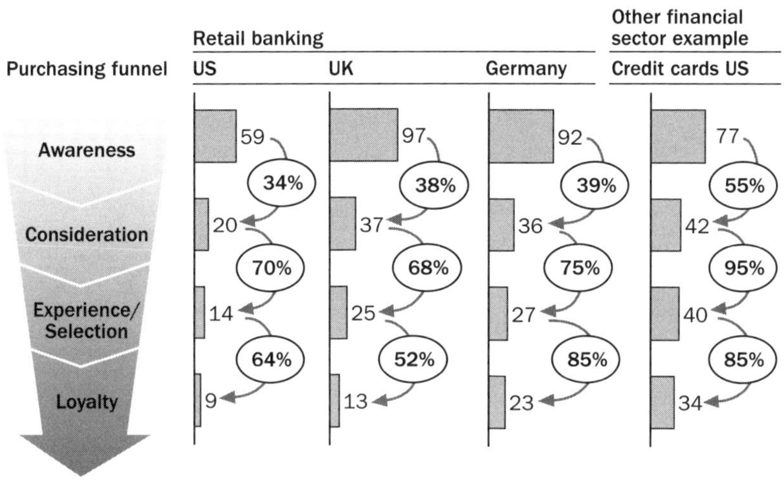

Figure 12.4 Conversion rates for retail banks vs. credit card companies (selected examples, percent)

Source: McKinsey US Brand Health Survey, 2000

experience. More sophisticated promotions can have multiple effects. In 1999, Charles Schwab—which makes substantial charitable donations—gave all commissions from online retail equity orders placed on Mother's Day to a breast cancer foundation and on Father's Day it donated the money to a prostate cancer charity. As well as a very targeted incentive to use its services, this also reinforced the broker's image as a concerned corporate citizen.

Loyalty. Cementing loyalty is probably the most critical factor driving brand profitability for retail banks. Inspiring loyalty requires offering customers an experience that reinforces their reasons for choosing that bank and encourages them to purchase more products and services. This means creating an emotional affinity between the brand and the consumer. Again, McKinsey's brand health research of retail banking brands shows very significant gaps between different players. In the US overall, 64 percent of people who were at some time customers of a bank were still customers. For the bank that scored highest, Wells Fargo, that figure is 85 percent. Wells Fargo is considered distinctive in resolving problems when they arise and in delivering a consistent service. At the other end of the scale, the worst bank manages just 50 percent. In retail banking, loyalty bottlenecks have left many struggling.

One bank faced a flat-to-declining market share among both its affluent and mass market segments—accompanied by a fall in customers' recognition of the bank's key attributes, such as being trustworthy. On digging deeper, it found sharp declines in customer satisfaction scores, driven by two factors. First, customers were demanding higher levels of service in banking—thanks to competitors' advertising and word of mouth—but they were increasingly disappointed by their actual experiences. There were mistakes on statements, high service fees, branch closures, etc. Second—and worse as far as customers are concerned—was the perceived lack of responsiveness on the part of the bank to problems that did arise. This was at the heart of customer defections, and, as negative word of mouth lowered consideration, new customer acquisitions fell off. The bank responded by reallocating nearly all of its marketing budget from advertising and promotion toward improving the customer experience. For example, it launched a specific problem resolution effort and overhauled its training and incentives for bank employees to improve service.

Box 12.1

Focus on bottlenecks: tips to get started

- Map how customers move through the purchase funnel.
- Measure indicators, drivers, and results at each stage of the purchase funnel.
- Ensure metrics and expectations are appropriate for the life stage of the brand and target segment.
- Look for performance changes over time as well as gaps vs. competitors.
- Understand root causes for bottlenecks.

Use the right vehicles to remove bottlenecks

Equipped with an informed view of a brand's bottlenecks, retail banks can then build programs that use the most appropriate set of presence-building vehicles and tactics to remove the bottlenecks. It is too easy to rerun last year's program or to fall into 'group think' and imitate competitors. There is no reason for one bank to have a near identical marketing spend to another, when they are each likely to be experiencing different bottlenecks and, even more importantly, unique root causes for them (see Box 12.2).

Given the increase in the number of different touchpoints, the importance of customer experience, the power of word of mouth, and other brand dynamics, marketers today have an unprecedented range of options for addressing bottlenecks. The key to building presence is to select the right vehicles at the right time to address specific bottlenecks. So, while television and radio advertising can be effective in building awareness, they are far less effective in driving selection or loyalty (Figure 12.5). For many retail banks, using the right vehicles to address key bottlenecks represents a significant opportunity, especially in terms of driving trial and loyalty which, as we have seen, is often a higher priority than generating awareness.

There are no limits to the creativity that can be brought to the challenge of developing new marketing tactics. In fact, the more innovative and fresh the approach, the more likely it is to break through the noise and achieve the desired objectives—as long as it actually addresses the bottlenecks. US insurance company State Farm addressed awareness and consideration bottlenecks head on by garnering free publicity and sparking positive word of mouth through its 'Dangerous Intersections' program. The company used its proprietary databases to supply the media with a list of the most dangerous intersections in several major cities. The media turned it into a big story, crediting the insurer. Citizens wrote to local authorities and politicians demanding that something be done, and, as a result, the insurer strengthened its image with millions of consumers as a concerned and caring institution and delivered real benefits, in the form of information, at a fraction of the cost of a major media campaign.

As the portfolio of brand-building vehicles grows, so does the challenge of main-

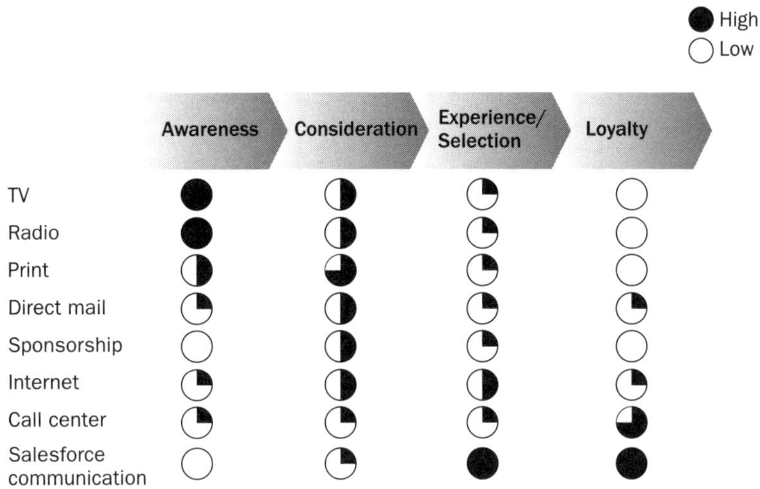

Figure 12.5 'Rules of thumb' for effectiveness and efficiency of vehicles

Source: McKinsey

taining a consistent customer experience wherever the customer comes into contact with the brand—be it through a television advert or face to face in a branch. For retail banks this is a very significant hurdle, as customer experience remains the single most important driver of conversion, but it is also the most difficult to tackle as it involves so many people and different organizational areas.

Progressive Insurance is obsessed with superior delivery at two important trigger points: the time when customers choose the insurance product and the time of an accident. At the time of product selection, being the 'reliable, trusted friend' of its customers has meant that Progressive even uses its multiple sales channels to facilitate price comparisons with key competitors. Progressive is convinced that the short-term tactical loss of revenue due to price comparison-shopping is more than offset by the long-term strategic gain in market share. Customers show their appreciation for the Progressive value proposition through greater conversion and higher loyalty. At the time of an accident, Progressive differentiates itself from the competition through responsiveness and a visible demonstration of caring. Not only does Progressive maintain a round-the-clock immediate response call center, but its claims representatives often travel to the site of an accident, sometimes bringing checks with them, so that customers can immediately get on with their lives. All these elements combined reinforce Progressive's brand image of being on the side of the customer.[9]

Once a bank has selected the most appropriate vehicles, the next breakthrough in marketing effectiveness comes when all the tools work together. Each part of the marketing program (advertising, sales activities, promotions, call centers, etc.) should contribute to a common goal. When this is done well, the branding process can assume a life of its own, creating a virtuous cycle of brand-building. These brand-building dynamics create a value greater than the sum of their parts. Looking at the combined impact of advertising and call center activities, for

[9] *The Power of Brand Delivery*, McKinsey Marketing Practice, 2001.

example, suggests that the combination of these activities drives cross-selling far in excess of the total gain achieved by advertising and call center activities conducted independently.

Box 12.2

Using the right vehicles: tips to get started

- Question old assumptions about spending mix.
- Evaluate the performance of existing vehicles against each stage of the purchase funnel.
- Experiment with new tools and consider changing how existing ones are used.
- Understand how to exploit fully all customer touchpoints in delivering desired messages.
- Ensure that vehicles are consistent with the desired image of the brand.
- Map relationships between vehicles, consumer reactions, and brand outcomes.

Invest smartly and have a clear message to accelerate brand-building

Having selected the right marketing vehicles, banks should ensure that spending levels are above the minimum level needed for critical mass and below the point of diminishing returns. They also need to make sure that the message and creative execution have the desired impact (Box 12.3).

An S-curve effect is both measurable and manageable, with a low impact from spending until a critical mass level is reached, followed by a rapid growth in impact from higher spending, followed by diminishing returns (Figure 12.6).

There are many players who are not even on the curve thanks to a very poor message impact. It does not matter how creative the execution is—if the message is not geared to clearing the bank's specific bottlenecks then the impact will be minimal.

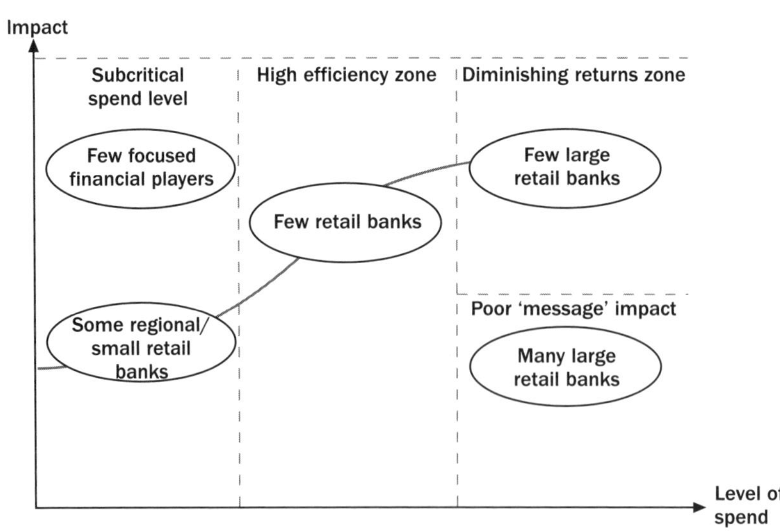

Figure 12.6 Efficiency of marketing spend in retail banks

Source: McKinsey

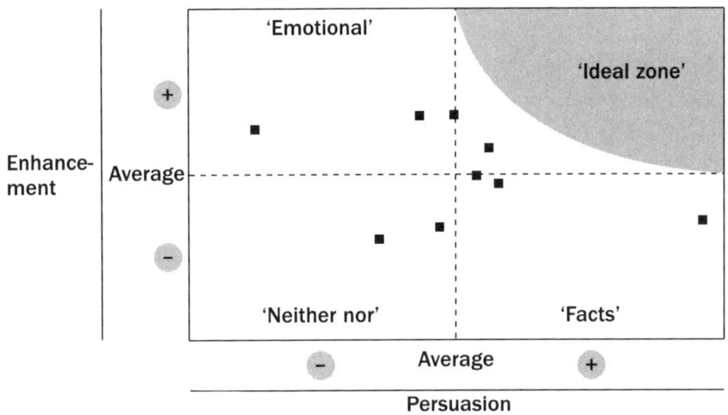

Figure 12.7 Impact of television advertising of German financial institutions

Source: McKinsey

In 2001/02, we conducted customer surveys to assess the impact of television advertising in German financial services. The effects of commercials were measured both quantitatively and qualitatively on criteria such as the appeal of the advert's story, the picture the consumer received of the institution, and the extent to which customers understood the explanation of benefits. The criteria were grouped into emotional and factual criteria. The results showed that no provider reached top scores in both dimensions (Figure 12.7). As a matter of fact, only one provider reached the upper right-hand quadrant. Many performed well in one dimension, but had a weaker result in the other.

The study also showed that although customers thought some adverts were creative and fun, these had a very limited impact when it actually came to enhancing the bank's image or getting the customers to consider using the bank. Other banks rated lower on their creative appeal, but had a much higher consideration score and therefore the impact was greater.

Adverts should always be tested against a set of criteria that are specific to the task at hand. McKinsey's brand health research in the US measured which elements actually drive consideration for retail banking customers. The study measured both the expressed and the derived importance of attributes.[10] The results show that the majority of the most important attributes were service-related: 'delivers what it promises', 'good customer service', 'provides good value', 'I can expect consistent service', and 'will not let you down if there is a problem'.

[10] Derived importance comes from an aggregated correlation between each individual's perception of brand and his or her likelihood to consider it in the future. Respondents were asked to define their experience of the brand, rate it against 35 emotional and rational attributes, and rate the likelihood to consider the brand in the future assuming they held no financial products at the time. The resulting correlation produces a set of attributes that appear to tie in closely with the likelihood of considering a brand.

Box 12.3

Investing smartly and aligning message: tips to get started

- Do not choose variables too far removed from the marketing activity. For example, link advertising to changes in consumer attitudes and not directly to sales.
- Create a library of rules of thumb regarding the zone of effectiveness for each major vehicle.
- Track internal and competitor data over time for the most important vehicles, as changes in competitor spending and behavior will shift effective zones over time, and thus the effective spending zone will also change.
- Ensure that message and creative execution are what is required to remove bottlenecks.
- Ensure that what you say is aligned to what you do; do not communicate what you cannot deliver.

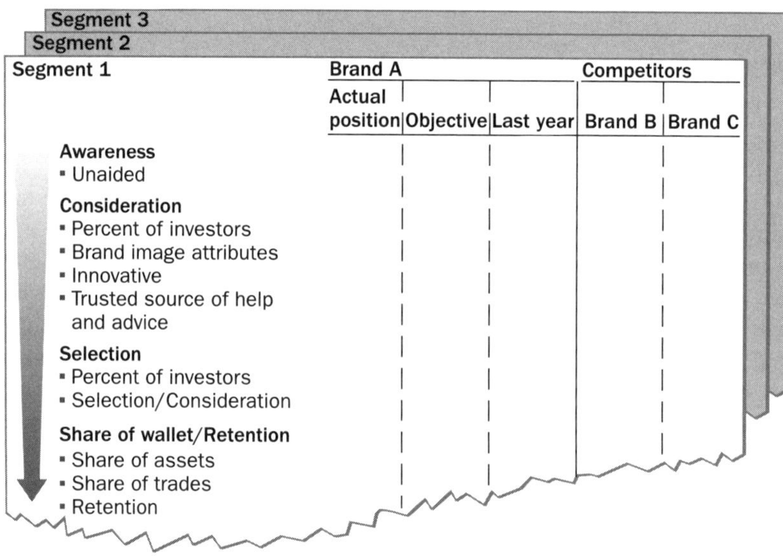

Figure 12.8 Scorecard to track brand progress

Source: McKinsey

Keep score and fine-tune

Once the marketing program has been redefined, progress should be tracked with a scorecard to ensure continuous development and refinement, and responsibilities for acting on early warnings of poor brand health should be clarified. With the pace of change in today's marketplace, a brand scorecard can monitor program results and, most importantly, help marketers adjust course when necessary. Relying on instinct or broad outcome measures can lead to the wrong moves. An effective brand scorecard tracks the most important metrics along the purchasing funnel and reports changes as frequently as monthly. Ideally, scorecards should be developed for each target segment with the metrics developed from the key bottlenecks along the funnel (Figure 12.8). The actual performance of the brand should then be tracked against objectives, the previous year's results, and the competition.

Only through a rigorous application of the lessons learned from the scorecard will the branding strategy truly develop in the right direction.

Every retail bank has a brand, and every bank has a marketing budget. But few banks understand how their brand works and how their marketing budget can best be allocated in order to maximize the brand's impact. Those banks that have already grasped this problem have put themselves several steps ahead of the rest, but with a combination of discipline, rigorous analysis, and a dash or two of creativity, other banks can also split out from the mass and start to catch the customer's eye—and wallet!

13

Sales Power: Maximum Effort and Maximum Reward

Reinhold Leichtfuss, Heinrich-Stefan Rolvering, Christian Schramm

Within marketing and sales, the presence of a strong sales culture has been the strongest differentiator between the outperforming banks and the others. It is, together with pricing, the most powerful way to grow revenue.

But how many bank leaders can put their hands on their hearts and say exactly how big their sales capacity is or to what extent sales effectiveness is accurately measured? Truly professional sales power management is still missing in 90 percent of all banks. For a long time, banks have followed the relationship–sales approach on the basis that once a customer relationship is established, cross-selling of further products will be easy. In reality, however, cross-selling requires continuous, relentless efforts, and a lot of banks have a high percentage of single-product customers.

Sales power is the product of sales capacity (number of salespeople and their share of time allocated to selling) and sales effectiveness (Figure 13.1). Sales effectiveness is the result of several factors: the number and quality of customer contacts, the closure rates, the volume per sale, and finally the mix of products and prices, which strongly influences profitability.

Very few banks manage all these factors systematically. Some certainly tackle several of the issues, but lack a vision of the whole picture and, as a result, miss out on valuable benefits. However, the best-performing banks achieve higher revenues per employee as well as higher cross-selling ratios than their national peers. They do so by applying the right mix of activities and by systematically increasing their sales power.

OPTIMIZE SALES CAPACITY

The task starts with simply identifying the salespeople, understanding their individual contribution, and learning how to free more capacity of the best performers. Once this is done, banks should then think about whether they have enough sales staff and whether each person is spending enough time selling.

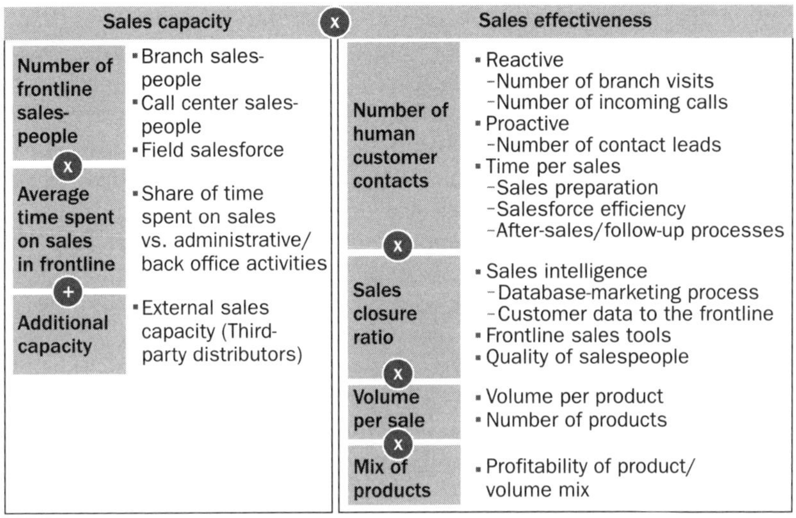

Figure 13.1 Formula for calculating sales power

Source: McKinsey

Install ideal number of salespeople

Banks, as a rule, do not have enough strong salespeople. Indeed, some still have more staff sitting in the back office than facing customers. This is not altogether surprising as many banks are still somewhere on the transition path from a payments and credit provider to a sales and service-driven organization.

The best practice banks have up to three-quarters of their total personnel working in sales and service functions (Figure 13.2). Reaching such levels is not easy, as it clearly does not make sense just to transfer people straight from the back office to the sales frontline where a completely different set of skills and personality traits are

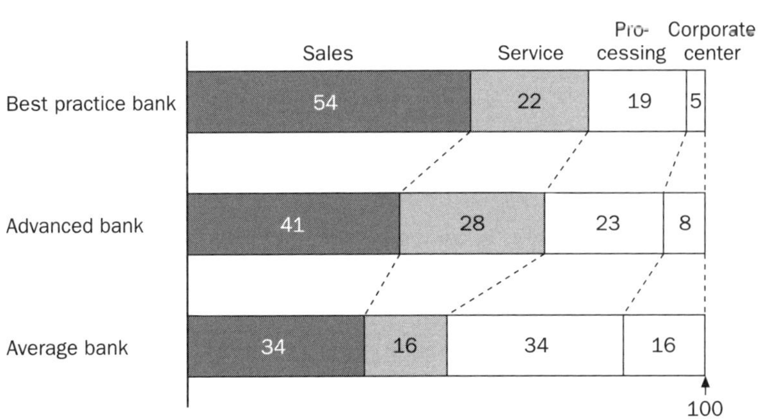

Figure 13.2 Allocation of bank personnel (percent)

Source: McKinsey

needed. Building a substantial salesforce takes time, and the recognition that recruiting from beyond the financial services industry is a good idea. Many sales-driven banks do just that, turning to traditional service industry personnel such as retailers or department store managers, even when their own staff are already more sales-oriented than the banking average. Nonbanking sales staff also often have lower wage levels and may consider retail banking a progressive step in their career path.

In order to determine the optimal size of the salesforce in all channels, it is important to calculate the cost–revenue trade-off. This will often lead banks to conclude that they can afford more salespeople. One North American bank analyzed the productivity of its mortgage salespeople and found that they were all generating good profits, but there was a lot of unmet demand. So it nearly doubled its mortgage salesforce and as a result increased revenue by 5 percent and profit by 10 percent within the first year.

As sales increases in size relative to other functions in a bank, its importance will also rise, and the subsequent attention of top management will further help to maximize sales power.

Use additional third-party capacity

Another way to increase sales capacity is by using third-party distribution channels. This has the advantage of being a variable rather than a fixed cost, and can often add specific expertise, sales drive, and additional customer contacts. Examples range from the short-term hiring of additional outbound call center capacity to long-term sales agreements with financial adviser or other distribution networks. Of course any cooperation with external distributors must be economically advantageous. Longer term sales agreements might make sense when a bank's products have a strong brand or if it can build on economies of scale. Deutsche Bank, for example, has a distribution agreement with DVAG, the largest German financial adviser network. Thanks to the strength in the German market of Deutsche Bank's brand and that of its mutual fund company DWS, the products are attractive for external distributors and both parties profit from the deal. Cooperation agreements with post offices are also common in Europe. In Spain, Deutsche Bank sells its financial products through branches of Correos (the Spanish postal group); and in the UK and Sweden, some banks use the post offices to offer transactional services to their customers thereby releasing the capacity of their own salespeople.

Maximize sales time per sales employee

In the 1990s, many analyses found that sales personnel were spending just 15 to 25 percent of their time actually selling, and even this was distributed unfavorably between proactive and reactive selling (i.e., responding to customer-initiated contact). By the mid-1990s, some of the best banks were aiming for 70 percent selling time, but frontline sales staff at most could manage only much lower levels. Some sales managers, notably in the affluent segment, were managing to spend around 30 to 40 percent of their time selling, because they were allocated 200 to

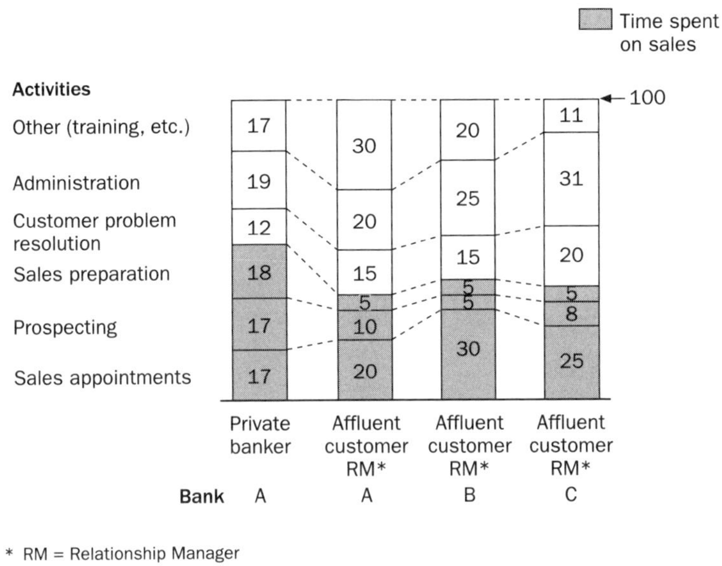

Figure 13.3 Time allocation of sales employees (percent)

Source: McKinsey

300 customers each and were largely freed from administrative tasks in the light of the importance of this customer group (Figure 13.3).

Today, the average proportion of sales time ranges from 20 to 50 percent in most banks. Raising it higher is difficult for several reasons. First, there is a certain amount of administrative work that sales staff should perform, for example, data entry for consumer credit should be done at the point of sale so that it is done only once. Second—and most importantly—IT support in many banks is often not advanced enough, leaving salespeople to draw on data from several systems, sometimes even transferring data from one to another. Third, processes are neither optimally defined nor consistently applied across an institution. Instead, each region, sales unit, or even individual sales person defines his or her own process. And, connected to that, fourth, some employees actually seek administrative tasks in order to avoid active selling.

There are many measures banks can use to counter such inefficiencies, both at their root cause or just tactically by allocating sales and administration time between different people in the sales organization, thereby at least freeing up the most effective salespeople as much as possible. Of course, to do that requires that the managers know who the most effective salespeople are. The tactical way to improve efficiency is to support the best people in doing pre- and after-sales work. Tackling inefficiencies more fundamentally requires redesigning processes to reduce back office workload for frontline staff through automation.

MAXIMIZE SALES EFFECTIVENESS

Maximizing sales effectiveness is a never-ending task. An analysis of sales effectiveness can make for sober reading: in many banks, sales employees sell only one product each day. In any advanced multichannel retail bank, maximizing sales effectiveness has become a complex task that requires not just a heavy dose of good traditional salesforce management but also a healthy helping of intelligent database-marketing, to enable better customer understanding and to send salespeople to the right targets with the right products.

Increasing sales effectiveness means getting more, higher quality customer contacts, higher closure ratios, higher volume per sale, and a better profitability mix of products sold. These effects can be reached by three major efforts, all of which interlink and influence each other: (a) improving sales intelligence, (b) strengthening frontline execution, and (c) improving sales force organization and management.

Improve sales intelligence

At the heart of an intelligent sales and marketing function should sit an advanced *database-marketing system* often referred to as *customer relationship management* (CRM) systems. Once it is being used effectively, it can help staff maximize the number and quality of both *proactive* and *reactive* customer contacts and ensure they are turned into sales.

Database-marketing. Some retail banks have spent a fortune on their database-marketing infrastructure. Yet despite the high investment, few are truly satisfied. Only 16 percent of companies that implemented CRM software say that it has exceeded their expectations, while 41 percent consider the effort a 'potential flop', according to a March 2001 survey conducted by the Data Warehousing Institute. Some other surveys cite even higher levels of CRM dissatisfaction.

The ideal process starts with a highly developed, accurate, and reliable database. Good analysis tools can then help develop targeted campaign ideas. A campaign testing process should then be established and linked accurately to the frontline in order to really close sales and collect customer feedback. Few banks manage to perform well in all elements of this process (Figure 13.4).

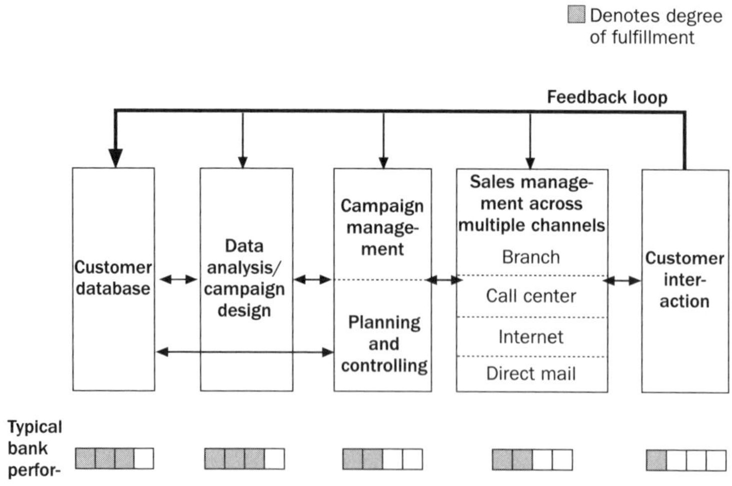

Figure 13.4 Database-marketing process

Source: McKinsey

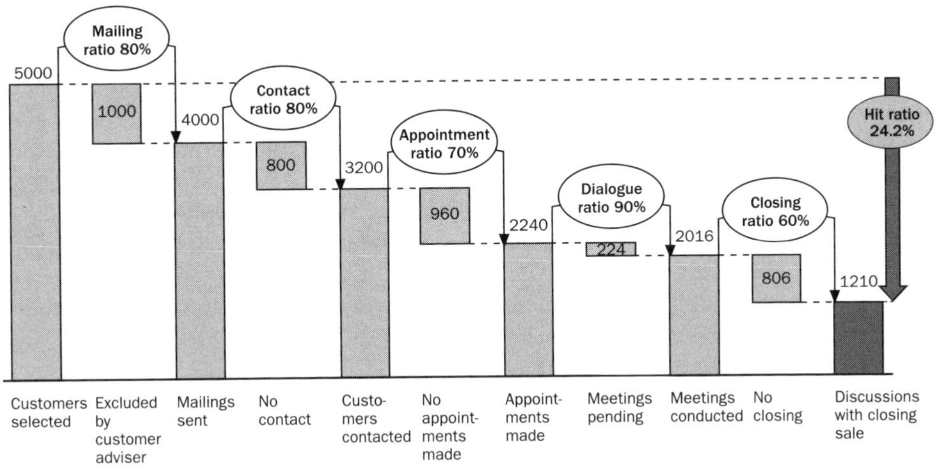

Figure 13.5 Activity-based sales-controlling

Source: McKinsey

Although most of the banks that have introduced database-marketing have actually made good progress in cleaning and analyzing customer data, as well as in developing campaigns, there has been less progress in connecting to the sales frontline. Ideas may be generated in the corporate think tank, but the sales staff often find there is no institutionalized method of providing input in campaign development.

One way to solidify the connections is to establish a 'brains trust', whereby the best marketing people, the best sales reps, heads of customer segment units, database-marketing experts, controllers, and heads of marketing come together. This group should then draw from the database and previous campaigns, think about the best possible campaigns, run statistical analyses, and launch event-based campaigns. The outcome will be thoroughly analyzed and used for new campaigns.

Once a campaign's products, timing, and marketing are finally designed, it can be rolled out. In an excellent campaign, the execution is monitored closely so that any problems can be identified at each step and be eliminated (Figure 13.5). There are usually many hurdles in implementation: salespeople may not like proposals coming from the center, they spot incorrect data (usually a result of insufficient care by the frontline employees themselves) or even ignore proposals completely.

Others just do not try hard enough to reach customers. But even those who do try hard will still have problems getting through to customers and convincing them on the phone or face to face. Therefore, it is important to introduce minimum targets to be achieved at each step (e.g., address by mail at least 80 percent of the target customers, contact by phone 80 percent of the customers mailed, and so forth in order to arrive at a hit ratio of 24 percent). In the introductory phase, these controlling mechanisms are necessary to exploit fully the power of sales intelligence. In this context, very simple data can provide the basis for success (i.e., home address and telephone number). To be valuable, the data must be up to date. In top-performing banks, contact telephone numbers are accurate for more than 90 percent of customers, the rate of undeliverable mailings does not exceed 2 percent, and e-mail addresses are available for at least 20 percent of the existing customer base. It is hard to reach these levels. Therefore, it is crucial that frontline staff understand the importance of data quality, starting with the accuracy at account-opening and ending with regular data checks during customer contacts.

Finally, the area of the biggest gap between excellence and the mainstream is the customer feedback loop by which a bank should exploit all possible opportunities to learn more about the customer. Banks on average have just exploited 25 percent of what is possible in this step. Only very few excellent banks in this area are making the best out of the learning opportunity.

Four banks that demonstrate how to use database-marketing systems successfully and economically are National Australia Bank (NAB), Royal Bank of Canada (RBC), Unicredito, and Stadtsparkasse Köln.

NAB has an integrated CRM approach that drives customer penetration. The customer database is constantly updated and can deliver real-time account information including the customer's lifetime value. Using simple analytic modeling, daily and weekly leads are generated based on predicted events or prioritized behavioral triggers. The information is delivered to all services and sales channels and agents are provided with tailored scripts. The campaigns are coordinated across all channels and continuous learning takes place so that the models and approaches can be constantly revised and improved. In 1999, NAB implemented a new sales leads program that manages the frequency, content, and channel method for contacting customers. During six months, the program generated 570 000 new leads that resulted in A$4.4bn in new business.[1] NAB reportedly has the highest share of wallet, customer satisfaction, and retention rates for high-net-worth customers in Australia. In recognition of these achievements, the Institute for Financial Studies in the UK awarded it the prize for best CRM strategy in 2001.

RBC, Canada's largest bank, has built a customer database that is integrated across branches, the call center, and the marketing department. It includes rolling three-month detailed transaction data and 19 months of summarized data and is linked to external data sets including geo-demographics and life-style indicators. The synthesized customer information is displayed to call center and branch personnel on their desktops and targeting models are run on a monthly basis to deliver lead lists. Campaigns are then targeted at specific customer segments, such as those likely to buy or defect as predicted from propensity models, or at customers moving to a new phase of their life cycle and hence to a new segment. As a result, RBC has achieved dramatic increases in direct marketing campaign response rates, reaching as high as 40 percent in some cases—compared with an industry average response rate of 2 to 4 percent. Revenue per marketing dollar has shown double-digit growth each year for the past three years, and the banking division has experienced a 20 percent year-on-year growth in sales for the last four years.[2] As a result, in 2001 RBC received the 'Innovator of the Year' award from the magazine *American Banker*, which cited the bank's leadership in CRM and cross-selling initiatives.[3]

---

[1] National Australia Bank, investor presentation, May 10, 2001.

[2] Teradata. *Customer Success Stories: Royal Bank of Canada*, May 2002.

[3] Gordon Nixon, President and CEO RBC. Leadership in integrated financial services. Presentation to Merrill Lynch Canada's *Canadian Banks CEO Conference 2002*.

Italy's Unicredito has a unique approach to CRM. The bank invested heavily in CRM and sales-monitoring systems, which are used daily to drive targeted product campaigns to various segments and monitor sales effectiveness. The campaigns are steered by a central unit that reports directly to the head of retail and that is staffed with highly skilled marketing specialists, some of whom come from nonfinancial marketing heavyweights like Procter & Gamble or Unilever. The CRM system also measures the sales agents relative sales productivity and guides them to product bundles that add greater value, based on peer comparison and segment experiences. Finally, the CRM system is used for setting stretch sales targets at the individual level, which are closely linked to incentive schemes. One or two people in each region (comprising 75 to 80 branches) translate the campaigns into locally specific action plans that account for the particularities of the regions and branches.

Stadtsparkasse Köln, one of Germany's biggest and most innovative savings banks, has successfully established a new campaign and event management process with relatively little investment. Instead of purchasing an expensive CRM system the bank developed the process on its own, focusing on intelligent data analysis and taking event data to the frontline. It went from conducting only five to ten campaigns a year to being able to run many campaigns simultaneously. Today, it conducts over 70 campaigns a year and has increased hit ratios significantly.

If used correctly, database-marketing can open a different world with hit ratios doubling, trebling, or even better (Figure 13.6). However, such success can be reached only by controlling and continuously improving the process step by step.

Increased sales intelligence is crucial for generating and using both proactive and reactive customer contacts more successfully.

Reactive contacts. The majority of a bank's contacts occur when customers approach the bank. A bank with two million customers, each of whom contacts a bank

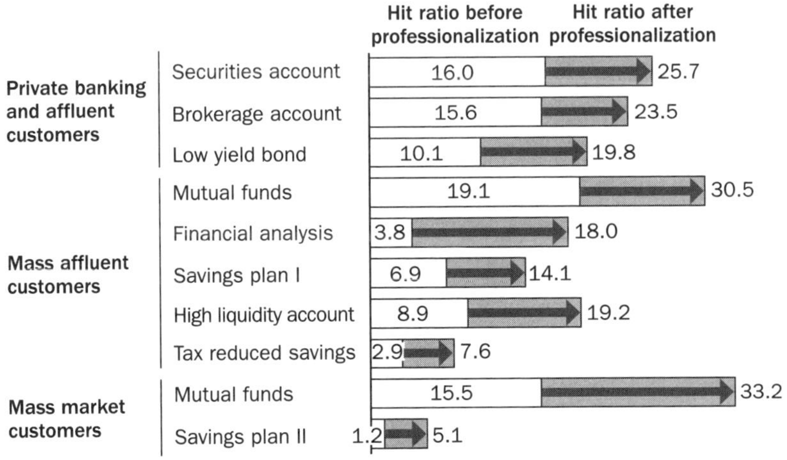

Figure 13.6 Hit ratios by segment and product at a European bank (percent)

Source: McKinsey

employee on average four times a year, makes eight million customer contacts per year. All these should be exploited to the fullest extent possible, which requires the database-marketing system described above. There are two ways of interacting with reactive contacts: the tailored response and the campaign focus.

In the tailored response, the salesperson can see on screen what the calling customer may need, either because they have asked for it before or because of their stage in the life cycle, or simply because they do not yet have the product.

Analyzing cross-selling and demand behaviors provides information on the likelihood of a customer buying the product. Some banks have designed customer propensity models that trigger event-based customer leads.

Each time that a customer contacts the bank during a campaign, the salesperson should discuss the product. This is especially easy if the campaign has an obvious talking point. One bank combined the offer of a consumer loan with displaying a luxury car in the most relevant branches. The number of consumer loans sold tripled compared with other months—helped by the emotional appeal of the car.

Proactive contacts. Generating business from scratch is much more expensive in both time and money. Traditional approaches here include using the branch network, a mobile salesforce, mass or worksite-marketing (e.g., offering financial advice on a company's premises or tailoring products for the needs of company employees and offering them via a corporate intranet), and advertising. Less common methods include partnering with retailers and using customer and employee referrals.

Sales staff should approach existing customers during any sales campaigns—either periodic or regular—with specific growth targets for products or segments. Some banks use campaigns only occasionally, while others such as Unicredito and RBC have built their whole business system around them. Because campaigns are expensive, it is important that they focus on high-value programs (i.e., those with high hit ratios and low costs per hit).

Many good regional banks invest time and money in local neighborhoods to help build their prospect pipeline. They sponsor local events, senior managers are active in the community, and a lot of local product campaigns are conducted. Little if any marketing money is spent on corporate brand-building, everything is directed instead toward hooking the local population with relevant products.

MLP (a German financial adviser network offering its own and third-party financial services and products) builds its pipeline of high-value customers by establishing relationships at universities, thereby attracting customers at a point in the life cycle where the need for advice is high. MLP advisers gather information on final-year students and invite them to career-specific financial seminars where the different options that best address their particular needs are explained. The seminars are often coupled with training on how to apply for a job and other useful skills. After the seminar, the students are invited to individual counseling sessions where concrete product offers are made. MLP has an 80 percent closure rate after these counseling sessions, partly due to the good fit between students and their counselor, who has usually studied the same subject. More than 60 percent of the contacted graduating medical students become MLP customers and the rate is approximately 38 percent for other core target groups such as engineering, law, and business students.

Another approach is to use employees' local knowledge. One bank put a referral program in place whereby employees with no customer contact were asked to generate two referrals a month and those with regular customer interaction were asked for ten. The program generated 80 000 referrals and €70m in new deposits. Referral programs are often combined with programs that make it easy for customers to change banks. One bank allowed its customers to open a new account over the telephone and then arranged a time the following day where a courier could call in person with the appropriate forms and pick up the initial deposit.

Taking an opportunistic approach to customer acquisition means having programs that take advantage of rare, but high-potential opportunities, such as a competitor being taken over or other high-profile industry events such as competitors closing branches. To exploit these events, 'SWAT' teams of salespeople are sent to hot spots (such as a branch about to be closed), acquisition kiosks are set up in local supermarkets, and targeted direct mail campaigns are launched in relevant markets. Other tactics include assigning account-opening teams to ATM locations where a high proportion of transactions are made by customers of other banks.

Strengthen sales execution

In improving sales execution at the frontline, it is necessary to differentiate between affluent, mass affluent, and mass market customers. For affluent customers, a relationship manager and financial planning are integral to the sales process. Mass affluent customers are usually allocated to a team, rather than an individual manager, and their financial planning meetings are generally shorter. The mass market cannot usually support relationship management nor financial planning; rather a product-oriented approach is appropriate.

Despite these different approaches, all three segments benefit from database-marketing and event-based campaigning. For the affluent segments, experience has shown that it pays to feed relationship managers with good campaigning ideas between customer meetings, leaving the relationship manager to decide to which customers they apply. Indeed, database-marketing and campaigns can establish new levels of sales activity for the affluent segment, ensuring they are contacted about all relevant sales events.

Overall, two things facilitate the improvement of sales execution: sales support tools and the skills of the salespeople.

Several banks use state-of-the-art *support tools* to this end. These tools include the links from the database-marketing system to the frontline, financial planning tools, and scripts for guiding customer interaction.

Ideally, the data from marketing systems should be accessible on all channels and are updated in real time. One bank has installed tools that estimate the volume of assets a customer holds outside the bank and the risk that the customer will leave the bank within the next two years. The salespeople in the branch get this information on screen, together with an indication of three products the customer is most likely to need.

The salesforce should use such tools to fulfill segment-specific targets. Cross-selling is usually the best way to enhance profitability (indeed, many of the high-

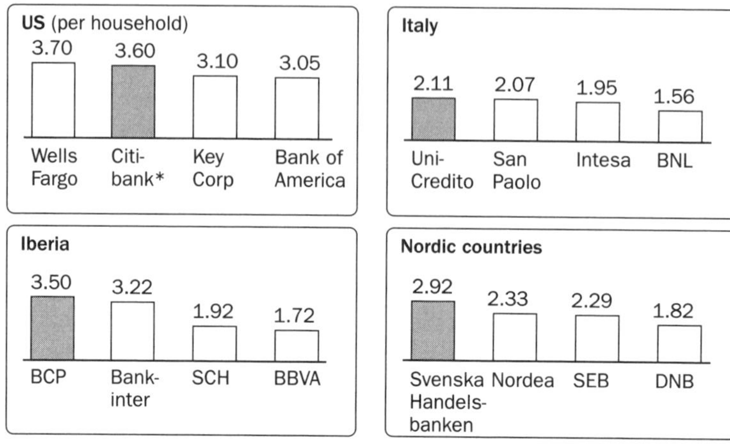

* Up to 6.7 in branches where Citipro has been piloted

Figure 13.7 Number of products per customer (2000–2001)

Source: Deutsche Bank; McKinsey

performing banks achieve outstanding product–customer ratios) (Figure 13.7). However, for some segments it might be more appropriate to focus on up-selling (i.e., migrating the customer to a higher value-added product such as a structured investment product). In the mass affluent and the affluent segment, increasing the bank's share of wallet could imply a very significant rise in profitability.

Financial planning tools support and structure the sales process and increase retention. In Europe, many banks have been using financial planning tools for years, mainly for wealthier customers. Citibank, however, reports outstanding cross-selling levels of 6.7 products per household in branches where it is piloting Citipro, a sophisticated but easy-to-use financial planning tool. Citipro starts by assessing the customer's financial situation and his or her plans for the future. In the next step, different scenarios are calculated based on figures such as the amount a customer would have to save each month in order to reach a certain net worth in five years' time. In the last step, the program offers concrete financial solutions such as cash management, automatic savings plans, etc. The whole process takes one to two hours. This is a successful example of a centrally driven financial planning tool that makes customers feel they matter and has helped produce those remarkable cross-selling ratios.

A third set of tools is the use of guidelines and scripts to standardize the sales process. In tests using mystery shoppers, substantial differences in a bank's sales process are often revealed. Depending on which branch the shoppers visited, consultation times for customers with identical profiles can range from 10 minutes to over an hour—and often result in totally different proposals. This has to be avoided. Often it is older, more experienced sales staff who reject the standardized approach, because they believe that they know how to advise; but defining best practice and adopting it universally is vital. The high-performing banks use these mystery shoppers, visiting a branch eight to ten times a year. They also use detailed customer satisfaction surveys extensively. The results of both are relayed back to branch managers and can affect their salary.

Having such tools is one thing, but staff need the *skills* to use them. This means training them and introducing measures to attract, motivate, and retain the sales leaders. There seems to be no shortage of training provided by banks—often considered to be a nice day out by employees—but whether it is always the most effective and targeted training possible is open to debate. To take a positive example, when Citicorp merged with Travelers Group, it immediately began a pilot program in Chicago to train its branch staff to sell products from both Citibank's and Traveler's portfolio.

In developing training programs, banks should consider where exactly the bottleneck to higher sales performance lies. In terms of training the frontline staff, both content-oriented and development-oriented approaches are important. The content-oriented part covers such topics as customer analysis and the needs-based sales approach and aims to come up with concrete activity-based improvements. Development-oriented coaching means training people in the art of selling, covering topics such as a sales closure technique or questioning techniques. What is often missing, but needed urgently, is effective on-the-job training to be provided by sales management.

Improve sales force management

Perhaps the most important way of maximizing sales effectiveness is to improve salesforce management. Here, sales has to be seen within the broader context of a bank-wide performance culture, especially in terms of reinforcing the passion for achievement down the line. Tasks here range from communicating an inspiring sales mission to counteracting underperformance decisively through effective coaching. We have already discussed how to build a performance culture including incentive systems in Chapter 4, but we would like to elaborate here on those areas that pertain specifically to sales: sales organization, communication of a sales vision, stretch targets, controlling system, benchmarking, and managerial training.

Sales organization. Before improving sales force management, banks should check whether responsibilities and accountabilities of sales units are defined clearly, whether they are directed toward the target segments and whether the interaction between customers and product units is working smoothly and beneficially for the whole operation. It is also necessary to decide which segments should be addressed and whether products should be sold by generalists or by specialists. This usually depends on the specific institution, although products that are further from the heart of traditional banking, such as property and casualty insurance, are usually dealt with better by specialists.

As we have already seen, one very important organizational task is the establishment of a central sales and marketing intelligence unit to fuel the sales machine. The unit should be staffed by both successful sales managers, who are accepted by frontline staff, and by statisticians who can use advanced analysis tools. Establishing such a unit is not always easy because it introduces processes in sales that interfere with the traditional freedom of sales units and regions; however, it can help pick up the speed of the sales process.

Any bank that wants to move toward a far more sales-oriented culture must *communicate* loudly and clearly the vision and the new importance within the bank both of sales as a function and of the salespeople themselves. Top management and sales managers have to generate a sense of urgency and create an environment where competition is encouraged as people strive for ever-more-ambitious targets.

The central marketing unit should help sales staff reach more exacting targets. Of course, calling for *stretch targets* is easy, but actually setting them—and then achieving them—is more difficult. There are two broad approaches to target-setting. At Fifth Third, one of the high-performing banks, CEO George Schaefer chooses general broad targets, such as his desire for people to 'raise revenues by 20 percent and grow costs by a single digit'.[4] Citibank PK in Germany used to follow the same philosophy, but when Christine Licci became CEO, she changed this, claiming that across-the-board targets are unjust and do not exploit the potential in growth areas. Now the bank is planning differentiated individual targets for each branch.

Within either context, to set targets properly it is helpful to know the market potential. In many banks, this is based only on volume per customer and product profitability, but using such basic metrics can cause problems when sales staff argue that their particular regional circumstances make targets unrealistic. The solution is to use a broader spectrum of factors including market penetration, cross-selling ratios, product utilization, customer retention and churn rates, share of wallet, cost-to-serve, or upward and downward migration. When combined, such a mix gives a more holistic view of the performance of a sales unit and thus provides the basis for incontestable target-setting.

Having set stretch targets, it is vital that a *controlling system* is installed to measure progress and overall performance, that it is accepted by sales staff, and is genuinely helpful for management.

There have been many different perspectives on exactly what, when, for whom, and how often to measure such data. Such debates arose because many banks felt constrained in measuring what they actually wanted to control (e.g., when work councils or trade unions would not allow individual, narrow controlling). There is no one right target to control, as the best performing banks show. While Svenska Handelsbanken controls cost–income ratios and profit per branch, Citibank chooses to measure activities (e.g., number of sales meetings). Behind these differences, however, the logic remains clear: whether you choose to control profits, contributions, volumes, product structures, or activities, all these data are logically connected and should be available so that a bank can actually control performance at the most appropriate level (Figure 13.8).

As a rule, the more decentralized a bank is the more it will focus on profits and the more centralized or the more it needs to push up sales, then the more it will have to control activities and new business. Existing business does not normally require significant additional activity. Using a net present value (NPV) system for new business fulfills several targets well, because it measures the profitability of new business as well as stressing the bias for activity in branches. As an example, in

[4] 'Robert A. Bennett, Happy warrior.' *U.S. Banker*, January 2002.

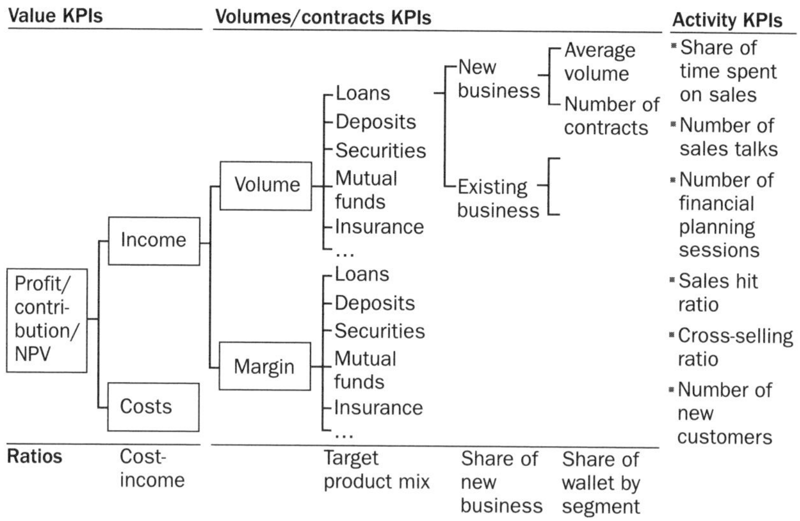

Figure 13.8 Different levels of key performance indicators (KPIs) for the frontline

Source: McKinsey

Deutsche Bank's retail network the salesforce can see the NPV of the business it closes.

The fact is that both activity- and profits-based controlling can work; ideally, the sales force should be monitored very tightly—daily and weekly. The closer a bank can come to daily, individual controlling the better, because the more attention paid to sales the better the results.

Internal *benchmarking* is another good way of improving activities and effectiveness. Some banks use benchmarking to identify their best performing branches and then talk to the staff there to uncover the secrets of their success. Underperforming branches are then given the information, together with names of colleagues in these branches who they can quiz. Benchmarking results can also stimulate competition within specific units, which helps show poor-performing teams who claim they cannot improve that higher levels of achievement are possible.

This takes us even closer to the core of the sales management task: hands-on *development of sales managers* and sales staff. For a sales manager to succeed, he or she has to understand the overall vision for the sales function and for the bank as a whole. They must be role models who can solve problems themselves. According to one article, 'Salespeople are likely to adopt their sales manager models. If the sales manager goes beyond the call of duty, salespeople are likely to accept such behavior as the rule of the firm and adopt it. If, however, the sales manager has high expectations of the salespeople but does not have the same expectations for himself or herself, sales personnel are likely to reject the sales manager's demands.'[5]

If they are to be effective, sales managers must know the strengths and weaknesses of their staff and must help them achieve their targets. They must learn to coach their

[5] Dubinsky, A.J. and Skinner, S.J., 'Going the extra mile: Antecedents of salespeople's discretionary effort.' *Industrial Marketing Management*, Vol. 31, 2002, 590.

staff with tangible results as the goal. As we said earlier, training for both sales managers and their staff should predominantly be on-the-job training.

Good sales management also requires the daily analysis of objectives and developments. Most of all, it means starting the week discussing targets and then ensuring that everybody stays on track to meet them. Too many bank managers have not been trained properly to do this and some do not even know it is what they should be doing.

Banks traditionally have invested in training frontline staff, but still lag in training the sales leaders and the development of their coaching skills. This is, if anything, more important because it has a multiplier effect, yet it has typically not been the focus of personal development initiatives.

Neglecting the importance of performance-oriented sales management would be a devastating mistake. The sales managers are vital cogs in the wheel when it comes to creating a performance culture that enables employees to perform at their maximum. When sales staff face up to the challenges, have good standing in the bank, and are involved in target-setting and target fulfillment, then they will feel like valued members of the bank. The end result is a sales culture that encourages everyone to go the extra mile.

14

Customer Service: Stand out from the Crowd

Luca Martini, Renato Martini[1]

Service has the potential to become the next battleground in the fight to gain a competitive edge in banking, as banks' product offerings otherwise look increasingly similar. But while other retail organizations learned long ago of the benefits to be extracted from establishing a first-rate service machine, banks have tended to be slower to react. However, as the business undergoes a process of progressive commoditization, retail banks would be well advised to take a serious look at service. Those that establish a lead in offering truly distinctive service stand to reap tidy benefits in terms of customer acquisition, cross-selling, and retention.

WHY CUSTOMER SERVICE MATTERS

When banks think about ways to acquire and retain customers and increase their share of customers' wallet, they often begin by looking at the products they offer, examining their sales skills and techniques, and thinking about prices and promotions. Recent research, however, suggests that a bank's level of service can make a tangible difference not only in customer retention but, more surprisingly, in customer acquisition and cross-selling rates as well.

Service is a major factor in a customer's decision to switch banks, and good service reduces customer churn. About two-thirds of the reasons given by customers for leaving their banking institution in Italy and the UK were service-related (Figure 14.1). This is an important insight given how much cheaper it is to retain a customer than to acquire a new one, and in recent years customer loyalty levels have dropped, with corresponding increases in churn rates. In Italy, for example, the churn rate doubled from 1997 to 2000, rising from 4 to 8 percent for mass market customers and from 5 to 10 percent for affluents.[2]

[1] The authors would like to express their gratitude for the contributions of Justo Alcocer, Pat Butler, and Andrew N. Davis.

[2] Eurisko ABI.

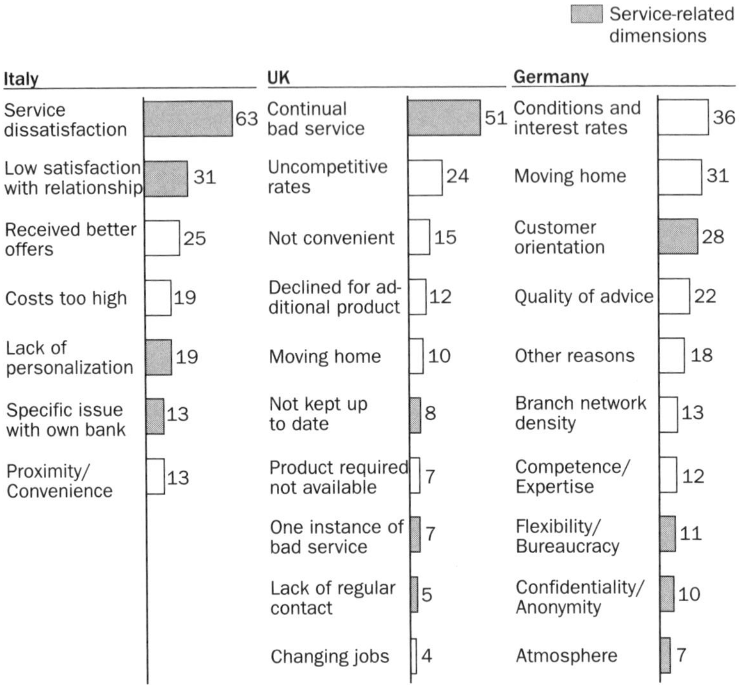

Figure 14.1 Reasons why customers switch banks (percent, multiple answers possible)

Source: Eurisko customer satisfaction (1999–2000); Mintel Customer Switching (2000); Soll + Haben 5 (2000)

The value-creation potential from reducing churn is significant. Shaving 1 to 2 percentage points off a hypothetical 8 percent churn rate (i.e., reducing churn by 15 to 30 percent) could open up 10 to 20 percent of market value left untapped due to poor quality of service. Take into account the potential additional improvement in acquisition rates and the value-creation opportunities are even more exciting. It could be worth several hundred million euro to a medium-sized European retail bank.

It may come as a surprise to see that service has such a large impact on customers' initial choice of financial institution. Traditional banking wisdom holds that branch proximity and price are the key factors in determining where a customer will bank. This has often been supported by market research based on the attributes that customers most often list as influencing their choice. Moreover, common sense would suggest that since service is something that a customer experiences only after opening an account with the bank, service quality should carry little weight in the decision. But the fact is that service is one of the few attributes that people actually talk about (they seldom mention price and never proximity). The importance of word of mouth is often underrated, and recommendations from friends are a source of customer acquisition that banks should not overlook. Recent research backs this up, highlighting the importance of service elements in determining where customers bank.

Service-related dimensions (shaded)

	UK	US
1.	Friendly	Resolves problems quickly and correctly
2.	Trustworthy	Quality
3.	Reputable	Gives good advice
4.	Professional	A bank for people in the know
5.	Offers solutions tailored to my needs	The bank delivers what it promises
6.	Flexible	Provides good value
7.	Fashionable	Provides good customer service
8.	Gives good advice	Is easy to do business with
9.	Provides good value	The bank for people like me
10.	Makes its customers feel valuable	Consistent performance

Figure 14.2 Top 10 attributes in choosing a bank (derived importance [by correlating individual rating of attributes with overall consideration of brand])

Source: McKinsey Brand Health Survey, 2000 and 2001

Recent McKinsey surveys in the UK and US set out to measure the derived importance of a host of attributes in customers' choice of bank.[3,4] Of the 10 most important attributes, the majority are service dimensions (Figure 14.2). Branch proximity, price, and product range all ranked low in derived importance because they are not perceived as real differentiators in today's market.

A benchmarking study conducted by an Italian bank supported this by showing that the difference in customer acquisition rates between the branches in the top and bottom deciles in customer satisfaction rating was between 3 and 6 percentage points. So, good customer service can indeed bring in new customers.

Finally, cross-selling opportunities can also get a boost from a strong service culture. One study carried out on 17 Internet banking sites in the US showed a strong correlation between satisfaction with service experience and willingness to buy again.[5]

Despite the clear importance of service quality, few European banks have explicitly positioned their value proposition primarily on service. This is mainly the result of two factors: historical precedent and the problems of managing the intangible nature of service issues.

Service has not traditionally been considered important; the focus has been on product offering rather than customer service. But products have been designed for efficiency or IT simplicity and are not focused on the customer experience. The design of the service elements of the customer experience is typically dispersed across several departments rather than centralized in marketing. Designing customer

[3] McKinsey Brand Health; US survey of 9 retail banks in 2000; UK survey of 12 retail banks in 2001.

[4] Derived importance comes from an aggregated correlation between each individual's perception of brand and his or her likelihood to consider it in the future. Respondents were asked to define their experience of the brand, rate it against 35 emotional and rational attributes, and rate their likelihood to consider the brand in the future assuming they held no financial products at the time. The resulting correlation produces a set of attributes that appear to tie in closely with the likelihood of considering a brand.

[5] Shopnow.com 2000.

forms, for example, is often a task relegated to the organization department or even IT.

Second, service is typically an amalgamation of many small factors and intangible elements, mostly related to the way branch employees behave. Hence, many banks struggle to achieve consistent customer service across all touchpoints. Changing the behavior of thousands of frontline staff across all business units is a process of considerable magnitude.

There is evidence, however, that the market is beginning to understand the importance of service excellence. The high-performing banks in our Excellence in Retail Banking survey (see Chapter 2) typically get good ratings in customer satisfaction surveys. Royal Bank of Scotland (RBS) in the UK, Fifth Third and Citibank in the US, Banco Popular in Spain, and Svenska Handelsbanken in Sweden all ranked the highest in their domestic markets.[6]

In addition, there are examples of other strongly performing banks whose value proposition includes service as a key element (e.g., Commerce Bank, Wells Fargo, and Washington Mutual).

At Svenska Handelsbanken, quality of service (and the overall success of the company) was secured by the use of a bottom–up model that uses a decentralized and entrepreneurial strategy. The strategy is based, first, on a high level of delegation to employees. Procedures are built to allow broad leeway in most decision-making (including price) delegated to branch employees. This gives each branch more scope to tailor customer service as appropriate. The second strand of the strategy is based on employee motivation. All employees own company shares, amounting to roughly 10 percent of the bank's total equity. This results in high-quality service on relationship dimensions (e.g., greater courtesy, commitment to solving problems), and the bank has had the highest customer satisfaction levels among the large Swedish banks for the past 10 years. Its strong focus on personal service in branches was one of the attributes that earned it the title Bank of the Year by *Privata Affärer* in 2001, an award historically reserved for niche banks.[7]

Wells Fargo makes no attempt to hide its strong focus on customer service, 'We want to be advocates for our customers and put them at the center of everything we do. We want to give them outstanding service each and every time, so they'll give us all their business, honor us with repeat purchases, and rave about us to their family, friends, and business associates.'[8] To accomplish this vision, it set up concrete goals for improvements. It accomplished most of its top ten customer service issues in the spring of 2002, a few months ahead of schedule. This meant it could set up a new top ten. Its achievements included reducing the error rate on customer statements by 78 percent and on new account opening information by 33 percent, and the virtual elimination of delays in getting customers their deposit account statement.

Notice that neither of these banks has a killer service application. Success rather lies in paying close attention to a combination of small details. All these details,

[6] Which Online 2000; MORI Excellence Model 2001; STIGA 2000, Harris Survey 2001, Svenskt Kvalitetsindex 2001.

[7] Svenskt Kvalitetsindex; *Privata Affärer*, November 28, 2001; *Affärsvärlden*, February 2, 2002.

[8] Annual report 2001.

spread across the various service delivery levers (mission and values statement, processes, people motivation, environment, incentive systems, etc.), steered in the same direction, and consistently improved over time can combine to produce spectacular results.

Defining customer service

We have shown how important high customer service levels can be. But to be able to offer them, a bank needs to be clear as to the elements that make it up. The whole customer experience can be divided into three dimensions comprising functional, process, and relationship elements.

The *functional elements* enable the customer to transfer, invest, and borrow his or her money. For a money transfer, the major functional feature would be the customer's ability to make a payment from his or her current account to another account. Also falling into this category are such elements as the channels available for making transactions (branches, ATMs, Internet) and product-related financial advice.

Functional elements are what is normally meant by 'product'—the answer to 'What am I buying?' 'Service' is thus the process and relationship elements of the customer experience.

Process elements relate to how products can be acquired, used, and disposed of by the customer. They include features such as the ease of the process of activating a credit card (number of signatures required, clarity of the language used for the brochure, etc.) and the time required to perform a banking task (the length of the queue in front of the teller or the hours the branch or call center provides service).

Relationship elements relate to how the customer feels when interacting with the bank. This includes the level of trust the customer has in the bank, the existence of a calm, welcoming environment where the customer is treated courteously, and, finally, the bank's professionalism (which encompasses everything from acknowledging bank mistakes to the professional attire of employees). Much of this is intangible and is thus evaluated by customers in terms of what they perceive it to be, rather than what it objectively is.

Traditionally, banks have focused primarily on the functional elements by providing products tailored to customer needs, introducing new ways of doing transactions (e.g., using credit cards), and offering new channels in order to increase convenience and boost the customer experience. But as retail banks' offerings converge, with even the smallest regional bank capable of providing online trading, for example, the importance of functional elements relative to the service dimension (process and relationship elements) is diminishing. As Dick Kovacevich, CEO of Wells Fargo, puts it, 'Like Wal-Mart and Home Depot, we view ourselves as a distributor. In our case, we're a distributor of financial services and products, whether we make the product or someone else does. We're not a product-centered company but a customer-centered company. We're focused not on selling checking accounts, credit cards or mortgages but on helping our customers succeed financially, satisfying their needs to borrow, save, invest, and insure their assets.'[9]

[9] Annual report 2001.

Given the commoditized product landscape, banks should turn to the process and relationship elements to distinguish themselves. Relationship elements have been shown in market research to be among the most important dimensions. They were deemed to be the most influential of all service attributes in determining churn (more important than speed, knowledge, and queue length). It is also, sadly, the area where a bank's performance is most likely to disappoint. In the remainder of this chapter we therefore focus on the process and relationship aspects of the customer experience.

HOW TO IMPROVE CUSTOMER SERVICE

It is vital to recognize that service is a fundamental component of the overall customer experience (and what the customer pays for) and therefore should be managed actively by the bank along the entire business system with an approach that is specific to its soft nature.

Retail banks are often astonished at the extent of the benefits they can gain from getting service right. Unfortunately, this astonishment is often accompanied by the realization that their business systems are inadequate to tackle the changes required.

Taking process and relationship aspects into consideration can radically change the business system of the bank over all three of its dimensions: the customer offer, organization and supporting processes and systems, and company culture.

Designing the service elements of the customer offer

The first thing to do before designing an offer is to understand what the customer wants, which in service terms can be achieved by looking at customer behavior. There are many tactics suitable here, such as hidden observation, running focus groups, and looking at interaction preferences. All can help banks understand what is important to customers, even on matters such as the degree to which they are willing to delegate financial matters or their particular style of managing their money. Alongside the normal sporadic checks, a more systematic analysis of customers should be conducted over time to reach a fuller understanding of customer behavior.

Banks can benefit from the experience of best practice retailers, for whom walking in the customer's shoes is a core skill. Home Depot, for example, claims that two pieces of knowledge lie behind its success: (1) 'We're not that smart'; and (2) 'We know we're not that smart.'[10] Starting from these premises, Home Depot's leaders listen closely to what their customers and staff members tell them, and the founders themselves actually spend much of their time walking the stores.

Car manufacturers have also honed their skills in this field. At one, corporate managers immerse themselves in the customer experience to gain insight into con-

---

[10] Bernie Marcus, Arthur Blank, and Bob Andelman, *Built from Scratch: How a Couple of Regular Guys Grew the Home Depot from Nothing to $30 Billion*. Random House, New York, 1999.

sumer behavior. The company sets up hidden cameras inside showroom cars to analyze customer behavior and find out what people look at when inside the car. Senior retail banking executives would do well to make occasional mystery shopper visits to small-town branches to learn what the customer experience is like at first hand.

The second step, based on these behavioral insights, is to redesign the customer offer to include the important service elements.

Traditionally, these elements have been treated merely as an ancillary aspect of products, mostly related to execution. This vision must change radically: service should be viewed as a portfolio of components, some tangible, some intangible, that need to be designed rigorously, much in the same way as product components are designed.

Again, banks can learn from traditionally strong service players. The Ritz-Carlton hotel chain has defined 'The Three Steps of Service' as a part of its Gold Standards (its values and philosophy). These are (1) a warm and sincere greeting—use the guest name if and when possible; (2) anticipation and compliance with guest needs; (3) fond farewell—give them a warm good-bye and use their names, if and when possible.[11] Another part of the Gold Standards is 'The Basics', which contains 20 guidelines for all employees.

Many of them are specifically related to serving the customer, such as 'To provide the finest personal service for our guests, each employee is responsible for identifying and recording individual guest preferences.'

Banks should start to design their service offers in much the same way. For example, rather than designing a new credit card just based on its functional features, the service components can be explicitly introduced to the marketing specifications. These could be process-related, such as the possibility of requesting the card online, the option of having it sent to any address, and guaranteed delivery within three days' time. They could also be relationship-oriented, such as the introduction of precise scripts to be used when dealing with customers and a mandate for reps to call the customer six months after activation to check that everything is all right.

Washington Mutual, a large US retail bank, has explicitly designed its customer experience. It recently introduced a new branch format, the Occasio store, which looks and feels like a shop. Instead of teller positions, retail assistants help customers by using 'teller towers' or hand-held terminals to perform transactions. There are also play areas for children and extended opening hours (including Saturdays and Sundays). This formula, set to be rolled out to several other locations in the US, has achieved impressive results: double the rate of new accounts and triple the rate of new deposits compared with traditional branches. The bank broke even on the program in one year.[12]

Build a supporting organization, processes, and systems

Having the right support structures is particularly important when it comes to ensuring consistency in service delivery. In fact, delivering quality means not just

[11] Company website.

[12] *Mortgage Banking*, June 1, 2001; *ABA Bank Marketing*, September 1, 2002.

trying to offer the best service, but being sure that the right amount of service is delivered consistently across the organization as planned. This is because a single instance of bad service tends to influence the customer's perception of the bank disproportionately and counteracts all the instances of good service received previously. Managing service therefore requires having the specific techniques in place to ensure the correct execution of process and relationship elements, techniques that are already well embedded in the systems of other service industries. We explore three of these techniques below.

A clear organizational responsibility for the customer experience. In many banks, a number of service elements are still defined by parts of the organization that are not in direct touch with customers and hence not designed based on customer needs. Having a business integrator or brand manager of the entire customer experience helps companies manage all the service elements comprehensively. Integrators are discussed in greater depth in Chapter 10.

Scripts and tools to manage frontline behavior. Scripts are very common in the world of retail. Indeed some, such as McDonald's 'Would you like fries with that', have entered the cultural consciousness. There are a couple of banks that use scripts both in the call centers and the branches. Commerce Bank in the US has introduced the 'Wow!' knowledge management system, which provides a database of answers that allow staff to respond to almost any customer situation. The bank also sends mystery shoppers to every branch twice a week to ensure consistent service delivery. In 2001, it conducted as many as 14 000 mystery shops, and every March, the CEO recognizes top performers at the company-wide 'Wow Awards'.[13]

A more advanced form of scripts are financial planning tools. These tools ensure a high level of consistency at the frontline and have traditionally been aimed at the affluent segment. Recently, however, they are being used also for the mass market (see Chapters 8 and 13 for more on this topic). Most of these systems contain scripts as well as offering products based on the customers' life cycle.

Processes to support delivery of the service offer. A service-offering also implies changes in a number of processes as well as use of tracking systems to deliver the bank's overall promise to the customer. First, the processes need to support the defined service offer. A US retail bank illustrates the power of adjusting processes. Following customers' complaints on the process of changing a customer's address, they rationalized it from six steps to four and introduced a problem-solving loop. Previously, more than 20 percent of address changes resulted in complaints, but, with the new process, the number of problems fell and customer satisfaction improved at a lower cost than before.

Second, tracking systems built into the process to control the 'production lines' are extremely important to ensure that quality is inherent. To give a specific, real-life example, banks should be able to spot that an ATM machine is eating cards or has depleted its cash reserve, or that the line is down, before customers complain. This can be achieved by implementing specific controls and monitoring procedures both within IT and through manual processes. For example, a major Italian insurance company uses an IT-based workflow tracking system to control its call center claims

---

[13] *Fast Company*, May 2, 2002.

unit. The system allows the company to record the customer call with all relevant data and attach an electronic copy of any relevant documentation to the file; automatically assign an external adjuster and tell the customer; settle a claim with a customer by electronic bank transfer; and produce regular reports to control workload, bottlenecks, lead times, and so forth. As a result the company has been able to reduce settlement time by 70 percent and rein in costs by 10 percent.

Instill a service culture

Up to now, we have been talking primarily about putting the mechanical elements in place. The real challenge comes when banks are faced with the task of instilling their entire organization with a quality-of-service mindset (i.e., building a service culture). Service must become an integral part of company performance if it is really to be considered an important part of the bank's value proposition. This entails undertaking several deep structural and cultural changes within the organization.

First of all, there must be *a system for measuring service* that works on similar principles to that measuring sales performance. In banks today, it is true that service is measured frequently, usually via customer satisfaction questionnaires, from which improvement steps are derived. This is helpful, but not enough to help build a true service culture. In order to make the difference, service performance must be measured regularly and continuously.

Measuring service performance also means going beyond the final economic (churn rate, customer acquisitions, etc.) or customer satisfaction outcome. It means measuring process and relationship performance. For process dimensions, key performance indicators (KPIs) will involve things like queue length (which can be measured by queuing systems) or mortgage approval lead time. For relationship elements, KPIs would be on things like courtesy (measured by customer interviews) or adherence to standard scripts (measured by mystery shoppers). Measuring service is standard procedure in the retail industry. A European grocery chain, for example, regularly records checkout lines, enabling it to gauge how well it meets its 98 percent 'one-in-front' target and giving it the chance to reorganize working schedules if the target is not met.

Some banks have invested heavily in developing these types of systems. Spain's Bankinter gauges customer satisfaction across 14 indicators, as well as hiring independent measurement agencies to monitor external measures.

Interestingly, Bankinter also measures employee satisfaction in terms of the level of service that they receive from the corporate center. This is important because it helps to foster an overall service culture that becomes the driving theme of the bank.[14] RBS—the UK's number one bank for customer satisfaction—has a similar system that reports an overall service quality indicator comprised of a number of measures, including: appearance, courtesy, efficiency, loyalty, product and service knowledge, problem-solving, queuing, and overall customer satisfaction.[15]

[14] Annual report 2001.

[15] RBS Retail Banking Presentation, October 2000.

This degree of measurement allows the high-performing banks to *link results to staff incentive plans*, both directly and by publishing rankings. At Bankinter, for example, about 30 percent of sales staff have their pay linked to service indicators, and quality awards are given to the best region and business division.

Staff will of course only achieve good results if they have received the right *training*. At Commerce Bank's Commerce University, the philosophy of customer service is driven home boot-camp style. As part of the 'Wow!' campaign, the bank also designed the SMART mantra to help it improve the frontline service culture. The bank continually repeats the meaning of the slogan to its employees:

Say "Yes" to customers!
Make each customer feel special!
Always keep customer promises!
Recover! To err is human; to recover is divine!
Think like the customers![16]

Training should help existing staff, but service can be boosted further by *incorporating service criteria into recruiting and career development*. Key decision criteria for hiring new staff should be customer orientation and other relationship skills. Commerce Bank has changed its recruiting policies to improve service delivery and new hires are now screened for an enthusiastic, positive attitude. Clear career paths have been introduced for those employees who demonstrate the necessary talent and motivation, with additional benefits such as reimbursement for education costs.

PRIORITIZE EFFORTS

It is not easy to transform the quality of service in any company, especially when the organization's mindset has to switch from a product to a service culture. Typical reasons for service programs failing are a lack of focus on what is really important for the customer, failure to reach a level of service that really makes a difference to the customer, accepting compromises due to implementation obstacles, the inability to create stable improvement conditions, and the lack of quantitative measures of impact.

Banks can get off on the right foot by understanding where the value really lies. This means establishing the quantitative relationship between actions taken on service and the value these actions will generate. The broad qualitative link is that satisfied customers tend to buy more, switch less, and even choose one bank over another if they think it offers better service.

However, it is important to understand that the relationship between service level and customer satisfaction tends to follow an S-curve with two breakpoints (Figure 14.3). If service levels fall below the lower breakpoint, customer satisfaction tends to deteriorate rapidly, giving rise to customer churn. From the lower

[16] Annual report 2001.

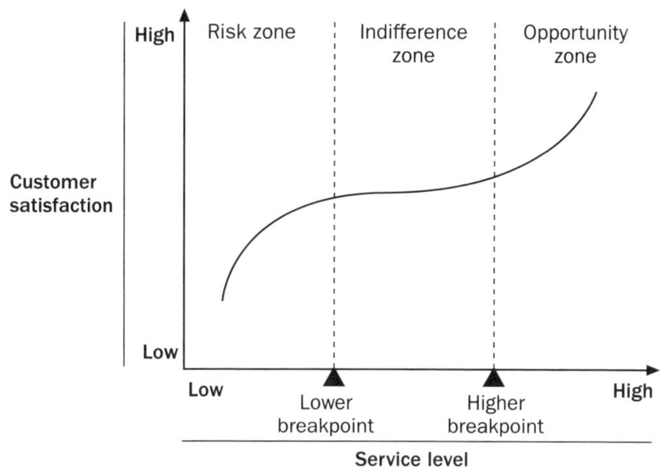

Figure 14.3 Relationship between service level and customer satisfaction

Source: McKinsey

breakpoint to the upper breakpoint customer satisfaction tends not to change significantly. Above the upper breakpoint it increases significantly, with positive benefits for the bank.

A good strategy is to invest where customer satisfaction tends to increase rapidly (below the lower breakpoint) and avoid investing if the upper breakpoint of customer satisfaction cannot be reached. In other words, invest in those areas where the bank is badly positioned.

Advanced market analysis techniques, such as conjoint analysis, allow banks to understand the exact shape of customer satisfaction curves and make decisions accordingly. For example, a Spanish bank conducted a conjoint analysis and thus calculated the conversion rate between service performance and percent increase in current account interest margin. The results were:

- image from 'popular' to 'prestigious': +4.3 percent;
- speed on operation *A* from 30 to 15 minutes: +2.2 percent;
- proximity from 10 km to 1 km: +1.6 percent;
- information availability from simple to detailed: +1.3 percent;
- speed on operation *B* from 15 to 5 minutes: +1.2 percent.

A US bank ascertained through market research which aspects of its service-offering would create the most value. It was able to define and act on those with potentially the greatest impact on customer relationships: account-opening, product purchases, and problem resolution.

As we have said, finding what the customer really values is the key to implementing any customer service program. By determining what economic effect a specific service-related action is likely to have on churn rates, share of customer wallet, and customer acquisition, a bank can prioritize the levers it must pull to create value.

Although retail banks are beginning to take the issue of delivering high-quality service seriously, service has yet to be fully acknowledged as a weapon by most of them. In a competitive, commoditized market, neglecting to tackle service quality issues diligently could be risky, especially if successful first movers show that investing in service is the road to take. In the quest for a competitive advantage, getting service right could put a bank several steps ahead—and keeping high service levels could make its position unassailable.

Part 4

Differentiated and Efficient Distribution

15
Lessons from the Decade of Distribution

Iacopo De Francisco, Reinhold Leichtfuss, Stefano Visalli

Back in the 1990s, bankers attending a series of workshops on excellence in retail banking clearly saw distribution as the hot topic. The 1990s was, after all, the decade of distribution; a period when banks restructured their networks and rushed to invest in new channels. But now that the dust has settled from this frenzy of activity, we can see that distribution has not emerged as a significant differentiator between the best performing banks and the rest.

Yet there is no doubt that the 1990s was a time of revolution in distribution: nonbranch sales of banking products and services now represent 15 percent of the total, with the trend toward acceptance of nonbranch channels likely to continue. It is true that some of the most recent channels have not turned out to be a holy grail—more of a white elephant in some cases—and the branch continues to be a core channel. But is the lack of differentiation simply a case of all banks following the same model, or could it be that, at the end of the day, distribution offers little opportunity for differentiation? Given that it accounts for up to 35 to 40 percent of a typical retail bank's cost, the issue is an important one for any bank. In what follows, we take a brief look at how distribution has evolved and establish what banks can learn from this as they go forward. Individual channels—branches, direct channels, and financial adviser networks—are discussed in separate chapters, and the part concludes with a chapter on how best to manage all these channels.

AN AVALANCHE OF OPPORTUNITIES: FROM ATM TO iTV

In the 1970s, after decades of inhabiting a static distribution landscape, retail banks began to take baby steps toward making it easier and more convenient for their customers to conduct transactions. Many of these developments have ended up almost fizzling out—despite often being introduced with a bang—but there is no doubt that the initial timid forays into alternative channels eventually triggered an avalanche of opportunities (Figure 15.1).

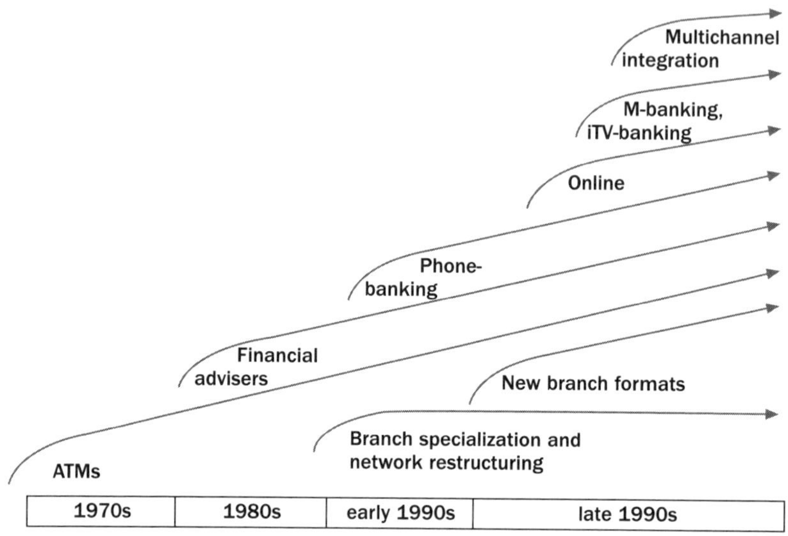

Figure 15.1 Key distribution developments since the 1970s

Source: McKinsey

Heavy investments in ATMs

The first automatic teller machines (ATMs) were introduced in the 1970s, but took a full 20 years to really take off in Europe. Today, life without them seems inconceivable. To date, the banking industry worldwide has invested upward of $30bn in buying over a million ATMs and several times that in servicing and running them. The annual investment in ATMs is higher than the total investment banks have made to date in their online channels. Between 1990 and 2001, the number of cash machines in Europe grew from 70 000 to more than 200 000, at a rate of more than 10 percent a year, and now virtually every branch is equipped with one.

About 60 percent of the ATMs in the US now have nonbranch, stand-alone locations. Almost 60 percent of customers in the US use the 'hole in the wall' on a regular basis for cash withdrawals and some 20 percent use them for cash deposits, thus freeing up considerable branch employee time.[1]

Ironically, by making cash withdrawal convenient and ubiquitous, ATMs have enhanced the role of cash at a time when banks would prefer customers to make full use of electronic payments. Thus, while it is hard to gauge the extent to which banks have profited from ATMs, customers have benefited tremendously. ATM networks recently experienced an accelerated growth, particularly in the US and the UK, where there has been a boom of stand-alone ATMs, reflecting deregulation of surcharges and the relatively low density of branch networks.

Financial adviser networks on the attack

In the mid-1980s the first mobile sales forces were deployed. These were financial advisers who offered customers personalized investment services at home. In some

[1] NFO Financial Services, *State of the Retail Market*, November 2002.

countries, they managed to garner a significant share of the asset gathering market. In the US and the UK, such networks have been established for some time, while in parts of continental Europe they are younger, but have grown rapidly, reaching sizable market shares. Examples include Banca Fideuram in Italy, one of the high-performing banks, and MLP and DVAG in Germany, which have both shown steady growth. Financial adviser networks challenged existing banks' value propositions for affluent customers, offering tailored, independent investment advice combined with push-selling. At the same time, they were able to attract the best salespeople by offering higher wages, better training, and more sophisticated support tools. In many European countries, financial advisers are the major channel for asset gathering, capturing more than half of inflows in retirement products and mutual funds. Chapter 17 elaborates on the significance of financial adviser networks and how retail banks can learn from them.

Phone-banking—the right focus needed

During the 1980s in the US—and in the early 1990s in Europe—phone-banking became more prominent. Citibank PK in Germany and First Direct in the UK were among the first players to introduce the channel successfully in Europe. Although a few direct banks offered phone-banking through call centers during the early 1980s, only a smattering of customers used it.

It became rapidly apparent that the potential cost advantage of this and other direct channels was being offset by a massive increase in transactions and the fact that inquiries and transfers were free of charge (Figure 15.2). However, as touch-tone technology improved, banks became aware of an alternative source of value in automated phone-banking. Instead of trying to make the service pay for itself, the banks saw that the channel could act like an ATM, shifting basic transactions away from the expensive branch network.

Today, most European banks offer a hybrid of automated and human-touch services. A typical European retail bank with 5 million checking accounts receives 59 million inbound calls a year, and retail banks must be equipped to handle as many

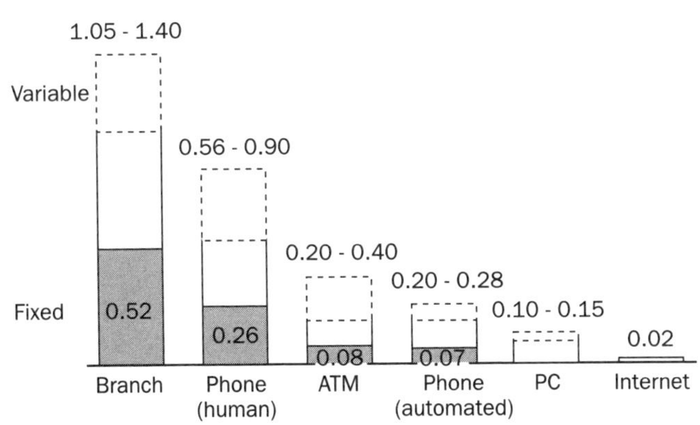

Figure 15.2 Cost per transaction by channel—indicative (average cost per transaction, €)

Source: Salomon Smith Barney estimates (1999); McKinsey

phone calls as branch visits. Nevertheless, banks still struggle with the right mix of inbound and outbound calls as well as making both efficient.

Banks' response: restructuring of networks

Pushed by these competitive trends and new entrants and spurred by new technologies, retail banks began to work on their branch networks as early as 1990 with the aim of increasing sales effectiveness and reducing distribution costs. Thus, they embarked on a path of specializing their salesforces and restructuring and rescaling their branch networks. Many continental European banks, recognizing that customer demand, products, and service quality vary between segments, aligned their sales forces and networks along these dimensions. They aimed to provide better advice and service for high-value segments by offering specific affluent or small-corporate customer centers. Banks also began to trim their branch networks and make them more efficient, drawing heavily on automation, especially ATMs.

Other innovative steps have been taken in this context, such as launching branches at points of high pedestrian traffic (e.g., at supermarkets) and, more recently, the co-location of branches in bookstores or coffee shops, with the objective of reaching a broader number of customers. Significant resources have also been invested in redesigning the branches and the customer experience itself, for example, by eliminating cashiers and cash-handling or through the introduction of different zones for advice, ATMs, and other transactions.

Online seemed to change it all

The second phase of direct banking took root in the mid-1990s, lifted up by the rise of online brokerage. This trend—already under way in the US—grew into the online boom that dominated mindsets and column inches alike by the end of the decade. Incumbents, alarmed at the growth rates of new online brokers, rushed to introduce online banking to defend their existing customer base but, by mid-2000, the hype surrounding online banking was starting to evaporate. Many new online players went bust and incumbents started to consider how to make money from their Internet investments under more realistic scenarios.

Finally, three other major technological opportunities had arisen by the end of the 1990s: mobile phone-banking, interactive TV (iTV), and broadband (high-speed Internet). Many banks again hastened to invest in the opportunities heralded to transform banking as we know it. Relative silence now surrounds these innovations, and their role in banking has been played down.

Experience suggests that new channels need time to take off—requiring significant investments on the way; and the time to gain sufficient levels of penetration becomes ever shorter.

Nevertheless, we are seeing ambitious innovators starting to expand their reach via one or more of these channels. We discuss the future of remote channels in Chapter 18.

The 1990s truly was the decade of distribution, as a combination of technological advances, increased understanding of the customer, and a desire to fend off attackers culminated in a range of channel-offerings that was unthinkable back in the 1970s. As banks look forward, there is a set of lessons they can learn from looking back.

MORE CHOICE FOR CUSTOMERS; SAME COST FOR BANKS

Although customers now enjoy a wide array of ways to interact with their bank, the branch remains the most frequently used channel. Furthermore, despite the growing usage of the Internet, the majority of customers continue to use branches and even visit a branch more than once a month, still unwilling to renounce the luxury of face-to-face interaction (Figure 15.3).

There had been predictions in the mid-1990s that only 50 to 60 percent of branches would still exist in 2000; in fact, the branch continues to have a pivotal role in banks' overall distribution strategies. In some areas of the world, such as Scandinavia, the UK, Australia, and Germany, the number of branches did fall by 3 to 5 percent a year between 1993 and 2001; however, in most countries the decline was slight and in some, including the US, there were even increases. On balance, therefore, the overall number of branches in Europe has remained more or less stable, as has the overall number of banking employees in Europe, the US, Canada, and Australia (Figure 15.4).

However, despite the longevity of the branch channel, banks are experiencing a clear shift to multichannel conduct, and new channels are now an essential part of the offer to customers. Even for mass market customers, the change has been dramatic with half their interactions now conducted away from the branch (predominantly at ATMs).

Although banks that have only direct channels still remain niche players, remote channels such as the telephone and Internet have been notably successful. In the US, for example, the total number of transactions in retail banks has increased by 9

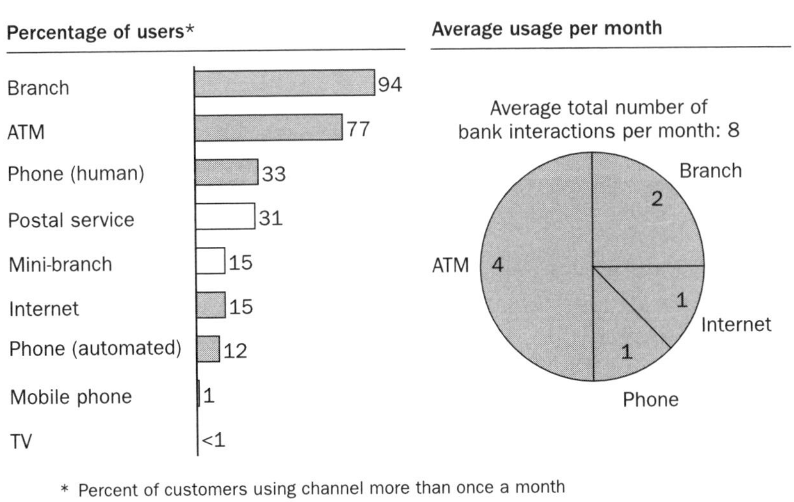

Figure 15.3 Channel usage in Europe

Source: McKinsey Mass Affluent Retail Banking research 2001).

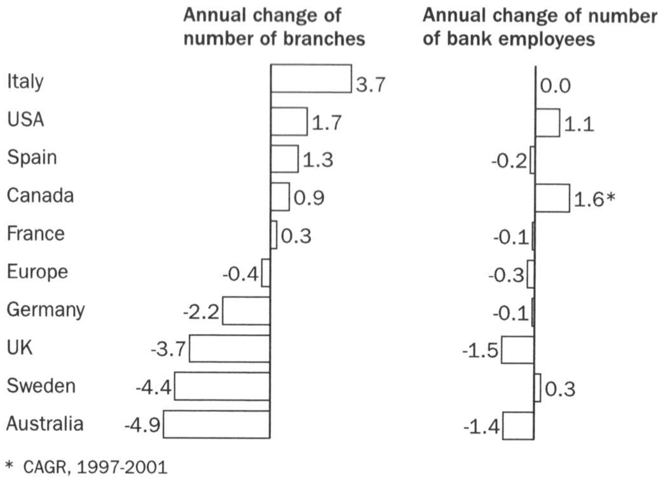

Figure 15.4 Branch and employee evolution (percent, CAGR, 1993–2001)

Source: statistical yearbooks; central banks; national banking associations

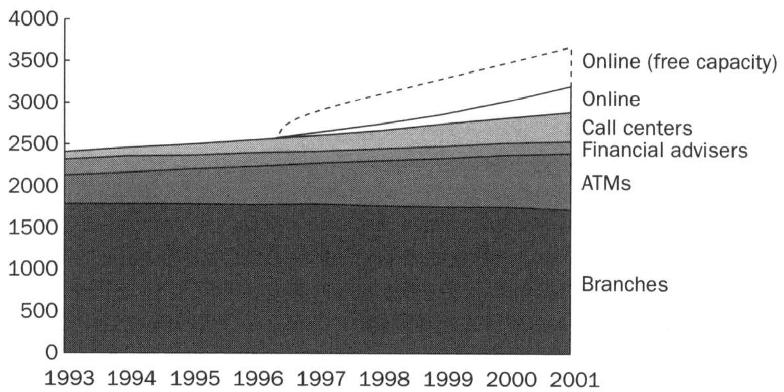

*Assumptions: Branch = 11 FTEs; ATM = 3 FTEs; FA = 1 FTE; call center = 2 FTEs (including interactive voice recognition capacity); online used capacity calculated at the same customer per FTE as call centers. Total online transaction capacity estimated at 50 percent of branch capacity in 2001.

Figure 15.5 Channel capacity development in Europe (full-time employees [FTEs], '000s*)

Source: Datamonitor; Forrester; J.P. Morgan; Blue Book; Statistisches Bundesamt

percent each year since 1996, with growth coming from all channels. Even though the branch's share of transactions fell from 52 to 45 percent, the total number of transactions in branches still grew at 5.6 percent. Meanwhile, Internet transactions increased at an incredible rate of more than 50 percent a year. Already today, four major channels are well established; with online banking attracting more than 10 percent of all transactions.

What is clear is that the overall distribution capacity of the industry has increased significantly. Totaling the number of branch employees, ATMs, financial advisers, call center staff, and online capacity introduced in the 1990s reveals that growth in capacity is approximately 20 percent, depending on the country (Figure 15.5).

As regards the scalable online platforms we have so far only included a proxy for the 'used' capacity. Since this capacity is able to handle many more customers, the potential capacity has increased much more.

The additional capacity has improved the service-offering relatively evenly across competitors, thus keeping its impact on customer acquisition comparatively low. As a result, despite efforts to improve the efficiency of the branch network and migrate customers to cheaper channels, distribution costs have not fallen significantly for many banks, and distribution still represents about 40 percent of a typical bank's cost base.

More channels has also meant more complexity, as banks struggle to figure out the roles of each channel in sales and service. Matching cost-to-serve, and thus channel (and product) proposition, with customer preferences and revenue potential for different segments is a big challenge. In Chapter 19 we discuss the issue of multi-channel management in more detail.

MAKING INVESTMENTS PAY OFF

With hindsight it is easy to argue that banks could have managed their distribution strategy better, but what would have happened to the competitive position of a bank that decided not to invest in distribution in recent years is not so apparent.

In fact, there have been innovators who have drawn clear advantages from being the first mover. A partial list would include Citibank PK in Germany with its phone-banking, some of the direct banks (especially the UK's First Direct), the financial adviser networks of Banca Fideuram and MLP, and Wells Fargo with its introduction of Internet-banking.

However, it is also clear that a large number of banks overestimated their ability to become true innovators and jumped at too high a cost into every new technology that was proffered at their front door without truly appreciating the high costs involved. It is revealing that the high-performing banks in our survey actually score below average in their investment in future channels such as mobile-banking and iTV. This is probably partly because they took a more thoughtful look at each business case, but also because these excellent banks are more likely to put their faith in the present rather than in vague promises of future riches. It also means—and this is a key lesson from the last decade—that excellence in offering new channels has been reached by migrating customers decisively once the investment has been made. The worst thing a bank can do is invest in new channels, but be slow in steering its customers toward using them. Getting a good return on investments has also involved making sure that specialized and dedicated salesforces really do serve customers better than they did before and that they achieve a higher revenue growth rate. In some cases this has been carried out successfully; in many cases it has not. Learning how to maximize sales power is a valuable lesson for making improvements here (see Chapter 13).

We have distilled four key lessons that banks should beware of in the years to come.

Do not simply stand by and watch the parade. There have been several successful first movers, and there are certainly opportunities for banks looking at new areas.

Moreover, if service levels improve across the board, those banks that do not follow suit may be putting themselves in jeopardy.

Avoid the 'lemming effect' and remain cost-conscious when investing. Many have overinvested in branch network restructuring and building new channels. Still others have not thoroughly thought through their value proposition, blindly copying instead what some of the innovators did—whether or not it fitted with their own model. In some cases, innovators took off in the wrong direction and realized it too late, while others pulled out as discreetly as possible. Some of the followers fared even worse.

Move toward cost-benefit-oriented thinking. Once an investment in new channels and different formats has been made, the entire journey needs to be marched through decisively step by step. Most importantly, investments must pay off. Unicredito has successfully reaped the benefits of a differentiated distribution network by simultaneously investing in new channels and reducing its cost–income ratio significantly. Many others restructured but increased the costs of distribution.

Work at multichannel management that creates value. This means cutting costs in channels where possible and exploiting income generation opportunities. Intelligent multichannel management builds on monitoring and steering customer behavior, makes the best use of channels, and provides the right incentives for network employees to work toward a common goal. Although the hype of online channels has subsided, more and more customers will be using these direct channels. Branches can be slimmed down further and move from transaction centers to sales centers. Some may just reduce the number of branches slightly, while others may move to a totally new mix.

Serving customers through multiple channels is a reality, both today and for the years to come. Distribution success for retail banks will require them to play with some or all of the options open to them: further trimming branch networks and developing new formats; expanding the roles of direct channels; and, finally, managing the entire channel mix more intelligently.

16

Branch-banking: A New Beginning

Carlos Beldarrain, Pedro Mateache, Bruno Montalvo, Ulrich Voss[1]

For the last 20 years, analysts and visionaries alike have been predicting the disappearance of retail bank branches. But here in 2003, there is no sign of this happening even given retail bankers' recent heavy investments in new channels. In fact, far from disappearing, branches are likely to thrive as the most important channel for sales and advisory over the next decade, with only a moderate reduction in their total number. Given a future landscape still replete with branches, success will come to those who can maximize the value of their branch network.

BRANCHES IN DISTRIBUTION—DOWN BUT FAR FROM OUT

Amid all the talk of alternative channels and new distribution concepts, branch networks have quietly continued to be the most important distribution channel for retail banking products. The branch is a key driver of a bank's economics: it is the major source of customer acquisition and sales activity (80 to 90 percent), and a remarkably high percentage of customers still carry out their service transactions primarily (or even exclusively) through branches (82 percent in Spain, 74 percent in Italy, 62 percent in Germany, and 56 percent in the UK).[2]

Extensive use of branches is common across all age brackets: the youngest group's usage rate is just 25 percent lower than that of the oldest age bracket (Figure 16.1). This means that it could take more than 30 years to reduce branch usage by just 25 percent on average in Europe. The need for branches would thus decline by less than

[1] The authors would like to thank Miguel Lucas, Matthew Usher, and Martha Whitmore for their contributions.

[2] McKinsey Mass Affluent Retail Banking research 2001 is based on 6000 interviews in 10 countries. Mass affluents are defined as individuals with more than €35 000 of household financial assets or personal gross income of more than €30 000 (which varies by country to make it equivalent in terms of purchasing power parity).

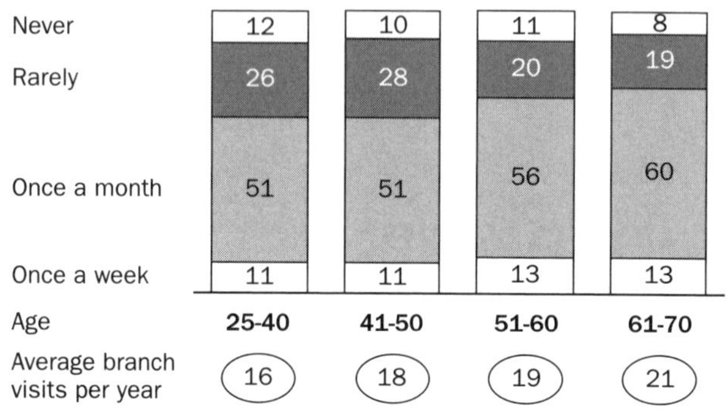

Figure 16.1 Frequency of branch use by age (percent of customers, 2001)

Source: McKinsey European Mass Affluent Retail Banking research 2001

1 percent per year.[3] Although this does add up over time, it certainly does not indicate that the European retail banking industry will undergo a drastic transformation over the next 10 years. Old habits simply die hard.

So, the demand looks set to remain. On the supply side, European retail banks have reduced the total number of branches over the past 10 years by less than 1 percent annually. There have been closures due to industry consolidation, productivity improvements, and channel migration, but offsetting this has been the expansion of some regional financial institutions.

We believe that the drivers of these trends will be in place for the foreseeable future, resulting in a slow overall decline of branches, but, as is already clear, the effects will vary greatly by country. Supporting this view (and contrary to common wisdom) the relative degree of branch saturation does not translate into a strong pull toward branch network consolidation; for instance, Spain, Italy, and France have relatively high branch densities, but their networks are still growing.

However, even between countries, there are some commonalities that merit attention. Branch closures related to consolidation have occurred mainly in small towns and rural areas, where the network overlaps of the merged banks offered the highest potential cost saving synergies. In fact, merger experience in Europe suggests that customer losses due to merger-driven branch closures are significantly lower in rural than in urban branches due to the reduced competitive pressure and further reach. On the other hand, in the absence of mergers, banks are closing a much higher proportion of urban branches, since their higher relative network density—and thus the typically close proximity of the next alternative branch location—permits significant cost synergies (Figure 16.2).

Banking productivity has also surged across Europe, with business volumes per employee growing at a rate of over 7 percent a year. A recent study by the McKinsey

[3] The underlying assumption is that each successive generation will have lower branch usage rates, while individual usage rates will remain constant over time. Whether this is seen as an aggressive or conservative hypothesis depends on whether the prevailing belief is that, as people age, they will tend to use branches more frequently or, on the contrary, they will further embrace alternative channels.

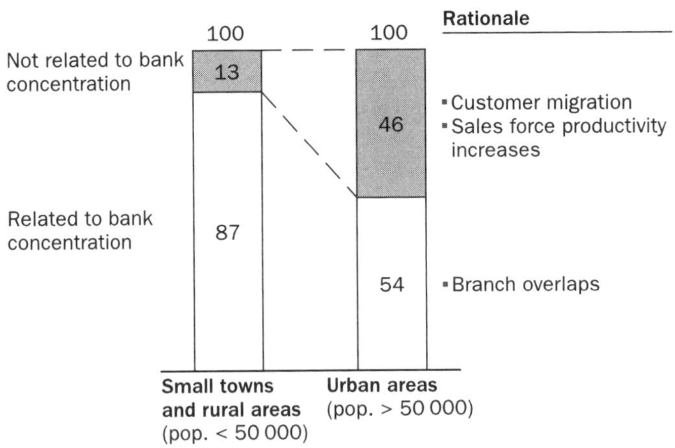

Figure 16.2 Branch closures in rural and urban areas—southern European example (percent, 1993–2000)

Source: McKinsey

Global Institute that examined retail banking productivity in France and Germany showed that the Internet-induced channel mix change has accounted for a significant part of the productivity improvement in the industry.[4] An obvious consequence is that the average branch volume will continue to grow significantly. However, as discussed in the next section, managing staffing levels for branch networks in high-density areas is a tricky balancing act between efficiency and customer convenience, which could result in either increases or decreases in the number of employees per branch. Low-density areas, on the other hand, will experience a branch size reduction driven by efficiency improvements.

Retail banks' love–hate relationship with their branch networks will therefore continue. Branches will remain critical to distribution, but the high cost burden will remain as well, since branches often account for more than 40 percent of a typical retail bank's cost base, depending on the level of back office centralization.

MAXIMIZING THE VALUE OF THE BRANCH NETWORK

If we accept that retail banks will almost invariably need a branch network as a crucial part of their landscape, then we need to look at how banks can get the most out of this bricks-and-mortar channel. Four tasks are important: optimizing branch network and individual branch size, emphasizing sales and advisory, selectively seeking new formats, and maximizing the value of the customer portfolio.

Optimize branch size and branch networks

Most retail banking branch networks have evolved without a clear strategy and common rationale. Few banks would choose the locations and formats they have

[4] *Reaching Higher Productivity Growth in France and Germany*, McKinsey Global Institute, October 2002.

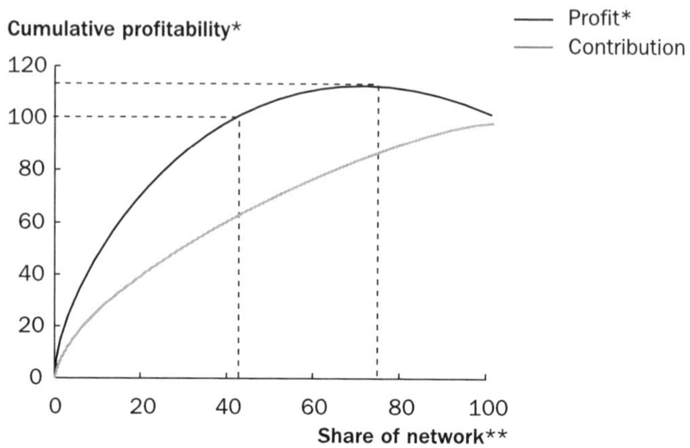

* After subtracting overhead costs and thus assuming that overhead cost is variable over the medium term
** Ranked by profitability

Figure 16.3 Cumulative profitability of a branch network after first wave of restructuring (percent)

Source: McKinsey

today if faced with planning a greenfield approach. Furthermore, branch networks are often not managed thoroughly for performance.

It is quite common that a large share of branches do not create any value. Forty percent of one large European retail bank's branches account for 100 percent of its profit; the next 35 percent added another 20 percent of the profit, but this was then eaten up by the bottom 25 percent of branches (Figure 16.3). Concluding that the bank should just close this underperforming quarter might be premature, as the economics of branch closures are not that clear.

The real savings from a branch closure are limited to the rent of the property, together with the economies of scale achieved in personnel (although these are limited). There is also always substantial uncertainty as to the actual customer attrition that accompanies closures even though experience shows attrition can be managed. In any case, rather than advocating mass closures, we believe that most European banks have substantial room for improvement in their branch network.

To return to our example above, when we look at the bank's branch network, four observations are startling (Figure 16.4).

First, branch size varies by a factor of more than 5, making structured management approaches and processes as well as economies of scale more difficult. Second, salesforce effectiveness—measured as profit contribution per branch employee—varied by a factor of more than 3, hinting at both structural and operational management issues and serious problems in the consistency of salesforce quality. Third, the range of customer penetration—in terms of both revenues per customer and profit contribution per customer—varied by a factor of 2.6, raising the question of why certain branches were so much more successful in cross- and up-selling. Fourth, salesforce productivity—measured as the number of customers per branch employee—varied by a factor of more than 2.

These puzzling facts force us to ask what drives these, at times substantial, differ-

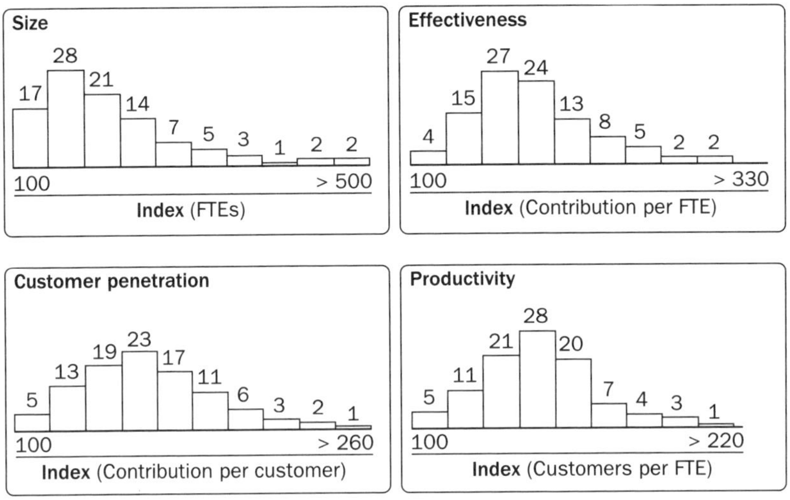

Figure 16.4 Example of distribution in branch size and performance (percent, 2001)

Source: McKinsey

ences in branch performance. We conducted a multivariate regression that identified four key variables in branch performance.

Location strategy is the first clear driver, as the built environment (e.g., city center, suburban, rural), exposure to pedestrian traffic, and regional wealth together account for 18 percent of performance variance. Product and service offering comes a close second, explaining 17 percent of branch performance. Those branches that offered the bank's full range outperformed smaller branches, which typically lack the critical mass of specialized knowledge. Branch salesforce productivity—the volume each employee has to manage—accounts for another 8 percent of branch performance. Finally, a number of important, but hard-to-quantify factors are responsible for the remaining 57 percent of performance differences between branches: local branch management quality, the motivation of the sales force, and the intensity of local competition may all play an important role.

Bank management can, in our view, significantly improve branch network performance by establishing a thorough sales performance program, while also optimizing the size of branches by aligning their staffing levels to local micro-market conditions.

Underperforming branches can—and should—increase their load per employee while at the same time taking a greater share of customers' wallets. Branch contribution can be split into salesforce effectiveness (contribution per branch employee) and branch size. Salesforce effectiveness is the product of customer penetration (contribution per customer) and salesforce productivity (customers per branch employee). Intuitively, it seems as if these two factors would counteract each other: increasing the number of customers per employee ought to have a detrimental impact on how well the salesforce can extract more value from each customer. However, our research found that successful branches actually perform better on both dimensions. When branches are compared with peers it becomes clear which benchmark they must reach.

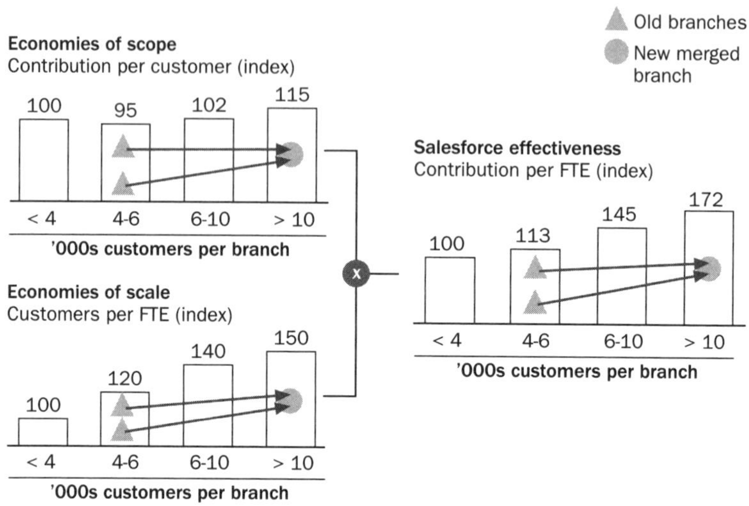

Figure 16.5 Advantages of branch size—disguised client example

Source: McKinsey

In high-density areas, merging two small branches will create more than the sum of their parts. In most markets larger branches tend to be much more successful in terms of contribution per employee. They consistently managed the double-whammy of more customers per employee and a higher contribution per customer. This performance difference per employee turned out to be 50 percent between branches with less than 4000 customers and branches with more than 10 000 customers (Figure 16.5). Behind these numbers, we see economies of scale, as smaller branches find it hard to work efficiently (a 4-person branch cannot allocate its customer-facing sales time as efficiently as a 10-person branch that can assign employees to specific profiles and tasks), and economies of scope, since larger branches are much better at cross-selling and up-selling (they can provide the expertise and have critical mass even for more unusual customer needs). This is particularly true in urban and metropolitan areas, where a bank's branch network may be dense enough to allow for quick consolidation without customer losses (in which case customer attrition can be kept to virtually zero), or where customer servicing (for individuals and small- and medium-sized enterprises [SMEs]) has been migrated to other channels, making a dense network of lower value to customers.

However, in low-density areas the rationale for branch consolidation does not apply. Often the geographical reach of branches is already stretched and the branch may be the only one in town. Some European banks have 40 to 60 percent of their branches in rural areas, at a rate of one branch per town. In such circumstances, there are only two choices for increasing branch contribution: either co-operate with a low-cost alternative channel (e.g., post offices), migrate the customer portfolios, and close the branches (at a larger customer loss rate than in the case of urban consolidation); or become a smaller, more efficient branch with a positive contribution margin.[5]

[5] Capital charges as well as direct costs should be included to calculate appropriate thresholds.

Emphasize the sales and advisory role of branches

Branches will continue to play several pivotal roles in retail banking. These range from marketing to customer acquisition and development to after-sales service transactions. Servicing, however, will to a large extent be migrated to lower cost channels so that branches can reinforce their sales and advisory role. This shift is likely to constitute one of the biggest challenges faced by many European banks.

Branches perform a key marketing role by conveying important brand attributes, often being the most visible advertising vehicle that a bank has. They are also crucial for building trust: 63 percent of European mass affluent customers do not trust financial institutions without branches. The proximity of a branch continues to be an important factor for retail customers when choosing a bank. Approximately 75 to 90 percent of customer acquisition takes place through branches, even though direct banking models threaten this near-monopoly by shifting attention and relevance to factors unrelated to physical presence; witness the success of ING Direct, Egg and Volkswagen Direct Bank in attracting deposits through competitive direct marketing and pricing.

To illustrate this, a recent study conducted by Royal Bank of Canada concluded that branches are far more important than they initially thought. This is not only because 70 percent of customers actually visit a branch at least every three months, but because their perception of the bank is driven primarily by these visits rather than by advertising, new product launches, or any other marketing effort.

Once banks get their customers into their branches, it is critical for them to push customer development. This means treating the branch as a sales center, with staff thoroughly focusing on proactive selling, Some 75 to 80 percent of mass affluent customers use only branches for their product purchases and about 60 percent do so to receive advice; conversely, only about 5 percent of mass affluent customers say they use only alternative channels for their purchases or to receive advice. Branch visits account for at least 30 percent of the customer contacts of a regular retail bank, with ATMs—typically located in or next to branches—accounting for nearly 40 percent of customer interactions. This shows the potential of the physical network to turn customer touchpoints into sales. Branches also serve as salesforce bases; they can be viewed as customer portfolio centers for teams of advisers, providing team interaction opportunities (e.g., for coaching, sales-planning, and individual motivation), which cannot be performed as easily with a mobile salesforce.

Notwithstanding these thrusts, the role of the branch as a center for customer transactions will remain important in the near future. Transactions are the inevitable consequence of product sales and could be considered after-sales services. Banks have been very concerned about these transactions: they are intrinsically unavoidable, and they typically do not generate revenue; thus they appear to clog up capacity. Technological innovation has helped migrate transactions to cheaper alternatives. Still, research reveals that customer branch transactions still represent a sizable percentage of the total (more than half in most European countries).[6] Some—especially transactions involving cash and document-handling—will move

[6] In fact, despite lowering transaction unit costs, the introduction of new channels has induced a substantial increase in the number of transactions (and the resulting overall costs).

only slowly to alternative channels; this is particularly true for SMEs, which will not convert all their paper-based and cash transactions to remote channels overnight. However, customer branch transactions are falling. Specific case examples show that, by using an alternative account with high pricing for branch access, transaction migration rates toward advanced ATMs and call centers can reach 60 to 70 percent in deposits and 95 to 100 percent in statement inquiries.

As the role of branches changes, banks with differentiated branch capabilities in the areas outlined will be better positioned to extract more value from their distribution networks.

Selectively pursue new branch formats

If the branch is the most important medium to reach customers, it is perhaps also the most likely to be attacked by competitors and new entrants. Banks must therefore constantly assess how to improve their customer interaction, and branch network innovation is one approach.

The transformation of the role of branches will happen in parallel with the trend toward specialization of functions and roles by customer segment. This specialization began with the in-branch allocation of segment-specific portfolios (mainly SMEs and affluents) to the salesforce, and, as a further step, the banks with enough critical mass have extended the concept to the branch network level, selectively deploying new format branches. Here we review five of these concepts.

Supermarket banking. Supermarket distribution models have existed for some years, seeking to capitalize on the flow of potential mass market customers. There are two different approaches. The US model, which consists of smaller, highly automated branches focused on the mass market, has had mixed results. While some banks have achieved cost reductions of around 40 percent and marked customer acquisition ratio improvements, others have withdrawn their supermarket presence.[7] The UK model developed by Tesco Personal Finance and Sainsbury Bank is quite different.[8] Here, the supermarket branch is not a real branch at all, but actually remote access to simple financial services (primarily transaction accounts and credit cards) marketed under the retailer's brand. This model seems to have been successful: the supermarket channel has proved to be 60 percent cheaper than the traditional branch model.

The UK experience might not be replicable for banks or retailers in continental Europe for four reasons. First, UK retailers are quite sophisticated and have very strong brands. Second, the high-margin environment has allowed levels of price differentiation that may not be feasible in other markets. Third, continental customers could well be more reluctant to swap the confidential environment of a traditional branch for the open environment of a supermarket or the more impersonal direct channels to do their banking. Finally, in countries with high

[7] Mostly under the bank-branding model, successes are TCF/Jewel–Osco, NCBC/Kroger, First Market Bank (first new branding in the US, between NCBC/Ukrop); Wells Fargo shows success with Basha and Lucky Stores and failure in Vons Stores, Safeway and Albertsons; Bank of America withdrew from Jewel–Osco and Kroger.

[8] Other banks have developed the US branch model type: HSBC/Morrisons, Abbey National/Safeway and Lloyds TSB/Asda.

traditional branch density, the convenience advantage of supermarket-banking is no doubt diluted.

Co-location with retailers/post offices. Some banks have tried to share distribution space with retailers in an attempt to access an additional flow of potential customers and to save money on rental. The UK's Abbey National is one of the more dynamic players in exploring this concept: it has launched ventures with food and furniture retailers, newsagents, mobile phone retailers, and a coffee shop chain. The latter, a joint venture with Costa Coffee launched in July 2000, has attracted substantial press attention and generated positive feedback from customers who appreciate the new atmosphere created. Whether the actual economics turn out to be sufficiently compelling is still up for debate. Wells Fargo's venture in the US with Starbucks, another coffee shop chain, did help cut costs through the sharing of space, but was unsuccessful at generating crossover traffic to the bank.

Branding seems to be one of the most important strategic levers for achieving success with this format, which implies that it will be crucial to anticipate how customers will perceive the banking brand associated with the specific retail brand and how to prevent potential brand contamination. Also, experience so far confirms that the physical format of the retail branch is an additional critical factor for success, as is a location with heavy foot traffic, high banking visibility in the facility, and highly automated service terminals affording customer privacy.

It is difficult to predict the degree of success of these formats. However, we do not believe they will represent a broad strategy among banks, as the potential new customer base is not necessarily compatible with the bank's and there may be a risk of brand-positioning conflict for the bank.

Partnerships with post offices are a special case and have been used as a way to penetrate new markets quickly and to be present in markets below banks' minimum efficient threshold (whether in expansion, rationalization, or consolidation moves). The good news is that costs for post office outlets tend to be lower than at traditional banking branches (e.g., €1.00 vs €2.50 per transaction in one European market), and—from the bank's perspective—these costs are variable rather than fixed. However, there are some drawbacks. Post offices can rarely offer more than simple transactions and product sales, severely limiting the potential for banks. It has also proved difficult in some markets to strike a good partnership. Finally, the model carries an inherent risk of nurturing a potential competitor, the post office itself. In any case, opportunities in this field may be dwindling, since a large number of European countries have already reached some sort of postal operator–banking deal.

'Light' branches. These are streamlined branches without tellers such as the Occasio format launched by Washington Mutual in the US. The bank substituted tellers with service representatives and financial advisers with hand-held computers, using a standardized design. It also built a retail sales area within its branches stocked with financial-oriented products such as software and books to help customers with their financial needs. This concept resulted in a 20 percent reduction in capital expenditure levels, while it achieved two to three times the business volume growth of the traditional branches and dramatically reduced break-even time.[9]

---

[9] *Mortgage Banking*, June 1, 2001; *ABA Bank Marketing*, September 1, 2002.

Another successful example is AutoBank in South Africa. It targeted a migration effort at low-income customer segments. The branches offered a reduced set of traditional banking products and services (savings accounts, instant account opening, and card-issuing and micro-loans through an alliance partner), along with other nonbanking products such as funeral insurance policies and prepaid cell phone contracts. The physical branch design also made full use of electronic service interfaces and an entertaining environment (e.g., TVs showing music videos). Results were promising, with 3.5 million customers captured in five years, more than 100 branches opened, and the model contributing 10 percent of the retail bank's profits.

We believe there is potential for this type of format, especially as a means to expand into areas with low critical mass for the traditional channel or to drive network segmentation aimed at migrating low-income customers to low-cost channels.

Affluent/High-net-worth branches. Following the trend of the 1990s in the US, this concept has recently been deployed by a few European players, such as Xelion in Italy and ActivoBank in Spain and Portugal. These branches are upscale high-tech-looking advice centers with real-time market information offering investment-focused advice and a limited range of banking services to their target affluent and high-net-worth segments. In many cases, the advisers work not in the investment center itself, but in a separate cheaper location (e.g., on an office building floor rather than at street level).

None of the attempts has reached a significant number of customers (either in Europe or in the US) probably partly due to the weak investment environment at the moment, but also as a result of both positioning and customer acquisition issues.[10] From a positioning standpoint, we think these centers need a broader offering than the one they currently provide, when compared with other affluent models, such as personal independent financial advice or traditional players' 'red carpet' model.[11] From a customer acquisition viewpoint, these business models need to deploy more innovative approaches to increase their current acquisition effectiveness and become more cost-efficient. Given the slim target market and the high costs inherent to the acquisition process, for most players these centers may serve more as flagships to convey an image of financial sophistication to the customer base than as a profitable sales growth vehicle.

Virtual branches. Spain's Bankinter has established agreements with corporate partners whereby the bank installs self-service devices at the partner's premises and offers virtually its entire banking product line to the partner's employees through their corporate intranet. Financial advice and additional product information are delivered through phone-banking, and the bank has a revenue-sharing agreement with the partner, whose personnel run the virtual branch at a very low incremental cost. Through these agreements, customer acquisition costs are low, as the corporate partners' employees are attracted by the convenience of making their recurrent transactions at the workplace and at competitive prices.

---

[10] In fact, Activo Bank's shareholders recently announced the closure of their venture.

[11] A more detailed definition of these models is developed in Chapter 8, dedicated to the affluent market.

These corporate-based virtual branches can yield excellent results as a means to acquire and service customers; however, opportunities are only available for banks with advanced technological platforms and will be limited, in each local market, by the size of the available spectrum of corporates with attractive employee bases.

The models described above illustrate that new formats have existed for some time and that although there have been some successes, it is difficult to imagine there being one killer concept. Many of the ideas have been tested in certain countries only, and some have not traveled well. Moreover, the success of these formats seems to be more dependent on the particular use of specific elements and on execution than on the overall robustness of the concept. We believe these new formats will most likely develop only in high-density areas, where there is a critical mass of the target segment and where the higher relative sophistication of customers will enhance the probability of customer acceptance. In lower density areas, traditional branches are likely to remain unchallenged.

Our view is that progress in branch network performance will most probably not come from any one single channel or format, but from a combination of them that captures synergies. New-format branches are likely to account for no more than 10 percent of the total number of branches by 2010.

Extract maximum value from the branch's customer portfolio

If a retail bank has to depend on branches just as a retail chain depends on its outlets to survive, then they may simply have to make the best of it. While a lot of attention over the past decade has been devoted to transaction automation and branch format, the branch's big advantage—its inherent sales power—continues to be neglected. In fact, it might be best not to consider branches a channel at all; instead they should be seen as the physical representation of a customer portfolio, with the branch staff responsible for maximizing the portfolio's value.

Bank branches are still not geared consistently toward sales: administrative work takes away time from selling. Employee profiles tend to be more teller-oriented and less sales-oriented. A sales culture and the sense of harvesting a customer portfolio is blatantly absent in many banks. Branches are more reactive than proactive, with outbound sales typically very small. Rather, branches open their doors in the morning ready to serve anybody who walks in, thus letting the customer—rather than the bank—drive the agenda and the day's economic results.

Banks need to go through a paradigm shift. They should—and we believe they will—manage their branches more like franchises: a concept where actual franchising (i.e., involving transfer of a share of the ownership in the business) is not necessary, but where a bank can get people motivated to sell. This can be achieved through team dynamics, performance management, incentives, and effective central support.

This is not to say that real franchises might not be the right way to go. Numerous banks have experimented with such schemes. A spokesperson for Abbey National reported that the bank's pilot in the UK had increased sales and made substantial cost savings. Australia's Colonial First State Bank reported a 30 percent revenue increase from a franchising model where the bank had to pay only the corresponding sales commissions to franchisees, which covered their own premises and labor costs. Dexia Belgium has been using a similar system for some time.

In order to achieve an effective change toward becoming primarily commercial organizations, branch network organizations and management processes will need to evolve from today's hierarchical, centrally managed models to newer ones that foster much greater entrepreneurship and a commercially proactive mindset.

This change must be reflected along several dimensions, dramatically increasing the variable compensation of the sales personnel linked to individual and team objectives, switching performance-monitoring from product holdings to new sales, developing core advisory skills, fostering individual and team entrepreneurship, and increasing staff specialization by product and customer segment (which can be partially achieved by using effective sales support tools). Implementing this change will also call for redesigning the role of the branch manager and the relationship between head offices and branch teams. The branch manager role will have to shift from one of an administrator of resources and budgets to one of sales team leader and coach, actually becoming more of a senior salesperson, coordinating and tending to the development of his or her sales cell. As for the head offices, their supervisory role of today will be transformed into one much more focused on supporting the frontline with client and product leads, as well as specialized product and sales support.

Retail banks should be able to manage their branch networks flexibly, adapting them to market conditions. In this sense, retailers can offer four important lessons. First, avoid the traditional reluctance to abandon locations for fear of losing volume and adopt a dynamic, systematic process to assess the impact of new locations. US retail chain Walgreens relies on an impact assessment process to close poor performing stores, while clothing retailer Gap actively uses stores to drive migration to alternate service channels. Second, reallocate resources following value-based customer segment criteria. Home Depot studies its customers' value in order to invest staff resources where they generate the maximum value. This also means transferring best practices across the network (McDonald's optimizes the design, merchandising, and marketing of its physical stores to facilitate customer flow) and stimulating frontline brand delivery. Disney and Ritz-Carlton invest time and money in understanding the importance and status of frontline performance and employ comprehensive strategies to ensure capability-building. Third, test new formats; and, fourth, tailor the approach to micro-markets. Victoria's Secret uses consumer research techniques such as in-store observations and creates tailored product/pricing-offerings accordingly. Both Sears and Wal-Mart use demographic and psychographic profiles and traffic patterns garnered from their customer base to tailor specific competitive offerings.

The successful branch network of the future will be integrated into a multichannel setup, commercially driven, and dynamically managed. The fundamental trends driving these changes are already under way. The success already savored by select players, along with the thriving interest of others in making further inroads in this direction, lead us to predict a lasting, healthy, and indeed reinvigorated life for the retail bank branch.

17

Financial Adviser Networks: Embrace the Enemy

Maurizio Donato, Lodovico Mazzolin, Ulrich Voss[1]

It should come as no surprise that the demand for advice is high and growing, given a market that offers such a range of sophisticated financial products. Pan-European market research conducted among mass affluent consumers revealed comprehensive financial planning and personal advice to be one of their overwhelming needs.[2] These are customers who seek tailor-made solutions and who want the personal touch of face-to-face financial guidance. Financial advisers (FAs), whether independent or tied to an institution, have been highly successful in capturing this market, drawing on their entrepreneurial skills, high-touch relationships, and their ability to give perceptive advice.

Almost three-quarters of Europe's major retail banks now own or have a special distribution agreement with an FA network.[3] But many are still unsure whether to consider FAs as their enemy or to embrace the concept further in order to complement their other channels. An FA network can certainly help banks address some of the issues they face in terms of offering qualified advice. It can compensate for less proactive and undermotivated branch staff, protect their most valuable customers, and increase their market share at variable cost. Taking the next step will require banks to grapple with how best to overcome a variety of hurdles and to gauge carefully local market conditions and regulations.

THE FINANCIAL ADVISER SUCCESS STORY

Traditionally, nonbank distribution networks have captured a significant market share in financial products that require advisory capabilities. The economics of

---

[1] The authors would like to thank Vanda Boscaratto, Bruno Montalvo, Stefano Visalli, Paul McNamara, Paolo Pellegrini, Pierre-Ignace Bernard, Martha Whitmore, José Antonio Ramos, Rudi Forster, and Richard Gradidge for their contributions.

[2] McKinsey Pan European Affluent Investors Market Research 2002 (10 countries, 6000 interviews).

[3] Top 42 retail banking groups by total assets in the UK, Germany, Italy, France, Switzerland, the Netherlands, Belgium, Spain, Portugal, and Scandinavia.

these products make them especially suitable for the sales-based commission schemes that are favored by independent agents. Life insurance, mortgages, and—to a lesser degree—mutual funds all tie the consumer into long-term financial obligations or contributions, which allows the producer to pay high, upfront sales commissions. Across key European countries, insurance agents, financial advisers, and brokers distribute almost 80 percent of life insurance, almost 60 percent of mutual funds, and more than 50 percent of pension products. The exact share of sales in the hands of financial advisers varies widely across Europe, depending on local maturity levels, regulations, and demand. In 2000, it ranged from 71 percent in the UK and 68 percent in Italy, to 14 percent in Germany and less than 5 percent in France and Spain.

Many banks have suffered at the hands of FA networks over recent years, losing distribution market share, particularly in mutual funds. The share of new sales for banks, for instance, fell from 83 percent in 1999 to 78 percent in 2000 and 63 percent in 2001. FAs have thus apparently not only been better at capturing the wave of equity investment than banks but also experienced the downturn later. In Italy, for example, FAs were the only distribution channel that posted positive inflows in mutual funds both in 2001 and in the first half of 2002, while in the UK, FAs managed to grab 81 percent of new 2001 net inflows against an initial market share of 61 percent of total stocks.

From an economic perspective, the FA channel enjoys respectable profitability as well as impressive growth rates. A comparison of the performance of Europe's top ten FA networks (in terms of return on equity [ROE]) and the top ten retail banks between 2000 and 2001 shows FA pre-tax ROE noticeably higher at 64 percent compared with 45 percent, thanks to FA networks' leaner capital structure. FAs also have much stronger revenue growth (12 percent compared with 6.5 percent). On the other hand, the FA networks' cost–income ratio was 20 percentage points worse than that of retail banks due to adviser sales commissions. FA networks' big advantage though is the high degree of variable cost: typically about 70 percent of costs are variable in an FA network, whereas in a retail bank 90 percent of the costs are fixed (Figure 17.1). It is clear, considering these indicators, why capital market expectations for FAs are higher than for retail banks. In fact, even in the downturn, all the leading listed FA networks boasted a higher price–earnings ratio than that of the leading retail banks (Figure 17.2).

FA networks have profited from the inability of many banks to serve attractive clientele appropriately. They have also provided excellent earning opportunities for their advisers, which has helped them recruit experienced staff, especially from banks whose compensation structures typically provide little incentive for performance and therefore little upside for talented salespeople.

While the market has clearly given financial advisers more than a helping hand in recent years, high-performing players have succeeded by implementing clearly distinctive formulae that benefit customers and advisers alike.

The German financial adviser network MLP (2600 FAs and 2001 pre-tax profits of €151m) is perhaps the best known example of an FA player that has a finely honed value proposition for a well-defined customer segment. Despite its simplicity, it has yet to be copied successfully in the market. MLP targets future affluent customers (i.e., law, medicine, and business students who will later need sophisti-

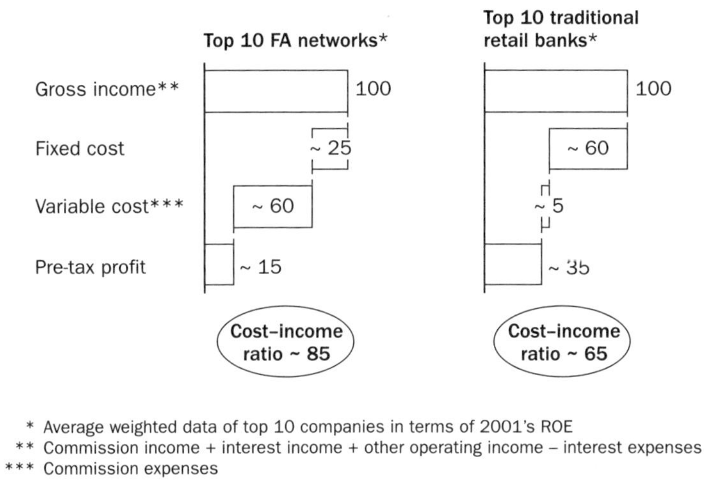

Figure 17.1 Cost structure of FA networks vs. retail banks (percent, 2000–2001)

Source: annual reports; McKinsey

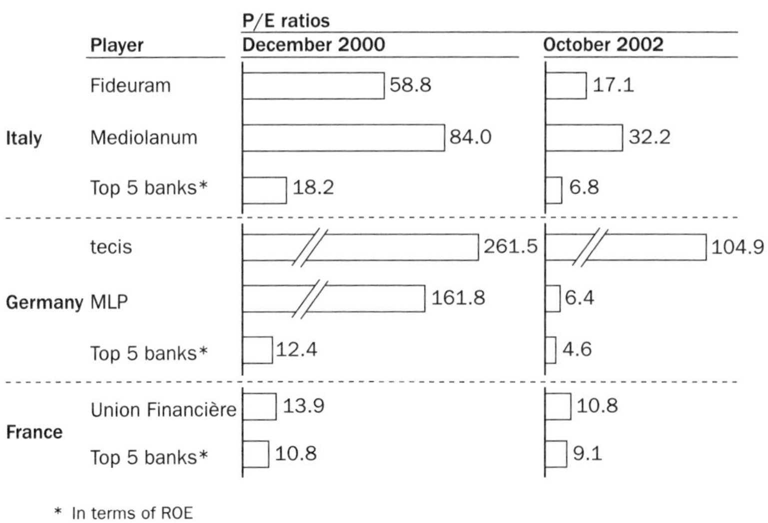

Figure 17.2 Price–earnings ratio comparison

Source: Datastream; Bankscope; Bloomberg

cated planning services). To capture them, MLP advisers organize career-focused seminars at universities, with the intent of establishing a long-standing relationship with the students. MLP advisers attend a two-year training program and generally have the same social background and standing as their customers. As 'peers' to their customers, they can build trust and confidence much more easily than the typical insurance agent or bank clerk. They start by selling low-margin financial products to students at the start of their careers, upgrading these products over the years.

One of the traits that FA networks share with their insurance agent counterparts is the ability to attract and retain a solid salesforce. This ability is one of Banca

Fideuram's key success factors. Banca Fideuram, owned by Sanpaolo IMI, is one of Italy's largest (3800 FAs and €229m in 2001 pre-tax profit), targeting affluent customers. Banca Fideuram's FAs are among the most qualified advisers in the Italian market and hold the largest portfolio (roughly €10m in assets under management [AuM] each). Banca Fideuram was among the first to recruit former bank employees, and its now ample experience has enabled it to build a veritable recruiting machine focused on finding high-quality people. It exploits its brand to attract people, assuring world-class operations and offering an appealing compensation package. From 1997 to 2001, Banca Fideuram recruited about 1050 people, with an attendant above-average portfolio, paying sign-on bonuses aligned to market standards. In the last two years, Banca Fideuram succeeded in increasing the size of the network by roughly 7 percent a year, an absolutely outstanding rate considering that it was so large to begin with.

However, Banca Fideuram is not Italy's largest FA network; that accolade goes to Banca Mediolanum (approximately 3850 licensed FAs, another 3000 nonlicensed FAs, and 2001 pre-tax profits of €119m).[4] Mediolanum uses a coherent multichannel approach that focuses on the mass affluent segment. Along with a very large salesforce, it provides remote channels and financial centers and importantly, extensively exploits its Mediolanum TV channel. The private digital satellite channel broadcasts both entertainment and investment-oriented programs for its customers and specific training and information programs for its salesforce.

The UK's Countrywide (2000 FAs and €9m in 2001 pre-tax profit) uses the skills of its parent company, the Misys software group, to provide distinctive service to its advisers.[5] The 'mi-solution' IFA desktop (dedicated software for financial advisers) provides end-to-end support, from marketing tools to fee-processing, thus increasing the time FAs spend on sales. Misys also provides training, compliance and marketing support as well as help in finding new FAs. Countrywide has one of the highest growth rates in the UK market with a gross income compound annual growth rate of 14 percent between 1999 and 2001.

THREE OPTIONS FOR BANKS

Predictions for the advisory market suggest that demand will grow at a rate of 7 percent a year over the next five years, with FAs retaining their position as the key distribution channel. Cost pressures will almost certainly continue (particularly at the lower end of the market), while revenues will remain stable: although volumes are likely to swell thanks to an increase in both customers and products, margins could shrink due to a combination of competitive pressures and the dissolving of ties between banks and FAs.

Banks serving the affluent segment through the traditional relationship manager model will need to refine their value proposition to compete with the FAs. This will

[4] Mediolanum's two largest shareholders are Ennio Doris (36 percent) and Fininvest (35 percent).

[5] Misys also owns another three important FA networks in the UK: DBS, IFA Network, and Financial Options.

require becoming more sophisticated through the use of financial planning tools and a broader mix of products. It also means hanging on to the best relationship managers and stimulating a more proactive approach to targeting affluent customers. At the same time, banks could exploit the FA option to grab market share from other players, assuming they can reach critical mass and create value within a reasonable time frame.

Retail banks that decide to pursue the FA channel option are faced with the issue of how to harness the apparent success factors of FA networks. From the many banks that have already started down this path, three basic strategies have emerged: placing products with existing networks, expanding distribution through the branch, and using a separate sales channel.

Place products with other networks. Banks can hardly avoid working with FAs. After all, in countries where FA and agent networks have captured a large share of the distribution of life insurance, mutual funds, pension products, and even—in some countries—savings plans and mortgage products, the banks are major producers and need the networks to place their products. Indeed, one would be hard-pressed to find a bank that does not have contracts with FA networks. Banks feel the same pressures that insurers have felt for many years: the problem has never been one of product range, but one of customer interface. They are standing in line to push their products to successful FA networks, but as more of these networks move away from exclusive deals to an independent stance, banks will have to cope with an increasingly competitive environment.

Expand the distribution power of the branch network. Banks today find it increasingly difficult to reach the more sophisticated customers through their branches. They may lack the regional coverage or the qualified and sufficiently incentivized staff to serve them. Many banks have therefore established independent FAs who—under the bank brand—act as independent agents and coordinate their sales activities with the branches. In some cases, these independent agents even run 'light' branches, particularly if maintaining a full-size operation is not economically feasible for the bank. For the customer, they are no different from the bank, and many will not even be aware of the agents' independence (and sales commission-driven payment schedule). While this approach is viable in certain circumstances (e.g., in low-density areas), its hybrid nature poses management challenges. A number of banks in the Italian market have pursued this strategy to strengthen the distribution capacity of their existing branch network (e.g., Sanpaolo IMI with Sanpaolo Invest) or to extend their distribution coverage (e.g., BipopCity), but, overall, the big retail banks such as Unicredito have abandoned this approach in favor of separate channels, thereby avoiding conflicts.[6] Some regional banks have continued to use the approach successfully, however (e.g., Credem).

Harness the power of a separate sales channel. In the mature Italian and British markets, banks have not hesitated to establish or acquire and run FA networks in parallel to their branch system. Although this can give rise to concerns of cannibalization and duplication of resources, this model may still be the best path to capturing the FA potential. Channel conflicts can be limited when the network

[6] Sanpaolo Invest was recently bought by Banca Fideuram; Unicredit Sim merged with Xelion; BipopCity integrated into the Fineco group, recently acquired by Capitalia.

Cross-border

Bidder	Target	Country	Value € bn	Year
Unicredito	OnBanca	Italy	83	2002
AWD	Tecis	Germany	369	2002
Banca Fideuram	Sanpaolo Invest	Italy	625	2002
ZFS	Bonnfinanz	Germany	n.a.	2002
AMP	Towry Law	UK	121	2001
Bristol & West	Willis National	UK	64	2001
AWD	Thomson's	UK	51	2001
Misys	DBS	UK	120	2001
Apax	Azimut	Italy	418*	2001
Skandia	Bankhall	UK	240	2001
Mediolanum	Gamax	Austria	n.a.	2001
Mediolanum	Bankhaus Lenz	Germany	n.a.	2001
Bristol & West	Chase de Ver	UK	177	2000
Bradford & Bingley	John Charcol	UK	160	2000
Towry Law	Advizas	UK	51	2000
Misys	IFA Network	UK	34	2000
Banca Fideuram	Wargny	France	n.a.	2000
Bipop	Safei	Spain	216	2000
Woolwich	Sedgewick	UK	64	1999
Misys	Financial Options	UK	64	1999
Mediolanum	Fibanc	Spain	n.a.	1999

* 5.7% of AuM; the deal includes profit sharing with Bipop and a soft loan by Bipop·

Figure 17.3 M&A in the financial advisory market

Source: press clippings

focuses on a segment that is harder to reach through the branch network (such as affluent customers). Separating the two distribution organizations also allows the bank to capitalize on the advantages of the sales commission-based agent network, which is usually culturally incompatible with a traditional branch network that lacks a true sales culture and incentives.

Unicredito has implemented such a parallel strategy. In 2001, it set up 1250 investment managers under a specific service brand—Dedicato—to strengthen its offer to existing affluent customers. That same year, to attract new customers, it set up a new FA network called Xelion (based around an existing group of about 750 FAs linked to the bank). Despite the market downturn, Xelion increased both its customer base and its assets significantly in its first six months and continues to grow both organically and through mergers and acquisitions (M&As).[7]

Banks considering having a network must contend with the *build-or-buy* question. Buying can be both expensive and risky. The acquisition price typically ranges from 7 to 10 percent of AuM and can run even higher. As a result, the payback period can be extremely long (i.e., 12 to 15 years), if synergies are not fully exploited. Furthermore, banks run the risk of buying an empty shell, especially if no lock-up clause has been written, meaning that advisers are free to leave the company after the acquisition. However, on the positive side, the number of acquisition targets should induce an increase in the M&A market, bringing prices down and making the acquisitions even more appealing (Figure 17.3).

Building a network can be cheaper, but risks lurk at every turn. Expanding organically or setting up a new network both entail recruiting FAs or bank relationship managers individually or in small groups. Recruiting costs, in the form of a

[7] Integration of other Unicredito networks and acquisition of OnBanca.

sign-on bonus, can range from 1.5 to 2.5 percent of the transferred AuM, significantly lower than acquisition multiples; but the recruiting process is a much slower process.

Launching a new network requires investing in infrastructure (IT, financial centers), which means that break-even for an initiative of this kind would be reached after roughly three to four years, assuming €7 to 10bn AuM. The initial investment can be trimmed by using the bank's existing infrastructure (e.g., branches, IT platform). These synergies can halve the cost and cut the payback period to between five and eight years; but experience has shown that integrating the FA network with the traditional branch channel can be perilous. Setting a few clear ground rules from the outset can help FA network builders avoid some of the pitfalls, such as any competition for business between branch personnel and FAs.

So, banks have to consider the trade-offs between the benefits of the FAs' sales culture, with the potentially problematic cultural and integration problems that they might encounter. But the revenue stream is too good to ignore, so even banks that are wary of any formal link with FAs would have to work on transforming their branches into sales centers—as we discussed in the previous chapter.

BUILDING SKILLS AND MEETING CHALLENGES

Retail banks considering how to compete in the world of FA networks should be aware that the road is often littered with stumbling blocks. But forewarned is forearmed, so those who decide to take this road can develop the skill set required to avoid the obstacles and meet the challenges.

The *sales culture* that is the lifeblood of an FA network, permeating through from top management down to individual advisers, is typically missing in many retail banks. FAs work and succeed as individuals, whereas branch banks thrive on team spirit. The professional ethos of FAs is more focused on performance and monetary benefits, whereas in retail banks a clear professional ethos may not even be clearly discernible. Learning to understand and manage the different sales culture of the FAs is probably the biggest challenge for a bank in managing an FA network, and they therefore need to work on their *salesforce management*. This involves recruiting the right people, providing them with the level of support to keep them loyal and happy (which includes making them feel like they are providing a service rather than taking orders), remunerating them at a price that is fair but which avoids eating into profits too far, institutionalizing the relationship with the customers to prevent the FA from having all the control, and ensuring advisers are productive.

As alluded to above, it is important for any retail bank deploying an FA network to pay special attention to *keeping costs at bay*. Fixed costs (e.g., compliance, recruitment, marketing spend, loans, office premises, and systems) in more mature markets can soar well above 30 percent, wiping out the variable cost advantage of the FA business model and increasing the importance of scale and individual FA productivity. A downturn exacerbates this trend, as the Italian market clearly demonstrates: in 2001, generally only big networks (AuM of more than €6 to 8bn) managed to turn a profit by, above all, exploiting economies of scale. Renegotiating FA contracts, introducing a cost-sharing mechanism for financial center costs and marketing actions (e.g., franchising), outsourcing noncritical operations, reducing recruiting costs through stock options, and attaining a significant scale are all means of combating these risks.

The narrow product range and scope of FA-offerings can expose a network to substantial *earnings volatility*. To compensate for this, FA networks should try to sell both a broader product range (e.g., insurance, capital guaranteed products, mortgages, etc.) and financial planning.

Banks need to ensure they do not miss opportunities for *generating leads*. Past experience has shown that mass advertising campaigns are far less productive, not to mention less cost-efficient, than drawing on a centralized database marketing system that can easily produce good contacts for FAs. Other marketing skills such as direct marketing, viral marketing, and sponsorships will also all help the drive for success.

Another concern for many banks is the *risk to their reputation*. The gold rush mentality with which FA networks are often associated is a regular cause of customer outrage over misleading advice or even cases of fraud. There is a degree of unseemliness attached to certain FA networks that makes some banks shy away from associating with them too closely. Branding, instilling good practices, getting closer to the customer, and monitoring the service provided can minimize these risks.

The FA network has shown itself to be an effective vehicle for serving the financial planning and investment needs of the affluent segment. Its capacity for producing better ROE and growth rates than the traditional retail banking model has certainly not gone unnoticed by many banks.

To harness the potential of the FA wave, retail banks should use the channel to increase product placement by making special agreements with FAs, expand distribution coverage, or, finally, create a separate channel to increase the market share in the affluent segment. Whatever the choice, establishing a successful FA channel is a long-haul journey, requiring robust business models and the right skills to embrace the 'enemy'.

18

Remote Channels: The Years to Come

David Chinn, Anupam Sahay[1]

The gold rush is clearly over. The early hopes from new channels have faded as investments outpaced demand, but customer acquisition turned out to be expensive, and increased transaction volumes have offset declining unit costs. Over 35 new direct banks were launched in 1999 and 2000—over a quarter of them are no longer with us.

But this does not mean a permanent retreat to traditional branch-banking. Behind the skepticism created by the Internet bubble, there has in fact been steady progress in the use and development of remote channels. While several prominent newcomers failed, Internet and remote channel usage at incumbent banks continued to increase steadily—and new channels such as wireless, broadband, and interactive TV (iTV) are on the horizon. Among affluent customers (who account for less than a fifth of the customer base, but the bulk of most bank's profits) usage is particularly encouraging.

The issue therefore, is not the relevance of these channels, but how to extract real economic value from investments in them. In this chapter we look at aggregate trends in direct channels, examine the role of individual channels, and shed some light on the central challenge of creating economic and customer value from investments in direct banking.

FIVE AGGREGATE TRENDS

We see five major trends in remote channels that will continue to shape the distribution landscape for banks over the next few years.

First, underlying use of remote channels will continue to increase, although branches will remain the dominant point of sale. In the US market, Internet usage has already hit 48 percent and is expected to stabilize at 60 percent by 2005. In Europe, penetration varies considerably with Nordic countries approaching maturity

[1] The authors would like to thank Simon Morrish and Matthew Usher.

at over 60 percent, while Spain, France, and Italy are underdeveloped with only one person in four or five using the Internet. There is considerable room for growth in Europe, particularly in southern Europe, but also in the two largest markets, the UK and Germany, which have penetration levels of about 40 percent. In populated developing markets, such as India or China, the rate of growth is even higher and expected to continue in double digits for the next decade. Today, branch and manned call center activity accounts for the bulk of customer interactions. Ten-year projections, however, suggest that remote channels could account for over 80 percent of customer touchpoints, forcing banks to rethink their approach to both sales and service.

Second, a range of new consumer devices will begin to change where and how banking activity occurs. Online-banking supplements call centers as the main remote channel today. Yet the underlying trend in consumer devices—quite independently from banking—does not favor PCs or fixed line phones. By 2010, by even the most conservative estimates, there will be 10 times as many wireless handsets and interactive television sets as there are PCs. Whether these devices eventually support innovative financial propositions or merely provide another form of access for straightforward transactional services remains open to debate—but there can be little doubt about the march of access devices and consumer technology.

Third, the highest use of direct channels will occur among the more profitable customers. Internet banking penetration rates range from 55 percent (Sweden) to 9 percent (Spain) with an overall European average of 15 percent of consumers banking online.[2] More telling is that these users are very active—logging on five times in an average month. Usage is spreading well beyond the technophile segment to the affluent, professionals, students, and over-50s. At leading retail banks such as Wells Fargo, the number of active users already numbers over two million. Over the next five years, it is a safe bet that remote channel usage will extend deeper into the mass segment, even if it is for limited purposes.

Fourth, the predominant use of remote channels so far has been in pre-sales or servicing activity—checking balances and comparing prices. However, in certain product categories, there is the potential for real sales and transaction impact. In the US, for example, over half of brokerage transactions occur over the Internet; in Brazil, over 25 percent of customers transfer money online, and 10 percent of sales of credit cards in the UK occur online. We are still some way away from a situation where most mainstream customers routinely purchase mortgages or long-term savings products remotely—but the role of remote channels in pre-sales and post-sales activity is steadily increasing, particularly in simpler product categories (Box 18.1).

Fifth, there will be continued pricing pressure, which forces greater innovation and efficiency. In some markets, such as the UK, pricing has triggered industry-wide change. When Internet-and-call-center upstart Egg launched its high-rate savings products, it forced mainstream banks to revise their rates upward or to innovate (Figure 18.1). This represents a real transfer of economic value to customers. While this may not be great news from a financial standpoint for banks, it does have the virtue of forcing these institutions to review their customer offers, institute retention

[2] McKinsey Mass Affluent Retail Banking research, 2001.

Box 18.1

Winning strategies for European online brokerage

The track record of online brokerage enterprises in Europe has been disappointing, despite healthy growth in both the number of competitors and the customer base. This is due largely to revenue volatility and the players' inability to achieve all the potential cost advantages. Despite nominal growth of the online brokerage customer base, for example, 25 to 35 percent of accounts are classified as inactive. Increased competition from new market entrants has also taken its toll on per-trade fees; in Germany, the average transaction fee generated by equity trades fell by 9 percent a year from 1997 to 2001. Online brokerage houses are especially vulnerable in bear markets because of their heavy reliance on volatile equity trading as a source of revenue (60 to 80 percent of online broker revenues come from equity trades compared with 25 to 30 percent for private banks). In the years ahead, addressing these issues through implementation of the best business model will be the key to success. Winners are likely to opt for one of the three strategies described below.

Integration into parent bank. This option enables players to reduce their cost base dramatically by drawing on the group's existing assets. The idea is not a fully integrated multichannel model, but more a loose integration, whereby the online broker becomes a business unit of the parent company.

The broker retains its own brand and value proposition, but benefits from the existing physical infrastructure and shared operating costs with its parent. The main economic benefits of this strategy are a lower customer acquisition cost thanks to the branch network, economies of scale through a common IT platform, and enhanced cross-selling to capture a larger share of customer wallet.

The prerequisites for successfully implementing this loose integration model are the technical capabilities to reduce the cost base effectively; an aligned value proposition; a specific incentive system for the branch salesforce to exploit synergies with off-line channels to the full; and superior segmentation.

Niche-targeting. The revenue pool of the online brokerage industry is concentrated in a small group of accounts. In fact, high-net-worth individuals (with assets over €1m) represent 5 to 7 percent of total accounts, but bring in 25 to 30 percent of revenues, while frequent traders (more than 22 trades per quarter) total just 2 to 3 percent of accounts but provide 45 to 55 percent of revenues. By aligning their product and service-offering to the specific needs of frequent traders or other high-revenue segments, online brokers can garner a significant share of the revenue pool.

One company that has implemented such a strategy is Twice.it. This broker has increased the sophistication of its offer over time from simple online stock market-trading to online trading in derivatives, short sell intraday or overnight, and margin-trading. The consistent implementation of this focused strategy has allowed Twice.it to take the lead in the online Italian derivatives market with a 34 percent market share.

Consolidation. Online brokers jumping on the M&A bandwagon hope to gain market share, size, and the potential synergies of the merged brokers. Cost synergies, estimated in the range of 10 to 20 percent a year, come from savings in operating costs (redundancies in back office, IT, and overheads, together with enhanced bargaining power with suppliers), depreciation from reduction in capital expenditure from the elimination of overlapping investments, the rationalization of IT platforms, and savings in marketing costs. Revenue synergies can lead to increases of 4 to 8 percent a year through the cross-selling of products to each player's customer base. In the US, online brokers have had a head start on consolidation, and the top three now have a market share of roughly 60 percent (compared with 35 percent in the more fragmented European industry).

Andrea Scerch, Luca Martini

measures, and accelerate their efficiency programs. In some ways, it simply accelerates the Darwinian evolution that is occurring among banks across the world.

DIFFERENT PROGNOSES FOR DIFFERENT CHANNELS

While the aggregate trends we discussed are undeniable, they can mask the nuanced evolution of individual channels. It is helpful to look at each remote channel

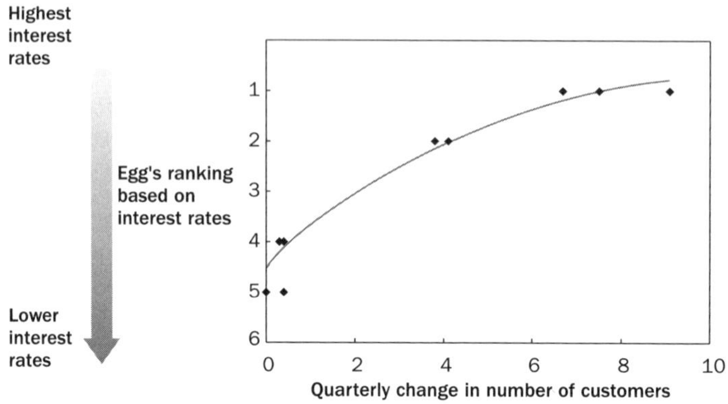

* Based on a sample of the 20 leading savings providers' best rates offered on instant access/no-notice accounts with £10000 balance

Figure 18.1 Egg's deposits interest rate and customer growth* (percent, Q3 1999–Q2 2002)

Source: MoneyFacts; Egg annual reports

individually to understand the complexity faced by banks, as these channels are at varying levels of maturity and have distinct sales and service characteristics.

The Internet: after the bubble

Several things have changed since 2000 when bankers chased Internet valuations with experimental business models rather than sustainable online revenue and cost programs. First, it has become clear that stand-alone Internet banks and brokers have lost out to incumbent banks—the costs of customer acquisition were prohibitive. Second, the Internet works best in concert with other channels, particularly call centers, in a multichannel environment—there will be few takers for monochannel offers. Third, it is apparent that the Internet can and will play a variety of sales and service roles for a variety of products—including mortgages (providing information and comparison), loans (applications), cards (straight-through processing), funds (purchase), broking (completing a transaction), or investments (post-sale information). Institutions such as Wells Fargo and Fidelity in the US, and SEB in Scandinavia, are leading the way in this field.

With this range of opportunities, banks should redouble their Internet efforts over the next five years—not write them off. The investment this time needs to be in upgrading skills and processes, rather than technology or customer acquisition expenditure. These include customer relationship management-enabled sales processes, multichannel contact center processes, and straight-through operations design. These skills do not come naturally to most banks, so a concerted organizational effort is required if they are to improve delivery and create tangible benefits from Internet investments.

In addition, there continues to be room for new, innovative propositions. Citigroup, for example, has introduced successful innovations such as the *My Citi* account aggregation service, which gathers together customer information from Citigroup as well as third-party financial institutions. Similarly, it offers the *C2it* service, which allows easy payments by e-mail over the Internet. Technology aside, the core of these innovations lies in some good old-fashioned business-thinking (i.e., finding the real problems customers face and addressing them in new low-cost ways). As Internet technology matures, the emphasis at banks must shift from the tools themselves to the customer offer and what will delight them, while adding to the bank's bottom line.

Broadband represents the Internet's coming of age. Broadband is being rolled out in most developed markets, through one of several competing technologies (DSL, cable, wireless, or satellite) that allow the high-speed transfer of data, images, and voice. South Korea and the US lead the way with 21 percent and 15 percent usage, respectively. In Europe, the Netherlands is fully cabled, and usage in Scandinavia and Germany is growing.

The early Internet offered convenience, choice, and price; now broadband offers the potential to bring back the lost soul of banking—the personal touch. The holy grail would be the ability to deliver personalized advice through one- or two-way videoconferencing. For this to be economical, it requires a visual and higher skill version of today's call center, as well as greater and more stable bandwidth availability. Therefore, it is much more likely that broadband will be used in limited settings—in branches, in an investment center, or a corporate site—than in mass retail. There have been several early pilots—Egg with mortgage advisers who can co-browse a site with customers or Fortis with private banking. However, commercial roll-out has so far been limited to investment banking and business-to-business innovators such as the UK's Raw Communications, which broadcasts live corporate and analyst presentations to fund managers. Banks would do well to watch developments closely over the next five years, as broadband may offer transformational opportunities when it matures.

Wireless channel: payments on the move

There is keen interest in the implications for banks of the growth and convergence of mobile devices. Over the last few years, several major banks have made big bets on mobile phone-banking: Barclays marketed subsidized handsets with Vodafone contracts in the UK, while Spain's BBVA went as far as forming a joint venture with Telefónica. These deals were predicated on a potentially win–win equation—the 'sticky' banking applications would reduce churn among telecommunications companies' (telcos) customers (which often runs at over 30 percent a year), while the telcos would open up parts of their customer base to banks in return. While the logic was reasonable, most banks and telcos have parted ways in today's more sober investment environment, having come to the unsurprising conclusion that specialization is good and banks will never be telephone operators.

More banking institutions are now focused on simple, but value-adding, customer applications. Most applications are service-enhancing, such as First Direct's text-messaging-based account information or mobile-banking from Japan's banks via the 'I-mode' service; a few, like Schwab's Pocketbroker, generate revenues from customers who value time-sensitive information. But the real mass market action is probably reserved for wireless payments. Mobile market leader Vodafone, for example, has begun offering a range of payment options to its subscribers for commercial transactions, including aggregation of payments to the phone bill and an e-wallet scheme that works with traditional credit cards. Similarly, Exxon now offers remote payments at its gas stations via a radio-frequency device. The financial impact of such initiatives in the short term for banks is small—but the relationship impact in the long term could be substantial if nonbanks take over the payments device, leaving banks with the plumbing. The challenge for banks, therefore, is to figure out the role they want to play in the payments value chain and to invent new classes of revenue-generating applications, just as telcos have been forced to do.

Interactive TV: a brighter future?

A number of banks have actively experimented with iTV. Among these are HSBC in the UK, BBVA in Spain, and Crédit Agricole in France. Some, like the Mediolanum group in Italy, have used television to interact with a dispersed advisory salesforce. Others use satellite coverage simply to transmit data and improve efficiency across dispersed branch networks.

This experimentation has been driven by simple, but compelling logic—mass market customers are much more likely to own a television than a PC, and a financial purchase that is set in an interactive advertising context (e.g., car finance with car-advertising) could trigger consumer interest earlier in the decision cycle. The results have been mixed, despite some promising early results. Consumers still associate television mainly with entertainment (and banking doesn't quite qualify), and iTV platform providers such as BSkyB in the UK, have proved costly partners. iTV is more likely to be a pre-sales information and service channel, with lead-generation capabilities in the medium term, rather than a mechanism for closing sales. Investments should thus be commensurate with this role in the short to medium term.

REDUCE COSTS AND INCREASE REVENUES

Faced with the proliferation in new channels—and recovering from mixed experiences with the Internet—banks are faced with a conundrum. On the one hand, they must offer these channels for competitive parity and customer experience; on the other, making them pay off financially remains a challenge. This section looks at how banks might marry prudence with innovation when investing in new channels.

Many of the excesses and failures of early Internet-banking can be traced to irrational exuberance. There is no substitute for the traditional management discipline of realistic and rigorous investment appraisal. Most new technology is expensive, large projects often go over budget and time, and customers do not change overnight; and they certainly do not start cross-buying products they do not need simply because a new channel appears. Therefore, banks need to return to formal business cases with reasonable assumptions, valuation based on cash flow and profit, rather than the subscriber number or revenue-based models that were in vogue. Equally, a portfolio view is required of such investments. Maturing channels such as the Internet require a healthy challenge process for second-stage investments; emerging channels such as wireless may require pilots for commercial proof of the concept; experimental or newer technologies such as broadband would benefit from

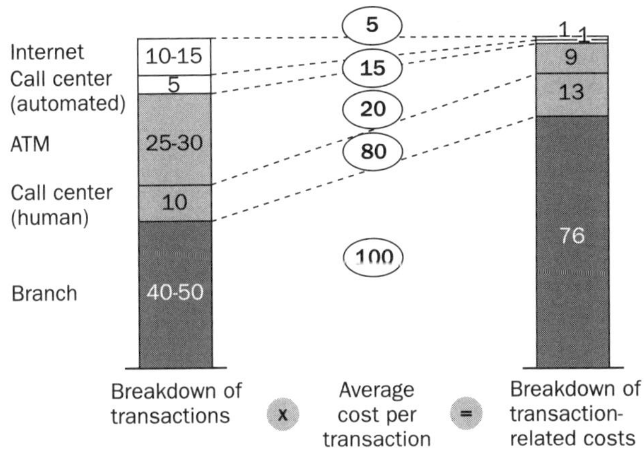

Figure 18.2 Breakdown of transaction-related costs—European bank (percent, 2001)

Source: McKinsey

research-funding to establish technological feasibility. In each case, the capital, business cases, and financial targets should be set according to the maturity and potential of the channel in its specific geographic context.

Reducing costs

The original premise that remote channels would somehow directly attack the fixed cost base—particularly branches—has proven to be false (Figure 18.2). Branch closure remains a largely independent decision, related to density and location, rather than the usage of remote channels. In fact, remote channels can mainly serve to reduce variable costs (e.g., the cost of processing an application or completing a transaction), provided volumes can be held in check.

One of the main lessons of the last few years is that cost-reducing channel migration does not just occur—it must be induced. This requires a mix of push-and-pull levers to influence customers, including differential pricing, customer education, and a redesign of the sales and service processes to minimize human intervention. Some of the changes required are mundane, but often overlooked—for example, having the same password or PIN across telephone, online, and wireless channels to make it easy for customers to use, ensuring a consistent look and feel across channels or creating effective routing between the phone bank and branches. Others, such as differential pricing across channels are more complicated, due to fears of cannibalization. Some banks have taken the logic a step further—instead of pricing differentially, they have baked channel access conditions into the product design itself. At The Woolwich, for example, a *Card Saver* account charges £1 for branch withdrawals, while ATM withdrawals are free.

Behind the efficient-looking front-end, transactions in some products, such as mortgages or mutual funds, still often travel through the back office, where things are often still disjointed or manual rather than automated. The real costs are hidden and can be eliminated only by taking an end-to-end look at the process from customer touchpoint to completed transaction. The gulf between distribution and operations functions in most organizations means that such a perspective is rarely taken, except in a few institutions such as GECC.

The challenge for banks, therefore, is to think holistically about channel costs across all channels, taking their brand, proposition, price position, and operations into account when creating a consistent lower cost offer.

Managing revenues

Although the emphasis has been on cost reduction, remote channels can also selectively serve to boost revenues. Banks can benefit from generating new leads, introducing new products, increasing customer retention, addressing new segments, and reaching a wider audience.

Examples are abundant. In the UK, for example, Charcol, a financial adviser, generates mortgage leads over the Internet which are then converted by call center or branch-based advisers. New products have evolved around direct channels. In credit cards, for example, Egg offers low-rate cards mainly serviced online; while Accucard allows customers to trade off and tailor rates, rewards, and transfers, as long as these generate the same value for the bank for a given risk profile. From the US, there is evidence that electronic bill payment and aggregated account information online leads to greater retention among depository customers.

Revenue potential is not, however, limited to existing banking customers. Online brokers, for example, opened up a whole new segment of retail investors: by 2001, over 30 percent of US trades came through the Internet, as middle-America switched on to an easy way to invest. Germany followed suit, with about 15 percent of stock investors trading online. At the opposite end of the wealth spectrum, the simple AutoBank innovation in South Africa, built around ATMs with straight-through transaction-processing, has allowed Standard Bank to address a large but impoverished customer segment that could not have been served profitably any other way.

The challenge for banks is to think afresh and put customers first. This is a reversal of logic for most banks, which tend to think about channels rather than customer propositions. Customers, on the other hand, react to offers. They want cheaper, better, faster. This gap in logic may well be the source of the gap in revenue generation that banks have thus far experienced with direct channels.

As with many technology-driven changes, executives and analysts tend to overestimate the short-term impact. In the longer term, they usually underestimate it. An unfortunate consequence of recent Internet experience has been a tendency to brush remote channels aside. It is time to look again at the fundamentals and, this time, to be better prepared for value creation and profitable innovation. Multichannel management, the topic of the next chapter, lies at the heart of this agenda.

19
Multichannel Management: Creating Value

Reinhold Leichtfuss, Heinrich-Stefan Rolvering, Mario Daberkow[1]

In the late 1990s banks became increasingly aware of the complexities of offering their services across a variety of channels and began a quest to find the best channel equilibrium. It readily became clear that the retail bank that masters multichannel management and establishes both a superior channel setup and the processes to support it cost-effectively will be able to improve its economic position and generate significant value.

Many banks have continued to make heavy investments in each new technology that emerges. They are caught between the desire to offer the ultimate service to customers and the very real problems that such a strategy poses. A survey by Forrester Research shows that European banks remain determined to continue offering all channels to all of their customers: 54 percent said that they want to give customers a choice for interacting with their bank, any way and any time they choose. Thirty-nine percent are trying to persuade customers to use the lowest cost channels through communications, service, or pricing differentiation, while only 2 percent are brave enough to cut costs by rationalizing or even withdrawing part of their channel offering.[2]

Whichever approach a bank thinks is suitable, one thing is clear: the bank must develop its own multichannel concept if it is not to destroy value. After all, the major channels show no signs of going away. But getting the concept right is a struggle for many—and implementing it to reap the benefits is an even greater challenge. A successful multichannel strategy requires, on the one hand, a thorough understanding of current and future customer behavior in each of the bank's segments and, on the other, comprehensive knowledge of the economics and value levers of multichannel management. The new multichannel strategy will require banks to redefine their management concept, which is likely to entail organizational changes and often a redesign of major sales and service processes. Finally, the whole concept will only generate the maximum benefit if banks are able to develop the appropriate multichannel IT architecture (Figure 19.1).

---

[1] The authors express their gratitude to Valentin Mihov and Sebastian Schneider.

[2] Remus Brett, 'European finance needs right-channeling.' Forrester Research, October 2002.

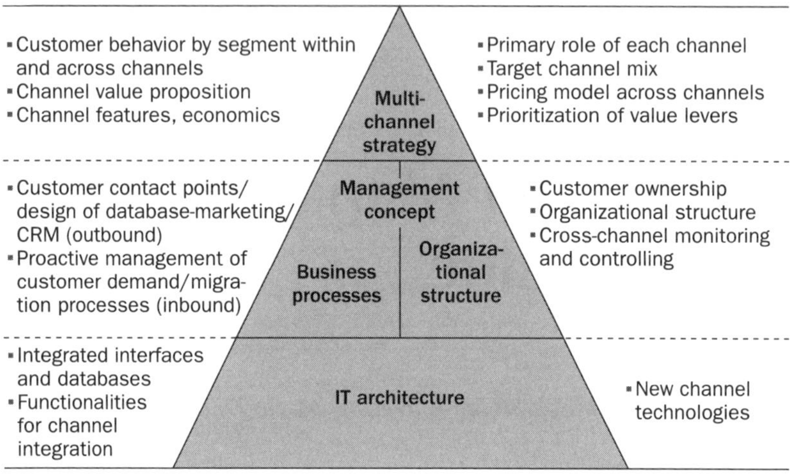

Figure 19.1 McKinsey multichannel development concept

Source: McKinsey

MATCHING CUSTOMER PREFERENCES WITH ECONOMICS

Defining a multichannel strategy that creates value requires working out how to match the cost-to-serve of various channels, today and in the future, with both the revenue potential and the needs of specific customer segments in terms of channel use. To do this, banks must determine the role that each channel will play and thus the level of integration required.

There are a few major trends in channel use that are likely to influence banks' channel offering going forward. First, the number of retail banking transactions looks set to continue rising across most channels. Second, banks will be reducing transaction capacity in their branches and manned call centers in order to help migrate customers to lower cost channels. This means, third, that while branches will maintain their important position, their role will shift to one focused on advice and sales. Lastly, customers will increasingly embrace multichannel offerings and will expect banks to give them a consistent experience. Certainly, not all customers will expect everything to be available online or through a call center, but the number of individuals using more than one channel is already quite high. Indeed, McKinsey research from 2002 shows that 30 percent of these valuable customers are already using four or more channels (Figure 19.2).

Recognize divergent customer needs

The first step in deciding on a bank's optimal channel offering is to understand how customers actually use each individual channel. For example, branches are the most important channel for sales, but only 13 percent of customers use them to invest money. However, over half still use the branch to check their account balance and more than two-thirds to make cash transfers. With the rise of Internet

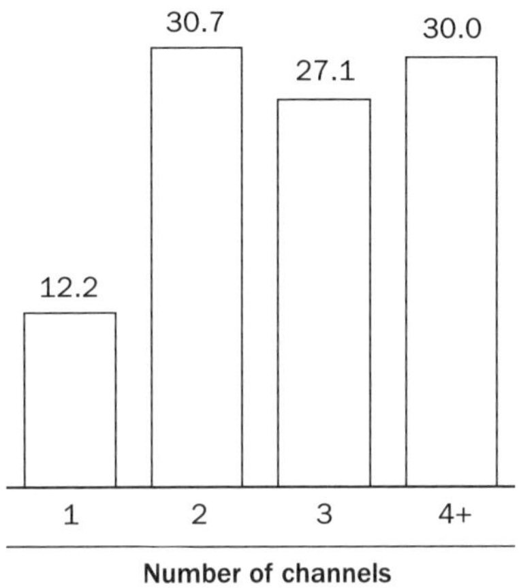

Figure 19.2 Number of channels used (percent of customers using)

Source: McKinsey European Mass Affluent Retail Banking research (2001)

penetration, the share of simple transactions and services conducted through automated channels is expected to double, possibly reaching 90 percent for money transfers and stock trading by 2005.[3] Banks should certainly look at market predictions when determining their plans, but they can act only as guides; banks must look closely at what their own customers expect and need.

An integral part of designing a successful multichannel strategy is quantifying the trade-offs that customers are willing to make in their choice of channels for different services. Market research McKinsey carried out in 2001 analyzed customer preferences and used conjoint analysis to derive the utility values for specific elements of the value proposition. The research confirmed that there are distinct customer segments when it comes to channel use, based on attitude (e.g., toward innovation) and financial sophistication. Thus, more than 40 percent of progressive customers (those open to innovation) with an intermediate level of financial sophistication assign greater value to the ability to transact online than they do to having access to a 24-hour call center. At the other end of the spectrum, less than 20 percent of the conservative and financially unsophisticated segment would be more interested in the online offering. The research also showed how channel preferences are not always considered at the design stage: reduced call center waiting time and toll-free phone-banking posts a considerably higher utility value than full multichannel availability—across all segments.

Based on such analyses, banks should be able to evaluate whether they really need to offer seamless access to the full product range, an integrated service, and comprehensive customer information at all touchpoints in real time. Given the increasing complexity and cost of channel integration, banks should be prudent when deciding how integrated they need to be with respect to customers' expectations, how integrated they want to be in order to develop a unique value proposition, and how integrated they can afford to be given the revenue potential of a specific segment.

[3] J.P. Morgan Online Finance Europe, 2000.

Customers do expect a consistent experience across channels; however, by and large, they neither expect nor need to have everything available anytime and anywhere.

Once banks have a thorough understanding of customer preferences and behavior, they can move on to the next step—clarifying the strategic role that each channel will play.

Clarify channel roles

Defining the strategic role of each channel for all customer-related activities means deciding on their primary and supporting functions (e.g., customer acquisition, customer development, customer retention, or customer service, across all products and customer segments) (Figure 19.3). If this is to work in practice, banks need to set pragmatic, achievable targets and control implementation rigorously.

One European retail bank identified three different segments and developed needs-specific branch formats with clear primary roles in sales and customer acquisition. The bank allowed only selected services in the branches. In order to fulfill this role, the bank developed very ambitious targets; for example, in the affluent segment, sales agents had to conduct at least five sales meetings or bring in €15 000 of business each day. For mass market customers, staff had to bring down the branch's share of particular transactions to less than 10 percent. In its call centers, the bank opted to push sales by setting up branch appointments and selling simple products directly and to relieve branches of certain services and transactions to enable them to increase the time they spent on sales.

Deciding not to offer all products through all channels, banks can avoid unnecessary investments and boost sales power, especially within the branches, by providing focus and reducing complexity.

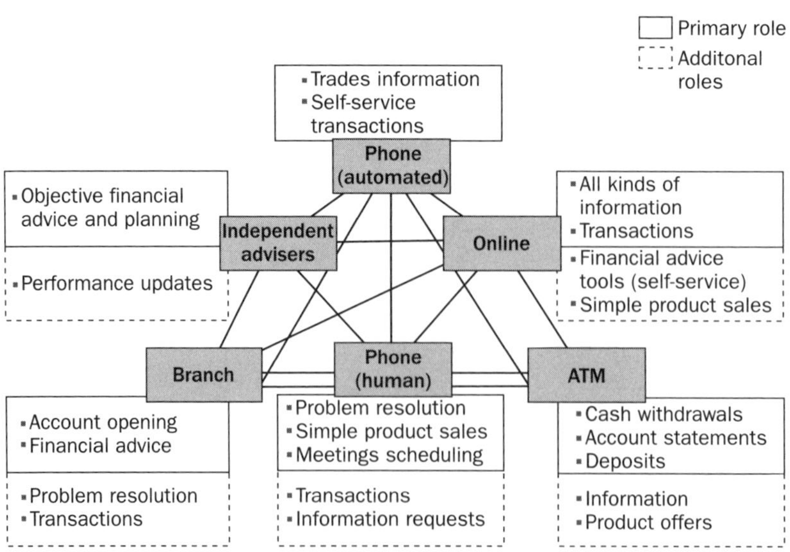

Figure 19.3 Clear roles for each channel

Source: McKinsey

Get the mix right

After setting each channel's role, banks need to set the right capacity. Analysis reveals a broad variety of multichannel business models.

Retail banks have traditionally had a multichannel mix that has relied heavily on branches, in contrast to financial adviser (FA) networks or new entrants who launched with direct channels. But although direct banks benefit from a favorable cost structure because they avoid the high fixed costs of branches, the branch still has the advantage of keeping customer acquisition costs low. Thus, branch density becomes arguably the cornerstone of a multichannel setup (Figure 19.4).

Charles Schwab is the archetypal successful channel innovator—and re-innovator! From its starting position as a US west coast discount broker in the 1970s, it evolved into the world's biggest and most profitable online broker, with almost eight million customers in 2002. In parallel, it successfully expanded its branch network by 60 percent between 1996 and 2001 to about 400 investment centers in 48 US states, in addition to setting up partnerships with independent financial planners through its Schwab AdvisorSource referral program.[4]

The primary role of its investment centers is customer acquisition and to act as physical account-opening points (70 percent of new accounts are opened in branches). The independent salesforce's role meanwhile is to provide objective, fee-based financial advice. Trades, transactions, and information, however, are offered online and through automated voice-response systems, while the call center agents focus on resolving problems. Each channel has a well-defined role, and the company understands how to use each optimally.

Citibank PK offers another example of how to get the mix of channels right. It restricted its number of branches to approximately 300 starting in 1990, while taking

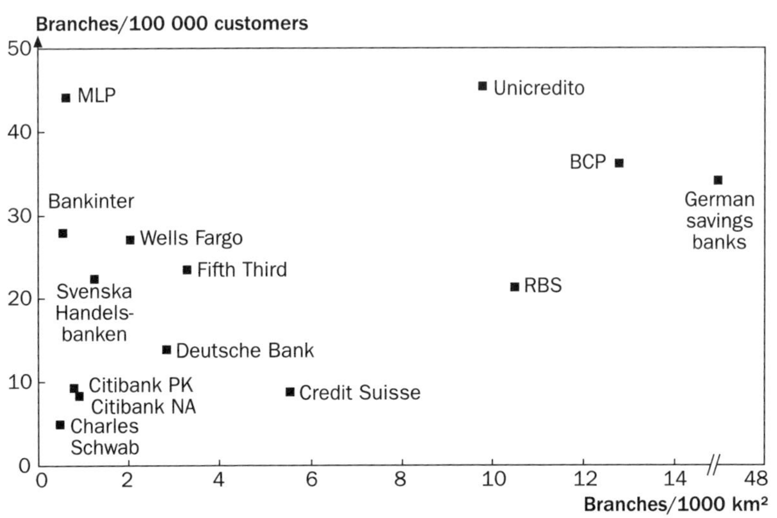

Figure 19.4 Branch density (2001)

Source: central banks; national statistics; McKinsey

[4] Charles Schwab, annual report 2001.

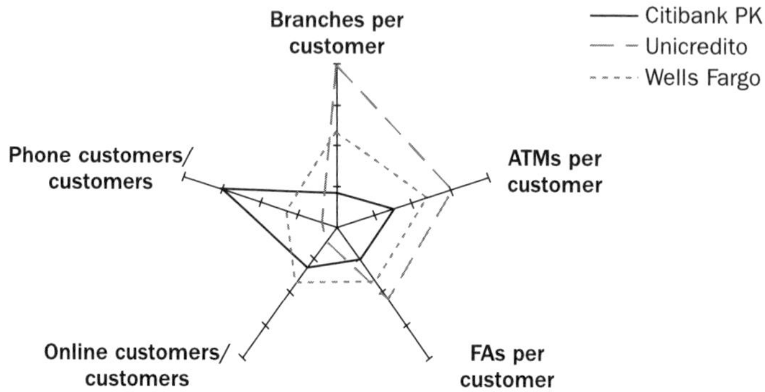

*Ratios are indexed based on the average of an international sample of 15 financial institutions. Wells Fargo provides the number of active online customers while all other banks use registered online customers

Figure 19.5 Multichannel profile (indexed*, 2001)

Source: annual reports; analyst presentations; McKinsey

full advantage of the opportunities provided by other channels, especially call centers. Citibank's branches cover all major German cities—about 60 percent of the population—and are predominantly focused on opening accounts and providing advice.

Also in Germany, Deutsche Bank's retail operation is moving from a branch-oriented model toward a more efficient multichannel setup. Its rescaling of the branch network (from 1200 branches in 1999 to around 800 by 2004[5]), combined with an above-average direct-channel penetration level, is expected to contribute to a boost in personal banking pre-tax profits and the improvement in cost–income ratio. Credit Suisse followed a similar route in the 1990s and improved both results and cost–income ratios significantly over the course of several years.

As we said earlier, the branch is still at the core of almost all multichannel setups, so, naturally, the way a bank shapes its branch network will define the rest of its multichannel setup and profile mix. A bank's multichannel profile tells us how much it has achieved in migrating, winning, and servicing customers through the alternative channels (Figure 19.5). Indirectly, the profile is a snapshot of the bank's multichannel value proposition.

Citibank PK in Germany has a relatively thin branch network, which it complements by promoting the use of remote channels. Indeed, it was the first bank to introduce ATMs and phone-banking. The bank's customers now execute more than 70 percent of total transactions by ATM, telephone, or online. Unicredito, meanwhile, started out by focusing on a physical presence in Italy, further developing its branch and FA networks, and investing less in phone-banking capabilities and online engines during the 1990s. As prices for building an Internet presence fell significantly and Italians warmed to the idea of remote banking, Unicredito started offering its customers state-of-the-art remote banking in a cost-efficient manner.

[5] Deutsche Bank, *Schroder Salomon Smith Barney (SSSB) German Banking Round Table*, September 25, 2002.

So, looking at these examples, we can draw a few lessons. First, there is no one winning multichannel mix *per se*; both dense and thin branch models can create superior cost–income ratios. Second, many of today's profitable multichannel models tend to have a bias toward one or two channels—partly to avoid the excessive fixed costs associated with strength in all channels—although this effect is likely to dissipate as multichannel systems evolve. Third, banks with particularly low branch density need very compelling value propositions as well as strong direct channel skills if they are to compete successfully with their branch-based peers. To take one example, Citibank PK is reaching customers via a TV sales channel and is experimenting with online audiovisual advice in 2003.

It is a delicate balancing act and one that is complex enough to elevate the issue beyond some other relatively straightforward banking tasks, even before considering the degree of difficulty involved in implementation.

Design for value creation

To determine the value-maximizing multichannel mix, rigorous modeling and business case calculation is needed. This requires a knowledge of the revenue potential, needs, and costs of the bank's target segments, as well as channel cost and capabilities for customer acquisition or development. The outcome will be a complex model of the entire chain of the channel service mix that will shape investment decisions on the mix of physical and direct channels, locations, formats, and capabilities (Figure 19.6). Depending on a bank's position, significant shifts in channel resources and budgets may be required.

To give an example, a European regional bank with a dense branch network in its home country planned to halve its network of traditional branches and simultaneously redesign its remaining branches and open new sales- and

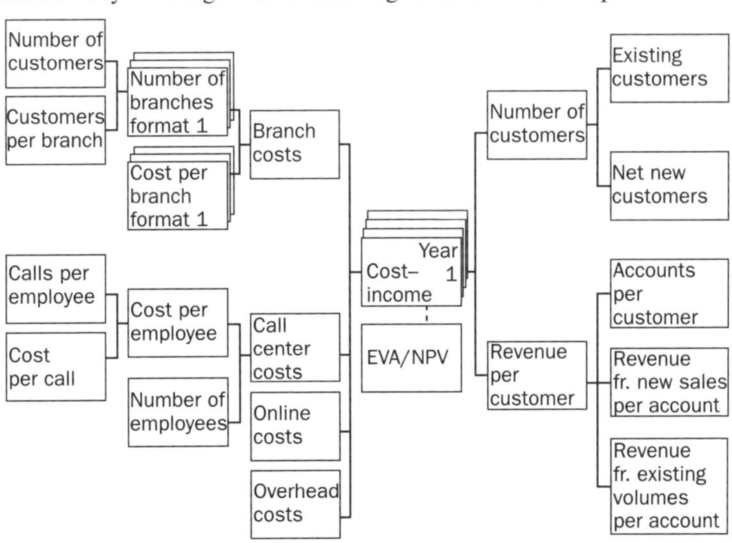

Figure 19.6 McKinsey value-creation model (excerpt) for multichannel management

Source: McKinsey

		Year 1	Year 5	Change Percent
Distribution	▪ Traditional branches	1000	500	-50
	▪ New branch formats	10	300	2900
Business structure	▪ Branch-based business	95%	65%	-30
	▪ Service transactions in branches	80%	40%	-50
Employees	▪ Traditional branches	10 000	6000	-40
	▪ New formats	–	3300	
	▪ Direct channels	200	600	200
Sales efficiency	▪ Mass customers per employee	750	1200	60
	▪ Affluent customers per employee	500	350	-30
Cost–income ratio		80%	60%	-25

Figure 19.7 Target multichannel setup of a European bank

Source: McKinsey

advisory-dedicated centers. Branch-based business transactions are expected to decrease from 80 to 40 percent, the call center has tripled in size and refocused toward providing sales support for branches as well as making simple sales. The ratio of customers per salesperson is eventually expected to increase in the mass market segment by 60 percent and decrease by 30 percent for the affluent segment (Figure 19.7). This combination of actions will enable the bank to drive down its cost–income ratio by 20 percentage points.

There are many other examples of banks that have changed their multichannel mix—either to a more focused or more comprehensive setup—and created value. A leading US bank followed a similar process of proactively changing its multichannel setup. It used a combination of price incentives, reduction of teller availability, and the temporary deployment of greeters to direct customers toward ATMs. As a result, it cut teller transactions by 30 percent, trimmed staffing levels, and improved pre-tax profits by 3 percent over six months.

Designing for value by changing the multichannel mix is in line with the principle of substituting capacity in one channel for capacity in another. As Citibank PK's Peter Buschbeck points out, 'Establishing additional channels makes sense only if these relieve existing channels. Such substitution is the recipe for an efficient, high-quality and cost-conscious multichannel distribution.'[6]

Price channels to reflect their value to customers

Attractive multichannel value propositions need to be supported by a pricing model that will both generate new revenue streams and help create the optimal channel mix. Leading players use pricing skills to differentiate their multichannel offering from

[6] Citibank presentation at *Privatkundengeschäft* conference, Frankfurt, February 19, 2003.

single-channel offerings, and the multichannel offering tends to be at the higher end of the price band. For many banks, especially those that have not clearly differentiated multichannel-pricing from pure online offerings, this may mean there is room for price increases. This is especially the case for brokerage and payments. One European bank, for instance, managed to revert a trend of falling revenues in the brokerage business in 2002 simply by adjusting prices. It altered individual price components while staying within the price band of its competitors' multichannel prices by taking a position at the upper end of the band for less price-sensitive fees and at the lower end for charges that customers use for reference and comparison, such as transaction fees.

Precisely because many retail banks have already used price incentives to migrate customers to direct channels, now may be the time to consider curbing unnecessary discounts. Transactions and services for which the use of direct channels is nearing the level of maximum penetration are especially suited to such moves. For all other products and services, banks should check whether price differences are really required and, if so, what form they should take. Pricing is not the most important driver for using online banking by any means. In Germany, for example, only 41 percent of customers say that price would be an incentive to use online banking if services in the branch were more expensive. The ability to understand how customers perceive value across channels will allow banks to price nearly all transactions to capture the maximum revenue potential.

As an example, National Australia Bank is targeting a 13 percent reduction in its total transaction costs per customer by 2003, although the number of transactions per customer will have increased by 50 percent since 1999. The path it has chosen to achieve such an impressive result gives customers the right to select the channel according to their own price sensitivity and preferences while matching prices with the bank's cost-to-serve.

DESIGN MULTICHANNEL PROCESSES AND ORGANIZATION

With the strategy in place, a bank must set about aligning cross-channel sales and service processes and a cross-channel organization.

Establish cross-channel sales and service processes

One of the secrets of success in the multichannel environment is to increase the efficiency of database-marketing-led sales campaigns by picking the channels with the highest conversion rates for setting up appointments, following up on leads, and selling products. Banks need to establish centrally managed, cross-channel sales processes that allow efficient multichannel sales campaigns. At one European retail bank, for example, the hit rates for selling mutual funds to a certain group of customers ranged from 1 to 22 percent, and the cost per hit was anywhere from €40 to €160. By optimizing its channel mix, especially integrating the call center into actively making customer contacts, the bank managed to double its average hit rate and significantly cut its acquisition costs (Figure 19.8).

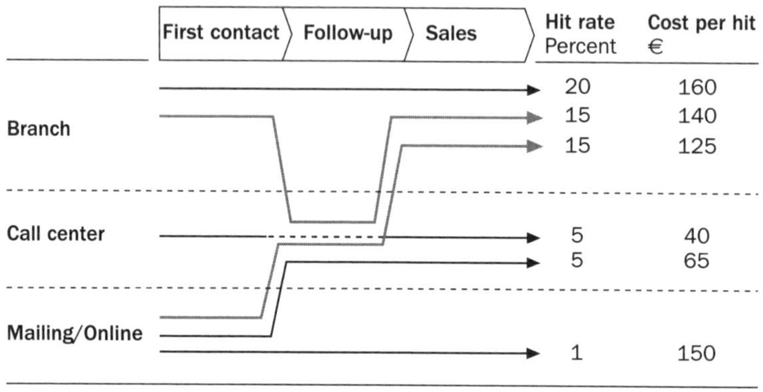

Figure 19.8 Cost per hit across channels

Source: McKinsey

By analyzing all the activities for each step in the sales process, banks can gain an in-depth understanding of which channel to use to improve the process. Given the complexity of the multichannel sales process, care in designing the interfaces between the channels involved is paramount. To ensure success in cross-channel sales, banks must continually refine their customer-oriented capabilities and instill a sales culture founded on transparent activity-based controlling.

In addition, banks should set up processes to redirect customers from branches to direct channels for simple, low-value-added transactions, and to guide customers to a branch if their needs cannot be served through the direct channel. Although there is a broad range of options for migrating services and transactions to low-cost channels, retail banks need to be aware of which are the most efficient. Business cases should be built on the share of migrated customers, cost of migration, and potential reduction in cost-to-serve.

A UK mortgage distributor escalates customers who are interested in mortgages from its online channel or the call center to its branches since the value of higher conversion rates in the branches is considerably greater than the higher costs. Other banks use leads created through the Internet (e.g., customers using advisory tools) or call centers to generate immediate, proactive customer calls.

Escalating customer leads also lets banks gain insights into customer needs, as existing customer profiles can be augmented with data on actual interest in a product. Even if no immediate action is taken, new data can sharpen customer relationship management (CRM)-based campaigns and increase hit rates. One southern European retail bank, for example, uses both inbound lead escalation and outbound sales campaigns through cross-channel sales processes. Whenever a bank customer asks for detailed product information—either on the bank's Internet site or from its call center—the request generates an automatic database entry in the customer profile and a link to a sales agent. The salesperson can then use the link for an immediate follow-up or the updated customer profile is used for fine-tuning any CRM-based campaigns. Consequently, the bank has increased its cross-selling rate to some four products per customer, 15 to 25 percent higher than its two biggest competitors.

Although such value-creation opportunities exist, cross-channel processes and cross-channel information must be scoped carefully to target customer needs and revenue potential in order to avoid overinvestment.

Establish responsibilities and cross-channel coordination

An organization geared toward multichannel management needs to resolve three key issues: how to ensure an integrated customer perspective, how to mitigate channel conflicts, and how to unleash the potential of centralized customer and channel management. A cross-channel perspective is required to align economics and customer experience, as decision-making must be customer-driven and cross-channel rather than being based on channels as individual 'silos'.

Banks must increasingly guarantee this integrated perspective on customers by installing managers who are in charge of coordinating customer access rights, customer-handling decisions, etc. To manage multichannel-banking, central marketing and segment management need to be more involved and their role must include designing or at least influencing products, services, and pricing across all channels, as well as defining customer ownership (i.e., the rights to contact customers). Thus, for example, call center agents can be allowed to contact affluent customers proactively, as long as the sales agent accountable for the customer relationship is informed and contacts are properly planned and coordinated. In some banks, however, affluent advisers claim the exclusive ownership and access to the customer.

Some tricky channel conflicts arise between mobile or third-party salesforces and branch-based sales staff. Although banks need to address the issue of cannibalization when introducing new channels and manage diverging business units' interests, this can be done centrally through pricing and revenue allocation. To minimize the potential for conflict between salesforces, it is crucial to establish clear rules. One bank, for example, introduced a 'first approach', whereby the first to enlist the customer becomes its owner and the customer may not be approached by other channels except after coordination. At another bank, mobile FAs receive—through branches only—a list of customers to approach with sales offers. Third-party FAs are then incentivized to transfer customer ownership to a branch within a certain number of months.

Revenue and profit allocation may become easier in the future. Channel performance management can rely increasingly on new sales-driven profit-and-loss statements rather than on statements based on previous periods' sales. In addition, channels should be managed by activity-based controlling to ensure that each channel meets its strategic role in sales and service. This will maximize the value contribution of existing business and, simultaneously, drive high sales performance through channels that can generate new business.

As banks develop their multichannel setups, central customer and channel management could become an important value creator. While the branch has remained the main location of customer relations and the owner of customer revenue, other channels have operated largely as service units and cost centers. With the development toward equal rights and equal importance of distribution channels, this model will not be able to provide customers with optimum service quality and will not allow banks to capture the maximum potential of their customers and channels.

Thus, banks will face the challenge of redesigning customer management according to new principles.

In the future, there will be more information available on customers as smart monitoring of customer behavior on the Internet enables better deductions of customer needs. Complications arise when this type of monitoring and data interpretation is extended to all channels—and all customer interactions with the bank. This will be possible only with systematic, standardized, cross-channel data management.

Customers expect their inquiries and orders to be recorded, regardless of the distribution channel used, and, if appropriate, transferred to other channels. Thus all of the bank's distribution channels must have comprehensive information covering all transactions and agreements. This requires some sort of central intelligence as advisers will not be able to keep a grip on all the information without system support. Central systems should ensure uniform quality and prevent contradictory recommendations being made (e.g., when advising on investments).

Central customer data management enables the capture of a greater quantity and variety of signals from the customer that reveal his or her needs. These data will trigger personalized marketing actions as the individual customer's needs change. In the future, the combination of a central, needs-oriented product-offering and the possibility of centrally selecting the optimum contact channel will allow for more focused marketing.

INFORMATION TECHNOLOGY AS THE FINAL DELIVERY STAGE

In a multichannel environment, IT has to align channel processes and data flows and integrate infrastructure software (middleware) in order to cope with channel demand. Ideally, IT therefore needs to provide customers with a transparent, consistent interface that contains the same information at any one time. Customers should not experience obvious discrepancies in service between channels, and the bank should be able to manage transactions from different channels with the same processes and speed, all of course at affordable costs. Standard software is available (e.g., for some financial planning and database-marketing), but it is needed in particular for integrating middleware infrastructure.

In a 2002 survey, two-thirds of banks claimed to have integrated their Internet or call center with other channels into a multichannel platform, while some 54 percent had already integrated their branch information system with their other channels. More than 45 percent of the banks claimed that if a customer meets an adviser to discuss a specific product or service and then contacts a call center agent an hour later, the call center agent would already be aware of the initial discussion. Just over a third of European banks state that their agent could pick up from where a customer abandoned an online form and be able to complete the process off-line. In the US the figure stands at 28 percent.[7] Overall, this seems to indicate that channel integration is indeed quite advanced; but such results sound optimistic.

In any case, the development of a multichannel IT architecture is one of the most

[7] Remus Brett, 'European finance needs right-channeling.' Forrester Research, October 2002.

complex and challenging tasks a bank faces. It makes sense to regard such an undertaking as a long-term investment; short-term results are hard to achieve and at least 12 to 18 months are needed to bring about visible changes.

Banks can avoid some of the major obstacles by following a few ground rules. Remember that such a development is a joint effort between IT and the business divisions, and it should therefore be treated as an integrated program that takes into account the needs of both. Avoid unnecessary risks by using only trusted technology and trusted partners. Learn to embrace the concept of central middleware—it may be complex, but in many cases it seems to be the only way to integrate processes over channels. Finally, be aware of the differences between stable back-end technology and the ever-changing hype at the front end. Such cultural differences between front-end and back-end mindset must be reflected when organizing middleware and process integrators.

To avoid dead-ends in the development of a true multichannel architecture, it is important for the business side and IT to agree on two very important questions. First, exactly what IT should be implemented at a conceptual level (i.e., thinking through to the end which multichannel requirements should or should not be implemented, such as channel-hopping, instant customer information, complete contact history with customers). Second, how IT and the business side should proceed to develop the systems (e.g., taking a number of evolutionary steps or undertaking a large-scale project). In general, a bank should think twice before risking a large project, often it is wise to follow the slow, but safer path of evolutionary development. In such a setting, a strong architectural vision on the part of IT is a core ingredient for success.

Lest we forget the lessons set out in the previous chapters in this part on distribution, make your investments pay off while creating options to benefit from changes in customer behavior and the multichannel distribution platform. Getting multichannel management right requires a comprehensive approach involving the three separate layers of strategy, processes and organization, and IT architecture. No matter how complex it may seem, simplification and cost–benefit awareness are crucial to designing and managing multiple channels for value. Remember, there is little point in installing state-of-the-art IT jewels if you are not doing everything possible to harvest the benefits of a better channel setup.

Part 5
Cost-efficient Processes and IT

20
The Eight Disciplines of a Cost Leader

Anupam Sahay, Pedro Rodeia, Reinhold Leichtfuss[1]

When Bank of Scotland launched its bid for NatWest in 1999, one local newspaper memorably announced that the bank would reduce NatWest to a 'brass plate'. As it happened, that opportunity fell to its thrifty Scottish cousin, Royal Bank of Scotland (RBS), which won the takeover sweepstake for the English bank. But what had made Bank of Scotland so confident in the first place?

At the time, both Bank of Scotland and RBS boasted a cost–income ratio of below 55 percent, built around a cost-conscious, lean operations culture. NatWest's, by contrast, stood at 70 percent, bedeviled by layers of cost and inferior service. Perhaps it was a cautionary tale for the first decade of the new century—cost leaders will thrive, but laggards will fight to survive. The logic is incontestable; revenue growth is slowing in many mature markets, emphasizing operational excellence and cost management as key value-creation levers. In other markets, where domestic consolidation is still in progress, cost leaders will surely be the predators and laggards the prey. More fundamentally, retail banking remains an intermediary industry at heart. It adds value through packaging, risk management, and distribution between providers and users of capital. As intermediaries, banks might reasonably be expected to be efficient—and not consume more than 60 percent of income along the way.

However, despite incremental advances throughout the 1990s, the goal of cost–income ratios reaching, say, 30 percent remains elusive. While the average bank today has a cost–income ratio of around 60 percent, the worst ones languish at over 80 percent. It is not that banks have not tried to manage their cost base at all. Indeed, throughout the 1990s, most banks went through several waves of restructuring. Many restructured following a merger or acquisition and made genuine progress through consolidation and rationalization. However, overall, progress in cost containment has been slow. New costs have sprouted while others were trimmed.

New channels, for example, were meant to herald an era of low-cost distribution. In fact, total distribution costs have grown as customers interact more frequently

[1] The authors would like to express their gratitude for the contributions of Mario Daberkow, Vito Giudici, Michael Kilka, Stefan Spang, and Cornelius Walter.

through these convenient new channels, offsetting the lower unit costs per interaction. Similarly, cheap bandwidth and increased processing power were to reduce technology expenditure. Yet, banks' IT budgets have risen faster than ever, but an in-depth study in 2001 by the McKinsey Global Institute could find little conclusive evidence of IT-enabled productivity improvement.[2] In fact the few improvements that the study did find came from changes in operating procedures—not IT. Intensive cost reduction activity applied to back office operations, however, has sometimes resulted in lower service and quality levels.

The issue, then, is how to sustain cost reductions and deliver a truly structural change while building operational excellence. In our work with leading retail banks across the world, we have observed eight disciplines that characterize cost leaders.

Discipline 1: 'It's all about management—strong cost-consciousness'

It may sound simple, but instilling strong cost and cost–benefit consciousness is perhaps the primary discipline for a cost leader. After all, avoiding avoidable costs is easier than eliminating embedded costs. Rigorous cost–benefit thinking takes this mindset further: investments are made only when there is a very high probability of quick amortization. In this respect, 'show me the money' means 'let me see the business case'. These cultural aspects are complemented by an eagerness for continuous improvement—even if it is only inch by inch. It is important to realize that a cost culture is driven top–down. Only cost-conscious leaders will inspire cost-conscious followers throughout an organization.

Avoiding avoidable costs. The way a bank's costs develop over time is largely due to cost culture and individual history. A culture of cost discipline can be recognized instantly at a bank. For instance, the headquarters are neither glamorous nor extravagant, with modestly sized entrance halls, and the location is often not the most prestigious. In continental Europe especially, the building will often be older than neighboring ones. Furthermore, the amount of office space per employee (including the management) will be relatively low.

It is probably no surprise, therefore, that stories abound of thriftiness in such banks. George Schaefer, CEO of US bank Fifth Third, for instance, is reported to have only reluctantly agreed to change the curtains in his room after 20 years. It appears that Banco Popular in Spain avoids buying overhead projectors, as it considers them superfluous equipment. All this may sound somewhat exaggerated, but a little of this attitude could benefit many other retail banks.

It must be realized that a cost-focused culture cannot be implemented quickly as flavor of the month when bad times arrive. On the contrary, it requires a continuous effort by top management and has to be driven through the organizational layers to reach every employee. Efforts centered on task forces or short-term projects may bring results, but they fail to change a company fundamentally to benefit shareholders and customers. As Svenska Handelsbanken wrote in its 2001 annual report, 'Companies wishing to slash their costs quickly, find it very difficult to keep their customer focus while embarking on such a tough process and thus they

[2] *Reaching Higher Productivity Growth in France and Germany*, McKinsey Global Institute, October 2002.

will almost certainly endure a period of deteriorated customer relations. But being thrifty means that you have always had to be focused. If you are thrifty, you have a strong incentive to get things right the first time. Mistakes are just too expensive.'

'Show me the money.' Demanding rigorous business cases for investment opportunities will mean fewer headaches. High-performing banks' growth has led to above-average cost growth, compensated by even higher revenue growth. This is the result not only of their performance and sales cultures but also their shrewd investment policies based on sound businesses cases. The careful analysis of business cases is a characteristic of many Anglo-American banks, with their long experience of responding to the pressures of capital markets and value generation expectations. For example, rigorous business-case-testing has been a strong cultural element of Citibank for many years. At Wells Fargo, the additional costs caused by new investments have to be financed by cost cuts in other areas to avoid negative effects on the bank's market valuation. In short, management and employees must act as if they were the owners and use the bank's money as if it were their own.

Drive for continuous improvement. The third element of a cost-conscious culture is continuous process improvement once investments are made. In this respect, for example, Citibank is well known for its relentless drive to improve inch by inch. Many players still need to learn this discipline, although retail banks often lack the capabilities to examine processes and improve them continuously.

Again, top management's position is a key success factor. Continuous improvement is possible only when constant pressure on costs is made visible, since these improvements are decided and implemented at the middle-management and employee level. In many cases, the top management need not know the details of every implementation measure. Instead, top management should focus on planning for the expected savings, monitoring the success of the improvement schemes, and rewarding the best performers. Managers who drive for constant improvement need to be matched by employees with a common mindset and the relevant skills to implement changes. As Svenska Handelsbanken puts it, 'In a thrifty company, the employees must be proficient at many things. To be proficient and knowledgeable, employees need long and broad professional experience. Thus, in a thrifty company, it is important to create the sort of working conditions where the employees are happy, want to stay with the company for a long time and are keen to keep on learning. Productivity will then increase so that the thrifty company manages with fewer employees.'[3]

Looking forward, managers with the capabilities to achieve continuous process improvements will be in demand. We expect to see more manufacturing-style chief operating officers in banks who can instill cost-consciousness and drive continuous improvement toward superior operations and cost platforms.

Discipline 2: Lean, value-added corporate and support services

Next to overall cost-consciousness comes cost-efficiency in functions that do not generate revenue directly. Corporate centers are a prime example, playing a significant role in a bank's overall cost-efficiency. In fact, the first step for any restructuring

[3] Annual report 2001.

	Bank Percent of total FTE	External benchmark* Percent of total FTE	Reduction potential Percent of functional costs
Strategic planning	0.08	0.05	38
Communication/Marketing	0.37	0.22	41
Accounting	1.25	0.80	36
Controlling	0.54	0.52	4
Auditing	0.70	0.46	34
Human resources	1.63	1.17	28
Legal	0.40	0.26	35
Total	**4.97**	**3.48**	

* Median of top 3 sample banks (sample size: 10 retail banks)

Figure 20.1 Corporate center headcount reduction potential at a European bank

Source: McKinsey

program should be to find the right size for the corporate center. An oversized corporate center sends the wrong signals to the entire organization about what is important and where the real power is situated. Second, if too many important second- and third-level positions are located in the corporate center and if there are more corporate center positions than market positions, then the laws of gravity dictate that a bank will focus more on its internal affairs than on the market. Third, a bloated corporate center tends to appropriate decision-making power from the frontline, thus hindering fast, market-oriented decision-making. Lastly, high corporate center costs have to be allocated to business units—a process that ends up being a source of unproductive debate.

There are many companies with efficient, tightly run corporate centers, and these can serve as benchmarks for the size of the corporate center and its individual functions (Figure 20.1).

Discipline 3: Efficient distribution formats

With some 30 to 40 percent of costs, distribution represents the biggest block of costs in many retail banks. In Part 4, we indicated how distribution could be made more efficient. In terms of controlling distribution costs, three mechanisms have proved universally powerful.

Eliminating service activity from branches. Huge progress has been made in stripping out administrative and service functions from customer-facing branches, but the journey is not over. Today, between 30 and 60 percent of branch time is taken up by such activities. Therefore, eliminating them by creating centralized service centers and rerouting traffic, particularly voice traffic, away from the branch is a key element in controlling back office costs or preparing select activities for outsourcing.

Managing branch capacity and formats. The old standard model of a branch, with a manager and eight employees, is in decline. Several new formats, such as thin branches and segment-differentiated networks, will allow for managing headcount more flexibly and space more efficiently, while continuing to deliver superior customer service.

Efficient multichannel setup and channel migration. It is key to capitalize on a multichannel mix (as outlined in the previous chapter); banks must migrate customers proactively to channels that are efficient and correspond to customer preferences. Simultaneously, focusing strongly on maintaining a single process model with a high rate of straight-through-processing (STP) for all channels is a key success factor in containing back office costs.

Discipline 4: Lean operations

Banks should take a leaf out of the manufacturers' book. Manufacturers have long focused on eliminating waste, variability, and inflexibility from their operations. To this end, they have applied a variety of techniques ranging from straightforward core process redesign to more sophisticated quality assurance concepts, such as Six Sigma. These techniques and approaches are just as applicable in a banking service environment. We give three examples.

Establishing service factories. This involves consolidating multiple, fragmented operating centers into centralized factories in which industrial disciplines can be established. It is all too common for a bank to have half-a-dozen or so centers doing exactly the same thing, but each falling short of achieving the critical scale and quality. Service factories are the conceptual equivalent of call centers for distribution (i.e., a managed environment where banks can centralize and industrialize their processes).

Executing core process redesign. To assure the cost-efficiency of service factories and to identify improvement opportunities throughout the entire value chain of a bank requires a continuous process improvement program. This involves taking an end-to-end perspective, from the customer all the way through to the operational process, with a view to re-engineering as a way to reduce cost and cycle time and increase quality. An important principle here is STP, which should be implemented whenever possible. STP has taken root in wholesale banking, but retail banking lags behind. There is an urgent need to redesign processes to eliminate hand-offs and reduce errors and cost, not just fix up the existing processes. This applies to the whole range of banking processes from payments to loan-processing.

Introducing customer- and product-specific target service levels. It is equally important to tailor service levels to customers according to segment, thereby aligning the cost-to-serve with customer value. This can result in fundamental changes to service levels; for example, it may not be necessary to process a mortgage application within 24 hours for a low-value customer, whereas it might be essential for a customer who is at risk of leaving the bank.

Discipline 5: Smart sourcing

Historically, banks have taken the view that the constraints of risk management and control mean that most banking activities must be performed in-house. In a few cases, there is growing disaggregation of the value chain (particularly for credit cards and mortgages) and the appearance of specialists that can deliver the same services at lower cost and greater scale. This will be the way of the future. Banks should rethink which services they genuinely need to operate in-house and which they can source effectively from players better equipped to deliver them. Moreover, they must think about *where* they will source such services. Given the significant differences in cost between the Western world and lower cost locations, such as Eastern Europe and Asia, the location of a provider is as critical as its service offering.

Outsourcing. It can be argued that banks should retain only customer-facing and corporate activity and contract out all processing activities. This is an extreme position; however, there is now a substantial range of suppliers and partners, particularly in the more mature banking markets, that can deliver services at cheaper rates and higher quality, for instance, by aggregating services for several institutions and developing specialist skills. Outsourcing models vary substantially, but two areas of outsourcing are emerging in the industry: one relates to full business process outsourcing; the other is more traditional IT-outsourcing. The banking industry has yet to adopt outsourcing to the extent seen in other industries.

Although there is no rulebook for succeeding in outsourcing, getting it right does depend on a few preconditions. First, that the bank fully understands its own cost structure and scale curve. Second, that it negotiates from a position where it understands its own ability to reduce costs internally (i.e., without engaging a service provider's support). Third, that both parties know that effective contractual negotiation should result in a win–win situation—neither party can afford to gouge the other, as this would destabilize their relationship. The actual selection of an outsourcing partner and negotiation of a contract should not be attempted if the above three conditions cannot be achieved.

In general, the North American and UK outsourcing markets are already quite developed, but continental Europe lags behind. For example, Fiserv and Alltel in the US offer application service provider-style services to smaller banks, so that the banks no longer need to own the technology or do the processing. More mainstream commercial models involve an arm's-length contract with pre-negotiated service level agreements; card processors, such as Experian and Certegy, have demonstrated the viability of this model. At the other end of the scale are collaborative models in which a number of banks pool together to create industry utilities that then offer services to a range of banks. iPSL in the UK—a joint venture between Lloyds TSB, Barclays, HSBC, and Unisys—is one such utility. In continental Europe, Interpay in the Benelux region and SIBS in Portugal offer industry-wide variants of the model. We explore outsourcing in more detail in Chapter 21.

Offshoring. This has sprung up as a second leg of smart sourcing. Offshoring involves establishing operations in locations beyond the home market to take advantage of factor costs, such as reduced labor costs, and a more favorable regulatory and fiscal environment. International banks, such as HSBC and Citigroup, are already quite advanced along this path. They have established hubs in low-cost locations in Asia that can process at 30 to 50 percent of the cost in western Europe or the US. We explore offshoring in more detail in Chapter 22.

Discipline 6: World-class purchasing and supply management

External costs (i.e., purchase costs) often represent between 10 and 20 percent of a bank's total cost structure. While retailers and manufacturers have been ruthless about the management of suppliers, banks have frequently been relatively lax in an area of such significant potential (Figure 20.2). Starting from a thorough understanding of a bank's current purchasing cost base, the key lies in a rigorous approach to each of five sources of opportunity.

Vendor management. Typically, banks have a large number of suppliers who can be squeezed by introducing new suppliers (or consolidating existing ones) and applying open price-bidding for key contracts. One bank saved 15 percent of its branch maintenance costs by reducing the number of existing service contractors to just two who could offer nationwide coverage in the form of a dedicated joint venture. Applying another tool taken from manufacturing—the 'total cost approach'—banks can actively identify cost reduction potential along the entire product/service supply chain and renegotiate prices with vendors—especially vendor-related costs for ordering and delivery.

Demand management. A simple, central revision of the purchase database using internal and external benchmarking usually reveals unnecessary—yet somehow institutionalized—spending, such as on corporate center office space (one of the most prominent examples). Banks need to define a purchasing behavior code and enforce compliance with its policies (e.g., defining a list of official suppliers, and refusing to settle accounts with nonofficial suppliers to eliminate maverick buying).

Purchasing processes and organization. An appropriate segmentation of purchasing processes, according to the importance and complexity of spending, is essential for a powerful purchasing organization. In excellent organizations, about 80 percent of purchasing is centralized; in the average retail bank, centralization varies from 20 to

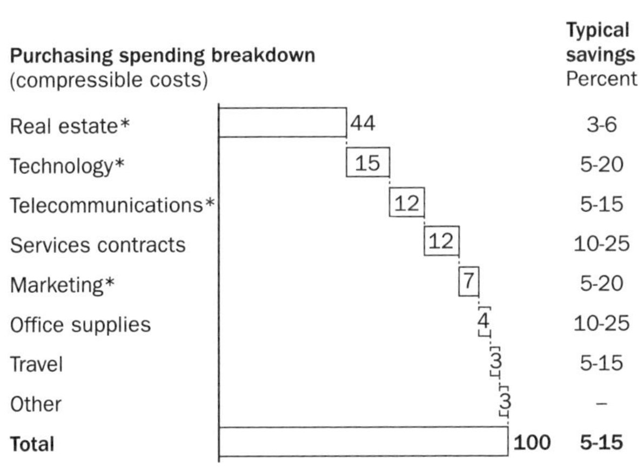

* Includes only acquisition and supply contracts, such as rentals, cleaning cost, security, software and hardware acquisition, advertisements, etc.

Figure 20.2 Typical purchasing savings potential (percent)

Source: interviews; McKinsey

50 percent. A major advantage of better segmentation is the separation of negotiations from administration in purchasing, with skilled central staff to manage the negotiation of all high-impact contracts and technical specialists to set the specifications. Banks should also consider investing in skills and hiring core people with solid purchasing competencies, preferably with an industry background.

Use of e-business tools. Introducing e-tools throughout the purchasing process can generate savings of up to 25 percent, resulting from price reductions (e.g., marketplaces, e-auctions), the optimization of internal administration (e.g., purchasing card, purchasing and supply management intranet, catalogs) and interaction processes (e.g., supplier extranets, automated ordering, etc.).

Discipline 7: Technology transformation

Technology has increased in complexity and cost. A cross section of a bank's IT systems today would resemble an archaeological dig, as layer upon layer of new technology has been added over the course of the last two decades. Even though the underlying models for technology have shifted from mainframe to client-server to distributed architectures, banking IT architectures have not kept pace. More often than not, banks are still running on mainframe machines in batch mode, with many applications that have been developed largely in-house, with only a selective use of off-the-shelf packages. This is not entirely a bad thing, as mainframes still provide the lowest running costs of all platforms. However, these architectures need to be upgraded in due course, and managed with a clear focus on costs. A technology transformation should address the following four areas: infrastructure, applications, architecture, and business-led management.

Infrastructure. This includes all production-related IT hardware, facilities, and people. The biggest impact here can be achieved through infrastructure consolidation, comprising logical consolidation (i.e., mapping similar activities onto the same hardware) and physical consolidation (i.e., moving the hardware and its management to centralized locations). Consolidation can reduce the infrastructure budget by as much as 10 to 15 percent. A careful analysis of the infrastructure (e.g., the resources used by applications and the [often exaggerated] service requirements), reveals a significant savings potential of some 20 to 25 percent.

Applications. Around 30 to 50 percent of an IT budget is typically absorbed by applications. For banks, a large proportion is used up in the maintenance of aging applications. There is no silver bullet for restructuring the application landscape, given the complexity of the applications (the result of the work of various programmers over time). Hence, maintaining an overview of costs in this area is mainly a task for management, backed up by rigorous controlling to create cost transparency for users and for the IT department.

Architecture. Long-term improvement comes only by intervening in the IT architecture. The *ad hoc* systems that have grown organically in banks over the years pose a fundamental challenge to any optimization plans, as it is very hard to replace entire mainframe-based architectures cost-effectively. However, it is possible to apply the logic of client-server architectures (i.e., the separation of applications, databases, and presentation) to reduce complexity and ring-fence costs. Given the growth of new channels, the separation of the presentation level, in particular, has become a necessity and not just an option. Having achieved the separation of the three levels, middleware is used to connect the multiple platforms in the front- and back-ends in order to create a coherent whole.

Business-led management. One dilemma that has not been resolved, despite numerous efforts, is the interface of business with technology. It is difficult for the business side to specify its requirements in such a way that the IT side can deliver them accurately. A dialog between the two is needed to ensure the right priorities and service levels. At one extreme, some banks have moved to a model where business units own the development budget for IT and are charged with setting the priorities; hence, IT effectively becomes a delivery unit. Other institutions, particularly wholesale banks, are beginning to use an approach where IT clearly establishes the products it can offer and the pricing levels for different levels of service, as a way of creating transparency on the cost and delivery structure of the technology. Either of these options—and others lying somewhere in-between—can be made to work. It is essential to ensure a constructive dialog between business and IT and instill discipline with regard to the prioritization of, and investment in, technology. To start such a dialog, certain basics have to be in place. First, transparent pricing for the products offered by IT has to be agreed. Second, jointly developed service level agreements have to clarify the needs of the business side; and, lastly, continuous budget-and-cost-controlling should be installed to focus IT and business efforts effectively. Since IT costs have soared for banks are are such a relevant topic, we cover reining in excessive IT expenditure in Chapter 23.

Discipline 8: Realizing cost synergies from mergers

Any bank can improve its cost position either by sliding along the efficiency curve or by compressing costs through better control and innovation. Some of the best-performing banks have achieved the bulk of their cost improvement by realizing cost synergies from mergers. Two prominent, focused multi-specialists that leveraged mergers to gain economies of scale and then used the momentum to take costs out of their business systems are Unicredito and Royal Bank of Scotland (Figure 20.3).

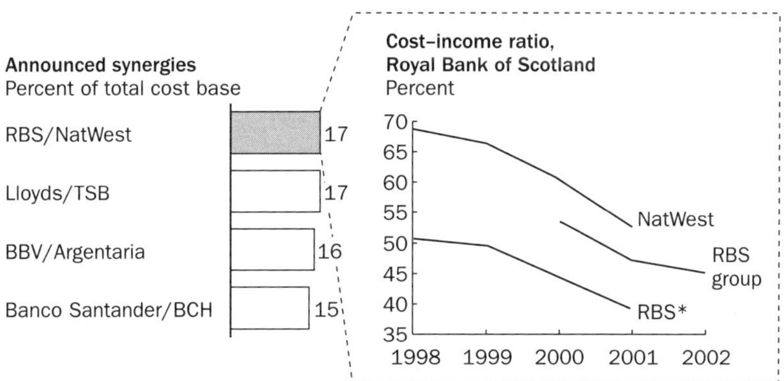

Figure 20.3 Role of cost synergies

Source: annual reports; McKinsey

The process of extracting the planned synergies frequently runs into problems due to a lack of strategic clarity, culture clashes, or delay and a lack of rigor in implementation. Nevertheless, the best-performing banks have been able to realize between a 15 and 20 percent reduction of the combined cost base over 2 to 3 years while still growing revenues significantly. We expect that mergers will become increasingly important as a source of cost savings in the years to come, as it becomes even tougher to shift the efficiency frontier and as the consolidation process in banking continues.

How to attack the cost base

Cost management and operational excellence are not about one-off initiatives or *ad hoc* measures. The focus must be on creating and sustaining a cost management culture and demonstrating the disciplines described above. This is easier said than done, as there are many obstacles (e.g., labor laws in continental Europe and governmental interference in parts of Asia). But, more often than not, the challenges are internal: targets are unclear, costs are opaque, responsibility is diffused across organizational silos, and top management, which is usually well versed in strategy, may not be as familiar with operations and technology.

Given the importance of costs to the strategic future of most banks, there can be no excuses for inefficiency. The cost base must be attacked. Cost leaders will thrive, but cost laggards are unlikely to remain independent. Consequently, the drive to operational excellence must come from the top, with clear aspirations, accountability transparency, and relentless focus. While short-term cost improvements are comparatively easy to achieve, the second and third horizons of cost-efficiency require not only breaking a few taboos but also a quite fundamental redesign and changes in the cost culture (Figure 20.4). Top management's cost-consciousness needs to

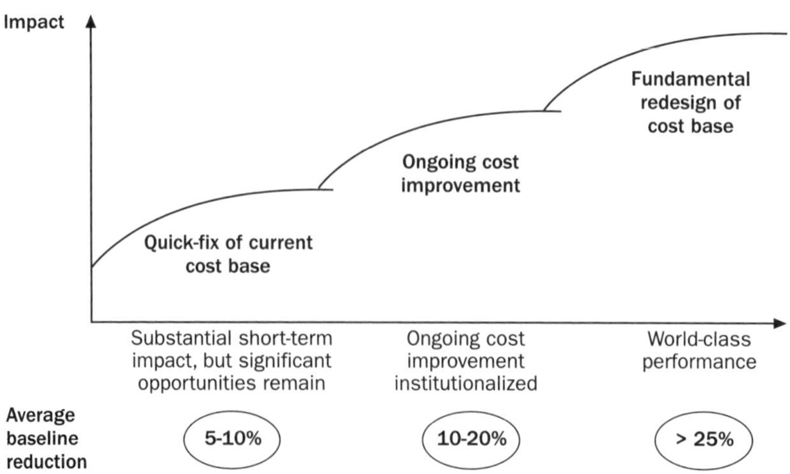

Figure 20.4 Impact of cost improvement efforts

Source: McKinsey

permeate the organization and the mindsets of thousands of employees. This is the challenge for banking leaders today.

In the subsequent chapters in this section, we explore three of the more compelling developments in cost containment. In the next chapter, we look at the trends in various areas of outsourcing, where specialist providers can increasingly help banks reduce costs and improve quality. The following chapter discusses offshoring, and in the final chapter we examine how to rein in IT costs, a task which has proved particularly tricky for banks in recent years.

21

Outsourcing: Increasing Opportunities

Roberto Lancellotti, Oliver Schein, Volker Stadler [1]

We define outsourcing as the process whereby the managerial control for the provision of certain services to a legal entity—the *client*—is transferred to another legal entity not fully owned by the client—the *provider*. The transfer is understood to be on a long-term basis and is regulated by a *service level agreement* (SLA) contract.

This definition encompasses a number of different concepts. First, the components of the outsourcing 'stack' (i.e., the IT infrastructure, the applications, and the related business processes) can be outsourced individually or bundled, as occurs, for example, in full business process outsourcing. Second, the service transformation—the so-called 'cleanup'—can be the responsibility of the bank itself or a provider and can be run as a separate project or as the first phase of an overall outsourcing contract. For example, in business transformation outsourcing, a provider carries out service improvements before an operational outsourcing phase.

The outsourcing of IT and operations is an important reality in banking today, as indicated by a large and growing market for such services and the widespread use of external providers by banks. Outsourcing is high on bank executives' agendas, especially in the current economic climate, as it is seen as a key option to enable cost reductions. However, it is far from being a panacea. Fewer than half of the deals—42 percent—reported by the respondents in a comprehensive survey of outsourcing in European banking had delivered the anticipated value creation in the form of cost reductions and/or service level improvements.[2] Value creation is determined by a provider's scale and structural advantages compared with the setup and running costs of an outsourcing arrangement.

In considering whether to outsource, banks should weigh up the case for external

---

[1] The authors would lke to express their gratitude for the contributions of Claudio Bombonato, Andres Hoyos-Gomez, Joakim Percival, and Stefan Spang.

[2] This chapter draws extensively on the results of a McKinsey IT and operations outsourcing survey; carried out from January to May 2002, the survey comprised over 70 face-to-face interviews with executives from 31 banks in western Europe (Benelux, France, Germany, Italy, Portugal, Spain, Scandinavia, UK, Republic of Ireland), as well as industry experts, and executives and experts from seven IT and operations services providers.

service provision compared with the potential value generated through internal improvements. Furthermore, it is important that banks clearly distinguish between the effects of a service cleanup (project-based) from the effects of outsourcing (ongoing operational phase of service improvement) to enable proper value attribution to the two phases. This establishes the basis for fair value-sharing between a bank and a provider. From a bank's perspective, however, value capture is hindered by significant feasibility barriers. These are related to *providers' capabilities* (i.e., a real or perceived lack of providers able to offer services at required service levels, especially in operations); *banks' readiness* (e.g., the degree of internal transparency on internal costs and service levels); and *sustainability*, such as the cost and complexity of reversing or changing an outsourcing relationship.

Banks in general recognize three cornerstones from which to overcome such challenges and achieve excellence in outsourcing. First, there is a strong consensus among banks to outsource only those services that they really know and control. Therefore, creating internal transparency on costs and processes is a key prerequisite, and banks emphasize the importance of being able to control service delivery. Second, most banks adopt selective approaches to outsourcing, even though providers push 'global' deals, which cover several services. A selective approach allows a bank to adapt the scope and depth of outsourcing to a desired level of ownership and control. Third, banks believe that chief information officers (CIOs) and chief operating officers (COOs) should continue to play a key role in outsourcing decisions as legitimate and credible stakeholders who are well placed to assess the real benefits and barriers of an outsourcing deal.

Whatever its individual strategy, any bank seeking excellence in outsourcing must draw rigorously on best practice. Our view is that outsourcing will continue to grow and will remain a key topic for banks. If there is no one single path to success in outsourcing, there are many valuable lessons to be learned from banks' experiences.

A GROWING MARKET

The size of the combined IT and operations-outsourcing market and the current provider landscape both indicate that banks do actively outsource.[3] Taken separately, the markets for outsourcing IT and operations services in western European banking are large and growing vigorously. Together, the IT and operations-outsourcing markets were estimated to be about €8bn in 2000, with an expected compound annual growth rate (CAGR) of 11 percent in 2005. The market for IT-outsourcing is the larger of the two and the fastest growing.[4] In addition, IT services

[3] The survey reviewed outsourcing for 11 specific IT (applications maintenance and development, desktops, data center, network, ATM/POS and call center infrastructure) and operations services (accounts, payments, loans, securities, printing) in the countries/regions mentioned above. These services are all key enablers for banks' core business, representing 30 to 40 percent of an average bank's cost base, and are closely related functionally and, often, organizationally within banks. Market data from proprietary research and public sources.

[4] Acutal growth 1996–2000: 20 percent CAGR for IT, 8 percent CAGR for operations.

are outsourced significantly more than operations, although the latter represents around 60 percent of combined spending.[5]

The IT market is characterized by an established experience base (data center-outsourcing began in the 1970s) and a relatively high degree of standardization across sectors and countries (with the exception of core banking applications, automatic teller machines [ATMs] and points of sale [POSs]). The supply landscape is competitive with a wide service-offering in most countries. The experience base for operations-outsourcing is more limited, especially for accounts and loans-processing, although payment (e.g., card-processing) and printing services are more mature. In addition, operations-outsourcing is very industry- and geography-specific, as the offering depends largely on the degree of product standardization and local regulations. The supply landscape is relatively small and fragmented for most services, but offerings can be found for the majority of service areas and countries.

From the perspective of CIOs/COOs, it is clear that outsourcing is a key enabler for many items on top management's agenda—notably the need to deal with cost pressures. In an economic downturn as banks focus increasingly on cost reduction, outsourcing is perceived as a major driver for lowering unit production costs and/or reducing the investment levels required of banks. Another critical management issue today is consolidation following a merger or acquisition, but here managers view outsourcing more as a barrier and an additional complication to the integration process. Nevertheless, some see potential even here: for example, external providers can maintain applications to be discontinued in order to release resources for critical development projects. Other management agenda items, such as improving flexibility to enable growth, handle new technologies, and access new skills/functionality, are also seen as major drivers for outsourcing, but are generally less urgent for management today (Figure 21.1).

CHALLENGES TO OUTSOURCING

Banks, therefore, clearly see outsourcing as a critical sourcing option. Despite this, of the deals set up by major European banks, over half—58 percent—failed to deliver the expected value creation.[6] What is it that prevents outsourcing from fulfilling its promise? Two key challenges are apparent: capturing the value created and overcoming the feasibility barriers.

Capture the value

An understanding of value sources, drivers, and their mechanisms is critical for banks to define their objectives. A prerequisite here is to establish transparency on

[5] Assuming certain direct IT costs are included in the corresponding figure for operations (which may include branch operations); amount may vary depending on a bank's individual situation and the accounting methods used.

[6] Value is often assessed only on a qualitative basis, as the real benefits generated are seldom tracked accurately.

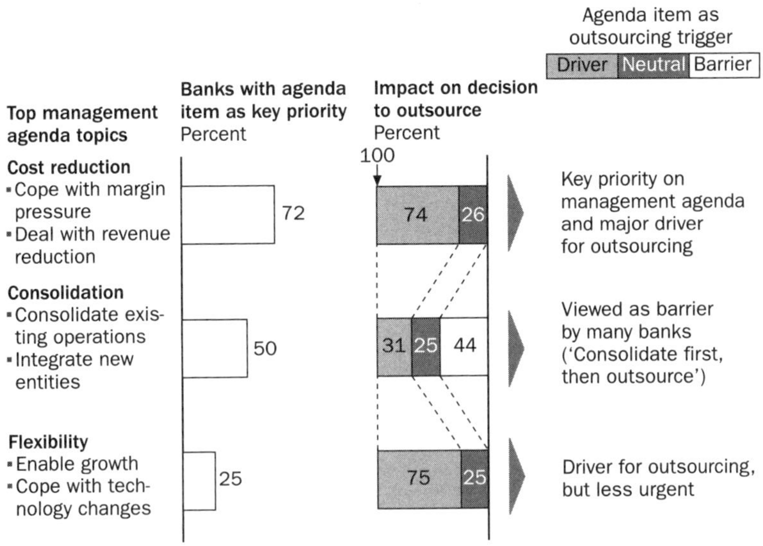

Figure 21.1 Management agenda and decision to outsource

Source: survey interviews; McKinsey

their service and cost positions. This is a first step toward gaining awareness of the potential advantages of using an external provider.

Banks recognize efficiency as the key value source of outsourcing; for instance, 44 percent of the banks in our survey stated that the single main value source was improving efficiency in service provision (e.g., reduced cost per trade in securities-processing or lower cost per million instructions per second for data centers). Other value sources cited were increasing effectiveness (e.g., superior functionality for loans-rating or higher network availability) and flexibility (e.g., facilitated ramp-up/down of call-center capacity).[7] We calculate, however, that a provider would need to realize a cost advantage of 40 percent, compared with a bank's former service costs, to deliver a 15 percent cost saving for the bank and still obtain an adequate margin (taking into account remaining costs for the bank and incremental value-added tax [VAT]), without counting the one-off implementation costs (Figure 21.2).[8]

Understanding a provider's potential advantages, therefore, is essential. These are economies of scale (e.g., from increased purchasing power or better resource utilization) and certain structural advantages (e.g., a superior infrastructure setup, lower cost of staff/location, pooled specialist know-how, or process best practices).

---

[7] 31 percent cited another value source in combination with efficiency improvement; 25 percent cited another value source without referring to efficiency improvement.

[8] Several financial services provided by banks to their end-customers are not subject to VAT. By outsourcing certain services to a provider, the provider may have to charge VAT to the bank. This would count as an additional cost to the bank on top of the provider's service provision charge. VAT exemption depends, among other things, on the scope of the service outsourced and the owner relationship between bank and provider. Any individual outsourcing situation has to be checked by tax and legal specialists.

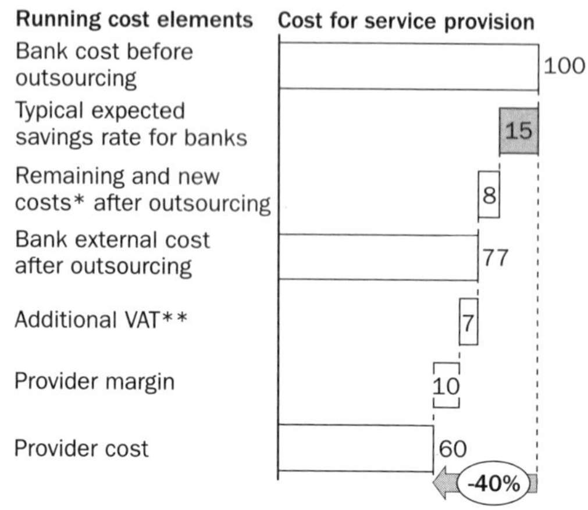

* E.g., costs related to provider management
** Assumption: 15% VAT payable on two-thirds of provider margin and cost

Figure 21.2 Efficiency gains and provider cost advantage (illustrative estimates)

Source: McKinsey

Providers' advantages are often not clear, because pricing models are complex or because services are bundled. Furthermore, banks often do not define the objectives of an outsourcing deal in concrete (e.g., service levels) and financial (e.g., target costs) terms. In our experience, too, objectives are seldom measured or tracked against the original business case once implementation is complete. One of the reasons is that there are likely to be frequent changes to outsourcing deals over their lifetime, such as in volumes, prices, and the services covered.

All of the elements contributing to the evaluation of value potential need to be considered and care taken not to underestimate the potential costs related to outsourcing. The time and investment effort required to set up a deal is often undervalued when preparing the business case; for example, IT systems integration is often more complex than foreseen. In addition, remaining costs can turn out to be higher than expected (such as those for internal staff that cannot be redeployed) or when provider-management requires a greater effort than anticipated. Sometimes, too, the potential remains unrealized because banks impose a specific *modus operandi* on providers, so that economies of scale or synergies cannot be exploited fully. For instance, banks may specify software or hardware configurations, instead of allowing a provider to draw on its own infrastructure.

Hence, a bank's prerequisites for an outsourcing deal are: identify the value sources and drivers for the service in question, define the criteria to measure the potential value creation, and set the objectives of a deal.

Overcome the barriers

Given the potential for outsourcing to create value, what are the factors that hinder its capture? There are three significant feasibility barriers relating to the capabilities of providers to respond to banks' demands, the readiness of banks to set up and manage an outsourcing arrangement, and the ability of both sides to maintain a sustainable partnership.

First, many banks remain unconvinced that providers have the capabilities to deliver services adequately. This real or perceived lack of capable providers, especially in operations, refers not only to the available offerings but also to whether providers can meet banks' requirements, such as the high security levels demanded for customer account data.

Second, banks may be inadequately prepared and lack specific expertise to enter into and manage an outsourcing arrangement. Many do not have a formal outsourcing policy and strategy in place, and internal service transparency is often inadequate (e.g., process documentation is lacking, cost structures and unit costs are unclear, service levels have not been formalized). Thus, it is difficult to determine the scope of an outsourcing opportunity and set cost and service level targets. Moreover, business cases for outsourcing opportunities are not systematically built up, and they may contain inaccuracies and gaps due to the difficulty of measuring value and feasibility. Organizationally, staff transfers can be a tough issue to manage, especially if opposition from labor organizations is anticipated. To avoid conflicts, staff are often not correctly redeployed or transferred to where they can add real value. If the skills and organizational elements needed to manage providers are not internalized, a high degree of organizational change is needed to professionalize them.

Third, sustaining a partnership—getting an agreement to function smoothly on a day-to-day basis—can also be problematic. Issues can arise concerning interface management, such as how to handle change requests or deciding which of the partners is accountable for which steps along the value chain. Part of the problem of sustainability is what to do when a partnership proves unsustainable: reversing or changing deals is often complex and costly because of contractual penalties or long changeover periods.

ASSESSING VALUE CREATION AND FEASIBILITY

What are the differences between outsourcing individual services in terms of the potential value and obstacles? To illustrate and compare the way the value and feasibility of outsourcing a particular service is perceived, we created a matrix based on banks' average assessments of the value creation and feasibility barriers for each of 11 services.[9] Value creation includes both actual and anticipated value creation (i.e., what participants had *actually* achieved and/or *expected* to achieve from outsourcing a particular service). The score plotted on the matrix refers to the absolute value creation with respect to the overall IT and operations budget (as

[9] See Footnote 3 for list of services; note that there was a spread in the banks' assessments for each service, which was a result of the specificity of each bank. Differences at the subservice level are not captured here, as the level of analysis is aggregated.

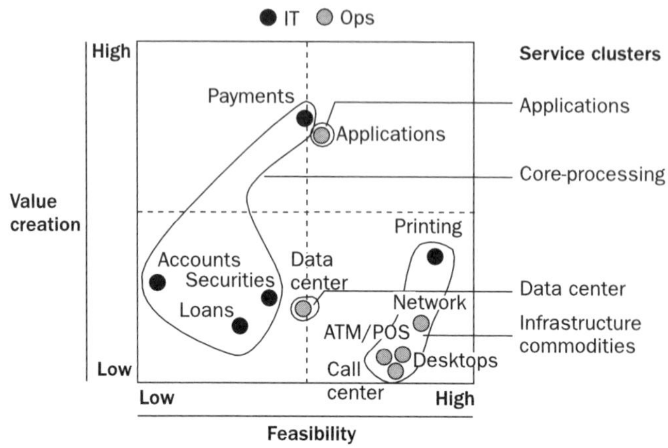

Figure 21.3 Average evaluation of services

Source: survey interviews; McKinsey

opposed to the relative value based on the budget for a particular service).[10] The feasibility barriers are those described above, which the survey participants rated according to the degree of difficulty they actually represent or are perceived to represent. The outcome can be structured around four distinct services/service clusters: applications, core-processing (e.g., payments, accounts, securities, and loans), data centers, and infrastructure commodities (e.g., printing, networks, ATM/POS, desktops, call centers) (Figure 21.3).

Applications is an important service area for banks, as it represents about 16 percent of the total IT and operations budget, making it an attractive target for outsourcing. The value-creation potential is high, as there are economies of skill (access to expertise in software development tools) and possibilities to redeploy staff (to focus on application design) and enable process best practices. However, applications-outsourcing is seen as a tough nut to crack. Its feasibility depends on having transparency on internal software development processes, especially the interfaces between functional and technical design, coding, and operating. In addition, the degree of control over critical skills, the stability of a bank's future requirements for an application (as change requests are costly), and the extent of providers' detailed banking expertise all play a role. At a more detailed level, the assessment of value and feasibility differs according to the type of subservice (maintenance is rated higher than development) and the degree of standardization of the particular application.

[10] Analysis based on a typical reference budget, split IT 40 percent and operations 60 percent. NB. This split assumes that certain direct IT costs are included in the corresponding operations figures; this may vary depending on the individual bank and the accounting method used. Value creation takes into account actual and expected value; the midpoint on the value-creation axis represents an efficiency gain of 2.5 percent on the total IT and operations budget (e.g., for the data center or securities budget of an average bank, this represents an efficiency improvement of about 25 percent). The midpoint on the feasibility axis represents minor feasibility issues but no major roadblocks; the degree of feasibility increases to the right.

Core-processing also has potential value to be unlocked; accounts and payments each represent around 15 percent of the total IT and operations budget. Value creation stems from aggregating volume and increasing the level of process automation (reducing the headcount and the wage bill), and adding extra functionality, such as a loans-rating engine. In addition, outsourcing can help banks avoid having to make certain investments (e.g., to comply with $t + 1$ settlement requirements). This means, however, that banks need to accept a certain level of standardization of processes and products.

There are also substantial barriers to outsourcing these services, as they are traditionally perceived as banks' core business; hence, the operational risk involved in outsourcing them is high. Banks also have security concerns with regard to customer data and related privacy issues. In addition, these services are very staff-intensive and, in most cases, staff transfers or layoffs need to be considered. Since core-processing services, especially securities and payments, are also very asset-intensive, banks may have to accept the need for substantial write-offs. Moreover, few providers offer such services, which leads to a 'hostage situation' (i.e., low—and potentially costly—contract reversibility). Overall, banks prefer to set up shared equity entities in order to retain operational control.

Data center-outsourcing creates relatively little value according to our survey participants, although it should be emphasized that the range of individual assessments is wide. Value creation from outsourcing is driven by lower staff costs (increasing the level of automation, economies of skills, etc.) and better use of assets (e.g., peak handling, as data centers have high fixed costs, but low marginal costs). Many large banks, however, believe that significant economies of scale can be achieved internally and that, as infrastructure is decentralized and heterogeneous, outsourcing is less attractive in terms of efficiency. Furthermore, data centers are often perceived by CIOs as a core service due to security requirements and the need for critical IT skills. Interdependency with other infrastructure and applications within a bank is high (indeed it may be growing due to multichannel architectures), which hinders carve-outs.

Infrastructure commodities generally face fewer obstacles, although the potential value from outsourcing such services is reckoned to be quite modest, as the respective cost buckets are rather small at around 2 to 7 percent of the combined IT and operations budget. Printing is the exception at about 12 percent of budget. Outsourcing such services appears to pose few problems for banks and, in addition, there are plenty of tried-and-tested providers and successful reference cases. Although there are staff transfer issues for the more staff-intensive services, most infrastructure commodities can be outsourced relatively easily as and when an opportunity arises.

The above assessments are reflected in the actual figures for outsourcing by banks. The data we collected show that whereas about one-third of IT services had not been outsourced, the corresponding figure for operations services is over one-half (57 percent). Furthermore, IT services are outsourced on a broader scope (25 percent of services) than operations (13 percent of services).[11] This reflects the difficulty that banks attach to outsourcing most core-processing services in operations; in

[11] Broad scope: service is outsourced to a provider 'end to end'. Limited scope: subservices or partial activities are outsourced.

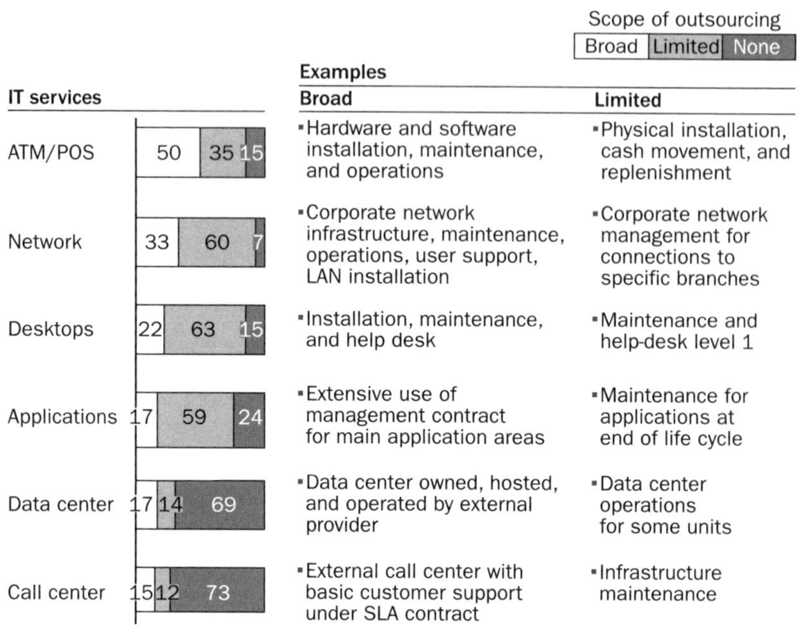

Figure 21.4 Scope and depth of outsourcing—IT (percent of services)

Source: survey interviews; McKinsey

particular, securities, loans, and accounts. Within IT, network and ATM/POS services are outsourced the most, data centers and call center services the least. All of these IT services are thought to create relatively low value, even though, with the exception of data centers, they are seen as quite 'easy to do'. This opportunistic approach to outsourcing leads to networks and ATM/POS being outsourced much more than call center services (Figure 21.4).

Within operations, payments (high value potential, although moderately difficult) and printing (relatively low value creation, but easy to implement) are the two most outsourced services, while securities, loans, and accounts have hardly been touched (Figure 21.5).

PUTTING OUTSOURCING INTO ACTION

A very clear viewpoint in terms of what outsourcing can actually deliver can help banks set clear and measurable targets consistent with their situation and raise awareness of the specific issues that must be addressed. Banks, in addition to carefully preparing and investing the time and resources needed, can draw on a number of best practices to achieve success in outsourcing. By synthesizing the insights we collected from the survey interviews, we can propose a three-phase, best practice approach to outsourcing deals. We see this as a road map to excellence for banks embarking on an outsourcing journey.

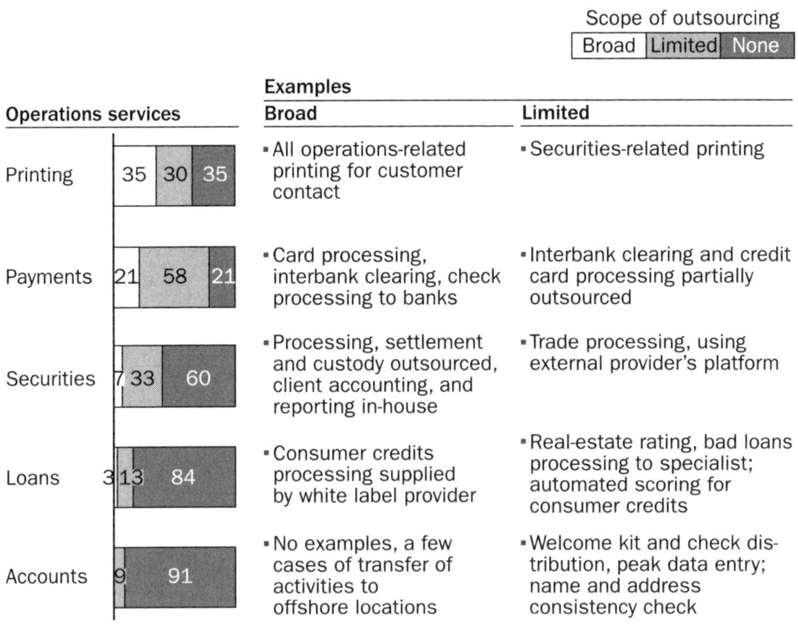

Figure 21.5 Scope and depth of outsourcing—operations (percent of services)

Source: survey interviews; McKinsey

Create the conditions, establish transparency, and define the opportunity

The basic principle is for a bank to outsource only what it knows and controls. To this end, best practices include institutionalizing internal provider-management capabilities and ensuring centralized knowledge coordination as well as access to highly skilled service and functional expertise (e.g., legal advice, human resources). It is also key to establish internal transparency, identify inefficiencies, and benchmark performance in order to set clear cost and service-level targets.

Analyze and assess the opportunity[12]

It is critical for banks to build their own independent business cases based on net present value (NPV) calculations. In addition, various options and scenarios (e.g., different pricing models, changes in volume) can be compared directly with the NPV calculation. There should be a clear separation between the effects of a service cleanup (a one-off project) and outsourcing (ongoing service improvement) in order to attribute the value created by each of the two phases. This establishes the basis for fair value-sharing between bank and provider. Moreover, alternatives have to be considered and the case for outsourcing compared with the internal

[12] The value and feasibility matrix developed for the survey is an example of how such an assessment could be initiated. Each dimension encompasses the relevant criteria and uses a scoring gridline mechanism to calculate the potential value and feasibility of outsourcing a given service.

improvement potential. In evaluating the provider landscape, banks should focus the screening and tendering process on the key criteria of service delivery, including obtaining service and industry-relevant reference cases, and the potential for creating a trust-based relationship with a particular provider.

Implement the deal to capture the full value

To capture the full value-creation potential, banks should actively manage the deal and invest in establishing a trust-based relationship with the provider. Service transition needs to be managed as a key project, for example, by defining a specific transition date and avoiding a 'big bang' strategy and by handing responsibility for the transition to a special unit made up of specialists from both the bank and the provider. Furthermore, banks should implement formal, detailed interaction processes, actively track performance, and focus on building up trust. Lastly, for the worst case scenario, it is in a bank's own interest to improve the reversibility of any deals by building clear exit clauses into contracts and determining the support that a provider must supply in such a situation. It should be stressed that entering into an outsourcing deal necessitates significant organizational changes, which should not be underestimated. In order to shift the focus successfully from execution and service delivery to managing the provider's service quality and levels, new roles need to be established, processes need to be adjusted, and the required mix of the professional backgrounds of staff will change.

These relatively high investments and efforts are the prerequisites to achieving excellence in outsourcing. Moreover, their justification becomes even more apparent given the increasingly important role that outsourcing will play in the banking industry.

LOOKING TO THE FUTURE

Outsourcing will continue to grow and will remain a key topic for banks, due to cost pressures, the disaggregation of service distribution and production, the industrialization of banking services, and regulatory and technological changes. Sometimes, one or other influencing factor will work in tandem with others. For example, new European Union regulations to align the price of cross-border payments to the level of domestic transactions will encourage outsourcing by putting pressure on banks to cut their costs in order to meet these price targets. Furthermore, outsourcing is a way to avoid making the significant investments that will be needed to comply with new regulatory requirements (e.g., Basel II). The increasing availability of core-banking software packages will also drive outsourcing. As more banks plan to introduce largely standardized packages, providers can build up essential expertise to offer to banks and leverage it for multiple clients.

Areas for growth

We can gain an idea about the potential growth areas in IT and operations-outsourcing by looking at banks' propensity to outsource a service in relation to

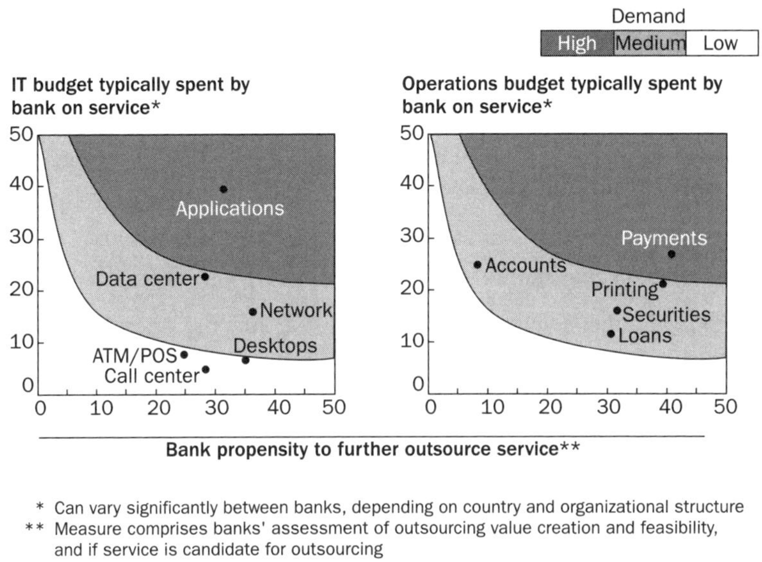

Figure 21.6 Outsourcing demand (percent, estimates)

Source: survey interviews; IDC; Gartner; client benchmarks; McKinsey

the typical share of (IT or operations) budget spent on that service by a bank (Figure 21.6).[13]

Thus, in IT, it would seem that a key growth area concerns applications. Applications-outsourcing has the highest potential for growth (in terms of contract value), largely because it represents a big slice (41 percent) of the IT budget. In operations, payments and printing are key growth areas: these services are not only more likely to be outsourced by banks but also spending on them is a large part of the operations budget (on average, some 27 percent for payments and 21 percent for printing). In addition, new service delivery models will develop to take into account banks' demands for innovative contract and pricing models and the growth in offshoring.

Increasingly, banks are negotiating consumption-based pricing (variable costs) and detailed SLAs for each service they outsource, as well as penalties for substandard performance by a provider. More emphasis is being placed on shorter contract lifetimes and the reversibility of deals to take account of faster technological cycles and industry changes, such as mergers and acquisitions (M&A). Providers are also being required to take on more of the risk to provide greater incentives to optimize services (e.g., through risk/reward-pricing or unlimited liability for disruptions to service delivery).

Offshoring is being applied progressively by banks, both internally and within outsourcing agreements. For example, of the banks in our survey, 26 percent have experience in offshoring, with the UK and the Republic of Ireland leading the way.

---

[13] Incremental propensity to outsource, calculated using banks' assessment of service as a candidate for future outsourcing (high/low) and average value creation and feasibility per service (i.e., if high, then propensity assumed to be high). Analysis at service detail level; there are differences at subservice level.

Banks that had already implemented offshoring did so mainly for applications services and, it should be noted, rather successfully. Other offshorers pointed out the high quality of their partners' work. A further 35 percent expressed their willingness to explore this avenue further—indeed many of them had already tried offshoring on a limited basis. On the other hand, banks that expressed no wish to experiment with offshoring mostly cited cultural and linguistic barriers as the cause.

Trends in the outsourcing market

We also foresee significant changes in both the IT and the operations-outsourcing market. In particular, the borderline between the two will become less distinct.

In the IT-outsourcing market, it is clear that banks are becoming more cost-sensitive and more experienced in setting up IT-outsourcing arrangements, while there is increasing commoditization of certain infrastructure services, such as desktops and networks. This will have the effect of squeezing providers' margins for some services. For example, one bank currently retains three different providers for desktop management, who are required to make competitive price bids at intervals. Increasing competition is the other major trend, especially with the arrival of several new players including consultancy firms (e.g., Accenture), telecommunications companies (e.g., Telecom Italia), and offshore companies (e.g., ING's deal with NIIT) in the European market. IT providers are attempting to build scale and develop integrated service-offerings; for instance, by adding consulting skills through M&As (e.g., Cap Gemini and Ernst & Young). Some providers are streamlining their portfolio to focus on core competencies and, in some cases, building alliances or subcontracting for other services.

The market for operations, on the other hand, will develop and mature with improvements in the service-offering and an increasing number of providers (in particular, bank-related joint ventures). The overall number of provider offerings will grow to meet the high level of interest that banks demonstrate for operations-outsourcing, thus increasing the availability of some service offerings. For example, banks will enter the market, either alone, as Deutsche Bank has done with etb, or as part of a joint venture with other banks or third-party specialists, like Barclays, Lloyds TSB, HSBC, and Unisys with iPSL. Furthermore, some already established operations providers will expand their services and geographical scope, while specialized providers will crystallize for certain high-volume services. The providers will aim to aggregate and exploit economies of scale (e.g., in securities-processing) by consolidating further and opening up their ownership structure or to leverage network externalities (e.g., for payments at a Europe-wide level).[14] Other providers will try to differentiate themselves by offering specific capabilities, such as loan-scoring models—although, even here, size will still matter. With the pressure mounting on IT providers, as outlined above, there will be an increasing tendency for such firms to target growth in the developing operations market. The traffic will not all be one way, however.

[14] Network externalities stem from a situation in which the value of a good to a consumer changes because the number of people using it changes (e.g., owning a phone becomes more valuable as more people are plugged into the network).

Looking in more depth at developments on the operations side, we can say that there appear to be first mover advantages in certain areas, such as payments, and that several providers are now targeting this market. However, many of these will not be successful given the tough nature of the challenges facing them. First, providers entering the operations market will face high entry costs (e.g., the cost and time of setting up multiple client systems). Second, geographical expansion may necessitate costs related to adapting a service-offering to local rules and regulations. In particular, banks intending to offer services to the external market (insourcing) will need to overcome other banks' reluctance to outsource parts of their business to a potential competitor (i.e., to other banks or joint ventures set up by banks). Insourcing will also mean extensive system upgrades for banks, as well as building new organizational skills for professional service delivery (e.g., contract management, sales orientation, service level definition, customer-reporting, systems integration, and project management). If setting up a shared equity unit is the preferred option, other issues arise, such as standardizing the various banks' offerings and systems that need to be moved to the new entity. Infrastructure may have to be written off or integrated and the scheme could inspire opposition from labor organizations if there are plans for staff transfers and/or layoffs. In addition, the governance structure and equity split need to be determined, and the partners have to agree on the future service offering and the opening of equity to new clients. Lastly, if partnering with nonbank, third-party specialists, such as property surveyors or IT providers, managing the different cultures and aligning objectives to the business models adds to the complexity.

Outsourcing might not be a new subject matter, but its relevance in banking is growing and new developments steadily reinforce the importance of its role. Although outsourcing can create significant value, its capture requires excellent preparation, implementation, and execution. We find that there is no one single path to success, but many valuable lessons can be learned from banks' experiences in outsourcing, not least from the application of best practice methods to achieve excellence in this field.

22

Offshoring: A New Road to Cost Reduction

Anupam Sahay[1]

A quiet revolution is under way in financial services operations, much akin to the radical change experienced by the global manufacturing industry in the 1970s. This revolution concerns offshoring: the internationalization of operations, through cross-border hubs in low-cost locations such as India, the Philippines, China, and select locations in Latin America and Eastern Europe.

Several major universal banks and international financial services companies have set the pace in establishing offshore operations. They are in the fast lane, while others are following more slowly. Although the potential will vary across banks, the basic rationale is common to all because the underlying economics of offshoring are highly attractive.

It is not too late for banks who have yet to decide on an offshoring strategy and, in the final section of this chapter, we describe how best to approach the offshoring decision and set out the key components of effective implementation.

THE THREE-LANE HIGHWAY

The pace of change in offshoring varies significantly between different categories of banks. This results in a 'three-lane highway' that has potentially far-reaching consequences for long-term competitive positioning.

Traveling at different speeds

In the fast lane of offshore operators are global players who already operate across international markets, such as American Express, Citigroup, GE Capital, HSBC, and Standard Chartered. For these institutions, centralizing operations in low-cost hub locations does not require major cultural change. Instead, it is a natural

[1] The author would like to express his gratitude for the contribution of his colleagues in McKinsey's Business Technology Office.

extension of their global business model. Standard Chartered, for example, is consolidating operations from over 40 countries into three large-scale, low-cost operating hubs: Chennai in India; Shenzhen in China; and Kuala Lumpur in Malaysia. Projecting forward over the next decade, a significant proportion of the cost base of these global players will be in new, low-cost offshore hubs, partly migrated from ultra high-cost locations in the western hemisphere and partly centralized out of previously disparate non-Western locations.

The highway's middle lane comprises institutions that are already actively pursuing offshoring, but (typically) lack the global reach of the leaders. These players do not have the same momentum as those in the fast lane; but they are all increasingly committed to a structural shift in their cost structure through offshoring. Their prevalent characteristic is that they are based, mostly, in the English-speaking world. Particularly among US and UK institutions, there is intense activity under way to evaluate, pilot, and roll out offshore activities. Most major UK banks are looking to set up offshore centres with (eventually) several thousand jobs each. Several major UK life and nonlife insurers are also active, including Friends Provident, Prudential, and Royal Sun Alliance.

The highway's slow lane is occupied by players from continental Europe and other regions. Here, there are very real barriers in terms of labor flexibility, language, and tax; as well as softer barriers concerning management mindset and international experience. These are impeding the realization of offshoring potential for continental European banks, and all the time the gap relative to the fast lane is increasing.

Far-reaching consequences

The most direct consequence is that banks in the fast and middle lanes are well placed to achieve a radically superior cost position. Depending on their pricing strategy, this may be turned into significant gains in customer market share through lower prices. But, potentially, the competition consequences reach further than this. In the longer term, offshoring results in a fundamental rebasing of cost structure relative to 'stay at home' players, and so may well shape the profile of future industry consolidation. Banks that are able to operate globally, with operations concentrated in low-cost locations, are much better placed to extract synergies from cross-border mergers and acquisitions. Benefiting from this virtuous circle, banks in the fast and middle lanes may well steal a march over the slow lane in terms of global competitiveness. This may or may not come to pass, but with today's trends we can envisage a scenario in which global financial services companies will have built an extreme competitive advantage in cost-efficiency.

THE ECONOMICS OF OFFSHORING

The driving force of the move to offshoring is the continuous pressure on banks to improve cost and operational performance. Offshoring presents a major opportunity for achieving a structural solution to the cost problem and, as such, it represents the

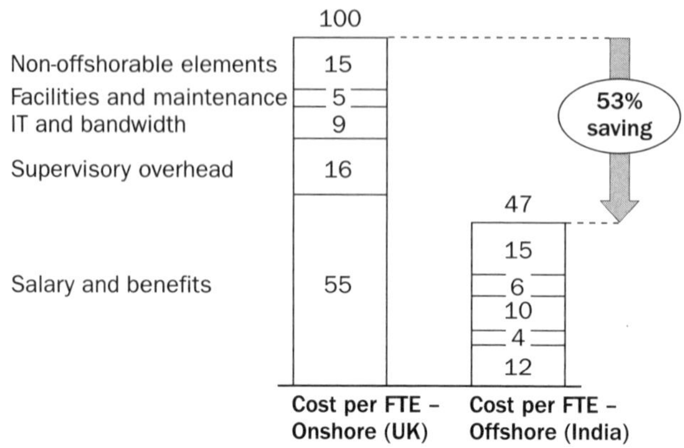

Figure 22.1 Operating cost-savings through offshoring (index, onshore (UK) = 100)

Source: McKinsey

next level of operational performance, moving on from incremental cost reduction through removing excess fat within the existing cost structure.

In this section, we describe the main sources of the operational benefit from offshoring. Collectively, they can deliver a sustainable cost reduction to the tune of 30 to 60 percent of the original cost of offshored activities (Figure 22.1).

Cost arbitrage

The first and most prominent benefit is lower labor costs. In well-chosen locations—particularly India and China—the availability of skilled labor is plentiful and increasing. This manpower is available at somewhere between 20 and 40 percent of the cost in advanced Western economies. Put another way, for any given level of wage cost, the skill available is much higher. The fear that offshore locations would compromise service quality has been dispelled by the early experiences of the global leaders. They have shown that a well-motivated offshore workforce is quite capable of delivering the same or higher levels of service quality and transaction productivity as its onshore equivalent (Figure 22.2).

Historically, the advantage in labor costs—and related costs such as occupancy—has been offset partly by inadequate and more expensive telecommunications. Ireland's advantage in this area (relative to non-Western locations) was one reason for its success as a tax-based offshore location for financial services in the 1990s. But in recent years, locations outside the western hemisphere have made radical improvements in telecommunications capacity, reliability, and unit costs. In India, for example, leased line costs fell by over 80 percent in the three years to 2001.[2]

---

[2] This example is taken from the NASSCOM–McKinsey Report 2002. (NASSCOM is the Indian National Association of Software and Service Companies.)

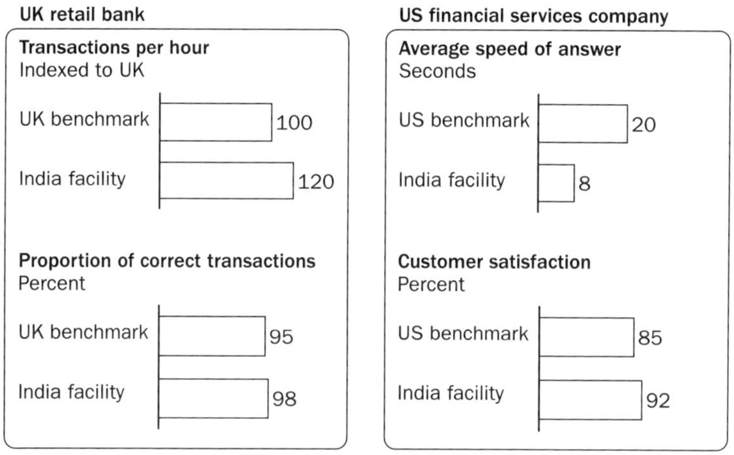

Figure 22.2 Onshore vs. offshore productivity and quality

Source: NASSCOM–McKinsey Reoport 2002

Access to scarce skills

In some categories, the labor advantage of offshoring is not just a lower unit cost per skill level, but the sheer availability of staff with the necessary skills. For example, software services skills are increasingly scarce in the Western world. Offshoring in India has proved an effective way to solve this problem. Over the past five years, the number of IT professionals in India has more than doubled to over half a million.[3] Similarly, Ireland offers a pool of investment professionals; a large proportion of the Italian fund management industry is now run from Dublin.

Government incentives

Governments in low-cost locations have acknowledged the employment and wealth-creation advantages of the trend to offshoring and provide incentives to lure offshore operators. These do not just take the form of tax breaks but can also involve tailored operational infrastructure. India, for example, provides a number of software technology parks, where the technology and premises infrastructure enables Western companies to start operations quickly, almost on a 'plug and play' basis. This is further sweetened by fiscal incentives, with several state governments offering a multi-year tax holiday.

Catalyst for a new business model

As a new start in a new location, offshoring provides a way around previously entrenched barriers to change. Hence, moving offshore can act as a trigger, enabling changes in the operations business model. These typically relate to centralization and standardization of activities. In particular, offshoring creates an opportunity to

[3] NASSCOM's website.

concentrate activities into a single center or into a few hubs, each supporting business activity in many countries. For example, Citigroup concentrates its trade-processing operations in Singapore.

SIX DECISIONS TO MAKE

Offshoring, particularly for the first time, poses significant logistical challenges. There is a wide gulf between formulating the business case for offshoring—which in most circumstances is robust—and the successful delivery of high-quality, low-cost operational capability in a new location. It is helpful to analyze and manage the offshoring decision across six components: opportunity-scoping, location, operating model, commercial model, partner selection and contract negotiation, and, finally, transition and rollout.

Opportunity-scoping

Several dimensions need to be addressed in assessing the potential scope of the opportunity. First, obtaining clarity of business logic for selecting processes to offshore. Second, assessing the financial advantage from offshoring the processes selected. Third, determining the sequence and phasing, so as to reflect the bank's priorities and risk assessment.

In retail banking, early movers in offshoring have already covered a broad range of activities, including noncustomer-facing-processing, basic activities within support functions (such as human resources [HR], finance, and IT), and customer interaction via call centers (both inbound and outbound). Clearly, not all activities are amenable to offshoring (e.g., those that require face-to-face customer contact such as complex advice). For others, telecommunications or other costs may override the benefit of lower labor cost (e.g., where document-imaging is a major part of activity cost), or there may be specific regulatory barriers. Nevertheless, in our experience, it is quite (and increasingly) plausible to consider offshoring for the great majority of operating and support activities of a retail bank.

Location

The main drivers of country selection are twofold. First, labor, including cost, quality, and type of skills, and fluency in the required language. Second, economic and political geography, including infrastructure (telecommunications, transport, etc.), time zone, investment incentives, and political risk. There is now a well-established marketplace of primary locations including, China, India, Ireland, the Caribbean, Mexico, the Philippines, and Singapore; and a second tier, including (among others) Eastern Europe, North Africa, and Mauritius. Across all the locations, India, the Philippines, and China are emerging as the leading low-cost countries in which to offshore (Figure 22.3).

Of course, it is not enough merely to select a country. Each one can offer several destinations with differing infrastructure and HR characteristics; and sometimes with significant variations in fiscal regime and investment incentives.

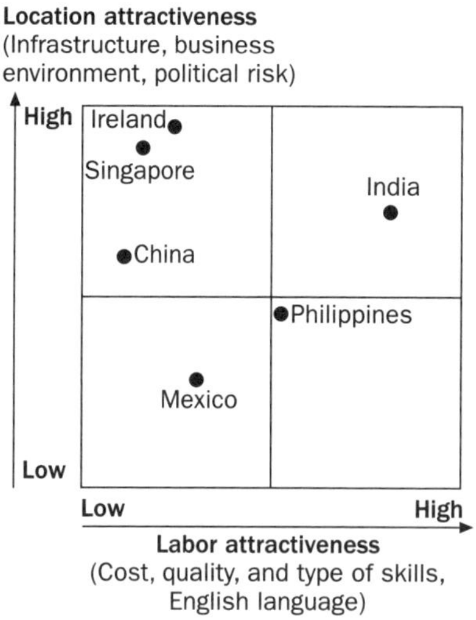

	Salary of new graduates 2000/01 US$ p.a.	Number of new graduates 2001 Million p.a.
Mexico	1400	0.14
China	2000	0.95
India	2400	2.10
Philippines	2900	0.38
Malaysia	7200	0.03
Singapore	16 000	0.01
Ireland	19 500	0.04

Figure 22.3 Comparison of locations

Source: NASSCOM–McKinsey Report 2002

Operating model

The operating model needs to address micro-level operational issues. Primary among them is the coordination of activities between an onshore and offshore location. Setting the right service level agreement is important, as is deciding on risk contingency and disaster recovery measures. It is critical to ensure that quality control is applied to offshore operations as stringently as it is to onshore operations.

The operating model also needs to address issues of operations structure—in particular, the degree of centralization, the appropriate number of hubs, and which business locations they serve. There is often a scale curve in operations, linking size and unit costs. For example, the minimum efficient scale for a call center is typically around 400 to 500 FTE equivalent positions; and around 1500 for a data-processing center (Figure 22.4).

Commercial model

The commercial model addresses the high-level organizational issues, including whether to outsource to a third-party vendor or to set up a captive operation offshore. There is no common best practice model here; instead, commercial arrangements need to be tailored to banks' individual capabilities and objectives (e.g., the time to market, the availability of in-house resources, the degree of control required, and the risk appetite). Many of the early movers adopted a captive model whereby they relocated a block of costs and continued to operate this in-house. This choice reflects the absence of credible outsourcing vendors three to five years ago, when the early movers started to migrate operations offshore. Today, a wide choice of commercial models is on offer, ranging from an arm's-length outsourcing contract to a

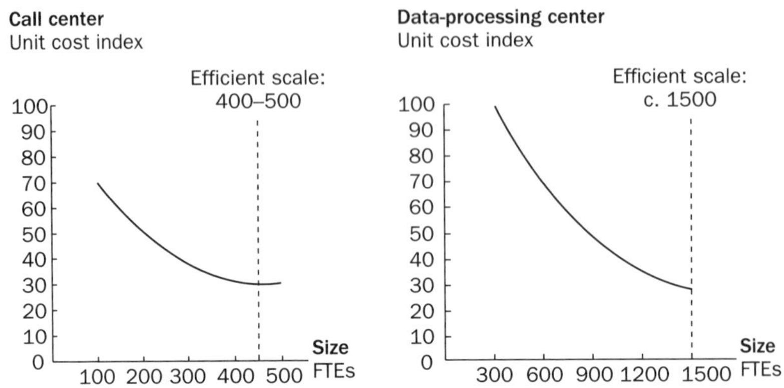

Figure 22.4 Efficient scale in operations centers

Source: McKinsey

Diminishing need for long-term partner involvement

Model	Examples from India
▪ Arm's-length outsourcing contract	▪ Egg + ICICI
▪ Strategic equity investment (minority stake)	▪ Citigroup + Progeon
▪ Joint venture	▪ N/A
▪ Assisted build-out	▪ American Express + bharti
▪ Buy-out of existing offshore BPO facility	▪ Conseco + Exlservice
▪ Captive service company (greenfield)	▪ GE Capital

Figure 22.5 Commercial models

Source: McKinsey

captive service company, and including several intermediate partnering options (Figure 22.5).

Partner selection and contract negotiation

The issue of partner selection is necessarily intertwined with the choice of commercial model. The availability and financial terms of a potential partner will be one of the key drivers of model choice. There is now a plethora of potential partners, including global players among the systems integrators and consultants; a new wave of indigenous players specializing in business process outsourcing (BPO) for offshore operators; and the third-party offerings of early movers' captive service companies.

Motivation and capabilities vary widely across potential partners: for example, negotiating stance and revenue expectations differ significantly between a systems integrator and a software house. Moreover, the partners best suited for call center activities—the most mature market in offshore BPO—typically differ from those most appropriate for transaction-processing or support functions (such as HR administration).

As with any outsourcing or operational partnership arrangement, a highly disciplined and fact-based evaluation of partners is necessary, followed by due diligence and contract negotiation. The total process of evaluation and negotiation—from initial sketching of the landscape of potential partners to signing the heads of agreement on a contract—can take three to six months.

Setup and roll-out

The final step is setting up a pilot and then rolling it out to full-scale operation. This involves several disciplines: governance, micro-level transition management (in moving processes from legacy structures to offshore locations), compliance (including legal and tax), performance management, human resource management (including redundancy programmes), operational risk management (including contingency-planning), and communication. A full discussion of all these disciplines is beyond the scope of this chapter. However, many offshoring programmes fail not because of operational difficulties, but because inadequate attention is paid to governance and communication.

First, governance. The success of the offshore model is often impeded by a lack of clarity and poor communication between the onshore and offshore organization. It is important to establish clearly delineated roles early on. For example, how the role of the country manager for offshore operations relates to a geographic manager onshore, and the mechanisms whereby senior management onshore monitors and incentivizes performance at a distant offshore location. The appropriate organizational solutions will depend on the bank's specific culture and structures. The key lesson is that these issues should be addressed and agreed before rollout, since an offshore operation can easily be jeopardized early on by a dysfunctional and mutually antagonistic organization.

Second, communication. Particularly in a first-time offshoring project, communication should begin onshore and encompass all relevant stakeholders. This typically includes employees, union representatives, senior executives, the press, regulators, and suppliers. External communication—such as to the press and regulators—should cover both onshore and offshore stakeholders. The communications plan should be positioned clearly around the rationale, trajectory, and impact of offshoring and should form part of an integrated change program across the organization. This is particularly important in countries with a difficult labour environment, such as many in continental Europe.

The activities amenable to offshoring are already wide-ranging, and their scope will increase as confidence is built from first generation experience. Indeed, looking a decade or longer into the future, the question is less which activities can be migrated offshore than it is which activities should continue to be performed in high-cost domestic locations. The distant vision—but one which clearly suggests the way forward—is that nearly all processing, functional support, and remote contact activity could be offshore. Some players are already on the fast track toward this vision. For most others, there is still a choice: wait on the sidelines and risk being left behind, or live life in the fast lane.

23

IT Costs: Reining in Excessive Expenditure

Andreas Etter, Ernst Sonderegger[1]

Retail banks face a particularly difficult challenge in controlling IT costs. There are few opportunities to improve cost-efficiency through large-scale purchases, such as a new hardware platform or network and software architecture. Banks that tinker with IT initiatives, either *ad hoc* or as part of the annual planning cycle, will certainly reap some rewards, but these will be inherently limited. Such a piecemeal approach simply fails to address the scale and complexity of the IT function. The route to effective IT cost control in the short to medium term lies in a periodic, structured review process that identifies and prioritizes key levers for cost reduction and in the disciplined implementation of the cost-saving opportunities generated through this process.[2]

THE COST CHALLENGE

Retail banks' IT costs have increased rapidly in recent years, and now represent 10 to 20 percent of annual total operating costs (Figure 23.1).

There are three drivers behind the seemingly uncontrollable escalation of costs: business demands, technological developments, and external factors. Banks looking to get a grip on these drivers face a set of inherent obstacles that they must overcome.

Drivers of cost escalation

Business demands continue to require the more intensive and wider application of IT. In the front office, banks are having to offer increased deposit automation; real-time

[1] The authors would like to express their gratitude for the contributions of Christian Casal, Thierry Seiler, Stefan Spang, Volker Stadler, and Martin Wechsler.

[2] The focus of this chapter is on levers that start to generate cost savings within approximately two years, including 'early wins' where the full run rate saving is achieved within a few months (e.g., six months at most).

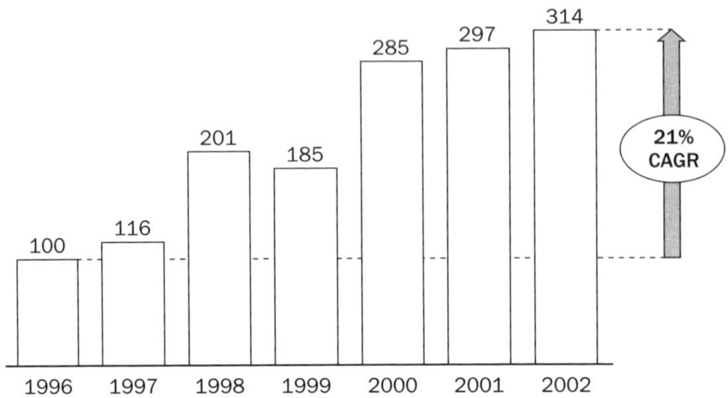

Figure 23.1 Growth in banking industry IT spend (index, 1996 = 100)

Source: Rubin Worldwide Benchmark Report 2003

banking; and enhanced IT support for sales and customer service at the branch, in the field, or at call centers. In the middle and back office, IT is having to cope with the automation of decision-making (such as behavioral credit scoring); straight-through-processing; and the application of advanced forms of image capture technology.

Technology developments over the past decade have been so far-reaching that they continue to exert considerable influence over IT budgets. The two most important developments have been the introduction of client-server architecture and the application of Internet technologies. Along with the direct cost of web-enabling banking processes, Internet technologies have given rise to costly new security requirements as customers now have direct access to banks' internal processes.

Despite a fall in IT unit costs, overall costs have continued to increase dramatically. For instance, the perception that IT was a relatively cheap resource—especially in terms of hardware—meant that IT managers neglected to manage growth in capacity. The IT buying frenzy of the late 1990s continued to push overall IT-spending upward, but not all of this was over-buying. The growth in volume during the Internet boom did justify a large part of the investment, but there still remain cases where IT managers bought excessive capacity and are now trying to improve its utilization.

Finally, the problems caused by *external factors* have not diminished with the passing of the millennium bug and the euro conversion. In coming years, new drivers may well equal—and, in some cases, surpass—the scale of these recent demands. The main external driver on the horizon is industry regulation; specifically, the IT support requirements of implementing Basel II (including the issue of operational risk), international accounting standards, and—for those banks involved in securities-broking, trading, or custody—international securities identification numbers and $t+1$ settlement.[3]

[3] At the line of writing, however, the objective of $t+1$ settlement appears to have been deferred.

Inherent obstacles

IT costs are inherently difficult to manage because of the complexity of IT requirements and the problems of short-term inflexibility.

Complexity arises from sheer size and the need for connectivity between heterogeneous systems. IT systems have often grown organically over a long time, as business requirements have expanded and changed, and they have various elements—sometimes highly customized—bolted on. This exacerbates the problems that already exist at the interface between business users and IT providers. The ability to adapt an IT system fully to new business demands can be limited. For example, one major European retail bank has declared certain older software components in its system as 'black boxes', prohibiting changes to them as the specific IT expertise is no longer readily available. Hence, any new functionality is built up with add-on patches, which, in turn, further increase the degree of complexity. Furthermore, the existence of highly specialized skills in the IT function can create a culture of organizational resistance to outsiders who lack the relevant expertise.

A significant degree of short-term inflexibility is built into a typical retail bank's IT cost base. At its most direct, inflexibility is embedded in the annual accounting costs of banks' IT. Depreciation of hardware equipment is a noncompressible sunk cost; as are software purchases or development costs for banks that capitalize these items. Depending on the particular item, the accounting cost in any one year may reflect investment from up to five years earlier. The full impact on annual accounting costs of curtailing immediate plans for capital-spending can therefore take several years to materialize. Many banks today are still living within the constraints set up by past decisions. Such a legacy also hinders a bank's ability to cut running costs of the prevailing hardware and software systems (Figure 23.2).

IT spend may seem a difficult area to tackle if it is dominated by a few, large, mandatory projects (although sometimes 'mandatory' is confused with 'pet'). However, on closer inspection, almost all projects—irrespective of size and

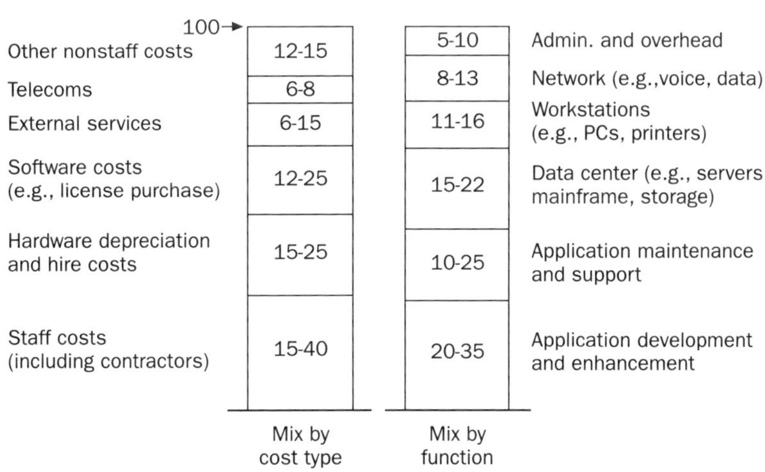

Figure 23.2 Estimated mix of IT costs in retail banking (percent)

Source: McKinsey

nature—can be a fertile source of short-term cost reduction opportunities as long as such opportunities are addressed systematically.

THREE LEVERS TO CUT IT COSTS

In identifying short- and medium-term IT cost reduction opportunities, the review process is best structured around three broad levers: increasing efficiency; sourcing effectively; and restructuring the project portfolio. At excellent banks, all three levers are used, they are applied across the full set of IT cost blocks, and their application follows a structured methodology.

Increase efficiency

To maintain the desired level of IT service at a lower cost naturally increases efficiency. In practice, however, such measures include initiatives where some trade-off is made between cost and service. In these cases, cooperation between the IT function and the business side is important.

The best way to identify efficiency opportunities is to ask the same set of questions across a wide range of IT resource units and service outputs—and to do so relentlessly. In particular, units should be challenged as to whether IT services can be eliminated, curtailed, consolidated, or reconfigured, or whether they are being replicated in another business area.

Excellent banks—particularly those that have succeeded in post-merger integration—have already captured the benefits of elimination and consolidation opportunities. For others, there are savings still to be made especially in areas where services are duplicated across different business units, where services add minimal value, where internal services lack a clear end-user, or where the level of service provision is no longer appropriate (often a legacy of past user requirements). Similarly, cost-saving opportunities also arise from consolidating multiple data-processing centers, servers, or decentralized systems.

Identifying reconfiguration opportunities is usually more complex. Some inefficiencies are spotted only after a full end-to-end process review, or require the standardization and automation of routine actions, or depend on exploiting synergies across several organizational units. However, there are potentially significant cost-savings to be had from comparatively simple reconfigurations. Two European banks illustrate this. In both instances, the savings were 10 to 15 percent of the corresponding budget.

The first relates to e-mail service levels. Cost-savings were generated from several simple, small measures: function-specific usage quotas, attachment size limits, and reduced data backup levels (taking into consideration any legal and internal requirements for archiving electronic correspondence).[4] The second relates to printing services. Here, cost-savings were generated through centralizing print jobs (including

[4] These cost-savings were primarily in the form of 'avoided' costs—rather than year-on-year reductions—through reducing or postponing investment requirements for data storage and network infrastructure.

some that were previously contracted out to third parties). Centralization enabled the smoothing of peak loads, along with the introduction of segment-specific delays to vary the speed of response according to the relative urgency of the task and relative value of the customer.

Some reconfiguration of technology can be undertaken directly by the IT function, without involving business users in a cost–benefit assessment. A good example is the use of Parallel Sysplex® technology.[5] By enabling many mainframes to act as a united cluster, the total number needed is reduced, thereby saving lease or purchase costs, maintenance costs, and, possibly, some software license costs.

Furthermore, costs for backing up mainframe capacity can be reduced, since, in the event of an individual mainframe failing, workload-processing can be distributed among the others.

Source effectively

Effective sourcing involves determining the appropriate mix of internal and external sourcing, in particular the use of external contractors, and the detailed application of purchasing and supply management techniques to externally sourced services and products. At the extreme, it extends to strategic outsourcing; but this is a larger topic, which is dealt with in Chapter 21.

The extensive use of third-party contractors is common in retail banks' IT functions. Indeed, it is a general feature of the IT labor market. This provides banks with a significant lever for their IT cost control initiatives if they can reduce the use of external contractors and tailor their use more appropriately to the pattern of a bank's IT-staffing demands. The key is to identify a level of core demand (i.e., the low point of fluctuating demand) and ensure this is met by a group of permanent employees (who are cheaper than equivalently skilled contractors). This basic service also includes low-value-added tasks, for which contractors are typically over qualified. Contractors are then used to meet increases in demand—with their remuneration structured to reflect time flexibility—and to fill in scarce skills. This approach can save substantial sums of money, both directly and by providing an opportunity to negotiate down the remuneration of the remaining contractors. At one bank, the net savings were 50 percent of external contractor costs. This comprised a gross saving of nearly two-thirds, partly offset by the cost of hiring additional permanent staff, mostly from the pool of redundant contractors.

Software license costs can be reduced significantly (e.g., by 10 to 15 percent of budget, sometimes more) by applying purchasing and supply management techniques. Long-established contracts should be monitored to ensure they reflect current license requirements and should be renegotiated to reflect software price decreases. Pooling negotiations and contracts creates a more powerful position from which to extract discounts from suppliers. This may sometimes mean selecting the main supplier's offering instead of entering into a new contract with an alternative supplier, taking into consideration the total cost of ownership over the life cycle of the software.

[5] An IBM term for the coupling technology that enables data-sharing across mainframes, configured in a parallel processing cluster.

Hardware maintenance costs can be reduced by up to 20 percent by using the same techniques. The main source of savings tends to be on the demand side (i.e., in reducing maintenance levels). A detailed review of maintenance activities can identify tasks that are redundant or over-engineered (e.g., noncritical backup or unnecessarily quick reaction time). Such savings occur irrespective of whether maintenance is performed internally or supplied externally. Indeed, one of the hallmarks of excellence in IT cost control is the application of the same purchasing and supply management techniques to the in-house IT department as to external suppliers.

Although the pricing of in-house and third-party IT support cannot be compared directly, benchmarking specific in-house services against suppliers' quotations can be used to put pressure on the IT department. Conversely, it can also elicit lower quotations from external suppliers. At one bank, this benchmarking process was used over a two-year period and led to successive reductions in both quoted external prices and internally submitted budgets.

Restructure the project portfolio

In order to restructure the project portfolio, there needs to be a comprehensive review of projects—both existing ones and those in the pipeline—from which to generate options for cancellation, postponement, or rescoping. Decisions have to be made in terms of the overall mix and prioritization of projects within the portfolio and in terms of the individual project value. Trade-offs are inevitable, and therefore decisions must be made with the cooperation of the business users and IT providers.

Where senior management has the appetite for aggressive cost reduction, a review of priorities across the whole project portfolio can be a powerful tool. Excellent banks have a clear picture of the total mix of projects that comprise the budgeted investment. However, in many large retail banks with multiple business units, such a holistic picture is often either missing or is inadequately drawn. The picture needs to include core information to facilitate decisions regarding high-level prioritization. This includes the scale of project spend (both capital and operating expenditure); assessed quantitative benefits (whether cost or revenue); categorization as mandatory (e.g., due to regulations), critical, or optional; and, for nonmandatory projects, the assessed risk from postponing or canceling the project. Ranking projects using such information enables senior management to decide on how aggressive to be. At one European retail bank, a review of 103 projects led to 27 percent being cancelled and 32 percent rescoped (at a high level). The total cost savings were just over 40 percent of the total budget, while 90 percent of the planned benefits from the projects were maintained.

Reducing costs at the individual project level requires the detailed involvement of middle management from both the IT department and business user divisions.[6] It is vital to carry out a granular project value analysis (i.e., break a project down into its component end products, such as specific functionality enhancements). From this, the estimated investment and return can be aligned for each component. This provides a quantitative context in which to generate micro-level cost reduction

[6] For some projects, such as those relating purely to IT infrastructure, business user involvement may not be necessary.

ideas (i.e., more efficient ways of achieving the same benefit or modifications to the project's scope). The process works well for both small, focused projects and large, multifaceted projects although, with the latter, it is often advisable to spin off reasonably self-contained subprojects and apply the process at this level.

Two examples from a large European universal bank illustrate the sort of opportunities that arise and the process involved. The first relates to an IT-restructuring project within a retail bank. The bank was successfully operating two front-end platforms, based on the same technology, but with different application architectures. Initial short-term cost-savings were realized by rescoping and aligning the scheduled development of the two platforms. Then, by evaluating and comparing the strengths and weaknesses of each one, the bank developed a target architecture for a single platform. The planned platform consolidation was supported by a positive business case showing expected savings in development, operating, and maintenance costs of some 10 percent over the first three years.

The second example concerns the process for reprioritization of the bank's project portfolio, which comprised around 350 projects. The target was to cut costs by 20 percent. After gathering information on the portfolio (as outlined above), prioritization workshops were conducted involving both IT managers and the appropriate business managers at which decisions were made to cancel projects or reduce their budgets, cumulatively building to the overall cost-savings target. Two things were particularly helpful in achieving the target: communicating the cost-savings target up front helped create pressure to reach it; and the transparency of the process was facilitated by working 'live' on the portfolio, tracking the effect of cancellation and reduction decisions using an online tool accessed in the workshop.

GUIDELINES FOR SUCCESS

In an era when costs have been running away from the control of managers, we have seen that there are ways to rein them in. To implement the ideas outlined above requires discipline and maintaining momentum through the necessary iterations. Even though these features to some extent are generic—they essentially apply to all cost reduction programs—it is worth emphasizing their importance to retail banks, in particular. There are few other industries in which IT accounts for such a considerable cost block as in retail banking (10 to 20 percent of annual total operating costs). IT cost-savings, therefore, can have a significant impact on retail banks' bottom lines, and not meeting the conditions outlined below almost certainly means failing to reach true potential.

There are four tasks in particular that banks need to perform if they are going to maximize the savings in IT. First, a bank should plot the types of initiatives or techniques against the time frame of impact. Having fixed dates in mind helps set and then meet expectations, be they of external stakeholders or of staff. A balance should be struck that allows for the immediate implementation of early wins while simultaneously developing and launching efforts that have a medium- and long-term impact.

Early wins also help to boost morale and sustain the impetus of the program, as well as providing a degree of self-financing for the program as a whole. They are readily available in each of the IT cost reduction levers. In increasing efficiency, banks can quickly eliminate low-value-added services and duplications; in effective sourcing, software contracts up for renewal can be renegotiated; and in terms of restructuring the project portfolio, low-value projects can simply be terminated. Long-term initiatives, where cost-savings start after one to two years, include consolidation initiatives; the outsourcing of specific infrastructure, applications, or developments; and the rescoping of complex, multi-year projects.

Second, the diagnosis for each lever should typically be applied across the full range of major IT cost blocks. This is partly to avoid missing any opportunities and partly because sharing the pain helps overcome organizational resistance to change. Individual circumstances may justify a departure from this approach, in particular where senior management already has a good understanding of more promising areas and where the organization's culture can cope readily with the apparent discrimination. However, it is rarely appropriate to designate 'no go' areas.

Third, cost reduction programs work most effectively when senior management takes a highly visible steering role, setting the goals for the overall program. For instance, during the reprioritization of the project portfolio at a large European bank, the physical presence of senior management in the room during the workshops enabled the whole process. Not only did it send an unambiguous signal with regard to the importance of the task but it also made sure that all participants were eager to be seen to share in the pain of making cuts. If the pressure from senior management is not applied consistently, however, the opposite can happen. A common problem, for instance, is that overall reduction targets are communicated and certain highly visible cuts occur in one unit that manages to achieve most of the overall target amount—even if not part of the original cost reduction program. Other units may then perceive further savings as noncritical and, in some cases, even renege on previously agreed savings commitments.

Fourth, it is important to involve relevant line management staff. Such programs should not be staffed solely by external consultants or through an internal projects division. In IT cost reduction programs, this implies that the active involvement of business unit management is often critical. There are opportunities that the IT department can identify and initiate off its own bat, but the program as a whole needs joint involvement. Indeed, one of the side benefits of a successful program is an improvement in mutual understanding between IT providers and business users.

If these principles are followed when applying the IT cost reduction levers described above, significant savings are achievable over a two-year horizon. McKinsey research has shown that—when taking such an approach to reducing IT costs—90 percent of the cases showed an aggregate reduction in the range of 15 to 30 percent; and, in many cases, savings of at least 5 to 10 percent were realized within the first year.[7] In short, given the right approach, retail banks' IT costs can be reined in quickly and effectively.

[7] Figures taken from an internal survey in 2001, which covered 135 IT engagements for financial institutions involving cost reduction.

Part 6
Superior Credit Policy and Skills

24

Changing Requirements for Excellence in Credit Risk Management

Uwe Stegemann[1]

The gauge of excellence in credit risk management has become significantly more demanding over the past decade. The days have long gone since balance sheet growth was acceptable as the dominant objective. Today, the watchword is value, and credit business needs to be profitable—after allowing for expected losses and the cost of capital cover for unexpected losses—to justify its demands on banks' capital resources. Moreover, it is no longer sufficient to rely solely on qualitative assessments of credit risk and on simple policy guidelines for the mix and volume of lending. The task of credit risk management is changing, requiring new quantitative techniques, which measure the balance of risk and return with increased precision.

In this chapter, we provide an overview of the radical change that is taking place in the nature of credit risk management.[2] First, we describe the traditional approach and identify the structural reasons that it is often value-destroying. Second, we describe recent advances in credit risk management techniques. These are opening up the prospect of a new approach that offers superior value-creation opportunities for banks that master them. Third, we explain why the current regulatory regime is out of step with this change and how the regulators are making major efforts to catch up with proposals for a new capital adequacy regime.

Our description of the nature of current change sets the context for the chapters that follow. They discuss the specific capabilities banks need to develop in order to meet the changing requirements for excellence in credit risk management.

[1] The author would like to express his gratitude for the contributions of his colleagues in McKinsey's Global Risk Management Practice.

[2] The underlying drivers of this change straddle retail and corporate banking. Moreover, banks differ (particularly across different countries) in their view of the appropriate boundary between retail and corporate banking. For these reasons, we at times take a bank-wide or corporate banking perspective on credit risk issues.

TRADITIONAL APPROACH OFTEN DESTROYS VALUE

For many European banks, credit business generates inadequate profits or, at worst, incurs chronic losses. Aggravating the problem of poor profitability, credit business is capital-intensive, often representing the predominant component of total capital requirements. This leads, almost inevitably, to value destruction. In this section, after briefly describing the scale of the problem, we identify the structural reasons that credit business is so often value-destroying, at least when managed with a traditional approach.

An unattractive burden

Credit business remains a key—and in some cases the dominant—shaper of balance sheets and profit statements at today's European retail and universal banks. A major reason for this is that many banks have—at least in the traditional approach—viewed lending as the lead product to secure customer relationships, particularly corporate customers but also retail, and allowed the profitability of plain vanilla lending to suffer in consequence. But, in practice, the expectation that lending is the relationship hook for cross-selling has often been disappointed.

The nature and scale of the problem become more apparent when looking at capital consumption and profitability. For corporate banking in the major European markets, we estimate[3] that the mainstream credit business ties up about 75 percent of capital and earns a return on equity—based on regulatory capital—below the cost of capital.

The picture in retail banking—more narrowly defined excluding middle-market corporate customers—is more mixed. Although this is not uniform throughout Europe, there are a significant number of banks that suffer inadequate profitability in retail credit business, if measured after expected losses and the cost of capital needed to cover unexpected losses. We have calculated recent performance in retail credit business, here defined as personal and small business credit, for a sample of German banks. Our estimate is that, on average, this business incurs an annualized pre-tax loss of 0.1 percent of outstanding loan balances, even before allowing for the cost of capital. A major cause of this loss is that default losses have absorbed over half of credit-related operating income (Figure 24.1).

Underlying this value destruction in banks' credit business are four structural drivers: flawed regulation, illiquidity, concentration risk, and mis-pricing.

Flawed regulation

Current capital adequacy regulation, as embodied in the Basel Accord of July 1988 and subsequent supplements, is out of step with modern credit risk measures. The granularity of risk differentiation across categories of borrower, as reflected in the regime's system of risk weights, is generally inadequate. The regulatory risk weights lack any direct correlation with the volatility in borrower default rates. The regime

[3] This is a joint estimate by McKinsey and Goldman Sachs, published in the report *The Future of Corporate Banking in Europe*, January 2001.

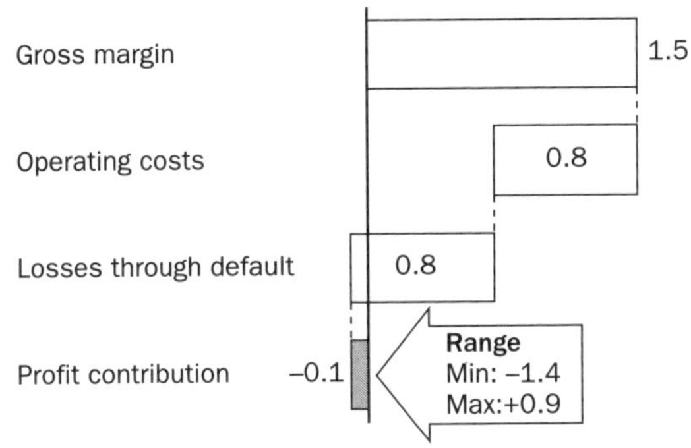

Figure 24.1 Retail credit profitability at a sample of German banks (percent of loans outstanding)

Source: McKinsey

also ignores other drivers of risk, such as the loan's residual maturity, the priority of the claim, collateral for products other than residential mortgages, or the use of credit risk mitigation techniques such as credit derivatives. Moreover, no allowance is made for the degree of portfolio diversification. Overall, lower risks are relatively over-capitalized and higher risks are relatively under-capitalized. The result, albeit unintended, has been a regulatory incentive for banks to downgrade the quality of their loan portfolio mix: arbitraging regulatory capital for lower risk-lending, through securitization and other structuring techniques; and expanding the volume of higher risk-lending, unfortunately often without the appropriate extra margin.

Illiquidity

Lending by retail and universal banks traditionally consists of largely illiquid exposures to retail and corporate customers. Medium- and long-term loans represent a significant share of total loan books, and short-term credit is often provided under committed credit lines. The traditional approach has been to retain these exposures on their balance sheet until maturity. The credit risk embedded in long-term loans is greater than the risk in short-term loans, other factors being equal.[4] With illiquid exposure in long-term contracts, it is very difficult for banks to respond speedily to new circumstances affecting the creditworthiness of specific borrowers or, more broadly, to changing macroeconomic conditions.

Concentration risk

Concentration risk arises from insufficient diversification of loan portfolios across one or more of several dimensions (e.g., individual customers, industry sectors, or

[4] Here credit risk is used in the narrow sense, being the risk that actual losses over the lifetime of the loan are not equal to the expected losses, with the difference usually called unexpected losses. Naturally, the uncertainty regarding the actual losses increases strongly with maturity.

geographic regions). It is a major source of overall credit risk, particularly for regional banks, but also for banks with nationwide coverage. We estimate that concentration risk accounts for 40 to 70 percent of total credit risk at some banks. One key reason for high portfolio concentration is that there are good business arguments—aside from the credit risk impact—in favor of banks generating credit business from the same customers again and again.

First, the shared cost of customer acquisition and relationship management can be leveraged for higher business volumes. Banks have greater insight into the needs and preferences of their established customer base, particularly for long-standing relationships. This insight translates into enhanced sales effectiveness. Second, concentrating on particular customer segments facilitates the development of industry expertise or specialist skills tailored to segment needs. In turn, the reputation established on the back of this expertise attracts additional customers in the same segment. Third (and to some extent mitigating credit risk), the superior information from long-standing customer relationships enhances credit assessment capabilities. Similarly, the more extensive information from deeper involvement in a particular segment enhances banks' understanding of credit risk factors specific to that segment.

However, in our experience, the strategy of high portfolio concentration is often carried too far: the business advantages are often outweighed by the additional credit risk. This applies to each of the dimensions of concentration; as an illustration, we use an example of geographic concentration risk. Banks with a regional focus in Bonn and its surrounding area faced a sudden increase in credit risk when the government restored the capital city status of Berlin, potentially resulting in the transfer of up to 50 000 jobs.[5] The impending loss of purchasing power undermined customers' ability to repay borrowings and threatened real-estate values, used as collateral for business-lending and home loans. This concentration risk could have been largely mitigated by lending or real-estate exposure in other regions; indeed, geographic diversification benefits are also observable across national residential real-estate markets (Figure 24.2).

The problem with concentration risk is not just the potential losses it represents, but the likelihood—at least in a smoothly functioning market—that banks are not rewarded through higher prices for taking on this risk. In our regional example above, a bank focused on Bonn may have to compete against banks with well-diversified loan portfolios. These competitors can—at least in principle—charge lower prices by leveraging the benefits of diversification, or earn higher profits at the same price level. Within efficient securities markets, asset prices tend to reflect only systematic, nondiversifiable risk, and hence do not reward risk that can be diversified away. The same tendency is at work in credit markets, but has to-date operated less effectively for several reasons: historically, banks have been unable to quantify these risks; have not priced the risks using a total portfolio perspective; and have not been fully able to trade the risks in liquid secondary markets.

[5] In the event, partly because of federal government aid, the impact was less than originally threatened.

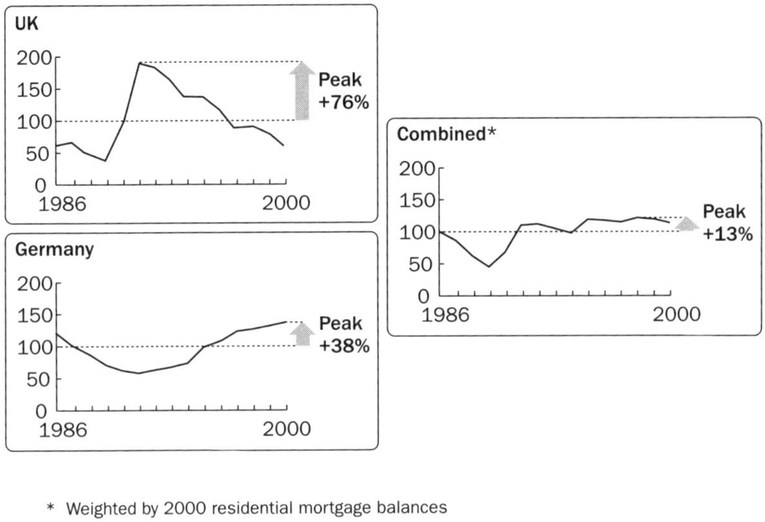

Figure 24.2 Mortgage foreclosures in UK and Germany (number p.a., indexed to 1986–98 average = 100)

Source: Council of Mortgage Lenders; Statistisches Bundesamt

Mis-pricing

Historically, in European banking, 'true' risk-adjusted pricing of credit has been rare, partly because, under the flawed regulation described above, there was limited incentive for banks to carry it out. An analysis we undertook of corporate credit-pricing in the late 1990s indicates that the degree of mis-pricing is significant. The corporate bond market charged an additional 200 to 400 basis points for B-rated vs. AA-rated risks;[6] banks on average charged an additional 15 to 40 basis points. Not only is banks' differential pricing much less pronounced than in the bond markets, but the absolute level of banks' pricing undercuts the bond markets for the less creditworthy borrowers (Figure 24.3). The result of this mis-pricing has been a continuing deterioration in the quality of banks' loan portfolios,[7] as low-risk customers tapped bond markets for cheaper funds and high-risk customers realized the cost advantage of borrowing from the banks.

The mis-pricing of default risk indicated by this comparison with the bond market is the most transparent—but not the only—source of overall mis-pricing of credit risk. Other factors that influence the true economic risk of bank credit—such as collateral, maturity, and contract-specific cash flow profiles—have typically also not been reflected adequately when pricing credit risk in the past. Under historical cost-accounting, banks have been able to hide the direct impact of mis-pricing, since

[6] The range partly reflects the presence of other pricing factors (e.g., maturity and other contract specifics).

[7] This primarily relates to corporate and institutional loan portfolios; but a parallel process—albeit not driven mainly by mis-pricing—has to some extent occurred through retail loan securitization, particularly mortgages.

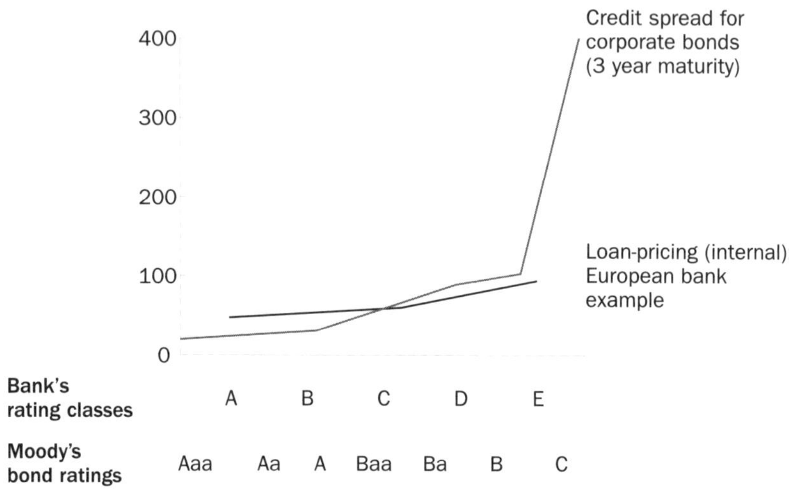

Figure 24.3 Comparison of bank loan-pricing with bond market spreads

Source: McKinsey

loans are reported at their face value. But in future this veil may have to be lifted, if the trend in international accounting standards extends to fair value-accounting for bank-lending. Moreover, even with today's accounting, the mis-pricing becomes apparent when the loans are packaged into securitized offerings and thereby sold in the market.

The combined impact of these drivers—flawed regulation, illiquidity, concentration risk, and mis-pricing—has been to make credit structurally value-destroying at many banks, particularly in small- and medium-sized enterprise (SME) and corporate business; though reflecting different competitive structures, this is not uniformly true across all European countries.

NEW TECHNIQUES OFFER SOME SOLUTIONS

At the root of the structural problems we have been discussing lie inadequate techniques at many banks for measuring and pricing risk and the historical absence of liquid markets and instruments for trading and managing—in the sense of unbundling and repackaging—credit risk. In recent years, the financial services industry has made impressive progress in developing new techniques for measuring credit risk and incorporating them into performance measures of profitability and capital usage. Linked to this has been the emergence of new markets and instruments with the common theme of facilitating the management, transfer, and trading of credit risk exposures: credit derivatives, securitization including collateralized loan-offerings, loan-trading, bilateral sales, and multilateral pooling.[8] In combination, these devel-

[8] This entails a group of banks pooling some of their loans (typically structured via a collateralized loan-offering) and buying back a repackaged tranche of the pool; some tranches may be sold to outside investors.

opments are leading to a new approach to credit risk management, often labeled 'credit-pipelining'. Although not a panacea, this new approach offers solutions to industry-wide structural problems and new, value-creation opportunities for individual banks.

New techniques

The new techniques in credit risk arise from applying and adapting concepts developed for price risk in the securities market. Academics and practitioners have adapted securities value-at-risk methodology to the measurement of risk in a credit portfolio, including determination of the capital required to cover this risk at any given level of confidence, known as 'economic capital'. Among leading banks, some have developed their own in-house version of the value-at-risk approach. Others use externally developed tools, particularly for corporate loan portfolios.

The outcome has been a radical enhancement in measuring credit risk, accompanied by the adoption of risk-adjusted performance measurement, using measures such as risk-adjusted return on capital (RAROC). The 'true' profitability of the credit business can now be evaluated by using internal risk-adjusted pricing, which incorporates a robust estimate of expected default losses and the cost of economic capital needed to cover unexpected default losses. It also becomes possible to evaluate the impact of illiquidity, concentration risk, and mis-pricing; and evaluation is the first step toward resolving—or at least mitigating—these drivers of value destruction in many loan portfolios.

At an industry level, the ability to evaluate credit risk paves the way for mutually rewarding transfers of risk among banks and between banks and non bank investors (i.e., smoothly functioning secondary markets for trading credit risk exposures). At one level, this means that a mutually beneficial price can be set for the bilateral sale of loan portfolios and for loan-trading generally. More interestingly, selling or swapping exposures can improve the risk–return ratio at both banks. This arises from portfolio diversification benefits and the nature of concentration risk. For example, a bank with very significant exposure to a particular sector can reduce concentration risk by transferring some of this exposure to another bank, with little or no such exposure. The acquiring bank thereby obtains portfolio diversification benefits. More generally, the differing portfolio structures of the two banks lead them to place different risk–return evaluations on the same sector; hence there will be an equilibrium price at which risk-adjusted profitability increases at both banks.

Credit pipelining

For an individual bank, the new techniques open the way to creating value through active credit portfolio management. We prefer the modern label of 'credit-pipelining', since much more is involved than just the management of portfolio risk through the use of securitization and credit derivatives. Credit pipelining affects all elements of the credit business system. It entails a profound shift away from the traditional approach of buy-and-hold (i.e., the originating bank holding until maturity) and introduces the new approach of originate, manage, and trade (Figure 24.4).

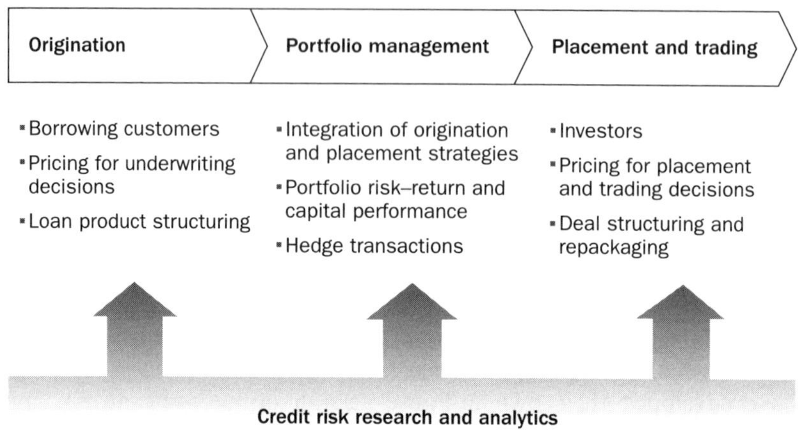

Figure 24.4 The credit pipeline concept

Source: McKinsey

Extensive new skills are required for banks to be effective in credit pipelining. In origination, advanced risk evaluation skills and product-structuring are necessary. Internal rating systems need to be able to generate quantitative measures of default probability and, as a further extension, support risk-adjusted pricing. Moreover, origination policy needs to anticipate the requirements of the portfolio management and placement functions (e.g., avoiding excessive product customization as this constrains subsequent trading). In portfolio management, robust tools are needed for measuring portfolio risk and return (e.g., credit value-at-risk and RAROC). These tools include decision support analytics to assess the 'what if' impact of new positions and economic capital methodologies to assess the capital impact of portfolio strategy. In trading and placement, financial engineering skills are required to understand and evaluate—and, at best, create and price—structured products, in which credit risk is unbundled and repackaged. Additionally, trading and placement requires access to investors other than banks and detailed market know-how.

These new skill requirements do not apply only to larger banks: smaller banks should also build pipelining skills, particularly in origination and portfolio management. While they may not be direct market participants for placement and trading, smaller banks can nevertheless access the market indirectly, via pooling or via larger banks.

New organizational capabilities are also required for effective credit pipelining. The possible organizational options range from a central portfolio unit for measurement, analysis, and advice to the creation of a profit-oriented 'credit treasury' to manage and trade the portfolio of credit risks (Box 24.1). To some extent, the concept of a credit treasury is analogous to the segregation of retail banking interest rate risks in the bank's treasury department or in a dedicated asset-and-liability management unit. However, the credit treasury concept, although interesting, is not—certainly not yet—on a par with the robust nature of money and capital markets treasuries. A major impediment arises from the special nature of credit risk and its pricing. The lending bank's privileged information on borrowers

Box 24.1
New approaches in credit organization

In recent years, some banks have begun to develop new central portfolio units, with enhanced roles and responsibilities, at least in relation to corporate and wholesale credit. Their aim is to provide organizational support for two interrelated insights from the credit pipeline concept: the value-creation benefits of a holistic portfolio perspective on credit management and the enhanced credit strategies facilitated by a functional perspective overarching different product–customer segments. In describing the basic concepts and practical issues, it is useful to identify three main options for such a portfolio unit—called a 'credit treasury' in the more sophisticated versions—differentiated by the aspiration for its role and responsibilities.

As a minimum, the central portfolio unit would undertake measurement, analysis, and advice to senior management. Its core role is to create and communicate portfolio information, so providing transparency for the credit risk and return performance of the bank's lending in aggregate. It would not have authority to alter the risk–return profile, whether through central transactions or by circumscribing frontline credit origination strategies.

Instead, it would provide advice—to individual business units or to the bank-level credit committee—to facilitate management (to some degree) of concentration risk and diversification opportunities. This option is a natural first step, which does not disrupt the prevailing culture and existing organizational responsibilities for profit and risk. Correspondingly, it is unlikely to constitute an effective support for active portfolio decisions.

The next step up is a credit treasury with 'backstop' responsibility for overall risk control. In this option, the credit treasury is tasked with keeping the portfolio within agreed risk–return limits. The least disruptive method (i.e., without effect on frontline operations) comprises occasional central transactions in hedge instruments and other secondary markets. Additionally, the credit treasury may set guidelines to influence—or limits to control—credit origination strategies. These may operate at a high level, such as the aggregate mix of mortgages and unsecured consumer credit or broad rules on product features to facilitate subsequent securitization, or at a fairly micro-level, such as *ad hoc* volume caps (e.g., on subprime mortgages) or even comprehensive limits for each credit-scoring band. The credit treasury is structured as a cost center in this option (e.g., the profit or loss from any hedge transactions is booked centrally and does not form the basis of performance appraisal) and frontline responsibilities are largely or wholly unaffected.

The most far-reaching option is for a credit treasury with profit center responsibility for the overall credit portfolio of the bank. (In large banking groups, some business units might even have their own credit treasury.) Here, the credit treasury would 'buy' the credit risks from the originating units—or pay them an introduction fee—and be fully responsible thereafter for active management of aggregate credit risk and return. In addition to transfer-pricing, arrangements would be established to govern risk aspects of origination strategy: these might be loose guidelines, perhaps accompanied by incentives via the transfer-pricing system, or might involve detailed rules covering volume mix and some product features. To complete a functionally driven structure, loan administration would be run by a separate unit, charging an internal servicing fee; and, once the normal lending relationship has broken down, problem loans would be 'sold' to an internal debt recovery department. This option supports, in concept, a culture of highly active management of portfolio risk–return in which the credit treasury may take 'proprietary trading' positions.

The credit treasury as profit center is a theoretically sound approach, but is not—certainly not yet—on a par with the robust nature of interest rate risk treasuries or asset-and-liability management units. For interest rate risk, there is a rich set of instruments and deep trading markets. This generates objective market prices that can be used as internal transfer rates—directly where customer-lending and deposit rates are explicitly market linked and, otherwise, as fairly reasonable proxies—and for mark-to-market revaluation of positions. Also, it enables the treasury, in principle, to hedge all or most of the interest rate risk originated by frontline units. In contrast, credit risk instruments and markets are relatively underdeveloped, albeit expanding rapidly. As a result, it is more difficult to measure 'fair values' and define objective transfer prices, and so avoid the potential for internal organizational conflict. Moreover, credit risk and its pricing often have a special nature, in that the lending bank's privileged information on borrowers—or confidential knowledge of current account behavior—provides the bank with insight superior to the market as a whole. This obscures the unbundling of value between an underlying price for 'pure' credit risk and value added by the frontline, and it complicates the interface between a credit treasury and frontline account officers. In particular, in business-lending (including SMEs except where solely reliant on automated scoring), it is difficult to structure incentives for the frontline to collect, interpret, and transmit information needed by the credit treasury for timely and appropriate portfolio actions.

Despite these implementation difficulties, the credit treasury approach points to a future of increasingly sophisticated central management of credit portfolios.

provides the bank with insight superior to the market as a whole. This obscures the unbundling of value between an underlying price for 'pure' credit risk and the value added by the frontline and complicates the interface between treasurer and frontline relationship managers.[9]

Credit pipelining creates significant benefits for individual banks in managing for value enhancement. In particular, banks gain enhanced flexibility in origination. Traditionally, a bank wishing to prevent undue concentration in a specific sector, or with a particular customer, seemed to have only one weapon in its armory: to reject the next loan application from this sector or customer or, equivalently, to tighten limits on revolving credit utilization.

Understandably, this could impair customer relationships. But structured products divorce the provision of finance from the absorption of credit risk. They enable banks to meet customer needs, while retaining flexibility in the amount of risk taken up and capital required. In essence, the ability to lay off credit risk at the point of origination—or to sell or hedge it subsequently—frees origination strategy from the constraints of the prevailing composition of the bank's portfolio. Banks can thereby free up credit lines and increase business with their core customers, and so extract greater competitive advantage from their core competence, reputation, and superior information.

In practice, this freedom will not be complete. Origination strategy is not wholly independent, and, conversely, a good-quality portfolio is still predominantly the result of a collection of good individual credit decisions. But the credit pipelining approach provides a new dimension. Leading banks do not just consider the risk and profitability of a loan—or block of retail lending—from a stand-alone perspective. They take a portfolio perspective in addition, evaluating the marginal impact of the lending on portfolio risk and return. Instead of passively allowing portfolio risk and return to be determined solely by origination decisions, they manage the portfolio through continuous feedback and signaling to the frontline and through active trading, directly in the loans themselves or via the use of derivatives and structured products.

Credit pipelining also generates common benefits for the credit industry as a whole. The trading of credit risk creates useful information for all market participants, primarily through the formulation and dissemination of market equilibrium prices. The secondary market liquidity created by active trading, if sufficient, leads to

[9] For example, it is difficult to implement a mechanism to incentivize the frontline to collect, interpret, and transmit the confidential credit information needed by the credit treasurer for timely and appropriate portfolio actions. This relates primarily to corporate banking; in retail, credit information can be transmitted (all or mostly) via the scoring system.

a more efficient credit risk allocation mechanism. Market participants can respond to changing conditions and offload specific credit risks to those who are better able and willing to take on the risk; for example, in the US mortgage banking industry, many originators often pass on most of the risk through secondary markets. The outcome is a better mix of ultimate credit risk owners and, consequently, a combination of greater availability and lower prices in the primary credit market. In short, it facilitates better macroeconomic performance by improving capital allocation in the economy.

REGULATORS ARE CATCHING UP

Advances in credit risk techniques have moved radically ahead of capital adequacy regulations. The result is that there is now a wide divergence between the regulatory regime and economic capital methodologies in allocating capital to different credit risks.[10] However, the regulators are making strenuous efforts to catch up. In this section we first outline the status of these efforts, as embodied in the proposals for a new regime (Basel II), and then assess the implications for banks.

Core features of Basel II

The overall theme of Basel II in relation to credit risk[11] is a finer calibration of risk-weighting and closer linkage between regulatory risk weights and the probabilities of default and loss. This will reduce, but not eliminate, the divergence between regulatory and economic capital performance measures. Indeed, elimination is not feasible as long as economic capital models vary significantly between banks and significant methodological dispute continues.

Banks can choose, subject to meeting eligibility criteria, between different options of increasing sophistication. In effect, these options are successively closer to a bank's own, internal economic capital approach; but even the most sophisticated option falls short of allowing banks to use their own economic capital calculation to satisfy regulatory requirements.

The base option is the 'standardized approach'. In retail credit,[12] the pattern of risk weights is broadly unchanged from the current accord; but their overall level is reduced by 20 to 25 percent in the July 2002 agreement. In corporate, institutional, and sovereign credit, the risk weights are more finely calibrated and linked to the

[10] Relative capital allocation is the key divergence; though even here different economic capital methodologies can produce significantly different outcomes. The aggregate amount of economic capital—as distinct from relative allocations to different risks—is much less determinate.

[11] Our focus is on credit risk only. The proposals are more wide-ranging, including other risk dimensions (such as operational risk) and the overall approach to supervision. At the time of writing, the details are not yet fixed: our description reflects the proposals issued in January 2001 and, in some instances, the agreement dated July 2002.

[12] In this context, includes exposures to small businesses, defined as having annual turnover below €1m.

probabilities of default. This is achieved by the use of external credit ratings to define regulatory risk-weighting bands; with unrated borrowers treated as equivalent, roughly speaking, to a low-to-middling rating class.[13]

The more sophisticated options are variants of the 'internal ratings-based approach', whereby the bank's own internal rating system is used to determine regulatory risk-weighting bands. For nonretail exposures, there are two variants: 'foundation' and 'advanced'. In the foundation variant, banks use their own estimates of probability of default, but the other parameters of a fully quantitative rating system—exposure at default and loss rate in the event of default including the impact of collateral—are predetermined by the regulatory regime. In the advanced variant, all these parameters are generated by the bank's internal estimates. These variants do not apply to retail exposures, where instead—broadly speaking—the key parameters are all derived from the bank's scoring system.

As a further refinement—agreed in July 2002—within the internal ratings-based approach, middle-market companies[14] will receive more favorable treatment than larger corporates. The impact is a lower capital allocation of up to 20 percent, amounting on average to 10 percent.

Finally, a further feature of Basel II is the recognition of other dimensions of credit risk, including the use of credit mitigation techniques. Here, we highlight two dimensions. First, the regime recognizes the risk impact of a loan's maturity; but, under current proposals, this applies directly only to nonretail exposures. Second, concentration risk is recognized, at least to some degree. Allowance is made for the concentration of individual exposures within nonretail portfolios, but not—at least not directly—for concentrations of customer segments—such as geographic regions or industry sectors—within retail or nonretail portfolios.

Implications of Basel II

The implications for regulatory capital requirements in respect of credit risk depend on the bank's business mix and whether it has the capabilities in place to adopt the internal ratings-based approach. Required regulatory capital is likely to rise—particularly under the standardized approach—if the bank has a portfolio of mostly low-grade corporate and institutional risks, including bank counterparties. A large universal bank, with a sophisticated internal rating system, is likely to enjoy a lower regulatory capital requirement. In particular, there is, potentially, a very significant benefit from adopting the internal ratings-based approach in place of the standardized approach (Figure 24.5).

Banks aiming to be eligible for the internal ratings-based approach will need to invest in skills to meet fairly demanding criteria and be able to demonstrate to the regulator that these capabilities are in place. Most large banks will aim to meet the requirements for the foundation variant; relatively few are currently aiming to be immediately eligible for the advanced variant. In broad terms, to meet Basel II standards for the foundation variant, the system needs to generate quantitative

[13] More precisely, unrated corporates receive the same weight as corporates rated from BB− to BBB+ inclusively.

[14] Defined as having annual turnover between €1m and €50m.

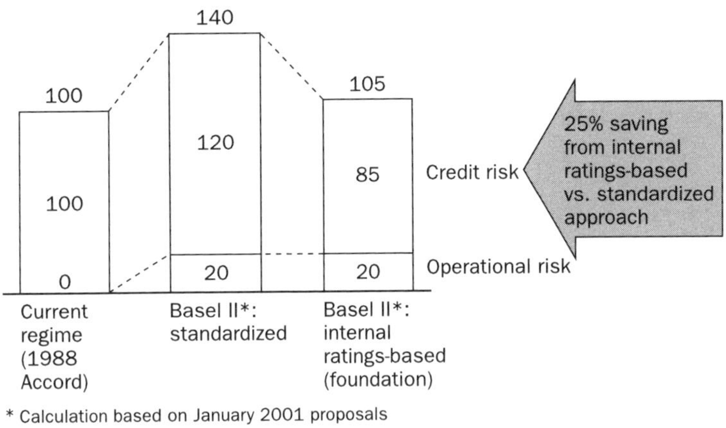

Figure 24.5 Impact of Basel II on capital required at a German bank (index, current regime = 100)

Source: McKinsey

predictions of default probabilities across a granular set of rating classes; use a conceptually sound approach; and be adequately validated, which in turn places significant demands on the collection, storage, and analysis of historic data. Furthermore, for the advanced variant in corporate and institutional exposures, banks need (*inter alia*) an effective system for managing collateral, including robust valuation and clear mapping of collateral to specific exposures.

The eligibility requirements for applying an internal ratings-based approach to retail exposures are similar in their essentials. In addition, banks need to meet fairly stringent risk segmentation requirements: by product type (e.g., credit cards, personal loans, or secured installment-lending, overdrafts, mortgages, and small-business-lending); by credit-scoring band; and, if material, by delinquency status and by vintage.

As well as the direct impact on capital requirements, Basel II has potential implications for banks' funding costs. Under the original Basel Accord, bank counterparties enjoyed a uniform low risk weight; but, under Basel II proposals, bank counterparties will receive different weights, reflecting their external or internal credit-rating.[15] Moreover, the set of risk weights in the standardized approach is radically higher than the risk weight applied to all banks under the current Basel Accord. Only if the bank is rated AA− to AAA will there be no change in weight. Otherwise, the weights will rise (e.g., more than double for banks rated A− to A+ and fivefold for banks rated BBB− to BBB+ or unrated.

Only combining assessments of impact on capital requirements and on funding costs will indicate whether a specific institute will belong to the winners or losers from Basel II (Figure 24.6).

[15] There is an additional complication, not analyzed here, whereby the standardized approach also considers the external ratings for the sovereign risk of bank counterparties.

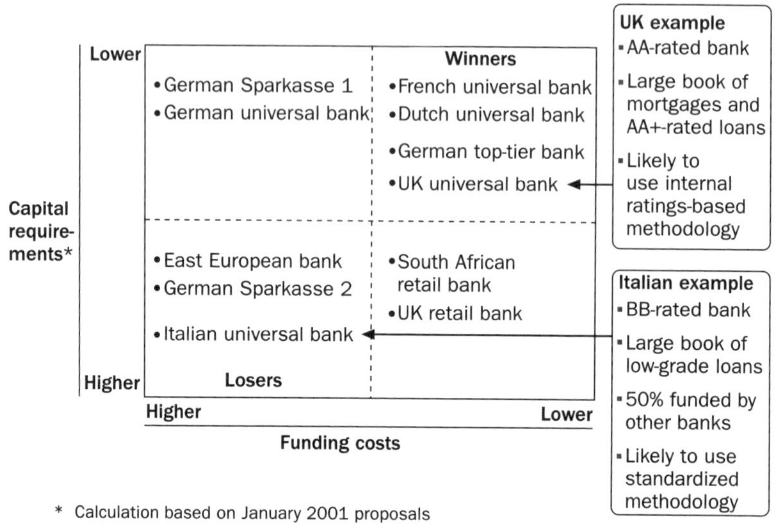

Figure 24.6 'Winners and losers' under Basel II

Source: McKinsey

The skills associated with credit pipelining provide some solutions for the losers from Basel II. Securitization and other credit-structuring techniques help along both dimensions: improving capital efficiency and accessing new, lower cost, funding sources. Low-rated banks typically have assets with a higher rating than the bank itself; or the assets can be restructured so as to unbundle elements that have a higher rating. These higher rated exposures can be repackaged to act, in effect, as collateral for specific lower cost funding. At least in principle, the underlying economic value from such strategies is available under the current regulatory regime; but Basel II acts as a trigger, intensifying the need for such strategies. In any event, in our view, banks should use the impending change in regulatory regime as a catalyst to review—and, where appropriate, upgrade—their approach to credit risk measurement, credit-pricing, and capital performance management.

CAPABILITY REQUIREMENTS

The arena of credit risk management has experienced a fast pace of change in recent years, and this shows little sign of abating. The capability gap between the leaders and the pack is already wide and at risk of widening. Aspirations for excellence will not be met by simply keeping pace with the regulators; though, as a minimum, ambitious banks should aim to meet the criteria for adopting the more sophisticated of the proposed regulatory options. For many banks today, this will represent a leap forward in credit risk measurement capabilities. Banks at the forefront should aim for best practice credit risk evaluation skills, integrated into an effective credit pipelining capability.

Meeting the challenge of these objectives requires improved capabilities—for banks striving for excellence, it requires best practice—across the whole credit management value chain. Internal rating systems form the bedrock of effective credit risk evaluation and pricing. They need to be conceptually robust and empirically valid to ensure superior credit decisions. A sound methodology in risk-adjusted pricing, coupled with appropriate IT support, is necessary to enable credit to be priced according to its economic risk. New skills and performance measures should not be the preserve only of the back office, they should be integrated into frontline management. Finally, systematic procedures—leveraging the rating or scoring system—are needed to ensure effective monitoring and review of exposures, leading to active management of exposure in response to the credit cycle. In the event of default, organizational focus and specialist skills are required to optimize debt recovery.

The chapters that follow address the issues involved in building and enhancing these capabilities. In Chapter 25 we explain the benefits of an internal credit-rating system and discuss how to reach best practice. Chapter 26 addresses adjusting for risk in loan pricing, focusing on the necessary methodologies and IT support. Risk adjustment also forms the basis of Chapter 27 where we look at the 'total RAROC approach' to measuring and monitoring credit performance. Finally, in the last chapter we see how banks can improve their credit workout and recovery by introducing proactive, systematic policies.

25

Internal Credit-rating: Building a Best Practice System

Axel Müller-Groeling, Uwe Stegemann[1]

A best practice internal credit-rating system has now become a core component of overall excellence in credit risk management. It provides the structural framework and insightful information necessary for superiority in credit-underwriting and credit exposure management. Used effectively, the benefits extend beyond the credit function: a best-practice system is a key enabler of value-based management.

In this chapter, we describe the features that characterize best practice rating systems, using a framework that we have found productive.[2] As context for this description, we first discuss the role of internal credit-ratings in improving credit management and, more broadly, in facilitating value-based management.

THE ROLE OF INTERNAL RATINGS

A good internal credit-rating system acts as a disciplined mechanism for individual credit-underwriting decisions—accept/reject, limit-setting, pricing—and for the subsequent monitoring of individual exposures, whether periodic review of all facilities or close monitoring of identified and potential problem credits. Furthermore, the rating system is a critical underpinning for portfolio metrics, since it provides a common measure across otherwise disparate exposures. It thereby enables aggregate

[1] The authors would like to express their gratitude for the contributions of Marcus Chromik, Jesko Frommeyer, Matthias Heuser, Max Neukirchen, Markus Rieder, Peter Strobel, and Nina Wessels.

[2] The framework is generic to retail and wholesale credit, but its primary relevance is where credit exposures are individually material: middle-market and large corporates, project and real-estate finance, leasing and other asset-based commercial credits, exceptionally large personal and small-business lending. In the personal market, it is current best practice to adopt a segment approach, focused on products rather than rating individuals; though some banks, at least in respect of affluent customers, do allow for customer limits across multiple credit product usage.

exposure measures for the outstanding portfolio over time and for the cohort of new advances during any period.

At their best, the portfolio metrics derived from an internal credit-rating system enables senior management to manage aggregate exposure proactively across the business cycle. The rating profile of borrowers varies with each phase of the cycle[3] and, in particular, deteriorates in the incipient phase of a downturn. A rating system that reliably captures the change in profile of existing, or indeed prospective, customers can provide an early warning signal. Armed with this information, senior management can respond with a timely change in credit stance: by revising formal credit policy and by modifying the criteria for individual underwriting or review decisions. This is not an easy task. It requires successfully integrating all relevant factors into the internal rating system; extracting and communicating the insights embedded in the system's information flows; and acting appropriately in response to these insights in day-to-day business decisions.

An internal credit-rating system becomes a key enabler of value-based management when the ratings also incorporate a quantitative measure of expected losses and can be linked to a quantitative evaluation of volatility in losses. The quantification of expected losses provides an 'economic' measure of the cost of credit risk (i.e., a conceptually sound, risk-based measure of expected loan losses). Used in internal management accounts,[4] it is instrumental in focusing management on underlying net margins—net interest income minus expected loan loss charge—rather than on gross margins, alone or combined with the potentially misleading accounting charge for the period. The quantification of volatility in losses provides the basis for an 'economic' allocation of capital (i.e., a risk-based measure of the capital required to cover unexpected credit losses for a chosen level of confidence).

Together, the expected loss measure and economic capital allocation provide the risk-adjusted performance measurement necessary for effective value-based management. Profitability, including return on capital, can then be measured so as to reflect credit risk at multiple levels: customer or customer segment; product sector; portfolio and subportfolios (e.g., rating classes, geographies); relationship manager or relationship management teams; and business units.

To extract the benefits from an internal credit-rating system, value-based management involves pulling several levers: credit decisions that reflect the understanding of differential credit risks; pricing hurdles that allow for material gradations in credit risk; and marketing and sales strategies that respond to the insights of economic profitability measures. The potential scale of the benefits is illustrated by a bank where the internal credit-rating system was upgraded to a new, objectively based approach. In total, the impact was an incremental profit of up to 30 basis points of credit outstandings. More accurate identification of customers with above-average default risk was used to help reduce total default costs by up to 10 percent. More

---

[3] In this context, the rating is a forward-looking assessment of current creditworthiness, as distinct from a 'through the cycle' rating based on ability to withstand the nadir, and, at least in principle, an assessment that is independent of current phase.

[4] Under current, accepted accounting principles, public reporting does not reflect expected credit losses. However, some banks disclose these as additional voluntary information (e.g., Barclays publishes 'risk tendency').

accurate identification of customers with below-average default risk was used to target a sales stimulation program, which generated a volume increase of around 4 percent. Tangentially, but nevertheless importantly, the introduction of the rating system facilitated extensive streamlining of credit processes. The greater clarity and objectivity of ratings acts as a catalyst to create a leaner and more efficient decision-making route: standardizing information-gathering and focusing information-processing on the final credit decision. The result in this case was a reduction in credit operating costs of around 20 percent.

CORE FEATURES OF BEST PRACTICE

In dealing with credit-rating issues, we have found it useful to structure discussion around a framework comprising five building blocks (Figure 25.1). We first introduce this framework, providing an outline definition of the building blocks. Then, taking each block in turn, we describe the characteristics of best practice.

A framework for internal credit-rating

The first block concerns the subject to be rated and the corresponding input data. This addresses whether the system rates borrowers or transactions (e.g., loan facilities) or is two-dimensional, rating both borrower and transaction. Drilling down, rating subjects may be split into different classes, each with its own rating system or at least its own version of some dimensions of the overall rating system. Typically, the different categories of rating subject would be customer segments (e.g., middle market, large corporates, financial institutions). In retail credit, at least for the mass market, the categories are typically product-based (potentially with subclasses driven by customer segmentation) (e.g., credit cards, home mortgages, personal loans). These categories, whether customer- or product-based, will have different requirements for input data, which is the full set of information contributing to assessing the creditworthiness of a rating subject.

The second block is the rating approach and model. This covers the methodology

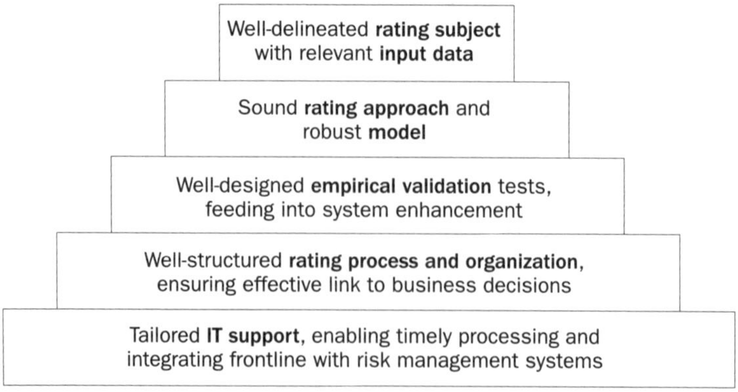

Figure 25.1 Building blocks of a best practice rating system

Source: McKinsey

and rules for analyzing input data and thereby assigning a rating class (i.e., a creditworthiness grade) to each borrower or transaction. The spectrum of rating classes represents a graduated assessment of creditworthiness. The most significant issue addressed in this block is the choice between causal and statistical models, and, within each, the specification of the model's parameters and internal logic. Causal models seek to identify the drivers of financial distress and the causal mechanism between these drivers and default. They are suited to rating subjects—such as project finance transactions—which are few in number, complex in nature, and characterized by unique features. Statistical models are not built on causal links, but are instead grounded in empirical observation. They seek to identify statistical correlations between input data (or subsets of input data) and default. They are suited to rating subjects—typical within retail credit—which are many in number, share simple common features, and for which a rich data set of default history is available.

The third block is empirical validation. However advanced its conceptual and analytical basis, a rating system is only as good as the accuracy of its actual predictions: the proof of the pudding is in the eating. Rating systems need to be back-tested against historical outcomes or calibrated with test portfolios. If successful, testing serves to validate the approach and provide senior management with the confidence to act upon the information the system provides. Testing also facilitates fine-tuning of model specification (e.g., the relative weight placed on different input factors), and repeated testing may even help detect structural change in the underlying risk behavior of borrowers.[5]

The fourth block is the rating process and organization. This covers the process for quality control of the rating system, in day-to-day operation and in periodic recalibration, as driven by empirical testing. The rating process also covers the mechanisms for ensuring an effective link between rating system information and business decisions. The organizational aspect is the allocation of responsibilities in the functioning of the rating system, in particular between risk management staff and the frontline salesforce and relationship managers. In particular, it addresses the potential conflict between risk control and the pressures from marketing objectives or individual performance incentives.

The fifth and final block is the role of IT support, in respect of both software application development and data-processing systems. Rating systems set demanding standards of timeliness and accuracy for the collection, storage, and processing of relevant information, and in the need for complex software tools.

We now turn to a discussion of best practice for each building block.

Subject and input data

Best practice rating systems distinguish between the customer (or other counterparty) and the transaction. This is because different loan facilities with the same customer may represent substantially different degrees of credit risk (e.g., because the facilities vary in the nature and amount of collateral or their seniority in a

[5] For example, at a northern European bank, the retail scoring system had been tailored to the needs of a specific customer segment, but volume growth meant that customers were drawn increasingly from outside this segment, with a different risk behavior profile.

liquidation). Leading practitioners make this distinction by separately identifying two aspects: the probability of default and the expected loss in the event of default, incorporating the recovery rate of exposure at the time of default.

Ideally, each category of rating subjects should be homogeneous in risk characteristics. This can imply a narrow segmentation of customers, to facilitate the identification of risk drivers common to all customers in the segment. But there are pragmatic advantages in wider segments. In best practice rating systems, this trade-off is judged well, adopting a segmentation sufficiently narrow for adequate homogeneity, but sufficiently wide to be practicable.

Even where each category of rating subject has its own rating system, a key feature of best practice is that there is a 'master scale' for rating classes across systems. This means that each rating class in any one system can be mapped as having the same creditworthiness as a particular rating class in another system. As a simplified abstract example, the probability of default in 'class C' in the rating system for mid-corporates is the same as in 'class 2' in the rating system for project finance transactions. Another way of achieving this is a single rating system—in the sense of a unique set of rating classes—but with rating approach and model tailored to each segment. The advantage of a valid master scale or single set of rating classes, based on explicit quantitative measures, is that expected default risk is directly comparable between different customers and products.

The final task within this building block is often the most difficult: identifying risk drivers and obtaining the related input data. We have found that performance improvements in this task can have a significant impact on the overall quality of the rating system. This can be illustrated by an example from real-estate-financing. Before improvements were made in the selection of input data, the rating system for real-estate-financing supported only four rating classes, which is a poor level of differentiation in grading risk.[6] Also, the performance of the rating system was unacceptable in empirical validation tests using a test portfolio approach. After improvements, the number of rating classes supported by the system doubled to eight and the system's performance in empirical validation tests reached an acceptable level. The main source of improvement was to introduce an additional risk driver, namely the volatility in the main input factors already selected such as contractual rent vs. market average and parking space relative to office space.

Approach and model

It is a key requirement of any credit-rating system that its conceptual approach should be methodologically sound and that its model should be technically robust. Best practice in these aspects is highly specific to the particular circumstances of each bank's credit business and its chosen model. Abstracting from these circumstances, we have found that a distinctive feature in achieving best practice is that the bank

[6] In general terms, best practice is probably at least 10 rating classes, including nonperforming and other problem grades; but the appropriate number will vary with rating subject. Under Basel II proposals (as published in January 2001), for a bank's internal rating system to be eligible for use in regulatory capital calculation, the absolute floor is eight classes: six performing and two nonperforming. And for banks with a wide spectrum of business lines, this rises to a minimum of eleven classes; nine performing and two nonperforming.

fully understands the model in use. By this, we mean that relevant staff in pivotal roles—in the frontline, in credit control, or in risk analytics—involve themselves in understanding the rating approach and model (i.e., its broad strengths and weaknesses, its specific limitations, and the specific context in which its advantages are realized). At the opposite extreme, the worst practice is to treat the model as a 'black box', cooked up in the back room of risk analytics or bought off the shelf. This understanding is perhaps best acquired by internal development of the model. If an external supplier is used, then the bank should nevertheless remain in the driving seat, ensuring that the model is adapted to the bank's specific needs and—most importantly—that supporting expertise is fostered inside the bank.

In-house understanding and expertise can be critical in interpreting doubtful or complicated outcomes from the model and, in the worst case, in avoiding entirely spurious outcomes. An example—again drawn from real-estate-financing—illustrates the importance of not taking a prospective model's outcomes at face value, but instead applying expertise to interrogate the results further. Two prospective rating systems at first appeared equally valid. When fed with a common set of input data—such as loan amount and maturity, property valuation, contractual rent, interest rate—the models generated very similar results, each predicting an annual default rate of around 0.6 percent. But when one of the input factors was changed—in this case, a 25 percent higher property valuation—the model outcomes diverged radically: one generated a lower default probability of 0.4 percent; the other, a higher default probability of 1.2 percent. As suspected by staff at the bank with property expertise, the original agreement at 0.6 percent was purely coincidental. On detailed investigation, it transpired that the first model lowered its default risk estimate because, when property value increased, the reduction in loan-to-value ratio fed through directly to a lower assessment of risk. The second model increased its default risk estimate, since it captured a causal link from increased property value to higher maintenance costs. This, in turn, fed through to a deterioration in the project's liquidity risk. Armed with this insight into the models' assumptions, it became clear which rating system had the superior model.

Empirical validation

The greatest challenge in empirical validation is for a bank to extract and make effective use of its own internal records on customers and transactions. A long time series of data is necessary for statistically valid results. It is debatable whether one full business cycle of data is sufficient; and the duration of one cycle is itself several years. And where there is a long run of internal data, complex validation issues may need to be resolved before reliable use is possible. At present, most banks do not have more than one cycle of internal data. But leading banks do successfully calibrate their internal credit-rating systems against internal data to the extent possible (e.g., in respect of part of the modeling[7] or some rating subjects) (Figure 25.2).

[7] The 'vintage' effect in retail credit risk-modeling is an example here. Internal data history may suffice to validate the modeled distribution of default risk in relation to vintage (e.g., how long since the customer acquired his credit card), but may be insufficient to validate how this distribution varies across different phases of a business cycle.

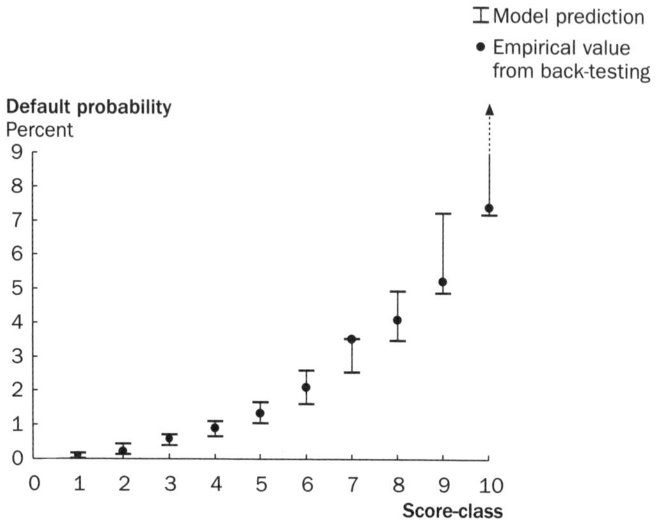

Figure 25.2 Model calibration through back-testing for retail credit

Source: McKinsey

An alternative to internal data is to import experience. Banks are unlikely to share their experience with others, at least voluntarily;[8] though anonymous pooling may be feasible. Instead, external credit-rating agencies are a key source. They have long-dated time series in bond default data, which—subject to qualifications, particularly for non-US exposures—can be mapped across to the rating classes of corporate and institutional bank customers.

Process and organization

We have found a tendency for issues relating to process and organization to be overshadowed by the other building blocks. They lack the intellectual interest of the rating approach and model, and they lack the high profile within the bank of the assignment of rating classes. This tendency is unjustified. In our view, it is particularly important to strive for best practice in process and organization.

Best practice process ensures that rating system outcomes reach decision-makers on a timely basis, and it prompts, or even forces, responsive action. Two examples illustrate the importance of these best practice features. The first example shows the consequence of process failure. In 2000 and 2001, a bank's rating system detected the deterioration of risk in the credit line facilities provided to two customers, both of which were other banks. The input data included the operating performance of the banks, and their deteriorating financial results fed through to a downgrading of rating class. But the rating system outcomes were ignored: both customers increased the utilization of their lines late into 2001, long after the warning signals were apparent. The increased utilization was very significant in both cases: one from

[8] In this context, it is at least interesting to note that the UK competition authorities have recommended that banks provide portable credit histories for their small-business customers.

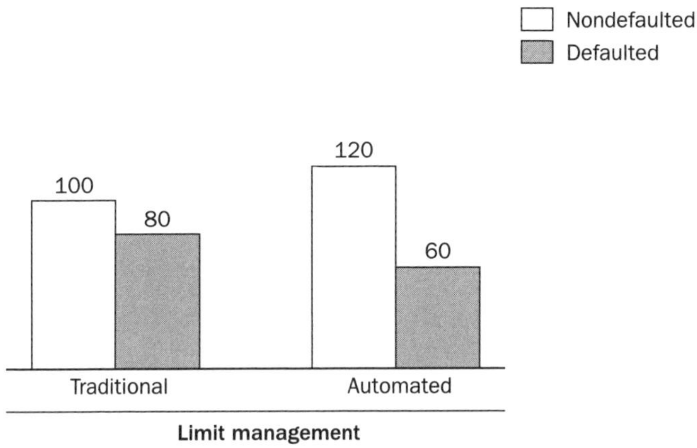

Figure 25.3 Impact of automating limit management at a European bank (limit per customer, indexed)

Source: McKinsey

€50m in October 2000 to €350m in December 2001; the other, from €100 million to €700m over roughly the same period. The second example shows the benefits of a rigorous process. A European bank implemented an algorithm into its overdraft limit management system, so that rating class assignments would feed automatically through to the limits set for credit lines. Previously, 'watch lists' of customers exceeding their preset limits were subject to 'manual' modifications, often leading to an increase in the limit. The new system led to significantly improved performance in reducing limits for customers who subsequently defaulted (Figure 25.3).

Best practice organization entails a clear separation of profit-oriented business roles from control-oriented risk management roles and an appropriate allocation of responsibilities between these roles. Applied to rating systems, this implies that the business units can propose new systems, modifications, or changes to particular operating parameters and should be involved in their development and enhancement; but the decisions cannot be theirs. The risk management function should agree and sanction the decisions, and ultimate authority should reside in a credit risk committee, with top management representation. In best practice, this is a board committee or has clearly delegated board authority.

The broad features of best practice are now also common practice, as banks react to—or stay ahead of—the demands of the supervisory authorities. Problems are more likely to arise at a micro-level, particularly with the allocation of responsibilities in assigning rating classes. Where the rating model relies solely on objective, quantifiable input data, the problem is largely obviated. The assignment of rating class can then be operated by the risk management function without involving the business units. But where judgment is involved—for qualitative inputs, such as an assessment of corporate customers' managerial competence—the issue is more complex. For large customers, there is a case to be made for allocating sole responsibility to the risk management function. This ensures rating class assignments are independent of the pressures of profit targets and individual incentives. But for small businesses and middle-market companies, this is impractical and uneconomic. The relationship manager or lending officer is then often the only person able to make the

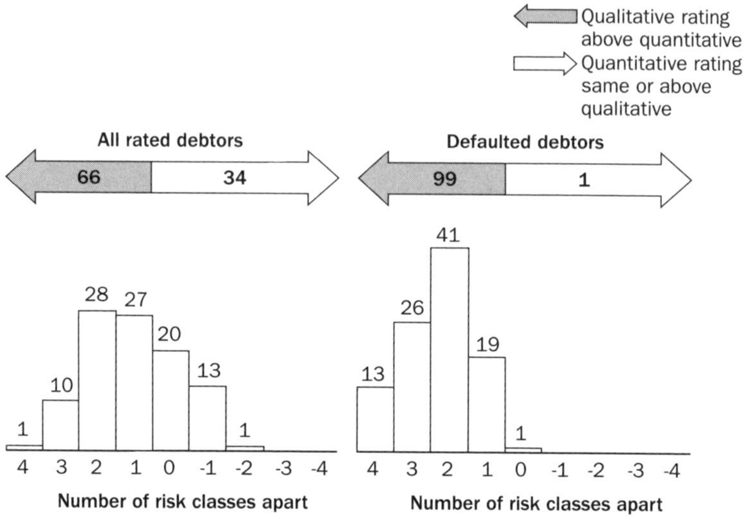

Figure 25.4 Qualitative vs. quantitative ratings at a German bank (percent)

Source: McKinsey

judgment; and, even with larger customers, he may be the best placed. This can go wrong, as can be illustrated by the experience at a German bank. An analysis of ratings revealed that, in two-thirds of cases, the qualitative assessment of management competence was graded higher than the quantitative measure of financial status. More importantly, when the analysis was run solely in respect of borrowers who had defaulted, in 99 percent of cases low grades on financial status were offset by high grades on management competence (Figure 25.4). It was transparent, beyond reasonable doubt, that qualitative input had been manipulated to improve the final rating class assignment. The solution to this problem lies in effective micro-level organization, ensuring that an independent risk management function monitors frontline input to the assignment of rating classes.

IT support

Although an important aspect, the issues relating to IT support are often highly specific to the context of each individual bank, and technical detail is inappropriate in this book. We have therefore kept our comments brief, highlighting three features of best practice. First, that IT systems are structured for effective integration between the risk management function and frontline business units. In particular, all relevant risk information should be readily accessible, in clearly expressed formats, through the sales support and relationship management systems. Second, that IT systems incorporate tools for testing and recalibration. These include, for example, software for statistical validation of scoring systems and for determining the statistical significance of individual risk factors, where used as input data for assigning rating classes. Third, that IT systems maintain a proprietary historical database—covering internal customer transactions—to facilitate future enhancement and back-testing of rating models.

The introduction and enhancement of internal credit-rating systems was widespread among leading banks in the 1990s. In the current decade, any bank striving for excellence in credit cannot afford to be left behind without a smoothly functioning system. A best practice internal credit-rating system is not just a key underpinning of superiority in credit risk management but also an important weapon in the armory of value-based management.

26
Loan-pricing: Adjusting for Risk

Matthias Effinger, Martin van Gemmeren, Wolfram Peters[1]

Risk-adjusted loan-pricing is a key component of leading-edge credit management. It creates the link between underlying risk management techniques, overall performance measurement, and operational business decisions. A robust capability in calculating risk-adjusted prices is important both for internal management purposes and for setting external prices that reflect risk differentials.

In this chapter, we first explain how risk-adjusted pricing can be used to address some of the key challenges facing European retail banks' credit business. Then, as an introductory guide to how to build this competence, we describe the two main prerequisites of a risk-adjusted pricing system: the methodology and IT support.

ADDRESSING CREDIT CHALLENGES

The ability to calculate risk-adjusted loan prices—and to make use of this capability in credit decisions and business strategy—is a vital skill in retail banking. It is not just an issue for corporate banking. Internal calculation of risk-adjusted prices enables banks to understand the true profitability of their credit business, in aggregate and across the bank (e.g., products or product sectors, customers or customer segments, business units and relationship managers). Armed with this understanding, banks are much better placed to succeed in addressing four key credit challenges: first and most importantly, to tackle inadequate profitability in the credit business; second, to measure and control the degree of cross-subsidization between credit and noncredit businesses; third, to avoid 'adverse selection' (a term we explain below); finally and more ambitiously, to adopt leading-edge value-based management techniques.

Tackling inadequate profitability

Segmentation is the key to using risk-adjusted pricing to improve the profitability of credit business. A tripartite segmentation of credit business profit performance is useful here. First, a 'highly unprofitable' segment, where the gross margin of net

[1] The authors would like to express their gratitude for the contributions of Gösta Jamin and Markus Pertlwieser.

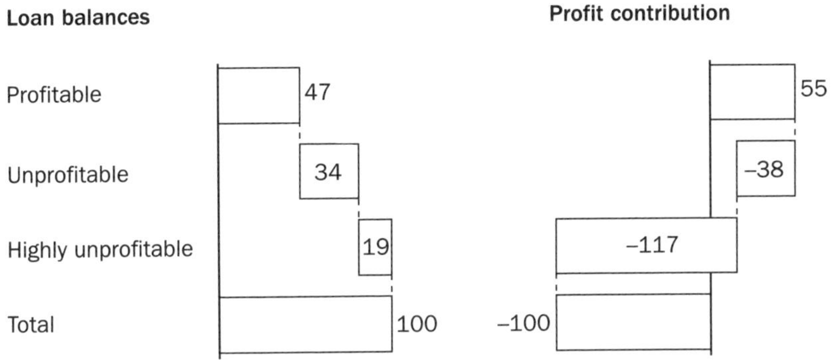

Figure 26.1 Retail credit segmentation at a sample of German banks (percent)

Source: McKinsey

interest and credit-related fees does not cover expected default losses plus the cost of capital. Second, an 'unprofitable' segment, where the gross margin covers expected default losses plus the cost of capital, but this contribution fails to cover relevant operating costs. Lastly, a 'profitable' segment, where credit business profits are clearly positive. It is not uncommon for the highly unprofitable segment to dominate overall credit business performance. Using a sample of German banks as an example, our estimate is that this segment comprises a little under 20 percent of total loan balances, but accounts for more than the total credit business loss (Figure 26.1).

Management actions should therefore focus on the highly unprofitable segment. In some instances price increases are accepted by customers, but otherwise the main task for management is to avoid new business in this segment and reduce existing exposures, including increasing collateral so as to reduce the net exposure. The best way to avoid new business is to integrate risk-adjusted pricing into frontline business management. Thus, minimum prices are set centrally as the hurdle level for the frontline in originating new business. A robust application-scoring system (albeit without linkage to pricing) is the next best alternative. Where neither is available, we have identified pragmatic measures that can be an effective short-term alternative. Based on insights into the key characteristics of the highly unprofitable segment, we have determined simple accept/reject criteria—such as demographic status or minimum collateral—as an initial approximation for specific bank contexts. These simple criteria are empirically validated and enhanced through piloting the approach in one or a few regions.

The management task for the unprofitable segment as defined above is different. This segment makes a positive, although insufficient, contribution to the recovery of operating costs; and without careful analysis of the structure of the cost base—particularly, the mix of shared vs. unique costs—a strategy of reducing exposures and thereby revenues could be counterproductive. Instead the focus should be on increasing collateral and, subject to an understanding of price elasticity, on gradually increasing prices.

In the context of a short-term profit improvement initiative, prices should be left unchanged for the remaining profitable segment. In tackling inadequate profitability, management should focus where the greatest potential lies.

Circumscribing cross-subsidization

European banks with poor profits in the credit business often argue that this is more than compensated by cross-selling benefits in noncredit businesses. To establish whether the extent of cross-subsidization is justified, it is necessary to identify and quantify cross-selling revenues—and profit contribution—for individual retail banking customers. In this context risk-adjusted pricing provides an appropriate benchmark of credit business profits for each customer segment—and, at its best, for individual customers—against which to assess whether cross-subsidization is justified. At some banks, this benchmark may well be reached, but, in our experience, more often it is not. We have analyzed cross-selling performance and profitability at several continental European banks and found that, typically, cross-selling does not justify unprofitable credit business. Our analysis revealed that the dynamic of customer behavior is a major reason behind this. Multi-product customers tend to be more loyal to their bank, are less price-sensitive, and are less likely to shop around for better prices. As a result, they may pay more for their mortgage or other credit products than single-product customers. The latter may negotiate for a lower rate on their mortgage, benefiting from the bank's expectation of subsequent cross-selling revenues, but then purchase their other products from competing banks, 'cherry-picking' the best deals.

Avoiding adverse selection

Where competitors set external risk-adjusted prices, banks following an undifferentiated pricing policy[2] may suffer from the problem of 'adverse selection'. Less creditworthy customers tend to select banks with undifferentiated loan-pricing, since their loans are underpriced relative to more sophisticated banks or the securities markets. Conversely, more creditworthy customers select banks that adjust loan-pricing for risk, since these banks can—justifiably—charge lower prices.

In Europe, risk differentiation of external prices is not yet common practice. This is partly because many banks' strategies is to use nonprice buying factors, such as brand attractiveness, convenience of access, innovative product features, and product-packaging or bundling. But pricing remains a very important buying factor, and, in recent years, some European retail banks have introduced a degree of risk differentiation in external pricing (Box 26.1).

Moving to leading-edge value-based management

At the most ambitious level, risk-adjusted pricing can be integrated into sophisticated value-based management. In this role, albeit subject to implementation complexities, it can provide an internal transfer-pricing system whereby separate value

---

[2] Or, *in extremis*, pricing that is less appropriately differentiated than the lead competitors, including the securities markets as a competitor for corporate lending.

Box 26.1

External risk-adjusted pricing in retail credit

It is already fairly common in the US—although not fully exploited—for banks to set external prices for retail credit that differentiate for risk. This reflects the existence of an industry standard scoring approach, which is used to accept/reject decisions, for maximum loan-to-value ratios in mortgage loans, and for price differentiation.

Europe lacks the equivalent of US industry standards, and retail price differentiation for risk is not yet common practice. Nevertheless, some banks are leading the way. The UK is probably in the forefront. In their internal management systems, the major banks employ risk-adjusted pricing techniques—typically introduced in the mid-1990s—using quantitative scoring approaches for personal and small-business credit. Risk differentiation of external credit-pricing is already common in business-lending, though the calculation is not transparent to the borrower; but it is still far from prevalent in personal lending. NatWest was the first mainstream player to introduce external risk-adjusted prices for personal lending, in 1996/97, via a subsidiary's direct personal loans operation. Abbey National's Internet-based entity Cahoot followed suit some years later. Both these examples relate to direct channel selling to new customers. The approach adopted by Barclays in its personal loan price differentiation launched in November 2000 differs by focusing on cross-selling loans to existing current account or credit card customers. As a result, Barclays is able to make use of internal management information about customers' account behavior. Thus, customers can obtain reduced prices on loans by 'good behavior' on their existing accounts: paying salary or other regular credits into their current account; avoiding bouncing checks or debit card payments; not exceeding agreed overdraft and credit card limits without prior warning. A side benefit of this approach is that the prospect of a lower loan price provides an incentive for customers to improve their behavior in managing their existing accounts.

Several banks in continental Europe have also introduced risk differentiation in retail credit-pricing. One bank adjusts mortgage prices for different levels of collateral: for example, the margin charged over EURIBOR is 170 basis points (bp) if the loan-to-value ratio exceeds 75 percent; 140 bp if the ratio is 50 to 75 percent; and 110 bp if the ratio is less than 50 percent. Svenska Handelsbanken adopts a similar structure in its mortgage loan-pricing. Citibank makes use of risk-adjusted pricing in personal loans (e.g., in its German subsidiary) and differentiates price according to loan duration.

Source: Barclays press release, November 9, 2000; *Financial Times*; and other press.

contributions are measured for the core components of the credit value chain: origination, portfolio management, and debt recovery. The result is a more sophisticated performance measurement system, aligned with the assignment of organizational responsibilities across the value chain. Origination manages the customer relationship and generates new credit business; its performance measures relate primarily to new business volumes and value added over and above the minimum price set by the risk-adjusted pricing system. Portfolio management is responsible for managing the portfolio's credit risk post-origination, including the efficient use of economic capital. Debt recovery takes over once the normal lending relationship has broken down and is targeted at maximizing debt recovery, after allowing for costs of pursuit and collection, plus the interest expense of delay.

We believe that these skills will become increasingly important in retail credit portfolio management over the current decade. Elements of this approach already operate in retail markets, particularly in the US mortgage banking industry but are reflected also in European securitization of mortgages and other retail credit.

DETERMINING THE METHODOLOGY

The first task in risk-adjusted pricing is to determine the methodology for calculating risk premiums, ensuring that it matches the specific nature of the bank's credit business; for example, using a fairly standardized approach for personal lending, but a more bespoke one for business-lending. In our experience, it is critical to strike a careful balance between complexity and pragmatism. Adopting some pragmatic solutions aids the technical implementation of the system and makes the system more transparent—and hence more acceptable—to the business users. However, the formulae and parameter estimates need to be conceptually sound and sufficiently precise for the specific context in which they are used.

Calculating risk premiums

In order for a loan to be profitable, the gross margin—operating income less funding cost—has to equal or exceed operating costs plus the risk premium. This has two components: the expected level of loss through default and the cost of—or target return on—the capital required to cover unexpected losses (Figure 26.2). We first discuss the measurement of expected loss and then consider issues relating to the capital component. Our discussion sets out the core concepts and touches upon—but does not analyze—some of the complexities. In our view, the theoretical subtleties are often of low priority in a retail banking context, and they are outweighed by more significant empirical issues in determining robust parameters from historical experience.

Expected loss

Expected loss in our definition is the average prediction of the possible loss through default, estimated over the lifetime of the loan. For pricing purposes, this expected loss is expressed in terms of the impact on interest spread (i.e., as an annual percent or basis points [bp] of the loan).[3] In turn, expected loss can be broken down into two

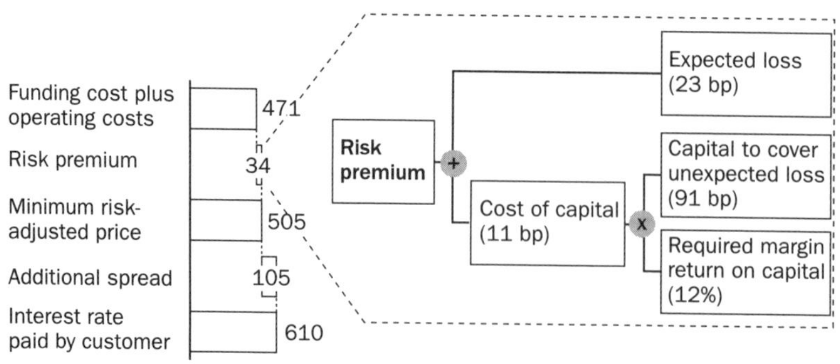

Figure 26.2 Risk-adjusted pricing for a retail loan (basis points p.a.)

Source: McKinsey

[3] More precisely, the expected loss component of the risk premium is the level of interest spread at which the discounted cash flow value of net interest income over the lifetime of the loan equals the discounted cash flow value of expected losses through default.

components: the probability of default and the expected amount of loss in the event of default, often called 'loss-given default'.

The primary methodological task is to determine the probability of default for each class in the internal rating system or each grade in the scoring system. We regard a reasonable rating or a scoring system as essential for risk-adjusted pricing; if not already in place, a system should be developed as part of the introduction of risk-adjusted pricing.[4] At the simplest methodological level, an estimate is made of the annual[5] average probability of default for each rating class or scoring grade; this is then assumed to remain constant over the lifetime of the loan.

As we forewarned, there are additional complexities. Here, we touch upon two methodological aspects of default probabilities.

First, the issue of time dependence. Particularly for longer term loans, the assumption of a constant annual probability of default is unlikely to hold true; for instance, the borrower's circumstances may change. Using a migration matrix is a practical solution to this issue. This approach not only specifies an annual default probability for each rating class or scoring grade but also the annual probabilities for the loan to migrate into other classes (or grades) during its lifetime. The result is a superior estimate of the annual average default probability for medium- and long-term loans. Even so, the migration approach is not a panacea; for instance, it does not capture the 'vintage effect' often observed in retail credit.[6]

Second, the issue of defining default. Practical considerations should play a major role in the choice, including compliance with the proposed Basel II definition of default. Usually, it is convenient to use the start of formal recovery procedures (i.e., when responsibility for the loan is transferred to the bank's debt recovery unit). However, at some banks, the transfer decision is judgmental (at least in part) and hence open to possible manipulation. An alternative is to use more objective criteria (e.g., a set number of days for which interest or scheduled repayments are overdue). This, in turn, raises complications. For example, the estimation of default probability has to allow for the possibility that the loan moves in and out of being in default as defined by days overdue. Practical considerations, however, dictate that banks should include days overdue as part of their definition of default, so as to comply with the proposed Basel II definition.[7]

Loss-given default

The second component of expected loss—loss-given default—represents the average prediction of the amount lost in the event of default, allowing for the realization of

[4] It is possible to start by some simple segmentation of the portfolio, using rudimentary criteria such as product and demographics. Such an approach amounts, in effect, to a rough-and-ready rating or scoring system and should be regarded purely as a stopgap, until a more robust approach is developed.

[5] Annual is used here for expositional convenience; the general concept is 'one period' default probability, where the period itself may be quarterly or even monthly.

[6] For example, in a cohort of new credit cards, the loss rate initially rises over time (as the 'bad apples' show up) and subsequently declines over time (as the 'good apples' survive).

[7] Proposals in Basel II (as published in November 2002) include a criterion of 90 days overdue.

any collateral. As the simplest approximation, the loss-given default can be measured as the nominal value of the loan, after deducting an estimated recovery percentage. For greater sophistication, nominal value could be replaced by 'fair value' (i.e., the discounted cash flow value of future net interest income and principal repayments). In our view, this is not a worthwhile enhancement in a typical retail banking context, unless it is already the case that fair values are used in the bank's performance measurement systems.

For credit lines, the amount of exposure—whether measured at nominal or fair value—is indeterminate. Hence, an expected line utilization rate must be estimated. We often use—at least as an initial approximation—a fairly conservative assumption of 100 percent[8] (i.e., equate exposure with the facility amount of the credit line). As a more sophisticated approach, utilization rates in the event of default can be predicted from historical experience, with the prediction tailored to different categories of credit line and different customer segments.

Estimation of the recovery percentage needs to address two main elements: the recovery of unsecured exposure and the realization of collateral. For recovery of unsecured exposure, the simplest approach is to assume a predetermined fixed recovery percentage. If possible, this should be based on an analysis of performance by the bank's debt recovery unit. As a more sophisticated approach, recovery rates can be tailored to different products and different customer segments.

The recovery rate on collateral poses a richer set of issues, partly reflecting the variety of forms of collateral, but the basic approach is the same as for unsecured exposure. What is needed is an estimate of the realization ratio—amount realized as a percentage of valuation—for each major category of collateral. Again, if possible, this should be based on an analysis of experience in the bank's debt recovery unit. Using external benchmarks for realization ratios is typically not a feasible option, mainly because the structure of collateral and the methods of valuation vary significantly between banks. Banks therefore need to create and analyze their own internal database. This can involve arduous analysis of historical paper-based files and require significant investment of time to resolve issues of data validity. In our experience, banks' collateral valuation guidelines are often optimistic and tend to overestimate the amount realized in the event of default. It is worthwhile resolving these data problems, since otherwise the overall risk of collateralized exposure can be significantly underestimated.

Finally, in respect of both the recovery of unsecured exposure and the realization of collateral, it is necessary to factor in the expected delay in recovery, by measuring the cash flow values discounted back to the time of default.

Cost of capital

Having discussed the measurement of expected loss, we now turn to the second component of the risk premium: the cost of—or target return on—the capital required to cover unexpected losses. This in turn comprises two elements: the percent charge for capital and the amount of capital. The minimum charge is the

[8] Proposals in Basel II (as published in November 2002) allow for a lower percentage: 75 percent.

hurdle rate for shareholder value creation. Alternatively, an aspirational performance target can be built into the risk premium.

The amount of capital should be 'economic capital', which is the amount required to cover—at a chosen confidence level—portfolio losses occurring above their expected level. As with the measurement of expected loss, the available economic capital methodologies can be highly complex. Leading-edge practice is to use full credit risk-modeling, with fully fledged portfolio simulation. Using such a model, the capital allocation for an individual loan is its marginal contribution to the economic capital requirements of the total portfolio. But there are some pragmatic solutions which, at least as a first step, are sufficient for risk-adjusted pricing in a retail banking context.

At the simplest level, economic capital can be set as a fixed proportion of the expected loss figure, by assuming that default probability follows the same standard statistical distribution[9] for each rating or scoring class. This implies a constant ratio between the expected probability of default—the mean of the distribution—and the estimated range of probabilities (up to a chosen level), known as the 'value-at-risk'. Alternatively, the ratio between economic capital and expected loss can be made to vary with the expected probability of default. A short-cut[10] model is needed to calculate this relationship. Unfortunately, it is not possible to determine empirically which of these alternatives is superior. The next step up in sophistication is to include portfolio effects. Large exposures would then, typically, receive relatively higher capital allocations, because of their knock-on effects on portfolio capital requirements. For a retail portfolio, however, these effects usually play a minor role.

Economic capital is the appropriate measure for decision support in value-based management; but some complications arise since, under the current regime, regulatory capital for credit risk is significantly out of step with economic capital. It can be argued that regulatory capital is only a boundary condition (i.e., that as long as consolidated capital exceeds aggregate regulatory requirements, only economic performance measures need to be considered in frontline business decisions). Ideally, in this case, the bank would communicate its economic performance measures to the investor community, and the capital markets would assess bank performance on risk-adjusted return on economic capital and the consumption of economic capital. However, currently this level of transparency is not practiced;[11] nor is it wholly feasible. Banks' return on equity—unadjusted for risk and using regulatory capital—is still an important performance measure, particularly as it is publicly available at consolidated level and (for some banks) at the level of individual business units. In their overall performance measurement systems, banks have developed varying approaches for managing the divergence of economic and regulatory capital performance measures. For some retail banks—with a relatively simple business

[9] Typically, this would mean using a gamma distribution. The normal distribution, used in simpler versions of market price risk measurement, is inappropriate, since it fails to capture the asymmetrical nature of credit default losses.

[10] This is a short-cut compared with full multi-factor credit-risk modelling.

[11] Some banks have published economic performance measures (e.g., Barclays and Deutsche Bank), but not at a very detailed level, and the underlying methodology and parameters are not transparent.

mix—this problem could be resolved under the proposed Basel II regime, since then they could use regulatory capital as a reasonable proxy for economic capital. At the very least, banks should use the introduction of risk-adjusted pricing as a catalyst for revisiting their overall approach to performance measurement.

ESTABLISHING APPROPRIATE IT SUPPORT

Once the methodology is determined, the next prerequisite for risk-adjusted pricing is appropriate IT support. An effective and easy-to-use IT tool is needed to embed risk-adjusted pricing in operational decision-making and performance measurement. The IT tool should support at least two main functions: minimum loan-pricing and loan profitability measurement. The detail of functionality and the technical features of implementation need to be tailored to the specific features of the business it supports.

Functionality

The first main function—minimum loan-pricing—calculates the hurdle rate for frontline pricing decisions, below which new lending destroys value. The risk premium needs to be calculated and combined with both a data feed on operating cost assumptions to generate the minimum margin and with a specified cost of funds to generate the minimum interest rate.

For standardized credits, such as mass market personal loans, the typical form of final output is a set of price quotation tables, built up from the minimum price—at which loans achieve the minimum target return on capital—plus an additional spread, reflecting the bank's strategy for price position in the market. The tables show prices for loan 'buckets', where each bucket is typically defined by two dimensions: scoring (i.e., the graded bands of the loan-scoring system) and collateral (e.g., the loan-to-value ratio).

For bespoke credits, such as business-lending, standard pricing tables are inadequate. Instead the IT tool for bespoke credits entails a 'query-and-response' approach. Common parameters, such as borrower default probabilities, are input and held in the pricing system centrally; otherwise, frontline staff enter parameters specific to the loan proposal and obtain a minimum price specific to that loan. This approach places considerable IT demands for fast response times.

The second main function—loan profitability measurement—incorporates the actual price charged to the customer, as distinct from the minimum price threshold. Loan profitability is either measured in absolute terms, as the amount of profit, adjusted for risk, and allowing for the cost of economic capital allocation; or, in relative terms, as the risk-adjusted return on economic capital. At its simplest, this functionality can be used to analyze specific loan proposals and so provide additional decision support in loan negotiations. But its use is much wider than this. Integrated with the bank's performance measurement systems, it facilitates the measurement of the 'true' profitability of the bank's credit business at different levels: bank-wide, business units, relationship managers, and product or customer segments. In such a scenario, a close link to the rating or scoring system is needed; at the extreme level, the rating or scoring system would be an integrated part of an overall credit risk measurement system.

Implementation

To date, banks have typically been developing their own tools in-house. In our view, a simple spreadsheet application is feasible—at least as a first step—to support standardized risk tables. This can be implemented in around one or two months, once the chosen methodology is in place.

The technical requirements of bespoke credit risk-adjusted pricing are more difficult. Moreover, ideally, the software application should be linked to a database capability. This is to allow frontline staff to revisit previous price calculations and to enable senior management to monitor the pricing process. In our experience, developing a stand-alone, bespoke credit pricing tool requires at least six months, and further time is needed to educate frontline users. The requirements are still more demanding if the credit-pricing tool is to be integrated fully with the bank's overall performance measurement systems. If the bank already has a data warehouse with the relevant portfolio data and flexible reporting tools, then credit-pricing can be integrated without developing a new interface application. But at many banks the IT architecture is fragmented; in this case, a new multi-interface application is needed to integrate the credit-pricing tool. The timescale for implementation is necessarily longer: an initial version can take up to one year.

Leading banks in retail and corporate banking are well ahead of the pack in the sophistication and use of their loan-pricing capabilities. Overall, however, European retail banks need to build and strengthen their capabilities in this area. At a minimum, there are pragmatic compromises—some of which we have described in this chapter—that will enable banks to keep pace with regulatory trends and the core demands of the competitive landscape. Banks striving to catch up with the leaders need to make a significant investment in modern—and still developing—credit risk measurement techniques.

27

Total RAROC: Bringing Economic Capital to the Frontline

Felix Budelmann, Edoardo Ginevra, Diego Polo-Friz

Over the last few years, risk-adjusted performance measurement (RAPM) systems have become increasingly widespread in the banking sector. Many banks frequently use RAPM indicators, such as RAROC (risk-adjusted return on capital), RORAC (return on risk-adjusted capital), and RARORAC (risk-adjusted return on risk-adjusted capital), in order to understand, monitor, and compare the aggregate performance of different business units and of a group as a whole.

In this chapter, we discuss how to take things a step further by introducing the 'total RAROC approach'. This is a more powerful tool for salesforce management that uses RAPM concepts to drive and monitor the performance of the account management frontline (particularly, when this is credit-intensive), directly focusing account managers on creating shareholder value. First, we discuss why RAROC is a crucial metric for assessing profitability and how it should be thought of as a bank-wide system. Second, we outline how the bank-wide roll-out of RAROC can refocus the frontline salesforce from being volume/revenue-driven to being completely committed to value creation. Lastly, we set out the prerequisites for a step-by-step implementation of a total RAROC approach.

WHY TOTAL RAROC?

RAROC is measured by the ratio of net profit to economic capital.[1] Net profit is made up of *net revenues* (calculated as the interest margin plus commissions) minus *operating costs*, *credit losses* (both expected and realized), and *taxes*.[2] The definition of

[1] We focus on RAROC (as we have defined it in this chapter), but there are other risk-adjusted performance measurement indicators; and different banks may use the same terminology to mean slightly different concepts.

[2] This is not intended to suggest that any component of losses should be double-counted, but that an expected loss accrual is set up when the credit is originated.

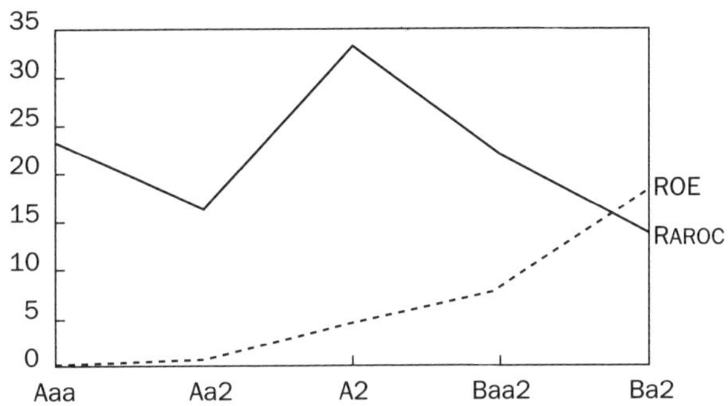

*Key assumptions: revenues based on historical average of corporate bond spreads; operating costs equal to 0.6 percent of bond market value; credit losses equal to average expected loss by rating class; economic capital is as reported in Basel II consultative documents; and regulatory capital fixed at 8 percent of bond market value

Figure 27.1 RAROC vs. ROE for different rating classes (illustrative example* on bonds, percent)

Source: Moody's; McKinsey analysis

economic capital derives from the concept of capital as a 'guarantee' protecting banks' creditors against unexpected events. In other words, the economic capital used by a bank is assumed to be the amount required to meet the maximum loss that could be incurred with a given level of confidence and over a given holding period. The level of confidence and holding period depend on a bank's risk appetite: the higher its risk aversion the greater the level of protection needed and, consequently, the amount of economic capital needed. Economic capital differs from regulatory capital, but the new regulatory approach proposed under Basel II will, to some extent, make these two concepts more comparable—another reason for banks to start exploring them now.

There are a number of reasons why RAROC is called for in banks. The most important is that traditional performance indicators, such as return on equity (ROE) (net profit over regulatory capital), may lead to unwanted risk-taking behavior. To understand this, let us look at an analysis based on data from the US corporate bond market comparing pre-tax RAROC and ROE (calculated as a spread, not as a rate) for different rating classes (Figure 27.1).

In the above—the logic of which is, of course, applicable to retail and/or to small-business portfolios, provided a sound internal rating system is available—the regulatory capital is fixed, so that increasing net spreads lead to an increase in ROE. On the other hand, economic capital increases with the level of risk, leading to a decrease in RAROC for debtors with ratings beyond A. By focusing on ROE alone, therefore, performance may appear suboptimal once it is adjusted for risk. Hence, banks that focus on ROE may be driven to take risks for which their desired level of economic capital is not sufficient to cover the potential maximum losses.

RAROC is not only useful in preventing such unwanted risk-taking. Its importance is also clearly recognized by external stakeholders. For instance, regulatory authorities, rating agencies, and investors assign increasing importance to sound, well-established, risk-related methodologies that can have a positive impact on capital requirements, a bank's overall creditworthiness, and the attractiveness of its stock.

Some examples will help to illustrate the type of benefits that can be derived from the introduction of RAROC; in particular, keeping risk levels under control, adopting a more profitable business mix, and increasing profitability by adjusting lending volumes and/or pricing. The introduction of risk-adjusted performance targets by a US bank allowed it, over three years, to reduce by over 50 percent its share of capital invested in businesses with returns below its hurdle rate. This was achieved through increased cross-selling and more accurate pricing and did not entail significant reductions in volumes. In another case, a continental European bank that introduced RAROC achieved an improvement in operating performance of about 15 percent by shifting its focus away from volume and toward margin after taking out costs and losses.

If these are key advantages of introducing RAROC-type indicators in a bank, the next question is what is the most powerful way to use them. The key issue here is who should use RAROC. In other words, should its use be restricted to the highest level of a bank's organization (e.g., the business unit) or can the concept of RAROC be used at all levels including the branches and by branch managers and account officers? Both alternatives have potential benefits. On the one hand, the complexity of the analytics and the aggregated perspective needed to measure performance at the bank level favor the use of RAROC at the top level of the organization only. On the other, a bank has to consider that an account officer—say, a corporate banker, a small-business portfolio manager, or even a mass market credit manager—not only owns most of the critical client information but also controls some very important levers, such as credit, pricing, etc. Moreover, the account officer is the one in a position to negotiate with clients.

The following is a description of the implications of adopting the latter (i.e., a deep implementation of RAROC throughout a bank), as we believe it is a more advanced system for managing performance. The implementation of this particular solution is called the 'total RAROC approach'. Obviously, this approach must be adapted at each level of an organization. At a typical commercial bank this works as follows: at the head office, regional, and branch levels, RAROC will be monitored with reference to the whole portfolio, while at business unit/segment and frontline levels, RAROC will be monitored separately for the relevant segments (i.e., corporate, small-business, and mass market). The private banking segment will not receive specific RAROC targets, while the affluent segment can be monitored in either of the two ways, depending on an individual bank's characteristics (i.e., largely in terms of the relevance of credit business to this segment).

INTRODUCING RAROC AT THE FRONTLINE

The implementation of total RAROC has the effect of profoundly changing the way account officers are considered within the value-based management process (i.e., from a purely volume/revenue-driven salesforce to professionals who are fully committed to value creation). This can be achieved by acting on two critical levers: *account officers' accountability* and *performance transparency*. On the one hand, account officers need to be made responsible for full value creation, in terms of net profit and return on capital, instead of being monitored, evaluated, and incentivized based on their volumes and/or gross margins. On the other hand, a strong performance culture needs to be established by working on performance transparency. The quantum leap involved is the shift from a very limited knowledge of costs, profitability, and capital usage at the account officer level to a frontline environment characterized by full information on revenues, costs, credit losses, and capital absorption at the portfolio, client, and transaction levels.

Account officer accountability

The need for accountability implies that each account officer is assigned performance targets aimed at value creation. In particular, these targets can be expressed in terms of three parameters: *net profit* ensures that capital deployed is used and growth is achieved; *ROE* ensures that the regulatory capital constraint is effectively managed, as well as supporting successful communication with the financial markets; lastly, *RAROC* ensures that economic capital is used effectively. This minimum set of instruments can be completed by introducing further tactical targets (e.g., volume of new mortgages); however, we will not deal with this topic here as it can be addressed using typical planning and control rules.

First, therefore, it is necessary to set targets for net profit, ROE, and RAROC. Specifically, ROE targets are set according to overall business plans at the bank or business unit level, whereas RAROC and net profit targets are set on the basis of internal benchmarking. Each account officer is compared with a peer group (based on seniority, geography, client portfolio composition, etc.) in order to extract best practice performances in terms of RAROC and/or net profit, which will represent the reference targets for these key performance indicators (KPIs).

Once such targets are set, an ROE/RAROC matrix can be constructed, in which the horizontal axis represents the relationship between current and target ROE (i.e., above or below target), and the vertical axis, similarly, represents the relationship between current and target RAROC (Figure 27.2). Specific guidelines are then associated with a position in each quadrant of the matrix. For example, if an account officer is in the top-left quadrant, he or she is above the RAROC target, but below the ROE target, and will be driven to increase ROE and net profit. An account officer in the bottom-left quadrant is below both ROE and RAROC targets and will be driven to increase ROE, RAROC, and net profit.

Account officers need to modulate their credit and commercial levers—the most important of which are volume, level of risk, price and cross-selling—to obtain a better mix within the structure of their activities and, hence, achieve all three targets. For each of the four quadrants, it is possible to show the potential causes of the hypothetical gap with respect to the assigned targets, and thus indicate the key levers to achieve the objectives.

A position in the bottom-left quadrant (i.e., below both the ROE and RAROC targets) is probably explained by inefficient pricing and/or too little cross-selling by the account officer, who should therefore focus on raising prices and increasing cross-selling. A position in the top-left quadrant (i.e., below the ROE target, but above the RAROC target) is most likely explained by the account officer being over-exposed to clients/products with low risk, who are absorbing more regulatory than economic capital. To increase ROE and net profit while keeping RAROC constant,

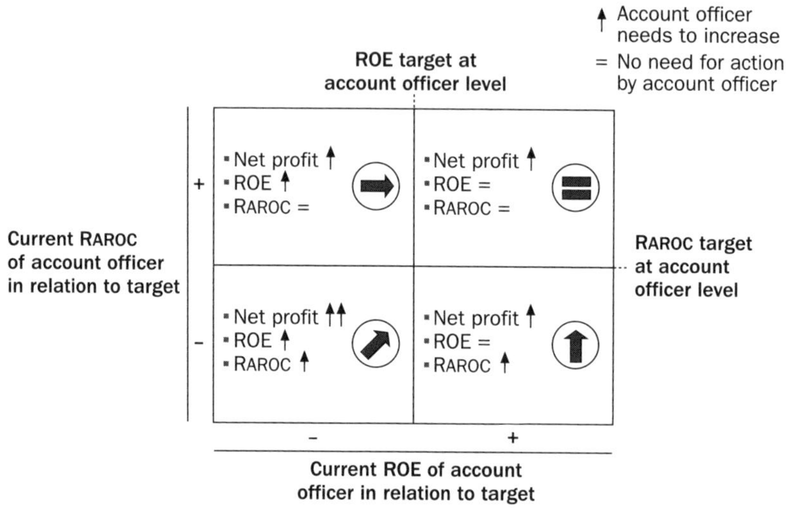

Figure 27.2 Action required from account officer for different positions in matrix

Source: McKinsey

this officer needs (all other things being equal), to shift to riskier assets, assigning less emphasis to volume, price, and cross-selling levels.

However, if an account officer is positioned in the bottom-right quadrant (i.e., below his or her RAROC target, but above the ROE target) it is probable that he or she is overexposed to clients/products with high risk, which are absorbing more economic than regulatory capital. To increase RAROC and net profit while keeping ROE constant, this account officer needs to shift to less risky assets; at the same time, the volume of loans must be increased to avoid a reduction in net profit. Lastly, a position in the top-right quadrant (i.e., above both the ROE and RAROC targets) would suggest that the account officer is applying best practice pricing policies and achieving a high level of cross-selling. In this case, the key to improved performance is to increase volumes, while keeping risk, prices, and cross-selling constant.

As mentioned, RAROC, ROE, and net profit should be the core targets that a bank must consider assigning to its frontline. It is possible to add to these core targets other KPIs, for example, in terms of revenue composition, the volume of specific products that the bank is pushing in order to increase cross-selling, market share, etc. Moreover, in some cases, RAROC or ROE need to be emphasized differently. For instance, if a bank uses much more regulatory than economic capital, ROE should be given more emphasis than RAROC, in order to incentivize account officers to use regulatory capital efficiently and vice-versa. Otherwise, if economic and regulatory capital absorption is more or less the same for the bank as a whole (which probably corresponds to most actual situations), RAROC and ROE must both be emphasized in order to ensure optimization at the account officer level for all possible situations.

Performance transparency

The key prerequisite to creating the necessary degree of accountability at the frontline is full performance transparency (i.e., account officers need to have a clear, accurate, and complete understanding of the revenues, costs, losses, and capital absorption of their portfolio). Each of these components needs to be carefully estimated—a task that is sometimes overlooked by even the most advanced internal accounting systems used in banking.

Revenues must be aggregated at the customer level, clearly representing the total gross revenues originated by each transaction at the group level. Account officers need to be aware of the total revenue earned from a particular customer—the gross revenue—without confusing it with the net revenue retained by distribution after payment is made to the internal 'factory' that provided the product. Let us take, for example, a small business customer who is granted a five-year loan, whereby he or she pays a given spread over market interest rates; the loan is provided by a separate group entity, which retains the spread and passes on to the distribution network only an origination fee. In this case, the full amount of the spread must be reported as revenue, while the amount retained by the factory will be included as a cost/transfer charge (see below on product cost). The key benefit of using gross, instead of net revenues, is that such a methodology makes it possible to align account officer and group targets. If the account officer's profit and loss takes into account an amalgam of gross and net revenues, he or she will optimize this aggregate, even if it turns out to be suboptimal at the overall group level. Moreover, a holistic customer perspective must be adopted, meaning that revenues reported to each account officer must include every component that arises from the clients in his or her portfolio, whether they were booked in the branch where the officer is based or in another domestic or foreign branch.

Costs must be allocated rigorously and charged to each account officer, using an accurate mix of direct and standard costing. Allocation techniques may vary according to cost type; for example, costs directly incurred by the frontline (e.g., account officers' salaries, branch rent), typically making up some 40 percent of the cost base of a corporate commercial bank, must be allocated directly. Product costs (i.e., costs of providing specific products like leasing, factoring, medium-term loans, derivatives, etc.), which are some 10 percent of the cost base, must be charged using predefined transfer charges aimed at recovering operating costs (including credit-related processing costs). Transaction costs (e.g., costs for money orders and other individual transactions) contribute about 30 percent of the cost base and must be allocated using predefined transfer charges, with the aim of recovering operating costs. The remaining 20 percent of the cost base of a typical corporate commercial bank is general costs (i.e., not specific to a given client portfolio or transaction), which are allocated using standard costs, predefined at business unit or regional level.

The key implication of these cost accounting rules is that every account officer will have visibility on and responsibility for all costs incurred, regardless of his or her capacity to influence them. An important rationale for this is that transparency is a value *per se*; moreover, one needs to consider that account officers directly originate—or, by their decisions, contribute to—a significant percentage of the cost base (e.g., by deciding on the product mix sold to their clients). This percentage is often considerable, as shown by the figures above: the total of costs under the control of or largely managed by account officers (i.e., frontline, product, and transaction costs) is typically some 80 percent of a corporate commercial bank's cost base. A brief example will illustrate this: for the same sum, a medium-term

Rating class	Expected loss Percent	Economic capital absorption Percent
1	0.01	0.56
2	0.02	1.37
3	0.07	2.75
4	0.23	5.42
5	0.64	9.08
6	1.54	11.95

Figure 27.3 Example of impact of credit decisions for different rating classes

Source: McKinsey

loan and a short-term overdraft generate completely different costs, and an account officer has a crucial role in the choice of the bank in granting one of these two credit instruments to a client. Account officers must therefore be fully informed of the cost implications of their decisions.

Credit loss allocation requires a clear distinction between 'expected' and 'realized' losses. Losses should not only be charged when they are realized at a default event—taking into account the expected severity, as well as any legal and financing costs—but also when credit is originated and during day-to-day management in order to account for expected loss components. Expected losses are inherent in any credit transaction and depend on a borrower's characteristics, such as sector, size, geography, etc.; they need to be accounted for not only in underwriting and pricing decisions but also during the life of a credit in order to track any changes in them.

Capital absorption—both in the 'economic' and in the 'regulatory' sense—must be made transparent to the frontline. Actual data help to show that credit decisions have a significant impact on expected losses and capital absorption following origination. An example derived from the internal ratings of one US bank is shown below (Figure 27.3).[3]

According to these figures, the decision to grant credit to a class 1 borrower from any segment (i.e., corporate, small-business, or retail) generates an expected loss of 1 basis point and an economic capital absorption rate of 0.56 percent of the amount loaned; in the case of a class 6 borrower, the corresponding figures are 154 basis points and 11.95 percent. Account officers need to be aware of this and be charged for the expected loss and the use of capital. Of course, all the components mentioned above should be clearly represented in the bank's management information system (MIS). One possible example is shown below, setting out the most important profit-and-loss items, at the required level of detail, that contribute to final results in terms

[3] Calculating economic capital is quite challenging in practice. The discussion of issues related to this calculation (e.g., the estimation of credit risk distribution, choice of confidence level and time horizon, treatment of diversification benefits, etc.) is beyond the scope of this chapter.

Profit information € '000s	
Interest margin on loans	800
Interest margin on deposits	200
Noninterest margin	1000
Total sales	2000
(Transaction costs)	(400)
(Product costs)	(50)
(Expected losses)	(200)
(Realized losses)	(200)
Value added	1150
(Frontline costs)	(100)
Margin before overhead	1050
(Specific indirect costs)	(30)
(Nonspecific indirect costs)	(50)
Profit before taxes	970
(Taxes)	(350)
Net profit	620

Profitability information € '000s	
Regulatory capital used	5000
ROE, Percent	12.4
Economic capital used	4000
RAROC, Percent	15.5

Complete management information needs to be available

- At product, client, and account officer level
- Current and cumulative of the year
- Vs. last year and vs. budget

Figure 27.4 Possible RAROC components in bank MIS

Source: McKinsey

of net profit, ROE, and RAROC at the transaction, customer, and portfolio levels (Figure 27.4).

IMPLEMENTATION APPROACH

The total RAROC approach described above implies the introduction of a widespread culture of value creation, which is able to change profoundly the approach to the client, setting aside volume as a value driver in itself and refocusing the frontline on profitability. The mindset of an account officer, instead of being credit-centered and accepting market prices will be reoriented toward cross-selling, capital optimization, and proactive price leadership. But this can be achieved only if a challenging change program is embraced. Such programs need to set clear, demanding targets, on both short- and long-term horizons, and imply a high level of ambition.

The prerequisites for successful implementation are threefold. One is to involve the CEO/senior management in key decisions, as this is the only way to endow such efforts with the necessary authority, at the same time as it permits its importance to be signaled to the whole organization. A second prerequisite is to assign clear responsibilities and ensure that information really does flow in order to make key management functions accountable for the success of the program and get the buy-in needed from inside the organization. In addition, it is necessary to keep the frontline implementation approach as simple as possible, avoiding any 'black boxes'. The process of introducing a total RAROC approach must be flexible (taking into account the specific characteristics of the credit salesforce) and sufficiently simple so it can be implemented in a reasonable amount of time and will be fully accepted by the frontline.

Once these requirements are met, it is possible to design a clear implementation path, which can be organized along the following steps: first, total RAROC needs to be institutionalized in a bank. By this, we mean aiming at the introduction of the holistic client perspective to calculate gross revenues (as described above) and factoring expected losses into pricing decisions. The key areas of impact are an increase in the capacity to negotiate and the ability to select the most profitable segment products. The second step is to carry out a rigorous cost allocation to define and implement the procedures of direct, indirect, and standard costing that are needed to measure correctly the net profit at the portfolio level. The most important result from this phase is an improvement in the efficiency of the cost mix. Third, rigorous capital allocation must be introduced, aimed at identifying the methodology for calculating economic capital and allocating it to the frontline, together with regulatory capital. The introduction of the methodology enables a bank to obtain the first results in terms of capital optimization. The last step we call 'total RAROC 100 percent', which, by defining RAROC-based targets for account officers, completes the implementation of the new approach and creates an integrated focus on shareholder value creation at the frontline level. The most successful system will likely be to proceed via iterations: the first iteration will be aimed at introducing the total RAROC approach, with subsequent iterations further refining the process.

Total RAROC is a best practice salesforce management system and its implementation in a retail bank needs to be thought of as a long-term change program. Although it entails challenging methodological and organizational issues, the expected impact is worth the effort, with the first results obtained early on in the process. In the end, the whole bank will be more focused on shareholder value creation; key value-creation levers will be transparent to the account officers, who are the key micro-decision-makers; and the entire organization will be driven toward higher effectiveness and efficiency.

28 Credit-monitoring and Workout: Proactive Management

Maurizio Donato, Andrea Mignanelli[1]

In looking at how best to manage credit risk post-origination (i.e., after the initial overdraft facility has been approved, the loan advanced, or the credit card application accepted), we concentrate on two functional areas in credit risk management. The first is monitoring and review, including active exposure management; the second is debt recovery and workout once the normal lending relationship has broken down. In both areas, leading retail banks have moved to more systematic procedures, involving widespread automation, and—particularly in debt recovery—have reorganized to create operational centers of excellence.

The value of improving credit performance overall is high; and improvements in credit management post-origination typically have a faster impact than those in underwriting, particularly where the flow of new business is modest relative to outstandings. This is an area, therefore, that justifies a major management effort in striving for excellence. We believe there is significant value for banks who can emulate the leaders.

STICKING TO THE RULES

In our view, the hallmark of excellence in retail credit-monitoring and review lies in highly systematic procedures: a well-structured credit decision system of codified rules, centered on robust automated scoring. This is not to say that there is no room for judgment. The involvement of staff expertise in credit decisions remains important in corporate banking. But leading banks have pushed the boundaries out in making extensive and intelligent use of automated decision rules in personal and small- and medium-sized business (SME) credit. Underpinning their ability to do this is the development of behavioral scoring models with high predictive power for the probability of default. Before discussing some of the features of best practice in

[1] The authors would like to express their gratitude for the contribution of Uwe Stegemann.

behavioral scoring, we describe the major benefits from rule-driven credit management procedures.

The benefits of systematic procedures

The most significant benefit is reduced credit losses. In the first instance, this arises where the predictive power of the scoring model generates credit decisions that are inherently superior—in avoiding or mitigating losses—to the judgment of staff experts.[2] This superiority is to be expected—if the model's input data are of good quality—in mass market personal credit and, perhaps, in lending to small businesses. In middle-market lending, automated scoring may not be inherently superior. Here, the benefit of a systematic decision process, driven by the rules of a scoring system, arises from the discipline it imposes. Under the pressure of close customer relationships or just from natural human optimism, lending officers—at least at some banks—have historically used their discretion in favor of lax treatment of potential problem credits. The imposition of rules avoids this distortion, leading to earlier or more stringent action when customers incur specific problems or suffer from deteriorating macroeconomic circumstances.

Perhaps the most significant reason for reduced credit losses is that monitoring and review can be focused systematically on those customers who pose the greatest risk. A good scoring model provides a granular categorization of customers according to risk (Figure 28.1). Combining this with other data, such as size of exposure or

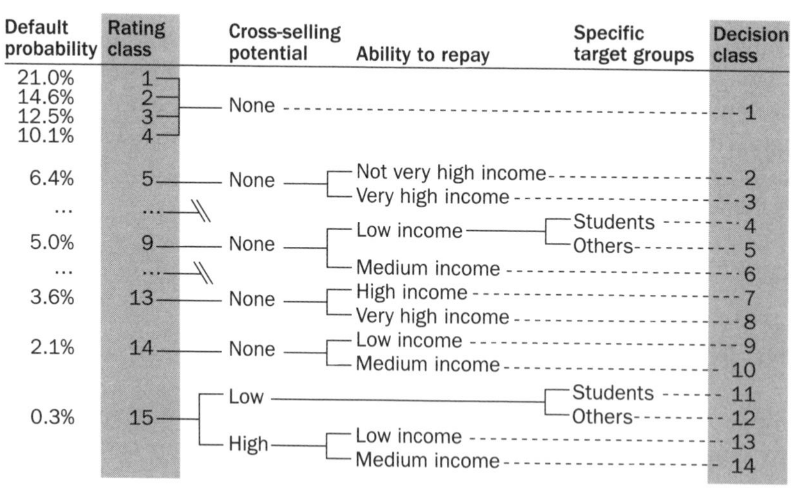

Figure 28.1 Illustration of redefinition of scoring-based rating classes into decision classes

Source: McKinsey

[2] Automation may be worthwhile even where the predictive power of behavioral scoring is modest. Where credit exposures are individually small, the cost savings from automated rules are likely to outweigh the impact of superiority in credit decisions from applying the considered judgment of staff experts.

industry sector, a systematic selection can be made to focus staff activity (e.g., which exposures to place on a watch list for close monitoring or which customers to review in-depth for decisions on credit line renewals). We have found that the increased focus can represent a radical change from previous procedures. One bank used to undertake in-depth credit risk analysis of 30 to 40 percent of its business customer base each year. It now focuses on customers categorized by the scoring model in the two most risky classes, and, as a result, undertakes analyses of 2 to 3 percent of its customers each month. Another has moved to a two-tier credit renewal system: for customers scored in the lower risk classes, there is a fast-track process that is close to automatic renewal, but subject to the back-up of biennial review; for customers scored in the higher risk classes, the review is now quarterly instead of annual.

Both these banks achieved lower credit losses, but also reduced operating costs by not double-checking low-risk customers; though the cost savings were partly used to fund the more intensive review of more risky customers. These cost savings arose from a complex rebalancing of staff activity. But the use of behavioral scoring also results in more straightforward reductions in the running cost of credit operations. This arises where automation reduces the workload in areas that were previously staff-intensive (e.g., the 'pay/no pay' decision for checks drawn on out-of-order accounts).

The final benefit is that senior management has greater control, amounting almost to the ability to calibrate the intensity of monitoring and exposure management. Senior management can implement changes in credit policy—such as a tightening in the incipient phase of a credit downturn—through central changes to the parameters of the rule-driven credit decision system. For example, this might entail widening the scope of watch lists—by changing the system's selection parameters—or imposing more stringent exposure reduction targets for customers already on watch lists. Ideally, senior management is able to calibrate how much it can tighten credit policy and be confident that the new policy will be implemented effectively throughout the bank's network, avoiding the uneven quality often associated with a more decentralized, discretionary approach.

Behavioral scoring

The ability to capture these benefits fully is dependent on a robust behavioral scoring model. Best practice models are distinguished by the range of relevant input data they use and by the extent to which they successfully incorporate data on customer behavior from the bank's internal information systems. Best practice models select the best performing parameters—or combinations of parameters—from a wide range of potential input data variables. The selection is made by iterative statistical testing to determine the greatest predictive power of default probability. In business credit, the range from which the selection is made includes: financial statements (i.e., balance sheets, profit-and-loss accounts, and corresponding financial ratios); segment-identifying parameters (such as location, industry sector classification, age of the company, age of the owner); credit bureau data (such as number of bank relationships, total borrowings by type, court judgments); and account data in internal information systems, comprising the current account used for payment transactions, loan accounts, and savings or investment accounts.

Best practice systems investigate not just the variables themselves but their multiple dimensions as well. This might be the scale or intensity of the variable, such as the borrowing level expressed as a utilization percentage of the facility, or the duration (e.g., days overdue on a mortgage repayment), or the frequency (e.g., how often 'out-of-order' transactions occur on the current account) of check pay-ins that the clearing system rejects because of insufficient funds, or the evolution, such as unusual changes in the pattern of debit or credit turnover on the current account. The final result is typically a multivariate model with up to 20 parameters. The most important parameters comprise the data from customer account behavior in the bank's own internal information systems. Effective use of these data radically enhances the predictive power of the behavioral scoring model.

It is not just the model itself that differentiates best practice. Excellent banks exercise the self-discipline of continuous improvement, through tracking performance of the model over time. Some areas of retail credit are particularly amenable to frequent tracking, as the quarterly—or even monthly—cohorts of new business in credit cards or personal loans provide data populations for statistical comparison. These comparisons track changes in the frequency distribution of both scoring outcomes and input variables, such as the job occupation of credit card applicants, and test whether these changes are statistically significant. The insights gained can lead to a change in the model or, where they indicate a change in underlying customer behavior, they can lead to a change in detailed credit policy (e.g., raising the minimum monthly repayment for particular segments of credit card borrowers). In small-business credit, these insights can lead, for example, to a change in the parameters for selecting customers for exposure reduction action plans.

REDUCING EXPOSURE

A well-structured credit decision system results in a systematic classification of all customers into decision classes. For higher risk customers, example classes include: place on watch list; prepare action plan for exposure reduction; transfer to debt recovery department. For customers where the normal lending relationship still holds, successful exposure reduction is a critical skill for banks to master, since it is the main route for avoiding or mitigating credit losses post-origination.

As with the other functions in the overall credit decision system, in our view the hallmark of excellence lies in highly systematic procedures, in place of an approach reliant on the discretion of the relationship manager. These procedures include: systematic selection of customers; action plans defining target reduction amounts and time lines; and monitoring of action plans by an independent specialist unit. Ideally, the behavioral scoring model—combined if necessary with other data inputs, such as identified vulnerable industry sectors—regularly generates candidates for exposure reduction action plans, and the credit culture and process ensures that action plans are regularly implemented.

In the absence of this ideal, we have found that a well-structured 'crash program' is an effective approach. A top-down analysis—using straightforward indicators, such as level of borrowings, type of collateral, customer's industry sector—can compensate for the absence of a behavioral scoring system in identifying the most risky customers, collectively representing, for example, 5 to 10 percent of the customer base. Once identified, target exposure reductions are set and relationship managers are required to formulate action plans over a horizon, for example, of three to six months. The key features of this approach combine to mobilize the organization: the steps are relatively simple, but concretely defined; they are carried out in parallel, within a common framework of clear targets; and results are closely monitored against clear time lines. At one bank, such a crash program was carried out on a business-lending portfolio of around €40bn, including medium to large corporate loans. The selection for action plans covered around 7 percent of the portfolio, and the final reduction in exposure amounted to around 25 percent of this selection. The bank estimated the economic benefit of this program as €65 to 70m, comprising avoided credit losses—of around €100m—less the present value of forgone margin and fee income.

An important element in achieving targets for exposure reduction is to make use of a rich set of exposure reduction techniques. These can include: reducing limits on revolving credit lines, either explicitly or via shadow limits;[3] nonrenewal of self-liquidating credits (e.g. in trade finance facilities); increasing collateral requirements; introducing or extending third-party guarantees; netting (i.e., ensuring legal offset of credit balances held at the bank against borrowings); restructuring of the credit product (e.g., accelerating the repayment profile on an installment loan or raising the minimum monthly repayment on credit card borrowing); switching to a lower risk credit product (e.g., replacing an unsecured personal loan with home equity leverage, or replacing a loan with a lease, or replacing an overdraft line with an invoice-discounting facility). Indeed, one of the advantages of the 'crash program' described above is that it can act as a catalyst in generating wider or more innovative use of exposure reduction techniques.

Nevertheless, individual exposure reductions are necessarily limited by contractual or marketing constraints. Hence, in best practice, they are supplemented by portfolio management techniques. These include selling or laying off risk through securitization, secondary market loan-trading, and credit derivative transactions. With the use of sophisticated portfolio risk measurement, risk exposure can be reduced even though the cash measure of credit exposure is unchanged or even increased. This can occur, for example, where increased credit exposure in one sector—directly with customers or, more flexibly, through market transactions—provides risk diversification benefits to the aggregate portfolio.

TRANSFORMING DEBT RECOVERY

Once the normal lending relationship has broken down, the primary objective becomes maximizing debt recovery, after allowing for costs of pursuit and collection, plus the interest expense of delay. In some cases, the most appropriate route is to

[3] Shadow limits are not made known to the customer, but operate in internal systems to trigger potential actions when the limit is breached (e.g., 'no pay' on checks, nonauthorization of ATM cash withdrawals or debit card purchases).

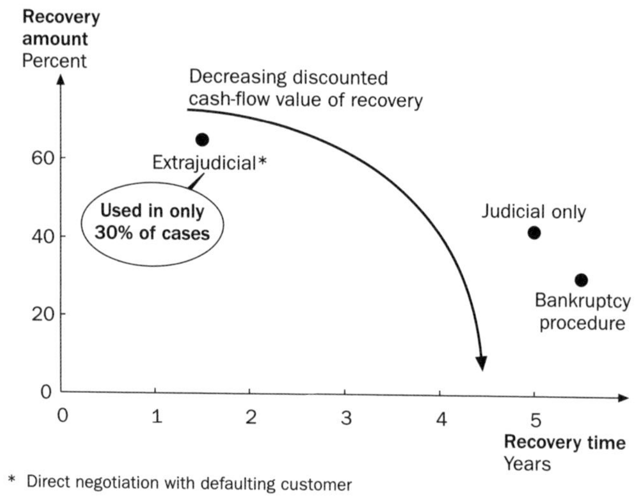

Figure 28.2 Comparison of debt recovery strategies in Italian banking

Source: Banca d'Italia; McKinsey

minimize costs, either by not pursuing the debt—a write-off in more than just the accounting sense—or by initiating insolvency or bankruptcy procedures. But other strategies may be more productive (Figure 28.2). These require skills in extrajudicial negotiation, in legal pursuit, and in workouts—ranging from relatively simple debt-restructuring to complex 'intensive care'.[4] Leading banks have recognized the value of these alternative strategies and have reorganized to create and sustain the necessary skills.

The features of a best practice organization in debt recovery can be illustrated by the approach adopted by a southern European retail bank. Prior to reorganization, this bank's debt recovery activities were conducted within the legal department, where the emphasis was on following correct procedures. The guiding motivation for reorganization was to introduce a performance culture of maximizing debt recovery. A new unit was established, specializing in recovery and reporting direct to the CEO. The direct report provides the unit with significant bargaining power in dealing with the bank's commercial business units (e.g., determining when a non-performing loan becomes the responsibility of the recovery unit and setting the internal price at which it is transferred). This has resulted in earlier transfers of nonperforming loans to the recovery unit, so increasing the probability of successful recovery, and has encouraged the commercial business units to be more vigilant in identifying potential problem loans.

Within the unit, activity is divided between three distinct departments: corporate recovery; retail recovery; and insolvency or bankruptcy proceedings. This structure reflects the different skills and approaches suited to each segment.

[4] 'Intensive care' is primarily relevant for significant corporate customers. It may involve complex debt restructuring; include the appointment of specialist turnaround managers; and, on rare occasions, entail new funds. Where successful, the customer is nursed back to a normal lending relationship.

Box 28.1

Third-party debt recovery in Europe

The market for third-party debt recovery services in Europe is underdeveloped and highly fragmented. There is, we suggest, an opportunity for some large specialist players to operate on a national or even multi-national scale. Large European banks that have mastered the necessary skills and processes in their internal recovery units, are well placed to create a profitable third-party business line.

At the end of 2001, the outstanding volume of nonperforming debt in Europe was around €900bn (Figure 28.3), and we judge that this volume is growing. The propensity for debt-holders to outsource their recovery is increasing. The intense pressures to improve profitability are resulting in a greater willingness to outsource, in search of superior competence and cost savings. Furthermore, the expanding number of debt securitization entities represents a natural market for third-party recovery services.

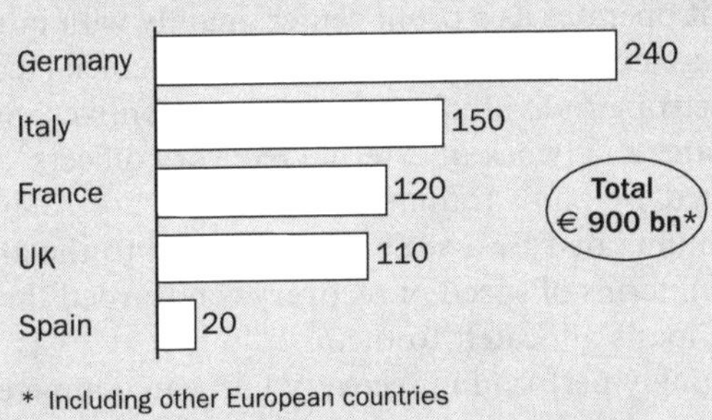

Figure 28.3 Nonperforming loans (including nonbank debt) (estimated balances, December 2001, €bn)

Source: McKinsey

The potential profitability is attractive for both the user and provider of third-party services. Using the Italian market as an example, we estimate that the leading banks are able to achieve around 10 percent superiority—against industry average—in credit risk performance through more effective debt recovery. A small or mid-sized bank, operating at or below industry average performance, can buy into this superiority through outsourcing and more than recover any incremental operating cost incurred through outsourcing charges. As a broad illustration, we estimate that the average net benefit from outsourcing is around 7 percent, expressed relative to the annual flow of nonperforming loans.

For the provider, the fees charged can amount to 10 to 15 percent of the amount recovered, sufficient to provide attractive profits for an efficient player with critical mass volumes. By adopting an *ad valorem* fee basis, the recovery agent avoids taking on additional credit risk. The original debt-holder retains exposure, but at least avoids the valuation risk of under-pricing loans in a sale; and, in any case, sale may not be a continuous option, where retail loan secondary markets are thin and illiquid.

Large European banks at the forefront of debt recovery skills and processes, are well placed to provide their services to third parties on a fee basis. The new income stream is not only potentially profitable but has the additional attraction of being counter-cyclical to their mainstream lending business.

Michele Cermele, Maurizio Donato, and Andrea Mignanelli, 'Good money from bad debt.' *McKinsey Quarterly*, No. 1, 2000.

In corporate recovery, the emphasis is on negotiation skills, targeted at accelerating cash in hand. The recovery officers are supported by significant investment in decision support software and in research to obtain the data input requirements of the new software. This provides valuable assistance in negotiations (e.g., the system calculates the present value of collateral, allowing for the expected delay in realization, and so provides a hurdle amount for an immediate cash settlement). In retail recovery, the emphasis is on containing the cost of pursuit and collection, through extensive use of remote pursuit by phone or mail—already a common strategy at nonbranch consumer credit companies, but not then typical for branch banks in the given bank's country of operation. Retail recovery is also supported by significant systems investment, particularly in an IT-based workflow management system. The system, for example, helps efficient selection and control of individual debt recovery strategies along a ladder of escalating action—remote pursuit by phone or mail, visits, court action—including a quantitative assessment as to whether the expected benefits outweigh the costs of moving up the ladder.

The recovery unit operates as a profit center, mainly with internal income from the commercial business units, and the emphasis on financial performance is further enhanced by very strong individual performance incentives. Supplementing its core staff, the unit operates a network of external recovery officers[5]—working to common standards, supported by bank training and IT, but not salaried employees of the bank. They are remunerated by a scale of fees linked to the amount recovered, and their performance in terms of speed of recovery is rewarded through the size and mix of the portfolio of loans allocated to them.

At its best, a strongly performing recovery unit can compete successfully in third-party debt recovery and so become a profit center in its own right (i.e., with external sources of income from other banks, particularly mid-sized players, from special purpose securitization vehicles, and from nonbank debt-holders). This is an underdeveloped industry in Europe, in which there are newly emerging opportunities for large-scale players (Box 28.1). We believe that it represents a profitable opportunity for banks that have honed their debt recovery skills in focused internal units, supported by robust systems and effective processes. It represents an opportunity, for some, to make good money out of bad debt.

In times of macroeconomic upturn, when credit risk is typically low on senior management's agenda, it is short-sighted of banks to ignore their shortcomings in credit management and debt recovery. In times of credit downturn, excellence in these areas will be a crucial differentiator of banks' financial performance. The key to achieving such excellence lies in organizational focus and systematic procedures, tailored to the requirements of different segments.

[5] Mostly, these are former relationship managers of the bank, but an increasing number are new to the role and include recently qualified university graduates.

Index